D0895013

PATRICK HENRY

PATRIOT IN THE MAKING

Patrick Henry

PATRIOT IN THE MAKING

BY

Robert Douthat Meade

J. B. LIPPINCOTT COMPANY

Philadelphia and New York

COPYRIGHT © 1957, BY

ROBERT DOUTHAT MEADE

SECOND PRINTING

PRINTED IN THE UNITED STATES OF AMERICA

LIBRARY OF CONGRESS CATALOG CARD NUMBER 57-9501

To my Mother and Father
Helen Douthat and Edmund Baylies Meade

By Robert Douthat Meade

JUDAH P. BENJAMIN: CONFEDERATE STATESMAN

PREFACE

AFTER completing an earlier book, I consulted numerous authorities in regard to another biographical project which I could approach with sufficient knowledge and interest. The late Dr. Douglas Freeman and a number of other distinguished scholars encouraged me in writing a full length biography of Patrick Henry. William Wirt Henry's three-volume life of his grandfather—the only complete study—contains much valuable information. But it was published in 1891, and since then a great deal of water has gone under the bridge. A mass of new data has been uncovered for historians: letters of Patrick Henry and his associates, newspapers, merchants' journals, diaries, official records. Modern science has developed the photostat and microfilm, and other duplicating devices which increase the available material (if delaying the final results!) of historical research.

When Victor Hugo wanted to describe the battlefield of Waterloo, he first visited "those terrible orchards, where every apple tree could show its scar of ball or bullet." Certainly, it is important for the biographer also to become familiar with his locale. He should not only examine all the written material even possibly relating to his subject, he should visit all the places the man frequented and become saturated with their atmosphere.

Virginia was a colony almost as long as it has been a state, and until the American Revolution many of her most valuable records were kept in the Mother Country. Moreover, Patrick Henry's father and tutor, Colonel John Henry, had undergone for four years the stiff discipline of King's College, Aberdeen, Scotland. In Hanover County, Virginia, Colonel Henry was a transplanted Aberdonian, even as Patrick's maternal Winston and Dabney ancestors of a few generations before had been transplanted Englishmen, from the West Country or elsewhere. Thanks to generous grants-in-aid, I was able not only to visit the principal manuscript sources of Henry material, the historic places in America connected with his life, but also I had the rare privilege of studying the English and Scottish background. I have worked in the records at Bristol, London, Aberdeen, Edinburgh, Glasgow, and even in remote British parishes. I have visited the Tower at King's College where John Henry heard "the musicall harmonie of costlie and pleasant bells." And I walked about Newburgh on the North Sea, the little Aberdeenshire village associated with the Scottish Henrys, even as I did Roundabout, Patrick's home in Louisa County, Virginia, or Red Hill, his last resting place, now converted into a Henry shrine.

After over twelve years of research and writing, I would not assert that I have uncovered a *trouvaille*, a major unpublished collection of Henry material. But I have found numerous batches of unpublished manuscripts which include Henry items. They are located chiefly in Virginia or in other manuscript collections listed in the List of Principal Sources, but the British research yielded invaluable background and supplementary material. From such discoveries, from individual letters here, public records there, from ecclesiastical archives, from diaries, reminiscences, and so on, I have assembled thousands of bits which together form a new, clearer, and more variegated picture of Patrick Henry.

To be sure, some of the data is of an unexpected nature. But on controversial topics the full evidence is presented, and the reader can judge for himself. No political figure of strong character, of burning conviction, could fail to take a stand on issues such as arose in Henry's time. In private life, however, he was genial and mild-mannered.

This first volume, subtitled "Patriot in the Making," covers Patrick Henry's career until 1775, or the events immediately presaging the Revolution. The second volume, to be published in a few years, will include his epochal "Give me Liberty" speech at St. John's Church, Richmond, his five one-year terms as Governor of Virginia during the war and postwar periods, his later career as lawyer and state legislator, his strong advocacy of individual liberties up to the enactment of the American Bill of Rights, and other events until he was buried at Red Hill overlooking the valley of the Staunton River in a tomb with the simple inscription: "His fame his best epitaph."

There continues his unexpectedly colorful private life centering around his young second wife, seventeen children, and sixty grandchildren, which led a great-grandson to contend in humorous verse that Henry should have been called the Father of his Country instead of Washington.

In conclusion, it seems appropriate that this first volume should be published during the year of the dedication of the Patrick Henry shrine at Red Hill and of the three hundred and fiftieth anniversary of the first permanent English settlement in America. It is good at this time to restudy the career of a Founding Father who gallantly met and surmounted problems just as difficult as those of our Atomic Age.

Henry believed that God helps those who help themselves. A product of a more rugged age, he would casually walk fifteen miles to and from his practice at Louisa court so that he could hunt along the way, and he thought little of riding horseback a hundred miles while defending back-country clients. If he were alive today, what would he have to say about the softening effect of modern mechanical inventions?

Unfortunately, it is impossible to thank in this volume many of the hundreds of people who have given generously of their time and talents, sometimes over considerable periods. For financial grants without which the long research and writing would have been impossible, I am indebted to the American Philosophical Society, the Patrick Henry Memorial Foundation, the Library of Congress, the Carnegie Foundation, and the Guggenheim Foundation. Randolph-Macon Woman's College, and especially its president, Dr. William Quillian, and president emeritus, Dr. Theodore Jack, provided release from extra academic duties and other needed time. The following gentlemen read all or the major portion of the manuscript, and, in certain instances, rendered valuable help in other respects: Dr. E. G. Swem, Williamsburg; James Easley, Halifax; Judge Leon Bazile, Elmont; Philip Thayer, Lynchburg; Samuel Schroetter, Charlottesville, all in Virginia; Hugh Lefler, Chapel Hill, North Carolina; and Bernhard Knollenberg, Chester, Connecticut.

Others who have materially contributed to the research, the typing over extensive periods, or in other respects include my wife, Lucy Boyd Meade; Dr. Douglas Simpson, Aberdeen, Scotland; Dr. Oliver Carmichael, formerly president of the Carnegie Association for the Advancement of Teaching; Mrs. Margaret Dabney Penick and her husband, the late S. Barksdale Penick, Montclair, New Jersey; William R. Shelton and other members of his family, Rural Plains, Hanover County, Virginia; Mrs. Elizabeth Rudasill Hunt, Charlotte, North Carolina; Gerard Tetley, Danville, Virginia; Miss Betty Woodsend of Norfolk, Virginia; Rosewell Page, Oakland, Hanover County, Virginia; David Mays, Richmond, Virginia; Mrs. Esther Ellis Fanfani, Mrs. Helen Knapp, Miss Gillie Larew and Mrs. Margaret Galloway Jones, Lynchburg, Virginia; Mrs. Ruth Aley and the late Maxwell Aley, New York City; Dr. Herbert Lipscomb, Ashland, Virginia; John Fontaine, Paces, Virginia; Mrs. Josephine Neal, Louisa, Virginia; Miss Tay Hohoff, New York City; Mrs. Elizabeth Spigner Lancaster, Columbia, South Carolina; Miss Nelly Preston, Seven Mile Ford, Virginia; Mrs. Mary Anna Castelvecchi Del Papa, Richmond, Virginia; and Raymond McCully, Philadelphia.

I also wish to express my gratitude for the service graciously given by the staffs at Randolph-Macon Woman's College and the Jones Memorial libraries, Lynchburg; the Alderman Library, University of Virginia; the Virginia State Library and the Valentine Museum, Richmond; the Library of Congress; and Colonial Williamsburg Incorporated.

[x]

CONTENTS

ILLUSTRATIONS

Grouped in this order following page 240

PATRICK HENRY

PATRIOT IN THE MAKING

1

The Earlier Scottish Influences

Ther is in this Universitie [of Aberdeen] a magnifick and
illustrious Colledge . . . called the King's Colledge.
————*Fasti Aberdonenses.*[1]

The greatest export of Scotland is men.————Old Saying

"You might as well go home and take off your Sunday
breeches," the Reverend Patrick Henry is reported to have said to
his nephew, young Patrick.[2]

Patrick had failed at storekeeping. He had failed at farming, and
again at storekeeping. Then he had turned to the law in a last effort
to earn a living for his wife and family. Now in late 1763 when he
was actually beginning to achieve a measure of success—to make ends
meet without help from his long-suffering father-in-law—he was risk-
ing his still shaky reputation in the seemingly hopeless Parson's
Cause.

Winter was descending upon Hanover when the gentleman justices assembled for the final hearing in the local *cause célèbre*. The
red and gold of the forests had faded to duller hues relieved only by
the green pines interspersed with red-berried holly and dogwood.
Any day the sand and red clay roads might change into treacherous
bogs seeking to engulf the struggling traveler.

Yet it would have taken impassable trails to hold back the crowd which overflowed the little brick courthouse that early December day. Besides Patrick's father, Colonel John Henry, who was presiding justice, and his associates, there were present a large group of clergy and a sprinkling of the country gentry with their powdered hair and knee pants. The bulk of the crowd, however, were plain folk, in leather breeches, osnaburgs, and the like, anxiously awaiting the appearance of their substitute, johnny-come-lately, champion. Many had never even heard Patrick speak.

The Parson's Cause had been initiated by the Reverend James Maury of adjoining Louisa County. The ministers of the Established Church in Virginia were paid in tobacco at sixteen thousand pounds per annum. But in 1758, during a period of economic stress, the colonial Assembly had fixed the clerical salaries for the next year at twopence a pound, much less than the market value. The clergy, laboring in a scanty vineyard, aroused considerable popular sympathy by their protests. They might have got relief from the Assembly had not several of their leaders launched forth into invectives and carried their case to the Privy Council in England. The clergy won and the Two Penny Law was disallowed, but not before their cause had become submerged in a far greater one—in this purely local matter of local taxation should any other will prevail than that of the colonial legislature?

Now in Hanover Courthouse, some eighteen miles north of Richmond, the Reverend Mr. Maury was suing for the back pay due him after disallowance of the disputed law. The justices upheld his plea; John Lewis, lawyer for the defendants, withdrew from what appeared a lost cause.[3]

It was at this desperate stage that Patrick Henry was employed to replace Lewis. A lean, sallow-faced young man of twenty-seven, Henry had built a considerable practice for a fledgling lawyer in Hanover and near-by Piedmont counties. This was his first important case, however, both from a legal and political viewpoint.

He began awkwardly, haltingly. For some trembling, agonizing moments it seemed likely that he would sink back into the mediocrity so devoutly wished for him by his opponents. His supporters hung their heads; his father, on the judges' bench, almost sank through his seat in confusion. The clergy, his avowed opponents, exchanged complacent looks as if already savoring their triumph.

Then Henry found himself. Somewhere from the depths of his heritage and experience, from the hopes and aspirations of his family and friends, he gathered the strength to ascend the heights. His words rolled forth; his spirit caught fire; his appearance, usually unimpressive, became striking—even awesome. His body became erect; his eyes, piercing; his gestures, graceful, bold and commanding.

His audience, discouraged by his irresolute introduction, now began to look up. They gazed in surprise as if they doubted the evidence of their senses. Then, caught in the spell of his eyes, his voice and words, they could not look away. . . .

What did Henry say to make the jury overlook the obvious legal rights of Parson Maury and give nominal damages of only a penny? From a contemporary letter by Maury and other accumulative evidence, we know that he soon left the technical legal questions and moved into a bold discussion of the compact theory of government and of natural rights. He questioned the very reasons for existence of the Established Church and he added, to the horror of the more sober and conservative portion of his audience: "A king by annulling or disallowing laws of this salutary nature, from being the father of his people degenerates into a tyrant and forfeits all right to his subject's obedience."

"The gentleman hath spoken Treason," ponderous Peter Lyons, the King's attorney, exclaimed to the justices. "I am astonished that your worships could hear it without emotion, or any mark of dissatisfaction."

"Treason, treason, treason," came also in a confused murmur from some gentlemen behind Parson Maury.[4]

Although Maury's version, in indirect discourse, does not give the style of Henry's moving, often poetic lines, a vivid impression is left by the traditional account, embellished by a few phrases handed down in the countryside. Certainly the following lines are in his

[5]

swift, bold style, the last sentence in almost identical words being confirmed by a long-time intimate of some of his grandchildren.

> "We have heard a great deal about the benevolence and holy zeal of our reverend clergy, but how is this manifested?" he asked. "Do they manifest their zeal in the cause of religion and humanity by practising the mild and benevolent precepts of the Gospel of Jesus? Do they feed the hungry and clothe the naked? Oh, no, no, gentlemen! Instead of feeding the hungry and clothing the naked, these rapacious harpies would, were their powers equal to their will, snatch from the hearth of their honest parishioner his last hoe-cake, from the widow and her orphan children their last milch cow! the last bed, nay, nay, the last blanket from the lying-in woman!" [5]

Granted that many of the Virginia people were too impoverished to pay their share of the clerical salaries, it is obvious that Henry's remarks were hardly restrained. They were the phrases of a young man warmed up to his argument and not stopping to weigh words. Delivered with his oratorical genius, they aroused intense feeling, especially since he described the bondage of a people who were denied the privilege of enacting their own laws. Even when displaying his masterly ability to sway a country jury, Henry was not a tear-jerker on the scale of Cicero. Yet not the least of his temptations in subsequent years would be to use his magic appeal to the masses for demagogic purposes.

Parson Maury, understandably angry with him, commented that his harangue to the jury had turned upon points as much beyond his depth and that of the jury as they were foreign to his purpose. But were they beyond Henry's depth? Or that of the jury, once he had expounded them in popular language?

Among the audience crowding the courtroom none was more surprised and enraptured than his own father, John Henry. Although the presiding justice, he was unable to suppress the "tears of ecstasy" which streamed down his face. Colonel Henry was a product of that stern discipline—not for intellectual or even physical weaklings—provided in the cold stone buildings of King's College, Aberdeen, Scotland. Not long before he died, he was reading, as stimulating diversion, the pages of a Latin dictionary, and in an extant copy of a letter to Parson Henry he used a Latin and Greek derivative to reinforce the point which he was developing with acute logic. Colonel Henry had been his son's only tutor for five formative years and in Patrick must have rested many of the dreams denied him in the New World—dreams which had seemed impossible of realization.[6]

From John Henry and his other Scottish forebears Patrick derived an intellectual and moral heritage no less important because little known. Patrick Henry's essential argument in the Parson's Cause was little different from what had already been written by a scholarly Virginian, Richard Bland.[7] But intellectual gifts can be used in brilliantly popularizing a subject as well as in descanting on it in a learned pamphlet. Life in the back country and experience with rustic jurors, added to an intuitive liking for and understanding of plain people, had taught him how to put the pedantic and complex into popular terms. On this background, superinduce an oratorical strain inherited from his mother's family, the Winstons, with other factors that can only be explained by the telling. Such positive qualities first appeared at Hanover Courthouse on that December day and later culminated not only in the masterly lawyer and orator but in the practical statesman. To develop the picture we must first turn to Henry's British background, in Scotland and England.

In Patrick Henry's lifetime Aberdeen was many weeks distant from Virginia even with fair sailing, and communication was infrequent. It is fortunate that a copy has been preserved of a contemporary letter, with information about his Scottish relatives, written by his first cousin, Margaret Donald of Aberdeen. On April 13, 1790, Margaret was living on Marischal Street there, a small thoroughfare climbing from a point near the docks to Union Street; a few old granite, dormer-windowed houses still hint of its antiquity.[8] A bequest of £200, left to Margaret and her sister by one George Donald in Virginia, had never been paid, and taking her quill in hand she

[7]

wrote Patrick, then a leading Virginia lawyer, that his intervention would be "very Seasonable." She also indicated a warm interest in the Henry family and gave Patrick news of his far-off British kin. His grandfather, Margaret wrote, was

> Alex Henry he married a Jean Robertson whos Brother came to Virginia and was living when my Br. Wm Duiguid was with your father. Jean Robertson had two sons your father and the Parson of hanover Three daughters who are dead long ago there is children living witness the two Mrs. Milns and my selfe to trass. the rest is out of my knowledge as I am a stranger at home.

Her mother, she continued, was Jean Henry, Patrick's aunt, and David Henry of London was a son of his grandfather's uncle.

All this Margaret thought that Patrick knew but David Henry seemed "desirous you should know again Sir I hop in return you will send me word how all is with you espisaly those I had the pleasure to know first My Dear friend Mrs. Merideth and her family next Miss Bettsy Henry and so." [9]

David Henry was a well-known London editor, printer, and writer, and some facts of his early career are sufficiently established to help distinguish Patrick's own family in the maze of Henrys, Hendrys, and the like, strewing the Aberdeenshire records. Obituary notices in the *Gentleman's Magazine*, which David had long been editing, stated that he was born on December 20, 1710, at Foveran Parish, about sixteen miles above Aberdeen. His family was, in his own words "more respected for their good sense and superior education than for their riches." At every neighboring gathering of the gentlemen they were described as among the foremost. His father, doubtless another poor but proud Scot, lived in "a genteel style" and was "at great pains" to instruct his children. David was entered in one of the colleges at Aberdeen but left in his fourteenth year and went to London. He was further described by an old friend as a man of ability and good taste. He had a well-stored mind and in all his writings he "never forgot the instructive moral."

At least so far as character and intellectual propensities are concerned, the description of David also applies to his cousins, John and the Reverend Patrick Henry, the American immigrants. In fact, one of David's obituary accounts mentions that several of his relatives sought their fortune in Virginia "where their name is held in reverence." [10]

Ancestor worship can reach unbridled proportions, and the Henrys have been traced by one enthusiast through Jean Robertson, Patrick's paternal grandmother, to a legendary Scottish king of the fifth century.[11] The historian, handicapped by the paucity of written records, must confine himself largely to a few generations before Patrick's birth. Enough can be found, however, to prove that the Henrys, while not demonstrably of royal or even noble descent, were not as obscure as is often inferred and possessed a significant cultural background.

Fragmentary parish records list an Alexander Hendrie, perhaps Patrick's grandfather, as living in or near Foveran in 1696 and a John Hendry in 1687. Patrick's paternal grandmother, Jean Robertson Henry, was doubtless one of the numerous Robertsons in this and adjoining parishes.[12] Probably about the time that Alexander and Jean were married, the feeble Parliament at Edinburgh ratified in 1707 the union of Scotland with England bringing to the smaller northern kingdom the benefits of the British mercantile system.

Alexander Henry brought up his family at a time when economic opportunity was at last opening for poor Scots. But it appears never to have been seized by the struggling Alexander, if we may judge from the scanty records winnowed in Aberdeenshire. He would never have been able to send his son John to college if John had not won a scholarship, and we do not know if he lived to hear of the family's improved fortune in America.

At that time most of the land in the area was owned by a few large proprietors and even the nobility often fitted into the traditional pattern of Scottish poverty. We have little reason to believe that, after their marriage, Alexander and Jean were able to better their worldly estate. They must have continued to eke out a living in Foveran or near it, for when their son, John, Patrick Henry's father, entered King's College, Aberdeen, he was assigned to the Buchan "nation." The nations were divisions of the students in accordance with their home address, and Buchan included some northern parishes of Aberdeenshire.[13]

Whatever might be stirring in the great world outside, life was not easy in the little community. During the last years of the seventeenth century parish relief, some four shillings to six shillings a distribution, had to be given an Alexander Hendry in 1688, to a John Hendry in 1692, and to Margaret Hendry, over a number of years. For most Scots before the Union of 1707, it was an achievement to live a full lifetime without ever having been on the parish relief rolls, and for many the effort was desperate, even hopeless, in the last grim decade of the century. The summers were so cold and wet that the essential grain crops did not ripen before the coming of winter. In Aberdeen many people were so weak for lack of food that they sank down and died on the streets. Tea had not been introduced, and there was not even enough malt for the common ale.[14] This was the period when Margaret Hendry was listed among the poor "in great Straits," and a bit earlier in 1687 "famer [farmer] Hendry" had doubtless been glad to receive £1.18 in payment for coffins and winding sheets which he had provided for the use of the Kirk.[15]

All this hardly fits the picture of the family described by John Henry's first cousin, David, even though David did characterize them as more distinguished for their good sense and superior education than for their wealth. The parish records show little to indicate that they were of the gentry. Could David Henry, the prominent London editor, have been guilty of the common sin of puffing his ancestry? A noted authority on Aberdeenshire local history, however, believes the contrary.[16] He indicated that the Henry family might have been members of the gentry some generations earlier. A laird might have a number of children and some of the younger ones be very poor. Their descendants would be reduced to the farmer class but would cling to the old family distinctions. Further evidence for this supposition is found on examination of the Foveran Kirk assessments

[10]

for June 12, 1665, which include Margaret Hendry—apparently the woman later listed as indigent—among the larger contributors.[17]

It is also indicative of a certain degree of circumspection if not respectability that no Henrys are included in a list of parishioners fined for disturbing people "in tyme of devine Service" and for various types of sexual immorality. The records show a degree of snooping by the Church authorities comparable to that of the Puritans in *The Scarlet Letter*. This was mostly moral zeal, carried to a fanatical extreme, but there was also a more practical aspect. In the Kirk Sessions Reports, Foveran Church, for one day in 1698 we find a notation that the clerk had reserved "12 pounds scots out of the penaltys" in partial payment of his salary. He helped to eke out his meager living by catching young couples in intimacies not blessed by the Church! In the 1690's we find two Sims including a "John Sim" among those cited or required "to stand on the pillar" in church for moral transgressions. Might they have been near relatives of the Scottish John Syme (pronounced Sim), with whom John and the Reverend Patrick Henry would later be closely associated in Virginia? [18] The narrow environment as well as economic stress contributed to the movement from the parish, not merely to Aberdeen but to more distant parts.

Nevertheless, although several of the Henrys, their friends or relatives, left early for Virginia, the roots of the family go back deep in Foveran or other Aberdeenshire districts. Robertsons as well as Henrys have long been associated with these and contiguous areas.[19] Foveran Parish, comprising only a few miles along the North Sea and inland, is near the northern border of Aberdeenshire.[20] Although some hundred miles north of Edinburgh, this northeastern county is emphatically not in the Highlands. The poor Celtic caterans from the mountains, periodically raiding the richer coastal areas, undoubtedly left their trace; but the district is predominantly Lowland Scotch in culture, and racially there is a strong Norse infusion. The northeastern coast of Scotland, jutting out farthest at Aberdeenshire, early offered an inviting field for Norwegian pirates. Sailing southward after reaching the Scottish coast, they must at times have come up the mouth of the Ythan, bordering Foveran.[21]

Norse pirates to the eastward, wild Celtic Highlanders to the westward, a stern climate with long winters and chilling winds: the Aberdeenshire Scotsmen early developed the rugged qualities that we note in many of the Henrys. And there was a persistent Norse strain indicated in the local dialect as well as in the predominant fair skin and blond hair. Long after John Henry lived in the countryside, the peasants still spoke Broad Scotch, even retaining a few old Teutonic words like *midder* for mother, *fadder* for father, and *stew* (or a similar word) for dust.[22] The Norse influence perhaps lingered in the blue eyes and sandy hair of Patrick and some of his descendants.

In the early days the Foveran people mostly walked the sixteen miles to or from Aberdeen. Nowadays the traveler still follows the highway skirting the North Sea. Low stone walls still separate some of the gently undulating fields. There are many cattle and numerous old houses of stone and plaster. Just before entering the village of Newburgh one veers toward the coast and, crossing a pretty brook, views at the left the Foveran Parish Church and quiet graveyard containing still legible tombstone inscriptions of a few Henrys. From this church it is only about a mile northward along the coastal road to the little village. In John Henry's time, Newburgh was only a cluster of straw-thatched stone cottages. Here were simple homes of the sturdy fishermen, herdsmen, and possibly smugglers making their meager living thereabouts; an old smuggler's cave is still pointed out.

This is a country of long winters and fleeting summers; the trees are stunted by their nearness to the sub-Arctic area. Just above Newburgh the Ythan wends its way through the sand dunes to the sea. And a half mile farther to the north stands the tall slit-windowed tower of Knock Hall Castle, ancestral home of the Udnys. From a hill a few miles inland, can be seen the Mither Tap of Bennachie, one of the most famous of Scottish mountains.

Visitors to Newburgh are shown a stone cottage, now greatly altered, in which the ineffectual James VIII spent a night during the

Rebellion of 1715.[23] A few of John Henry's relatives were doubtless among the Aberdeenshire men who were "out" in "The Fifteen." Probably some of young John's earliest memories were of the bedraggled Jacobite gentlemen who, after the Old Pretender had prudently decamped, fled northward along the coast to Peterhead and a French boat. Jacobitism and Episcopalianism, then persisting strongly among all classes in Aberdeenshire, again felt the heavy hand of the government. As Episcopalians, if not Stuart sympathizers, some of the Henrys must have fallen on evil days. Yet John's brother, Patrick, was perhaps first ordained as a minister in the struggling Scottish Episcopal Church whence, after ordination in the Church of England, he left for greater opportunity as an Anglican minister in Virginia.[24] And a half century later his nephew, Patrick, a devout Christian, would live to see the separate American Episcopal Church find its sanction in the distant land on the North Sea where his ancestors had lived. After the American Revolution, Samuel Seabury was elected as the first Episcopal bishop of the newly emancipated colonies. Journeying to England, he found that the Anglican bishops were legally restricted from consecrating him. He was later ordained in Aberdeen by a bishop of the Scottish Episcopal Church. The American Episcopal Church thus had an Aberdonian origin now regularly commemorated.[25]

But it is an earlier Aberdeen with which we are now concerned, that of the early 1720's when John Henry had just entered as a student at King's College.

The town, with some ten thousand inhabitants,[26] had not then developed into the large fishing and trading port of the present day. Many of the houses were in the old Scottish style, standing gablewise to the street, with space between for eavesdrop from the heavy thatched roofs and for pleasant gardens. The rude, half-barbarous Scotland of the Middle Ages was not yet entirely faded. John Henry might still witness a public scourging at the Market Cross or view a corpse swinging in the wind on Gallows Hill as a warning to evildoers.[27] But about the time of Mar's rebellion in 1715, Sir Samuel Forbes of Foveran wrote, not too boastfully, that no Scottish city

[13]

had a more valuable maritime commerce than Aberdeen.[28] And this estimation ignored its cultural influence. Long one of the principal Caledonian towns, it was remote from the ravages of invading armies and intellectually quickened by its grammar school and colleges.

In one of his last letters David Henry had spoken of his family's zeal for education. For poor Scottish laddies there were the coveted bursaries or scholarships at Aberdeen University. Ambitious boys, burning with zeal for learning, would walk from their little coastal farms or highland glens to Aberdeen for the fall scholarship competition at King's or Marischal. This consisted of stiff examinations in Latin composition, for the university authorities believed that college was a place only for the intellectually superior, for those with qualities of brain, not of brawn, to distinguish them from the masses. John Henry, probably after preparation in a parish school, was a winner in the competition at King's College.[29]

He was probably about fourteen or fifteen years old. Students then devoted themselves sooner than they do now to completing their education, wasting little time in extracurricular activities. In a picture of King's a few decades before John's admission, we see turreted stone buildings, laden pack horses, men in great black hats, and what appear to be little boys.[30] Actually, the latter must have been students who in accordance with the prevalent custom had entered the college when still in their early teens. Perhaps few matriculated as early as Elizabeth's dashing Earl of Essex, who received his M.A. from Cambridge when fourteen. And yet it will be recalled that David Henry had left an Aberdonian college to go to England at this tender age, while John Henry doubtless entered King's when little if any older, and was in America when twenty-one or less.

There is a tradition at Aberdeen University that the poor country boys used to bring a bag of oatmeal on which they lived for the term. John Henry, we hope, had something to supplement this classical Scottish diet or, at least, learned to eat fast at the bursar's table as did Sir Walter Scott's Captain Dugald Dalgethy when at Marischal. "If you did not move your jaws as fast as a pair of castanets, you were very unlikely to get anything to put between them." [31] In any event, John would have appreciated Carlyle's later description of "Marischal College, Aberdeen . . . where, for a few, in those stern granite Counties, the Diviner Pursuits are still possible (thank God and this Keith) on frugal oatmeal." [32]

There was a saying that whoever could survive on the northeast coast of Scotland could survive anywhere. And this statement applied to the rigors of the Aberdonian education as well as to the climate. Of the boys who succeeded in passing the entrance examinations at King's and Marischal during this period, only a relatively few ever graduated. John Henry's older brother, Patrick, was at Marischal sometime during 1713-1718 and was the proud possessor of an M.A. degree.[33] He had been preceded at one of the Aberdonian colleges by numerous students bearing his family name. Perhaps some were his relatives and were ancestors of other Henry families now scattered through the United States.

There is this specific record at King's for John Henry, Patrick's father, during 1720-1724:

> Joannes Henry, Buchanensis,
> burs., B.S.T.M.

"Burs." refers of course to John's bursary or scholarship and "B.S.T.M." are abbreviations for Bajan, Semi, Tertian, Magistrand, the Latin terms for the classes corresponding to the American Freshman, Sophomore, Junior, and Senior. The harsh struggles of the young students are indicated by the fact that of fifty-one members of the class of 1724 only four are recorded as attending for four years.[34]

We have noted that John Henry was listed under the Buchan "nation." The custom of dividing the students into "nations," derived from the Universities of Paris and Bologna, was symptomatic of the atmosphere of ancient culture, of learning dignified and precious, in which John was to spend the next four years. He could see at King's the bull or decree with its leaden seal (*bulla*) by which Pope Alexander VI in 1494 sanctioned the establishment of the university. Bishop Elphinstone, the chief promoter and first chancellor, modeled St. Mary's College, as King's was first called, after the University of Paris, where he had been a professor, and in certain respects after the University of Bologna. The first principal was Hector Boece, historian and friend of Erasmus.[35]

The first decade of the eighteenth century, just before John Henry and the future Reverend Patrick were in attendance, was a low period for the Aberdonian universities. In 1713, however, Queen Anne, "pitying learned poverty," gave a goodly sum to each college, and in general they had come into better days when John Henry was a student. There were still pointed jokes about how the professors cut capers when away from the university and there were sly references to their incompetence, as in the exaggerated ditty circulated about one Dr. Bower:

> Wondrous things don by me
> Who weel can count both 2 and 3
> Likewise I can count 3 and 4;
> All this is done by Thomas Bower.

But on the whole the professors were an excellent group of men, truly cultured and worthy of a student body making great sacrifices for learning and advancement. They were still well versed in Latin, and were at pains to enforce rigid standards.[36]

Although John Henry attended King's for four years, he did not graduate. Perhaps he had never learned to work his jaws fast enough at the bursar's table or, more likely, he found opportunity to leave for America. In the 1720's Aberdeenshire had not yet benefited greatly from the economic changes which were to alter the whole face of Scotland during that century. Soldiering for a price in a foreign army did not offer the traditional opportunity for poor Scots in this interregnum between wars. Nor did John have the inclinations of such hired soldiers as the fictional Quentin Durward or Dugald Dalgethy. But the American trade had begun to open up in Scotland after the Union of 1707 with England and the consequent removal of commercial restrictions. Much was heard of the chances for settlers in the new country. *The Gentleman's Magazine* refers to several of the Henry family who tried their fortune in America, just as a later Henry would try to "better himself and see the wu-r-r-ld" by going to Africa.[37] In addition to the reports sent back by friends already in Virginia, John Henry may have heard tales of other Scots who were flourishing in the plantation colony, including John Syme, his future wife's first husband and, notably, the redoubtable Commissary Blair. A poor bursar at King's, like John Henry, James Blair had later studied at Edinburgh, and, becoming an Anglican missionary to Virginia, had soon risen to be Commissary or head of the colonial church, a member of the Governor's Council, and the founder and president of William and Mary College.[38]

"The greatest export of Scotland is men." It is not altogether surprising that two military officers of Scottish descent largely determined the outcome of a crucial battle in the American Revolution. Major Patrick Ferguson, a slender young officer from Pitfours, Aberdeenshire, was the British leader at Kings Mountain, South Carolina. Despite Ferguson's bravery, this became the first link in a chain of British defeats which led straight to Yorktown. During the desperate melee on the wooded mountain slopes, Major Ferguson had seemed almost ubiquitous, "his voice, his presence, and his whistle" almost everywhere, until he proved too easy a target for frontier marksmen.[39] With Ferguson bullet-riddled and the battle over, a towering red-haired man with blazing blue eyes stalked among the enemy—Colonel William Campbell, Patrick Henry's brother-in-law. In shirt sleeves and with his collar open, the stern Campbell was not at first recognized by some British officers as the American commander. But he had fought his irregular troops with a genius, a dogged persistence, that did honor to his Scotch Presbyterian breed.

To return to venturesome John Henry, it was just as well that he was young and possessed of the hardy Scottish heritage. After walking or riding to Greenock or some other embarkation port for the Virginia trade, he had to make the long, rough voyage by sailing vessel across the Atlantic, then endure the radical change to Virginia diet and climate. Larger ocean vessels usually landed at York (Yorktown) or Hampton, from which ports it was only a short ride up the flat Virginia Peninsula to Williamsburg, the budding colonial capital.[40]

And here John was located by February, 1727, when he petitioned Governor Gooch respecting some land on the headwaters of "Great Rockey Creek" eighty miles northwestward in Hanover County.[41]

It should be noted that the tract John sought was newly surveyed land in the wild back country. Although hundreds of acres of such land could be bought for a few shillings, he petitioned for only four hundred.[42] We may be sure that he possessed little more of this world's goods than when he had entered King's on the scholarship.

Just what qualities did he now possess that would help him and his future children in the strange New World? If there were any doubt of the value of the stiff Scottish university training, it was fast being dispelled by the record of the select few alumni settling in America. Besides the forceful and plain-speaking James Blair, there was, for example, Donald Robertson, reputedly of Aberdeenshire, who after studying at Aberdeen and at Edinburgh, would establish a school in King and Queen County, adjoining Hanover, and teach two of Patrick Henry's eminent political associates, "Jeemie" Madison and Edmund Pendleton. "All that I have been in life I owe largely to that man," President Madison reportedly said.[43] Another of these Scottish university men was the Reverend James Keith. He had received in Aberdeen "the precise and methodical training of a Scottish college," and much of this he passed on to his daughter, Mary, who in turn deeply influenced her son, Chief Justice John Marshall.[44] Still another was William Smith, D.D. of King's. Slovenly and with more love for strong drink than was becoming to even an Anglican parson, yet a man of "genius, taste, and learning" withal, he was the organizer and provost of the University of Pennsylvania at Philadelphia, where Patrick Henry doubtless met him during the first session of the Continental Congress.[45]

Intellectually, and in all the qualities that make for character, John Henry undoubtedly brought to his son Patrick a superior heritage. This was augmented by the influence of John's brother, the Parson. The only member of his father's immediate family with whom young Patrick would have close association over a lengthy period, the Reverend Patrick followed his brother to Virginia, where he also soon

[18]

settled in lower Hanover. Here in 1735 he wrote the Bishop of London, in whose diocese Virginia was included, a letter thanking him for his endorsement and other favors. Along with many valuable colonial manuscripts, this letter narrowly escaped the German blitz of the 1940's and survives to give further indication that the Scotch Henrys were a family of some influence as well as excellent education.[46]

But what help would John Henry's education and connections be to him in Virginia? Among the noteworthy Aberdeen and Edinburgh alumni in America whom we have cited, Donald Robertson found a road to success in the teaching profession, James Blair and William Smith in the ministry. But John Henry, although essentially a scholarly type, appears to have arrived in Virginia with ambition to make his way in a more practical field. Probably while looking for a better opportunity, he went to live in the family of John Syme and his wife at Studley in lower Hanover. The Symes—and especially the comely young wife—would affect his career and that of his future children in a way that he little imagined.

2

The English and Hanover Progenitors

Genius is a flower that may rise anywhere, but the steely oak requires a deep and hard-knit soil.
——ALLEN NEVINS, *Grover Cleveland*

This small cheerful world, which . . . produced the greatest list of great names ever known this side of the ocean.
——HENRY ADAMS, *John Randolph*

IN THE FALL of 1732, the clever and urbane William Byrd II was traveling as pleasantly as possible, we may be sure, to his mills in the upcountry and back to Westover. Arriving at Shockoe's in present Richmond and crossing the river to the mills, he was disturbed to find both mills standing as still, for lack of water, as "a dead woman's tongue, for want of breath." Then, after further peregrinations, on the evening of October 7, he was conducted to the home in lower Hanover of the young widow Syme, lately Sarah Winston, where he intended to spend the night.

"The lady, at first suspecting I was some lover," Byrd wrote, "put on a gravity which becomes a weed, but as soon as she learned who I was, brightened up into an unusual cheerfulness and serenity. She was a portly, handsome dame of the family of Esau, and seemed not to pine too much for the death of her husband, who was of the family of the Saracens. He left a son by her, who has the strong features of his sire, not softened in the least by any of hers."

[20]

Byrd, a connoisseur of feminine charms, found Mrs. Syme a lady of lively and cheerful conversation. She was much less reserved than most of her countrywomen, and he observed that this trait set off her other agreeable qualities to advantage. They tossed off a bottle of port, relished with a broiled chicken.

"At nine I retired to my devotions," Byrd continued, "and then slept so sound that fancy itself was stupified, else I should have dreamed of my most obliging landlady."

That was on Saturday night. The following Sunday morning Byrd drank a quart of milk and tea "which I found altogether as great a help to discourse as the juice of the grape. The courteous widow invited me to rest myself there that good day, and go to church with her, but I excused myself by telling her she would certainly spoil my devotion. Then she civilly entreated me to make her house my home whenever I visited my plantations, which made me bow low, and thank her very kindly." [1]

John Syme probably had come from Aberdeenshire and John Henry's connection with him was based on their similar background in Scotland. Colonel Syme—the leading Virginians in every county seemed to have a militia title—had been a large landowner and surveyor, member of the county court and of the House of Burgesses. While preparing to survey the boundary line between Hanover and newly created Goochland County in 1731, he became ill and soon afterwards died.[2] His widow's "gravity" when she first met William Byrd was largely due to her husband's recent death. But it is likely that she was also thinking perhaps less soberly of the young Scotsman, John Henry, who lived on the plantation. At any rate, they were soon married.

Although there are notable exceptions, great men seem on the whole to have been influenced more by their mothers than by their fathers. Whether or not this was true of Patrick, his mother was unquestionably a woman of superior qualities, with an abiding influence on her famous son. Except when there was a church service, a dance or other neighborhood gathering, the young Virginia matrons then devoted themselves chiefly to their families. A British traveler spoke of them as generally handsome, though asserting that they were not to be compared with his fair countrywomen in England. He also conceded that they made as good wives and mothers as any in the world. But they had few educational advantages and not quite so much "tenderness and sensibility" as the English ladies.[3]

What the Virginia women may have lacked in sensibility they made up for in sturdiness, a quality needed in attending to their large families, their servants and slaves in the rough countryside. This sturdiness Sarah Syme Henry appears to have had in abundance along with some other characteristics that set her far above most of her countrywomen. Besides William Byrd's informal tribute, there is other testimony to her mild and kindly disposition, her undeviating honesty, correct understanding, and easy elocution. She is said to have happily united firmness and gentleness in the management of her family, and to have possessed notable intellectual gifts. A surviving letter which she wrote about 1771 shows rather correct spelling and punctuation with a clear and even felicitous expression, indicating an education superior to that of the average woman of her time and place. Further proof of her estimable qualities is found in her will, of which a copy still survives. She was or became deeply religious and in co-operation with John Henry, a devout Episcopalian, gave her children the full benefits of a Christian home.[4]

Sarah could appreciate John Henry's amiability, his family background and college training, in such contrast to that of the average uneducated settler. To the young widow he must have seemed a romantic figure, at least in comparison with John Syme.

In a new country, husbands and wives are both at a premium. John Henry married a widow who had been married to a widower.[5] Women were scarce during much of the colonial period in Virginia, and especially on or near the frontier. Widows, by virtue of their proven charms and inherited estates, rarely lacked suitors; there were instances of remarriage when the grass had scarcely grown over the deceased spouse's grave. Among the great Virginians born during the next few decades, George Washington, Thomas Jefferson, and James

Madison were all to find solace and a spur to ambition through marriage to widows, and John Henry was no less discriminating.

There were all the components of what was then considered a prudent marriage. Sarah had doubtless learned much about living amicably with a husband, or at least managing him discreetly; and she was well trained in the eighteenth century precepts of feminine subservience. "Never dispute with him [your husband] whatever be the occasion," advised a writer in the *Virginia Gazette*, May 20, 1737. "And if any Altercations or Jars happen, Don't separate the bed whereby the Animosity will cease . . . by no means disclose his imperfections, or let the most intimate Friend know your Grievances; otherwise you expose yourself to be laugh'd at. . . . Read often the Matrimonial Service and overlook not the important word O B E Y!"

Soon the young couple were merging their resources—John Henry's hopeful stake in the new land with his wife's more varied and established holdings.[6] On January 28, 1733, Governor Gooch had granted John Henry, "Gent.," twelve hundred acres in upper Hanover, about forty miles northwest of the present Richmond. Spreading out from Fork and Roundabout creeks in present Louisa County, the tract was carved out of wilderness territory with such boundaries as a "Hickory Thence North Thirty nine Degrees East Ninty one poles." Only one adjacent property owner is listed, Mrs. Syme, who had inherited the property from her husband.[7] In May, 1735, John Henry was granted a thousand more acres which adjoined his Roundabout Creek tract and was also included in one patent with 1,554 acres patented by Sarah Syme (now Sarah Henry) on both sides of the same creek in Hanover County.[8]

There is no patent formula for breeding great men. Although we know that certain factors of heredity and environment are more stimulating than others, there remain imponderables only to be determined by the Almighty. Nevertheless, on the maternal as well as the paternal side, Patrick was sprung from superior people. His mother, Sarah Winston Syme, was the daughter of Isaac Winston and Mary

[23]

Dabney, descendants of ambitious English emigrants to Virginia a few generations earlier.

The progress of the British nation toward a higher civilization has at times been tortuous if not imperceptible. Yet, as compared with inhabitants of more despotic countries, their citizens had by the seventeenth century developed a sturdy independence, a mental awareness which made them ripe for further change. For the British who remained in their own island stronghold the necessary incentive would soon be provided by such historical movements as the Intellectual and Industrial Revolutions. And for those emigrating to America there was the stimulus of cheap land, a flexible society, and a usually beneficent government—that is, until the change of policy not long before the Revolution.

The English people were once likened, with some truth for the eighteenth century, to a flagon of ale: froth on top and dregs at the bottom. Patrick Henry's maternal ancestors, the Winstons and Dabneys, belonged to the intermediate levels. They were of sound farming stock, and, like the Henrys, they appear to have inherited none of the queerness which plagued certain brilliant colonial families such as Jonathan Edwards' or one branch of the Virginia Randolphs. From his maternal line Patrick inherited a good English background, with qualities of character which would play a noteworthy part in his development. Within a few generations before his birth, both the Winstons and Dabneys had risen to be leading families of Hanover. Prolific and enterprising clans, not debilitated by wealth or leisure, they brought to John Henry, by his marital alliance, social prestige and influence which would, in turn, affect Patrick's political career.

There is a tradition that the Winstons were from Yorkshire, but the best evidence seems to indicate that the family was from Bristol or near by in the West Country, a region closely identified with colonial America.[9] When the first Winstons emigrated, Bristol was one of the most important ports for American trade, and Virginia emigrants were drawn largely from that city, from such English counties as Devon, Somerset, and Gloucester, and from some adjacent Welsh shires.[10] In addition to their profits from the usual plantation trade, now beginning to include the sale of numerous Negro slaves, the Bristol citizens made a pretty penny by beating the streets and highways of the city and near by counties for prospective American settlers.[11] If they lacked money for their passage they could obtain it or the equivalent by agreeing to serve for a specified time as indentured servants; in Virginia fifty acres of land was granted for each person imported.[12]

In an old section of Bristol, with its network of crooked streets and alleys, there are records in the city archives of one Winston hiring servants for the plantations and of two others signing indentures to pay for their passage to Virginia.[13] Several of Patrick Henry's ancestors in the colonies secured most of their landholdings as a reward for such human importations. One of his favorite boyhood playmates was a family "dependent," doubtless an indentured servant.[14] As late as 1774, on the eve of the American Revolution, Patrick's half brother, John Syme, Jr., was offering for sale some seventy of these servants, newly arrived in York River from London.[15]

The Winstons and other of Patrick's maternal ancestors became established in America largely through these inter-related devices for encouraging settlement. In fact, it is only through the records of indentured servants and headrights [16] given for the importation of these and other colonists that we are able to learn certain essential facts regarding Patrick's forebears and the society in which he himself was nurtured. Of course, a great many Virginia emigrants could pay for their passage, even in hard times, and indeed an appreciable number belonged to the upper classes; but numerous others, having little more than courage and ambition, signed indentures.

Before Negro slavery had gained its unfortunate hold, there was little stigma attached in England and the colonies to the trade in white servants. Not a few of them were political prisoners or educated persons who for some reason or other lacked the money for their passage. Most were excellent emigrants in the sense that they were willing to risk the long voyage on crowded, unsanitary ships and to labor for a perhaps unknown master in the hot tobacco fields. Of the Virginia House of Burgesses, a contemporary writer said in 1662

[25]

with some truth that it was usually composed of men who had been sent over as servants.[17] Many of the indentured servants were teachers, and as a class they frequently intermarried with free persons.

Virginia was the most important American terminus for this migration of freemen as well as servants. West Country folk by the thousand ventured to the colony. Vessels sailed out of the Severn, frequently in September, with goods for the plantation trade and with aspiring emigrants, and returned laden with tobacco or other raw products.[18] It was all a part of the prevailing mercantilist system of economics and worked to the great profit of the Bristol merchants if not so often of the planters.

From Gloucestershire in the West Country came many Virginia voyagers, a few of high degree. From there sprung the family of the brave but tyrannical Governor, Sir William Berkeley, and others of his name in Virginia. The Winston name was borne chiefly by farmers and tradesmen, many from the sturdy stock of which John Ridd in Blackmore's *Lorna Doone* is a prototype. Some were perhaps connected with the most prominent contemporary representative of the name, Sir Henry Winston of Standish, Gloucester, for it was a time when younger sons often had to become small farmers, emigrate, or go into trade. Sir Henry was the great-grandfather of the first Duke of Marlborough and ancestor, therefore, of Winston Churchill.[19] A small landed gentleman, John Churchill, rose a step in the world by marrying Sir Henry's daughter, Sarah, "an heiress in a small way." And Sarah Winston "bequeathed her Gloucestershire name" to the Churchills—a name that would have "a resounding reverberation." [20]

Another Winston, whose career may have had more influence on the Virginia branch, was Thomas (1575-1655), son of a carpenter in Painswick, Gloucester, near Standish. An M.A. from Cambridge, student of medicine at Padua and member of the College of Physicians, London, he was an active member of the Virginia Company.[21] There are also various seventeenth century records of Bristol Winstons or Winstones, notably of vestrymen or leading contributors at St. Philip and Jacob Church, on Tower Hill near Old Market Street in a section which residentially speaking has seen better days.[22] Since nearly all the contemporary Winstons were derived from the West Country, it seems highly likely that William Winston, Patrick Henry's first ancestor of the name in Virginia, was a member of the clan.

Records of York County in lower Tidewater Virginia show that one Henry Tiler [Tyler] was given eighteen hundred acres in 1666 for importing thirty-six emigrants, including a William Winston.[23] Not for a few generations would slaves provide the prevailing labor supply in the colony; it appears likely that Tyler's profitable importations were mostly indentured servants. But William Winston's name is not included in any available records of such servants, including those at Bristol, and he seems to have been a man of some education.[24] After 1666 we lose sight of him, at least for a time, among the scanty records of the period. He must have worked hard, clearing land and cultivating the tobacco fields, perhaps as a laborer for a planter, so that he could get a stake in the new country. In any event, one William Winston, probably the immigrant of 1666, began to acquire, near the end of the century, extensive landholdings, chiefly through the importation of settlers into the colony.

In 1687 Lord Howard, the Virginia Governor, granted to a William Winston a small tract of land in New Kent County on which he was then dwelling.[25] This was some fifty miles up the York River and its tributary, the Pamunkey, in new territory to which land-hungry settlers in York County would naturally move. By 1691 William was able to secure with an associate eight hundred acres in New Kent upon the lower side of Mattadeum Creek. The grant, signed also by William's wife, Sarah, was for the importation of sixteen persons.[26] During the decade from 1693, William patented some five thousand more acres, either personally or with a co-owner, in this area—land which had been granted him for the importation of nearly a hundred other settlers. One of his land boundaries listed was a gum tree on a southern branch of Totopotomoy Creek, a branch of the Pamunkey.[27] Fertile low grounds near navigable streams were in particular demand, for there were few roads and they were often impassable.

By the opening of the eighteenth century the Virginia Winstons were becoming one of the leading families in the upper part of New Kent from which Hanover would soon be formed (in 1720). Not that conditions were stable in this frontier region or that even hard-headed settlers did not fail in some of their visionary plans. We find William Winston's son, Anthony, receiving in 1701 a grant of 1,079 acres in St. Peter's Parish, New Kent County, which had been granted to William "and by him Deserted"—that is, he had not fulfilled the meager requirements for settlement under the patent.[28] William Winston, the Virginia progenitor of the clan, died about this time, and left numerous descendants who appear in the parish records as landowners, land processioners or vestrymen in New Kent and Hanover.[29] Among them was Isaac Winston, Patrick Henry's maternal grandfather.[30]

He married Mary Dabney of Hanover, and, like most couples of the time who lived a free country life, they had numerous progeny. Among their six children was a daughter, Lucy, who married William Coles and was the ancestor of Dolly Madison and of Edward Coles, an early, Virginia-born, Governor of Illinois. There were also three sons, Isaac, Jr., Anthony, and William, and two other daughters, Mary and Sarah. This Sarah, who bore the same given name as the wife of William Winston, the progenitor, was the mother of Patrick Henry.[31]

The first of these Virginia Winstons seem shadowy figures, not to be brought fully to light by the occasional references in court records or vestry books. But when we come to Isaac the family becomes more distinct and interesting, the period not quite so distant; we even know his children by their nicknames. Patrick's mother, Sarah, was Sally; his Uncle William was Billy or Langloo; and Isaac, Anthony, Mary and Lucy were respectively Ike, Tony, Molly, and Luly. Old Isaac, their father, had an "exceedingly bald head." We are gravely informed that baldness was a never-failing characteristic by which the male Winstons were distinguished. Hair simply would not grow on the top of their heads and even their wigs very soon had a dingy, half-burnt look, becoming much too thin in spite of the free use of salves.[32] Perhaps it was from the Winstons that Patrick got the thinly covered pate of his late years as well as more important characteristics.

Like the Winstons, his maternal grandmother's family, the Dabneys, would become one of the leading Southern families and include a remarkable number of military officers, educators, writers, and editors, in addition to the usual run of plantation masters and local officials.[33] Cornelius, patriarch of the breed in the colony, is said to have been an English farmer from Norfolk or Cambridgeshire. He is thus linked with the Daubeneys still known in that region of eastern England. There are numerous Daubeneys and Daubneys in the alumni records of Cambridge University.[34]

In Virginia the Dabneys proved to have the sturdy qualities needed for the frontier life. At a later period when the pioneer virtues were less cherished, some of the tribe made much of their fancied relationship to the genteel French d'Aubignés.[35] But whatever the characteristics of that checkered family—including Agrippa d'Aubigné, the Huguenot hero, and his granddaughter, Madame de Maintenon, pious favorite and wife of Louis XIV—the English Dabneys brought to America qualities useful in clearing a wilderness and starting a civilization. Cornelius Dabney, Patrick Henry's great-grandfather, settled in a border country with fresh memories of Indian raids. He lived long enough among the savage Pamunkeys, still inhabiting the area, to learn their language, and it was this founding Dabney who in 1678 translated and forwarded a missive which the Pamunkey Queen Cockacoeroe sent to the Virginia authorities at Jamestown. In all probability Cornelius was the "English interpreter" who accompanied the dusky queen when she appeared before a committee of the Burgesses wearing her regal attire: a plat of black and white wampum and a mantle of dressed deerskins, the edge cut in fringes.[36]

In the letter which Cornelius translated, the Indian queen craved pardon for a "running away" two years before during Bacon's Rebellion.[37] This was the Great Rebellion of 1676, a century before the American Revolution to which, indeed, it bore some remarkable similarities. Bacon's Rebellion against the tyrannical royal government, like that against the British in 1775, was largely the result of oppressive taxes and trade laws, of arbitrary rule by men who were appointed to office more because of family name and connections than ability. In 1676, as in 1775, the governmental policy was worse than a wrong, it was a blunder.[38] During both revolutions Henry or some of his ancestors lived near the center of important events, even when they were not actually involved.

Memories of stirring events remain vivid in a quiet, untroubled countryside. During Patrick's youth in Hanover County, cut off from the upper New Kent of Bacon's time, stories were still handed down of the arrogant Sir William Berkeley, the old Governor with the large nose, the dark piercing eyes, and small mouth (giving that deceptive impression of weakness),[39] who had crushed the liberties of the Virginia people. And always in the drama was Berkeley's shining counterpart, the aristocratic young Nathaniel Bacon. Marvelously, he had led the common people in successful revolt against all the power of the colonial government until, worn down by marches and countermarches in forests and swamps, he had died of the "bloody flux" in a Gloucester farmhouse.[40]

In the back country, New Kent or other counties where lived some of Patrick Henry's ancestors, Bacon had largely recruited his grim bands of frontiersmen, small landholders, and former indentured servants. From New Kent, Thomas Hall, well known to Henry's forebears as clerk of the local court, had gone forth to fight and then meet his death on the scaffold. William Drummond, the dauntless Bacon leader whom Berkeley taunted before his execution, was caught hiding in Chickahominy swamp. Not far distant, on the York River, some of Bacon's ragged followers had made their last stand.[41]

There are remarkable similarities between Patrick Henry and the ill-starred Nathaniel Bacon. Both strove mightily to maintain the

[30]

hard-won rights of Englishmen in a new and distant land. The broadly educated Bacon, admitted in an account of the King's commissioners to have "a pestilent and prevalent Logical discourse," made one of his stirring speeches to his men at the Falls of the James near where Henry delivered several of his notable orations. Henry was just twenty-nine years old when he delivered his philippic against the Stamp Act in the House of Burgesses at Williamsburg. "Caesar had his Brutus, Charles the First his Cromwell, and George III— [cries of "Treason, Treason"]. . . . If this be treason, make the most of it." Bacon was only a few years older when he issued his fiery and pathetic manifesto of 1676:

> . . . if there be as sure there is, a just God to appeal to, if Religion and Justice be a sanctuary here, If to pleade ye Cause of the oppressed. . . If after the loss of a great part of his [Majesty's] Colony deserted and dispeopled, freely with O'r lives and estates to indeavor to save the remaynders bee Treason, God Almighty judge and let [the] guilty die.

The comparison between Henry and Bacon extends in a measure even to personal appearance. Bacon was "indifferent tall" and slender, of "an ominous, pensive, melancholy Aspect," but black-haired and it would be inaccurate to ignore Henry's basically genial temperament, his blond hair and Scottish features.[42]

When Henry was a Southern chieftain of the Whig forces before the Revolution, the *Virginia Gazette* published a complete front-page account of Bacon's Rebellion.[43] Certainly there was no leader of a Revolutionary cause whose career remained more freshly before him. In the gallant Bacon who died, louse-ridden and exhausted in 1676, we hear the voice of Henry a century later.

The Indian queen whom Cornelius Dabney had served was wife of Totopotomoy, killed while an ally of the white settlers during a bloody fight with other Indians in 1656. Eight years later, Governor Berkeley granted to Dabney two hundred acres at the mouth of Totopotomoy Creek, named for the Indian king.[44] The biographer must piece together his story from numerous bits of information. It is curious how much of Patrick Henry's life would be intertwined with this tiny stream, hardly more than a brook, which snakes its way through the sandy bottom land of lower Hanover into the Pamunkey. Along this creek, with its rhythmic Indian name, William Winston and Cornelius Dabney had staked out some of the first land Patrick's ancestors owned in the New World. At the old brick house still standing on the hill above the stream Patrick would court and marry Sarah Shelton, the love of his youth. As a lawyer and rising political figure he would ride across Totopotomoy Creek hundreds of times in his travels through the lower county.

In Virginia the Dabneys were staunch Episcopalians, though there would be a Presbyterian offshoot. In Patrick's youth they might have been described as generally amiable, upright, and unambitious, at least politically. Although careful and industrious, they did not aspire to great wealth. But they were beginning to hold a number of offices in Hanover or adjoining counties, and in the succeeding generations they would be singled out in emergencies where there was a need of men with ability, quiet courage, and integrity.

Through the Dabneys, as well as through the Winstons, John Henry had become connected with a leading family of Hanover. Shortly before his son Patrick entered upon public life, one Dabney would be sheriff of the county and another a member of the county court, and the Dabney influence would be increasing in Hanover, Louisa, and neighboring counties, to Patrick's benefit.[45]

John Henry would be more successful in leaving his son a good name and a superior education than in accumulating a large worldly estate. But the records show that John made an ambitious if somewhat visionary effort in the latter direction during his early married years. He acquired large holdings in the vast unclaimed lands of western Virginia. Through the prevailing land speculation he hoped to add to his income, now embarrassingly small as compared even with the modest estate inherited by his wife from her first husband.[46]

Large grants in what is now Albemarle and other western counties were being carved out of the wilderness. Smoke from an occasional settler's cabin now curled through the valleys and from mountain-sides in a portion of Virginia hitherto little known except to the Indians, trappers, and wild animals. In the early 1730's there were several dozen patents in Albemarle County, two by fathers of illustrious Americans.[47] Peter Jefferson, a tall brawny surveyor-farmer of Goochland County, purchased for a bowl of Arrack punch the land near present Charlottesville upon which he built Shadwell, birthplace of Thomas Jefferson.[48] A few years earlier, John Henry and two associates had been granted over nine thousand acres in other sections of Albemarle County or near by, and John held property in the county for many years. Indeed, he had an overseer there as late as the 1760's and, in view of the requirements under the law, must have erected one or more buildings on the property to retain possession. But beyond these facts evidence of his actual residence on any Albemarle property soon enters the realm of the nebulous.[49]

John Henry—striving for an estate which he was never able to build to more than modest proportions—also secured in 1735 a joint title to thirty thousand acres "between the two Ledges of Mountains" in what was then Goochland County. The next year, with the Reverend Patrick Henry and several other associates, he patented thirty thousand acres on the south side of the James River, upon "the first creek below the great Mountains," and by himself 4,850 more acres on Roundabout and Fork creeks. That all of these purchases were speculation based on the potentialities of a new and unsettled country is indicated further by the fact that John Henry gave only five pounds of good and lawful money for his patent for the 4,850-acre Roundabout tract.[50]

Perhaps it was just as well that the land speculation required relatively little cash, for in addition to John Syme, Jr., children were now being born of Sarah and John. Already there had been William, named presumably for Mrs. Henry's brother or grandfather.[51] Then in late May of 1736 she knew that her time had come again. On the twenty-ninth when the green hue of the trees at Studley, the chirp of crickets on the quiet nights, the preoccupation of menfolk, white and

black, with the growing crops, all proclaimed the nearness of the
sultry Tidewater summer, she was delivered of another son. He was
born at Studley homestead and named Patrick, doubtless for his
uncle, the Parson.[52]

3

Early Plantation Life

They [the Virginians] are the most hospitable generous People I ever saw. . . . And really they have the Art of Enjoying Life, I think, in a Manner to be Envied.
———THE REVEREND JONATHAN BOUCHER in 1759 [1]

A time, there was, ere England's griefs began,
When every rood of ground maintain'd its man.
———GOLDSMITH, *Deserted Village*

On an upcountry trip in 1741, William Byrd notes that he left Westover, his James River mansion, about seven o'clock one April morning and took eight hours to travel the forty miles northward in his chariot to Major Henry's. There, next day, he had an early breakfast of chocolate and eggs, and then rode to Hanover Court and dined near by on fowl and bacon at Parson Henry's. Returning to John Henry's, he played cards and retired about ten o'clock.

Byrd had no occasion to mention Major Henry's second son, a blue-eyed, red-haired boy of five.[2] Not surprisingly, we have no exact data on Patrick until he entered school. The child of obscure though estimable parents, he had no legends told of him such as Plutarch retailed of Cicero: that his mother was delivered without pain and that his nurse was told in a vision he would one day render great service to Rome. The exaggerations regarding Patrick's childhood relate more to his teens and there take a different twist.

It was a time when children were not supposed to be underfoot; and the precept was easier to enforce when they roamed over a great plantation. With the large families then prevalent, Patrick was hardly likely to be a victim of oversolicitude. On the other hand, his father and mother maintained a moderately comfortable establishment in which the pleasures of rural life were not marred by too severe struggles for a living.

The original Studley house, some eight miles from Richmond and from Hanover Courthouse, has long since been destroyed by fire. But from its brick foundations lately rediscovered, from insurance records and other reliable sources, we are able to get a picture of the plantation where Patrick lived until his early teens. To his dying day he would recall the simple, two-story brick house with the many outbuildings so interesting to an inquisitive boy.[3]

Then there were the Negroes, not only nurses for the Henry children but playmates and friends, able to unfold the delights of the plantation world and of streams and forests. Scipio, Dill, Nell, Bartlett, Peter, Phil, Rose, Judy, Moses and so on—the Syme slaves as listed about a generation later must have included some of Patrick's beloved childhood associates.[4]

These Negroes, however, were all close to primitive Africa. The idea that their descendants might later develop into competent citizens would hardly have occurred to Patrick even when he reached his teens, especially since it was almost unconsciously rejected even by ministers and other leaders of enlightened local opinion.

Queried by the Bishop of London in 1724 as to the number of "Infidels" in his parish and his efforts to convert them, the overburdened minister in adjacent New Kent had replied: "None, but Negro slaves most of which are not capable of instruction." [5]

During his early years Patrick had the opportunity to see a number of slave auctions, among them perhaps that at which two new Negroes from Gambia were sold at Newcastle in 1745. Any childish compassion that he might have felt for these two slaves when they later ran away, clad in their new, buttonless cotton jackets and breeches and their osnaburg shirts, was probably dispelled by tales of the valuable goods they had stolen. At least one of them, a large yellow fellow speaking no English and with three slits on each side of his face (marks of the African savage), was manifestly unready to participate actively in an advanced British government.[6]

And yet as an intelligent boy, child of religious, sensitive-minded parents, there were some aspects of the slave system even under beneficent conditions which must have left him a bit uneasy. On visits to the courthouse he could hear the screams of the Negroes at the whipping post. Flogging of Negroes (and often whites) commonly took the place of imprisonment for minor offenses. Then there were stories bandied about of slaves such as Roger, the young Angola Negro, who had run away from a neighboring plantation. Perhaps recalcitrant as well as half civilized, such Negroes could not be left to lurk in a neighboring woods or swamp and were pursued by armed patrols. But hiding with the desperate and despairing runaway, his striped cloth breeches and old cotton waistcoat now doubtless torn by thorns and brambles, was his Virginia-born wife, Moll, a thick, squat woman only about eighteen and "very big" with child.[7]

Besides the slaves at Studley, with the complex problems they were already beginning to create, there was the fascinating realm of stables and horses. Later we hear of two stables and a race track on the Studley plantation, and the *Virginia Gazette* would carry numerous advertisements of the imported stallions with which Patrick's half-brother, John Syme, was helping to improve the Virginia stock: Sampson, for instance, got by Morton's Old Traveler out of a hunting mare imported by Syme, and now covering at twelve shillings, sixpence "a leap" or forty shillings the season.[8]

In his adult years Patrick would have to bear more than his share of strain and responsibility. Perhaps it was as well that during his childhood he lived a joyous, out-of-door life enabling him to store up a strong physique and tranquil memories. Henry Adams would speak of the "small cheerful world" in Virginia of this period which nurtured so many great men,[9] and certainly Hanover was cheerful

[37]

enough in those years before bad crops, wars, and trade restrictions made life difficult even for hearty extroverts like Patrick's neighbors.

We have the program of a contemporary St. Andrew's Day celebration in Hanover, surely not to be missed by Scotsmen and their families. Besides the races in which twenty horses or mares were to run for the entertainment of the ladies and gentlemen, the advance newspaper report tells of a hat valued at twenty shillings to be cudgeled for, the drums beating for the challenges (and none to play with their left hand), and of a violin to be played for by twenty fiddlers, none having the liberty of playing unless he brought a fiddle with him. Country fiddling was a happy pastime in which Patrick would gain proficiency when a mere lad. There were also foot races for small boys, an ample dinner followed by toasts to the King, the Governor, and so forth, with other quaint details, reminiscent of Merrie England transplanted to a land of greater opportunity. Here are the concluding plans for the celebration as published in the *Virginia Gazette*: [10]

"That a Quire of Ballads be sung for, By a number of Songsters ... all of them to have Liquor sufficient to clear their Wind-Pipes."

"That a Pair of Silver Buckles be Wrestled for by a Number of brisk young Men."

"That a pair of handsome Shoes be danced for."

"That a pair of handsome Silk Stockings of one Pistole value be given to the handsomest young Country Maid that appears in the field. With many other Whimsical and Comical Diversions, too numerous to mention. . . ."

For Patrick there were also increasing impressions of the adult world. Almost with his mother's milk Patrick drank in the family talk of public affairs, of law suits and the King's law as somewhat informally administered at Williamsburg and Hanover Court. Governmental affairs in Virginia were chiefly conducted by the Royal Governor, the House of Burgesses, and the Council. The Governor, the chief executive authority, had powers much like those of our American state governors today. During Patrick's boyhood and indeed until several years after he had become a member of the House of Burgesses, the Governor's office, with most of the fat salary, was retained by a succession of British noblemen, the Earls of Orkney, Albemarle and Loudoun and General Sir Jeffrey Amherst, none of whom bothered to come to Virginia. Lieutenant-governors such as William Gooch, Robert Dinwiddie and, finally, Francis Fauquier had to shoulder the work and responsibilities.[11] The House of Burgesses, in functions and powers a Virginia House of Commons, had two representatives from each county and a few from the college and boroughs. The Council, whose members were appointed by the King usually on the suggestion of the Governor, was the chief advisory body of the Governor and the upper house of the General Assembly. Although the legislative influence of the Council was now small as compared with the Burgesses, its members enjoyed great social prestige. Moreover, they comprised the supreme court of the colony, the General Court at which Patrick would practice in the anxious years immediately preceding the Revolution.

In this governmental world John Henry soon began to take a part which, if never of great significance, at least set his son an example of public service. As a planter, a surveyor, and schoolteacher, successively, he never had more than indifferent success, but in other fields he did become a leader in county affairs. In refreshing contrast to unfortunate manifestations during other periods of history, in the colonial Virginia of this age there was hardly a spark of anti-intellectualism. John Henry was one of the few college-trained men in Hanover, and his neighbors admired him for his learning, even though many could not understand its niceties. With his rigorous training at King's College, his good character, and county connections through his recent marriage, it is not surprising that by 1737 he was made an acting gentleman justice, then justice sheriff, and, finally, the presiding justice of the county court.[12] The Virginia counties were then ruled by a tight little group of gentlemen, holding positions somewhat corresponding to the interlocking directorates of present-day corporations. The Established Church was in the late 1730's virtually the only one in Hanover County and, since it was connected with the state, the vestrymen had important civil as well as ecclesiastical functions. Some six months after he was appointed acting justice in 1737, Major John Henry was ordered to be sworn as a member of the vestry of St. Paul's Parish; William Meriwether, the presiding justice, was one of the seven vestrymen signing the order.[13] By this time John seems to have been appointed a major in the militia, and later he became a colonel in charge of all the raw county levies.[14]

At the same time, Patrick's grandfather, old Isaac Winston, was an established leader of the back-country area. In 1732 Isaac Winston, Gent., already a land speculator, had obtained a grant for some seventeen hundred acres on Beaverdam Creek, Hanover County, and in 1735, with John Henry and William Robertson, for thirty thousand additional acres in Goochland. The next year he was listed as a captain and merchant of Hanover, and within the next fifteen years he became a leading landowner in adjoining Henrico County, where he had acquired property on the south side of Chickahominy swamp, near Richmond. A man of some education and considerable ability,[15] Isaac died in 1760 without including his then unpromising grandson, Patrick, among the numerous bequests in his will.[16]

In addition, a considerable number of Patrick's relatives served in various colonial offices. We have noted that several had already become vestrymen, sheriffs, gentlemen justices, or burgesses. Some years before, it had been said that if a case involving those landed nabobs, the Burwells, came before the Council, over half the members would step aside because of family relationship to the litigant. Economic power and resulting political power was now spreading to the up-country. Of the twelve gentlemen justices appointed for Hanover County in 1752, six were members of Patrick's family circle: John Henry, William Dabney, "Essex" William Winston, William Winston, Jr., Anthony Winston, and John Syme, Jr.[17]

John Syme was now also elected to the Burgesses along with John Chiswell, the grandee of upper Hanover, but had his election cast aside on the ground of undue influence.[18] The prestige of the family was becoming noticeable in adjacent counties; Patrick's grandfather, bald-headed Old Ike, was appointed that same year a gentleman justice of Henrico County and James Winston attained a similar honor in Louisa County.[19]

The duties of the county justices were individually not of major importance: recording deeds, granting licenses for inns and ordinaries, ordering bridge or road repairs, trying debt cases and other civil suits and defendants presented by the grand jury for failing to attend church, profane swearing, unlawful gaming or, at intervals, for more serious criminal offenses. But Virginians, trained as plantation managers, as vestrymen and county justices, would step confidently into a larger governmental scene.[20]

In moving toward the main events, the epochal years, of a great man, we can easily overlook some of his youthful influences. So far as the records show, Patrick Henry never failed to secure any office he sought from the people of Hanover. Since he was elected to his first public position before he was twenty-nine, many Hanover citizens already established in their lifework when he was a boy would be active citizens throughout his early political career. They and their children would stand solidly behind him even when he was accused of treason to the Crown. To this day his name is a part of Hanover folklore, tales of Patrick or "Pahtrick" Henry coming down from father to son.

In order to know the Hanover of Patrick's boyhood, the people and the places, one needs to ride over the country roads, some of them unused nowadays. And at times it is necessary to roam the woods and fields, especially when they are sites of eighteenth century farms and even of two abandoned towns. In 1736, when Patrick was born, there was no Richmond market and the rural life was built on the Pamunkey River trade. Some of the earliest Hanover farms spread along that meandering stream, then deeper and clearer than the present muddy river; with a little imagination motorists crossing it on the present Richmond-Tappahannock highway bridge may still envisage boats from England mooring at near-by ports.

Once the Pamunkey low grounds were claimed, new settlers pushed back to its principal tributaries, the North Anna and South

Anna rivers, and to other streams with fertile bottom lands. The original Studley plantation as Patrick knew it was much larger than it is today.[21] It is said to have stretched southward to the Totopotomoy and was only three miles from Page's Warehouse, the later Hanovertown, head of navigation on the Pamunkey and a rising market for tobacco and English goods.[22]

From Hanovertown it was only a few miles down the sluggish Pamunkey to Newcastle, once a thriving port. A plat still survives of this trading center made by John Henry, surveyor, when Patrick was three years old. The plat shows a hopeful town of twenty-seven acres with warehouses on the river, a main street sixty feet wide, and some fifty lots laid out with the owner's names including John Henry's.[23] Newcastle, like Hanovertown, would become a ghost town, symbolic of John's vanished hopes of financial success. But in Patrick's youth it was a growing mart, the largest town with which he had more than a speaking acquaintance. Here John Syme, Jr., conducted some of his trading enterprises[24] and here his desperate half-brother, as the British had it, would assemble the Hanover volunteers for a memorable event in the Revolution.

From Newcastle it is five miles southeastward to Studley. The intervening countryside is slightly undulating, with the Totopotomoy and numerous small tributaries intersecting what, when not misused, is productive sandy or sand-clay soil. An early account describes the area as containing a forest of full-grown trees, so that Patrick was in truth the forest-born Demosthenes that Byron depicted.[25]

Hanover County, about twice as large as it is today, comprised 205,936 acres in the 1730's (or 322 square miles). It was in strong contrast to a number of the older Virginia counties such as James City, York, Charles City, Middlesex, and Warwick, each with less than 100,000 acres. Sparsely settled as Hanover was, especially in the more remote region, it had, nevertheless, 1,941 tithables in 1726, chiefly white men and Negroes over sixteen, or more than any of these eastern counties.[26] And yet Hanover had only two representatives in the House of Burgesses: the older counties were tenaciously holding to their privileges.

There is no single source which gives more accurate information on life in Virginia during that period than the court records. Fortunately, a volume of the Hanover records for 1733-1735 has been preserved [27] which, with other contemporary evidence, gives a picture of the county social order about the time of Patrick's birth.

There were then a few great families in Hanover, with plantations embracing thousands of acres and, often, assured seats in the county court, the vestry, and the Burgesses. Nicholas Meriwether, whose daughter John Syme, Jr., married, was a member of a family whose baronial holdings in 1727 included 13,762 acres in the western part of Hanover which became Albemarle. Besides the large grants to the Symes and Winstons, such proprietors as Colonel Charles Chiswell and Nathaniel West Dandridge, Patrick's future father-in-law, inherited estates of some five thousand acres with many slaves and other personal property.[28]

But most of the Hanover transfers, recorded during the 1730's, were for small holdings, usually only some fifty to three hundred acres, with the majority a hundred acres or less. They were bought chiefly by poor people, hearty Virginians who enjoyed opportunities for fun and frolic, yet sweated in the sun, braved the rains, frosts, and snows and, aided by a few slaves and indentured servants, cleared the new country. How new may be surmised from the Indians who still lived near its boundaries, and the inventory of one John Hudson, dying about 1734, who left a tomahawk among his meager tools and furnishings. He also owned a Negro man valued at £23, a Negro boy at £14, "Amey a negro with a Lingering Sickness £5," a Negro boy worth £6, and two other Negro girls listed at £5 and £6 respectively. But modest as his estate appeared, it was larger than average. Of some two dozen Hanover citizens whose inventories were recorded during 1733-1736, nearly all owned no slaves and had estates valued at less than £100, while the others owned an average of one or two Negroes.[29] No record is given for indentured servants, but it is unlikely that by then they outnumbered the slaves. After John Henry moved, about 1750, to a new plantation, he could hardly have afforded more than a dozen slaves and an occasional indentured servant, even though his wife could provide some capital. The prevailing slavery system in Hanover at this time did not encourage aristocratic propensities as it did in the easterly counties where some masters had power over hundreds of toiling blacks. Where there were only a few Negroes in a family, there was closer association and more natural affection.

Another characteristic of this semi-frontier society was scanty education facilities. With no free public education available and relatively few inhabitants, it is not surprising that John and the Reverend Patrick were marked men in the community. The majority of their Hanover neighbors could, apparently, neither read nor write. This was true of virtually all the Negroes and of a majority of the white women if not of the men. Of some 513 principals or witnesses for legal papers during 1733-1735, over four-fifths could write but this group consisted largely of property holders. It included no slaves and probably few indentured servants. Of a total of forty-one women's names affixed to the records, sixteen signed their names and twenty-five made their mark. Obviously, the opportunity for feminine education in Hanover County was meager.[30]

Not that Hanover, even in 1736, lacked a sprinkling of men and even a few women with both education and refinement. Before Patrick left the county it was to take on a complexion much like those counties established years earlier. And yet it is not surprising to find that the 1733-1735 inventories usually include only necessary furniture and household and farming implements. There were only occasional references to parcels of books, valued at small amounts.

When it came to matters pertaining to land, the mature Patrick Henry would have the restlessness of a frontiersman (not to speak of a canny eye for a bargain). After his marriage he would live on some half a dozen plantations, none for as long as a decade. But during his boyhood John and Sarah Henry kept their brood at Studley some thirteen years. Here he spent his early youth in a household largely taken over by little girls. For after Sarah had given birth to three boys, John Syme, Jr., by her first husband, then William and Patrick, she and her second husband turned to girls, indeed a bevy of them: Jane, Sarah, Susanna, Mary, Anne, Elizabeth, and Lucy. By John Henry, Sarah had some eleven children, a sizable number even for colonial Virginia but one which Patrick would equal through his second marriage to Dolly Dandridge. Moreover, since his sister Elizabeth was born in 1749, at least five of the girls must have been added to the family circle within a decade after his birth.[31]

Patrick was encompassed by girls, first little sisters with dolls, then older ones with beaux and husbands. To these associations we may partly attribute an amiability and gentleness later characteristic of Henry in private life. Between him and his sisters the ties were unusually close. In the words of his neighbor, Samuel Meredith, who married Jane, the sister nearest Patrick's age, "He interested himself much in the happiness of others, particularly of his sisters, of whom he had eight, and whose advocate he always was when any favor or indulgence was to be procured from their mother." [32]

In 1739 the interlude of peace was broken, and England and France soon became engaged in the War of the Austrian Succession, another phase of the wearisome second Hundred Years' War. For several years the fighting had little effect on Virginia except for the tightening curbs on trade, immigration, and western settlement. But late in 1745 the Henrys received news of vital interest to all British citizens, especially those with Scottish Episcopalian (and Jacobite) connections. Thirty years before, Patrick's father and Uncle Patrick had witnessed the miserable results of a Jacobite revolt that sputtered and failed; now they read that the Old Pretender's son, Bonnie Prince Charlie, had taken advantage of English preoccupation with foreign enemies to make a desperate bid for the throne of his ancestors. In January, 1746, the "wicked and horrid Rebellion" had reached such a stage that Parson Henry and other Virginia clergymen were being urged by Commissary Dawson to inculcate in their parishioners "a firm Adherence to our most gracious Sovereign," King George II.[33] By late March the *Virginia Gazette* was publishing as news of middle

November that the city gates of Carlisle, England, were being opened to the rebel army.[34]

But a few months later word arrived that Charles' dwindling army had been cut to pieces at Culloden. There was a public celebration at Newcastle, with a handsome dinner and much drinking, huzzaing, and dancing. Never before had there been such a concourse of people at the little port, wrote the correspondent of the *Gazette* with real or pretended fervor; the few supposedly disaffected were declared to be quite out of countenance.[35] It had long been obvious that business was better under the stodgy Hanoverian rulers. After Culloden the Jacobite cause was as dead as Hector; John Henry as a magistrate and militia officer in all likelihood attended the Newcastle celebration along with Sarah and the two older boys.

What were John Henry's real sentiments regarding the rebellion in his homeland? And how did they affect Patrick? Later, after George III's accession in 1760, Colonel Henry was seen marching at the head of his regiment and celebrating the King's birthday "with as much enthusiasm as his son . . . afterward displayed in resisting the encroachments of that monarch." [36] But that enthusiasm perhaps contained its elements of expediency along with natural pleasure in a festive occasion in which he played a leading rôle. A generation before, in 1738, the Reverend Patrick and probably his brother John had taken part in the organization of a local Scotch society; a sermon was to be preached in the Parson's church on St. Andrew's Day.[37] During the Jacobite revolt their feelings must have been stirred by the dashing bravery of Prince Charlie's Scottish volunteers, and, after Culloden, sickened by the burning of the Episcopal meeting houses in Aberdeen or other episodes of the anti-Jacobite persecution.[38] Certainly, young Patrick absorbed from family sources a tradition of Scottish uprisings against the English yoke as well as of Bacon's Rebellion, close at home. To revolt against King and ministry was no light thing, but neither need they be considered sacrosanct.

By about 1750 John Syme, Jr., had reached his majority and might soon need Studley for his own family.[39] It was past time for the

Henrys to move elsewhere, and John Henry now set out with his family, including the fourteen-year-old Patrick, for Mount Brilliant. This was a large estate which they had acquired in the upper part of the county. The house, the first that the Henrys could really call their own, was twenty miles west of Studley, a day's journey over the rough roads that traversed the still largely uncleared forests. Only at occasional intervals did they get a glimpse of human habitations, but the wild game frightened in its native haunts promised fine sport for the boys.[40]

As if to secure funds for building or stocking the plantation, John Henry had during the past few years raised some £160 by selling several of his westerly land holdings.[41] In 1749, after the Treaty of Aix-la-Chapelle had brought promise of better times, he couldn't resist another small speculation, paying only £6.5 for 2,284 acres of land then in Albemarle County on the east side of Tye River under the three ridged mountain.[42] Late in 1748 he had been still listed as a vestryman of St. Paul's Parish but soon thereafter he was settled in St. Martin's Parish at Mount Brilliant.[43] Here Patrick lived for about three years and must have often visited until after his father's death shortly before the Revolution.

From Studley in the Tidewater region of Hanover, the Henrys had moved to its upper Piedmont section, in the rolling land near the South Anna River. The "compleat gentleman" of the period usually showed good taste in his choice of house, and John Henry appears to have been no exception. According to a well-founded tradition, the Mount Brilliant residence was a story-and-a-half frame structure with dormer windows, sturdily built with brick foundations and hand-hewn oak framing with wooden pins instead of nails. The dwelling stood on one of the highest points in Hanover with the land falling away on each side. Thus there was excellent drainage, while even on hot summer days a cool breeze rustled the foliage. Near by were primeval forests of oak and pine, though John Henry must have cleared some of the land stretching down to the South Anna.

Like Studley, Mount Brilliant has long since been destroyed and the very house site is covered by a cultivated field. But bits of crockery, upturned along with a few English coins and what was apparently a surveying instrument, evoke memories of a teeming life two centuries ago, while a tomahawk, Indian arrowheads and a bead found in the neighborhood recall the even earlier savage inhabitants.[44]

For some time the Studley neighborhood had been becoming more thickly settled, and at remote Mount Brilliant young Patrick would acquire greater experience with back-country men and manners. For days on end he would see no one but the plantation folk, fellow schoolmates, or the visiting relatives who then did so much to cement family ties. But when attending the chapel at Allen's Creek or the new Fork Church, he would enjoy the informal social sessions in the churchyard. During trips to the courthouse also, to the mill, stores, or other plantations, he would see something of friends and neighbors. John Syme, Jr., owned a plantation conveniently close,[45] and it was an easy ride to Scotchtown, the imposing mansion with which Colonel Chiswell had emulated Tuckahoe, an estate of his Randolph in-laws. Thus Patrick had some contacts with the gentry; but many more were with the small farmers and backwoodsmen upon whose favor would depend so much of his future career. The Mount Brilliant environment taught him a great deal not to be learned in books, but for a few more years the scholarly John Henry would make sure that these were not neglected.

4

Artistic Romancing

or the More Prosaic Facts?

There is reason to believe that [Patrick's] aversion to books and his indolence, have been exaggerated by Wirt's artistic romancing.——CAMPBELL, *History of Virginia*

U NFORTUNATELY, the general impression of Henry's boyhood has been greatly affected by the account of his first biographer. William Wirt seems to have adopted, not too wisely at times, the method of Parson Weems, an early biographer of George Washington. Within a generation after the deaths of Washington and of Henry in 1799, there appeared the well-known life by Weems and, soon thereafter, that by Wirt. Weems, not satisfied with Washington's authentic greatness, did not hesitate to add stories about him of the most doubtful accuracy. "I can't tell a lie, Pa . . . I did it with my hatchet," he wrote in his famous anecdote of Washington cutting down the cherry tree, cheerfully accepted by an uncritical public. But fictionized as it may be in no small part, Weems' biography was the second best seller of the day in America, has since run into over seventy varying editions including five in German,[1] and has left an inaccurate impression of Washington which is being removed only by the strenuous efforts of later historians.

[49]

William Wirt, the first biographer of Patrick Henry, was far more accurate than Weems. Although he never knew Henry,[2] he wrote soon after his death and was able to collect valuable reminiscences from his contemporaries. But Wirt was a busy lawyer and political leader who would not have had much time for painstaking historical research even if most of the Henry material had then been conveniently assembled. Moreover, he wrote shortly after Weems' noteworthy success and must have been influenced by it. There is unpleasant truth in Van Wyck Brooks' comment that the image of Wirt's hero depended on a "vague, gigantic shadowy memory in the marvel-loving minds of the people," and in consequence his book was not actually a biography but rather "a discourse on rhetoric, patriotism and morals."[3] Like Weems, Wirt indulged in romanticizing and painted vivid contrasts without always considering the final effects of his efforts. Somehow it would not do to give Henry credit for a normal upbringing, for all the results of tutoring by his learned father. Genius had to spring forth full blown or, as Dryden would have it:

> Time, place, and action may with pains be wrought,
> But genius must be born, and never can be taught.

Wirt also deferred too much to the statements of the great Mr. Jefferson which, as we shall note, are not among his most accurate recollections. Printed in several editions and drawn on heavily by later writers, at least indirectly, until the present time, the biography has created an especially inaccurate impression of Henry's youth.

Wirt did not even make adequate use of invaluable Henry reminiscences which he had himself collected. He could hardly have obtained more accurate data on Henry than that provided by relatives and associates such as Samuel Meredith, Spencer Roane, and Charles Dabney.[4] Could it have been that some of their recollections were too prosaic, too commonplace for the biographer? Perhaps this explains why he sometimes substituted country legends or even more fanciful material. Thus from Colonel Meredith, Henry's early neighbor and companion and later brother-in-law, Wirt obtained, and in part disregarded, this honest account of Patrick's youth:

> He was sent to a common English school until about the age of ten years, where he learned to read and write, and acquired some little knowledge of arithmetic. He never went to any other school public or private, but remained with his father, who was his only Tutor. With him he acquired a knowledge of the Latin Language and a smattering of the Greek. He became well acquainted with the Mathematics, of which he was very fond. At the age of 15 he was well versed in both ancient and modern History. His uncle had nothing to do with his education.

Until Henry attained eminence as a lawyer, there was nothing very remarkable in his "person, mind, or manners," Colonel Meredith continued. He had a "very mild, benevolent, and humane" disposition, was quiet and inclined to be thoughtful, though fond of society. And he added a few more details which would scarcely set him apart from other boys except in one or two particulars. He said that he seemed inattentive to the appearance of his outside dress except for having clean linen and stockings. How many back-country boys of his age were more scrupulous in this respect? But as Meredith was at pains to emphasize, young Patrick was not remarkable for either an uncouth or a genteel appearance—and indeed there was nothing in his early life for which he was remarkable except an "invariable habit of close and attentive observation." [5]

And yet, disregarding or distorting much of this and other accurate testimony which he himself had collected, Wirt stated that Henry's person was "represented as having been coarse, his manners uncommonly awkward, his dress slovenly, his conversation very plain, his aversion to study invincible." [6] He spun an account of Henry's laziness which has died as hard as some of the fables about Washington.[7] Henry's faculties were "almost entirely benumbed by indolence," Wirt asserted. Nothing could persuade him to read or to work. He ran wild in the forest, and divided his time "between the dissipation and uproar of the chase and the languor of inaction." [8]

Thus it could be seen how little education had affected the formation of Patrick's mind, Wirt continued. "He was, indeed, a mere child of Nature, and Nature seems to have been too proud and too jealous of her work, to permit it to be touched by the hand of art." Only in his talent for observing and commenting on human nature did he appear to have been superior to his youthful companions.[9]

Describing Washington's youth, Weems asserted that he was never guilty of so "brutish" a practice as that of fighting and in reading and spelling . . . he was "indeed famous." [10] But in ability to exaggerate Wirt could occasionally outdo the master. Let us now consider his assertions that Henry as a youth ran wild in the forest and that he was "a mere child of Nature" which, unwilling for her work to be touched by the hand of art, gave "him Shakespeare's genius and bade him . . . to depend on that alone." [11]

Until he was about ten and his education was taken over by that scholarly gentleman, his own father, Patrick's formal study was indeed of the most rudimentary type. Apart from the sketchy training he obtained when under ten at a "common English school," [12] his education, in the broader sense, came during this period from a free country life and from family training and associations. These influences remained strong throughout his youth. Few of the great Americans of this and subsequent eras—not Thomas Jefferson or even Abraham Lincoln—seem to have got more beneficial results from their frontier environment. It was a broadening, toughening, and almost wholly enjoyable experience. The frontier, its distinctive customs and people, helped to make Patrick Henry a flaming apostle of American democracy. At the same time he was fortunate to live in an educated, Christian household and to receive what for the time and place were the rare benefits of its training.

Colonel Meredith speaks of Patrick's fondness for his gun.[13] The muzzle-loading guns of that period, single shot and requiring several minutes to load and fire, were truly sporting weapons, never slaughtering the game as do some of our modern repeating or pump guns. Not that any curbs on hunting were then needed in the forests and uncleared expanses of upper Hanover. Deer, wolves, squirrels, rabbits, partridge, and other game abounded, at times to the nuisance level. There were great flocks of duck at easy riding distance on the Pamunkey and wild geese settling in the fields near its banks. And there were foxes in abundance, with dogs and horses to chase them.[14]

From his uncle, the mighty hunter, William (Langloo) Winston, and other men in the county Patrick could learn forest lore. William, who married his cousin Sarah Dabney, was a far different type from the powdered and bewigged gentleman of the Tidewater region. He camped with the Indians and dressed as a woodsman; he shot deer like a true Buckskin and Long Knife. At his quarters in Bedford or Albemarle County he spent half the year hunting deer. He was fond of the Indians and they returned the friendship, but his relations with an Indian chief's daughter who was reportedly engaged to another chief almost ruined the friendship. For a week the Indians besieged him in a log fort, where he defended himself with the aid of three Negroes armed with rifles. Tom, one of the Negroes, had to stand guard every night; but finally the favorite "squaw" went out and stopped the fighting.[15]

During his last years, when living at Long Island in Campbell County, Patrick showed Spencer Roane a "slope" or fish trap he had made across a branch of the Staunton River and which furnished fish for his family. And he spoke with pleasure of a buck recently caught in the trap after having been brought down the river in the current.[16] Such traps were then common, and Patrick probably learned to make them when a boy. There is other testimony of his fondness for the woods and streams and of his fun-loving spirit, normal for a youth in his teens. When crossing the South Anna with two companions, he enjoyed upsetting the canoe. Each time this was supposed to be an accident but his playmates would always have their clothes on while Patrick had somehow managed to be rid of his.[17] He also liked playing with a "dependant" noted for his agility and dexterity. Patrick would give him a pistareen to climb a tall pine in the neighborhood, feet foremost, and sometimes he would deliberately entangle his fishing lines, getting them in the hardest knots possible to observe how well the little fellow could untie them.[18]

Then there were water sports. In recent years a canoe, hollowed from a single log, was found buried in the river near the site of Mount Brilliant.[19] The South Anna, which here rushes down boldly from the Piedmont hills, still retains much of its pristine charm. At the road crossing are the great grindstones and ruined buildings of the mill where the Henrys traded and, near by, an old swimming hole presided over by some ancient beeches.[20] In such retreats, as in the great expanse of unspoiled countryside, Patrick found a beauty for which he had a greater appreciation with the passing years. In a disciplined form it appears in his oratory as well as in that poetry which he would write, then self-consciously destroy.

When Patrick was living at Red Hill in his last years, one of his servants, Jack White, a half-Indian and expert woodsman, asked his master to tell him about the boyhood sports on the South Anna. Patrick replied that during his solitary rambles his purpose had been to learn the language of the birds.[21] He might have added stories of his fishing and hunting. There was then an abundance of fishing in the South Anna; but even when the fish were not biting he would lie under the shade of a tree watching the motionless cork. When hunting deer, also, he is said to have preferred the silent stand where he could enjoy his solitary thoughts.[22]

All this does not greatly distinguish Patrick from thousands of other American boys of the period. In the careful opinion of Campbell, "the glowing fancy of Wirt has, perhaps, thrown over these particulars some prismatic coloring." [23] It is fortunate that we have a few other facts about his youthful years. When about twelve years old, he broke his collar bone and, while confined, learned to play on the flute.[24] He also developed some skill with the violin, and even, it is said, with the lute and harpsichord. Later his household would join in sacred music on Sunday evenings while he accompanied on the violin.[25] His interest in music, however, was not as deep or as discriminating as that of Jefferson.

His "delight was in conversation, and in the society of his friends and family, and in the resources of his own mind," wrote Judge Roane.[26]

Altogether, there was little about Patrick's early life to indicate his future greatness. Obviously, he was not the wild "child of Nature" described by Wirt; his genius did not spring forth full-blown without the benefits of education. But both Colonel Meredith and Judge Roane stressed his acute power of observation. Meredith recalled that from his early boyhood Patrick attentively observed everything important that occurred near him. "Nothing escaped his attention." [27] Judge Roane not only emphasized this characteristic but also its influence on Henry's future career.

"Mr. Henry was remarkably well acquainted with mankind. He knew well all the springs and motives of human action. This faculty arose from mingling freely with mankind and from a keen and constant observation." As a result of this ability and his mastery of his temper, Wirt said that Henry would have made a great negotiator. "In fact, he was a great negotiator, for in managing a jury or a popular assembly he measured and gauged them by a discriminating judgment. He knew how much they would bear, and what was the proper string to touch them upon." It was the "same faculty and discernment which enabled him to fathom the views and feelings of Courts and Cabinets," Roane added.[28]

With Patrick's remarkable power of observation went a similar capacity for reflection. Like nearly all of his colonial contemporaries, he read in his youth relatively few books, perhaps no more than some dozens. Of Montesquieu's *Spirit of Laws*, with which Patrick became acquainted in later years, Roane quoted him as saying that it was a good book to read on a stagecoach; one could read enough in half an hour to provide reflection for a day. And this was more or less the proportion between Henry's education as derived from reading and from observation and reflection. He read good books as he would from a text, and he filled up the picture not only by his acute and penetrating observation and reflection but by mingling with men.[29] Moreover, these habits would soon be sharpened by the prac tice of law in the county courts, a school remarkably adapted to ac quaint a person with human nature.

With the exceptions noted, all Patrick's early education was obtained from his father, possibly aided by his uncle, the Parson. In our own era of mass education, largely furnished in public schools, it is easy to underestimate the value of such tutorial education as was common among the upper classes in the eighteenth century. Probably John Henry, with his various public and private obligations, did not put his son through the educational paces as did another Scotsman, the Reverend Mr. Craig, tutor for Richard Henry Lee and his brothers. These gifted boys, rung into their little brick schoolroom by seven in the morning, had a round of instruction before breakfast, then again until five in the afternoon, with only a few hours relief.[30] But if John Henry did not enforce such a Spartan regime, still he was concerned with the education of his intelligent though not unduly studious son, and he was then apparently under contract to teach a number of pupils in the customary fashion.[31]

The tutorial system or individual instruction did not give opportunity for democratic association with large groups of students, as do our present public schools. But there were obvious advantages for precocious students. We can picture John Henry as he checked on how well Patrick did his arithmetic problems or read the history text or assignment in Horace.[32] How could a King's College alumnus fail to stress industry, thoroughness in scholarship? A letter which John Henry wrote to his brother, the Reverend Patrick of Mount Pleasant, indicates the kind of intellectual diet which John appreciated and, to a certain extent, must have offered to his own sons:

> I sent you two letters which I received at Williamsburgh from Mr. Blair Jr. They, together with one in my hands are in answer to a letter I wrote to Col. Bland long ago in defina of the Doctrine of Eternal Punishment. You'll perceive he wanders remarkably from the point in question. But what he chiefly labours at is to prove that the Greek word Aiwvios is always taken for a limited duration—wherein he is much mistaken.

That it is often to be understood in that sense I grant; but deny that it is always to be so understood. And indeed were I to give up the word Aiwvios to his sense thereof, so long as we can prove that Adavabia immortalitas is constantly predicater of the souls of men, both in sacred & profane authors, I can't see much advantage he can gain. I shall be glad to have some of your strictures & I will contrive you the third letter soon. The boy being in haste, I can't enlarge. With love to Sister, I am

Dear Brother
Your affectionate Brother
JOHN HENRY

Henry was correct in the point about the Greek word which he follows with such logic and scholarship.[33]

Further evidence as to the extent of Patrick's education, with the trend of his reading and his intellectual aptitudes, is given in the inventory of his library recorded after his death. There were nearly two hundred volumes, almost all solid treatises on law, religion, history, and politics and including some textbooks. The greatest number, about a fourth of the whole, were lawbooks but there were also numerous volumes of the classics.[34]

Among these classics were a considerable number of Greek and Latin books.[35] Wirt believed that Patrick could read the Greek characters but not translate the language.[36] On the other hand, one of his grandsons stated that when he was a student at Hampden-Sidney and Patrick was living near by he dreaded his grandfather's quizzings to determine his progress in Latin and Greek much more than he did his recitations to the professors. Patrick is also said to have talked in Latin with a foreign visitor during the Revolution, and, again on the testimony of his grandson, to have had some reading knowledge of French.[37] This is further substantiated by a book in which he wrote "Le don de Pierre de la Fontaine" and "Patrice Henry le Jeune. Avrille 18th, 1760." [38] Two French books are listed in his inventory.

It is easy to overemphasize the extent of Henry's early education even if we allow for his very retentive memory.[39] But, thanks chiefly to his father, the old Aberdonian, this education was more thorough than is commonly recognized. Among the fathers of some distinguished eighteenth or early nineteenth century Virginians—Washington, Jefferson, Madison, Pendleton, Monroe, and Marshall—none was as well educated as John Henry and none transmitted as much book learning to his son.

5

⌒〰⌒

Orator and Statesman:
The Seeds Being Sown

The child is father of the man.——WORDSWORTH

Nothing is a misery
Unless our weakness apprehend it so.
                        ——BEAUMONT AND FLETCHER

Two distinguished historians have stated that the generation which "came to maturity between the Peace of Paris and the inauguration of President Washington had to solve more serious and original political problems than any later generation of Americans."[1] Perhaps they would revise their assertion in view of the grave and bewildering problems of this atomic age; but in many respects the problems of our Revolutionary ancestors were more difficult and burdensome. The popular leaders of the Revolution, Sam Adams, Henry, Washington, Jefferson, Franklin, and the others, braved death on the scaffold or in a foul prison. The Continental armies were well-nigh crushed and the soldiers often ragged and half-starved. The government was at times financed almost from day to day. In several states there were nearly as many Tories as patriots; in all a depressing number of the indifferent or time-serving. Only a grimly determined minority fought the long battle for independence and national stability.

Patrick Henry's rôle in these times that tried men's souls is now best understood for the period preceding the Revolution, though even here there are many misconceptions. His later career, as we shall trace it in these pages, is less known: Governor of Virginia for five terms during the critical period; an outstanding lawyer and legislator; an opponent of the American Constitution, partly counterbalanced by his influence in securing the Bill of Rights; and, it should be added, a family man, with so many children and grandchildren as to evoke the poetic mirth of a great-grandson:

> The Belgian hare could nothing to you show,
> Prolific Patrick—what a family man! [2]

With his two wives, seventeen children, and sixty grandchildren would come far more joy than sorrow, but altogether Patrick would have to cope with personal and family problems that would have broken many men.

What inner resources did Henry draw upon to live serenely in those parlous years? For our immediate consideration, to what extent had these resources been built up in his youth? In view of his early training and subsequent events it appears likely that from his youth upward he was developing a religion based on deeds rather than words. Or, to use the homely phrase, God helps those who help themselves. At St. John's Church in early 1775 he would passionately exclaim:

> Sir, we are not weak, if we make a proper use of those means
> which the God of nature hath placed in our power.[3]

And soon afterwards he would tell the Hanover volunteers that "it was for them now to determine whether they were worthy of this divine interference." [4] There is indeed much reason to think that he early began to build a religious philosophy, based on family teaching and other experience, that would be reflected in his later career. Surely the highest form of statesmanship is based on deep conviction. Without it there could be no great oratory and Henry's noblest utterances might seem little more than words and gestures.

The twin strains of deep and comforting religion and of what is often related to and strengthened by it—a moving eloquence—were passed down in several generations of the Henry family. The religious heritage was largely through his parents and also his uncle Patrick, the learned rector of St. Paul's, Hanover County. Although he was a conservative, at least in his zealous defense of the Anglican Establishment, the Reverend Patrick seems to have preached a religion based on both faith and works. The expression was in the moderate, gentlemanly style but the philosophy was implicit. The Parson's cultured, formalized sermons, heard if only through one ear by his young nephew week after week, year after year, must have not only strengthened his religious convictions but also offered his first continuous model for speechmaking.

The unformed oratorical gift was already present within him as a heritage from the Winstons. And it would be bolstered by the influence of one and probably two great preachers and orators associated with the Hanover of his boyhood—George Whitefield and Samuel Davies.

Parson Henry became rector of St. Paul's in 1737 and through clerical teaching and intimate family association brought his namesake under the long-time influence of another educated Christian gentleman. Considering the conflicting testimony of Colonel Meredith and of Judge Roane, we must discount Roane's story that the Reverend Patrick, "a very learned and pious clergyman," taught his nephew the Greek and Latin classics. The influence of the cultured Parson seems to have been chiefly through association and example. We can, however, reasonably assume that he instructed the boy in the catechism and that Patrick received from him those principles which helped to make Virginia of that period a "nursery" of great men. In the words of his grandson, he was taught:

> "to be true & just in all my dealings. To bear no malice nor hatred in my heart. To keep my *hands from picking & stealing*," (*which kept him poor while he was Governor*)—"not to covet other mens goods; but to learn & labor truly to get my own living, & to do my duty in that state of life unto which it shall please God to call me." [5]

Some five or six years after John Henry came to Virginia, his brother Patrick had followed him, to become rector of St. George's Parish in the newly formed county of Spotsylvania. But St. George's was large and remote, even by Virginia standards, and some of the Reverend Patrick's purported flock were actually German Dissenters, brought in by Governor Spotswood to work his mines. Parson Henry was doubtless delighted when he received in 1737 a call to St. Paul's Parish, Hanover, where his brother's family was located. John Henry had probably used his influence to help secure for the Reverend Patrick the new charge which he would manage to hold through vicissitudes until his death some forty years later.[6]

The ties were close between the two brothers, removed from faraway Aberdeenshire to the new country. Visiting back and forth with the people at the glebe seat of Mount Pleasant or sitting with his parents in the new gallery or front pews reserved at St. Paul's Church for vestrymen, gentlemen justices and their families,[7] Patrick was under the constant influence of his uncle. That the Parson's conservatism did not shed off to Patrick is evident, but he does appear to have affected him otherwise by precept and example. Proof that the Parson's convictions were not of the passive type is found in a letter, still preserved in London, in which he tried to prevent an applicant whom he deemed unworthy, from entering the Anglican ministry because of his unfitness "in point of *Learning*" and of character.[8]

A sermon by Mr. Henry gives further indication of the example in morals, and to some extent, in speechmaking, which he offered his nephew.[9] It was a burial sermon preached from Hebrews 12:1-2: ". . . Let us run with patience the race that is set before us, looking unto Jesus. . . ."

"Our present life is a state of tryal and probation," the minister declared. Our conduct here will determine whether we shall enjoy "an eternity of happiness." In demonstrating just what this conduct should be, he stressed the importance of industry ("the Christian Life is an active and industrious life"), of patience, and of following the example of Christ and looking to Him for aid. He developed each of these points in order and drew some general conclusions.

When Parson Henry particularizes by opposing excessive drinking, a censorious critic might accuse him of hypocrisy. A contemporary merchant's account lists him as buying within some nine months "1 gro. corks" and "2 gross of Bottle Corks," surely more than were needed for his sacramental wine.[10] But he was truly opposed to intemperance. After praising in the sermon the honesty and diligence of his dead parishioner, he added an injunction worthy of full consideration in that heavy drinking period. The parishioner was a person of "exemplary temperance and sobriety, keeping within the bounds of that moderation of his appetites, that becomes the character of a Christian, and which I wish were universally practised among us. It would greatly tend to the Honour of God, and the Credit of our holy Religion."

He then followed with tributes to the religious convictions of the deceased, his domestic virtues, and his relationship with his servants and slaves to whom he was a compassionate and indulgent master. Far from exercising any rigor or severity toward them, he had a temper which was happily framed to do good to every one. Mr. Henry's description of the Christian serenity which he had helped to inculcate in the parishioner was much like that which would characterize his nephew Patrick. The happy frame of mind the deceased was in before his last sickness enabled him to bear it with "a wonderful deal of Christian patience." [11]

The impression here is certainly of a religion based on both faith and works and presented in a logical fashion by a cultivated gentleman. But if the Reverend Patrick had any oratorical gifts, they were not enough to keep many of his congregation from being lured away by the more spectacular Dissenting ministers. In a back-country region, where the influence of the ill-educated could be pervasive, he offered a groundwork of cultivated taste on which his nephew could later build. Beyond that, any conclusions are highly conjectural, and the search for sources of Patrick's oratorical powers must move to more fertile fields: the Winston heritage and the example of one or more great evangelists.

There is no contemporary written evidence of the Winston influence, as there was for the principal ideas in Henry's speech on the Parson's Cause. But, judging from later reminiscences, Henry seemingly inherited oratorical talent from his mother's people. It was like the military ability passed on for several generations by the Lees. His uncle William (Langloo) Winston offered him the influence of a natural oratory, a gift akin to that of such untutored orators as the Indian chieftains, Cornstalk and Tecumseh.

From the intimate and somewhat imaginative account of the son of Old Isaac Winston, we get this comparison of William and his famous nephew. Patrick's oratory is described in superlatives as one would expect:

> "Patrick, when he speaks, stirs the boys so that I've seen them jump up and crack their heels together, and slam their caps on the ground and stamp them. I have seen a fellow, under Patrick's inspiration, seize another by the collar and wheel him around off his feet for no other assignable cause than that inspiration, and the other hardly conscious what he was doing."

Then he compares Patrick's uncle William:

> "Billy, you see, don't come up to that quite; but I have heard him speak on election days, and he would roll his rich words into the crowd until the very hair would stand on my head, and I would cry like a baby." [12]

"I have often heard my father, who was intimately acquainted with William Winston, say, that he was the greatest orator he had ever heard—Patrick Henry excepted," recalled Nathaniel Pope of Hanover.

"During the French and Indian War and soon after Braddock's defeat," Pope continued, "when the militia were marched to the frontiers of Virginia against the enemy, William Winston was a lieutenant of a company. The men, indifferently clothed, without tents, and exposed to the rigour and inclemency of the weather, discovered aversion to the service, and were anxious and even clamourous to return to their families." But at this critical point William

Winston mounted a stump and addressed them with great eloquence on liberty and patriotism.

"Let us march on! Lead us against the enemy!" was the general cry after he concluded. So forceful was his speech that the recruits were now anxious to meet the dangers which shortly before had almost produced a mutiny.[13]

The oratorical talents which Patrick inherited were also passed to others of his family. His sister Jane was one of the remarkable women for which the family was distinguished. The noted Presbyterian minister, Archibald Alexander, was not only strongly impressed with her character but even asserted that she had oratorical gifts as great as her brother Patrick's.[14]

His sister Elizabeth was described by his grandson as resembling him in both person and intellect. He recalled her as possessing the same vivid imagination. She had the same flexibility of voice, grace of elocution, and interplay of features expressive of every phase of her feeling. Much younger than Patrick, she would live to offer prayerful wishes for James Madison when Madison was a presidential candidate. Madame Russell, as she was then widely known, pressed Madison to his knees and prayed for him as the incoming chief executive.

"I have heard all the first orators of America," Madison said, "but I have never heard any eloquence as great as that prayer of Mrs. Russell on the occasion of my visit to her." [15]

Piety such as Mrs. Russell's was evident in another of Henry's sisters, Lucy, who also inherited the family eloquence. The gift was even passed down to a third generation.[16]

But if Patrick owed much of his oratorical talent to family heritage, he was also influenced by notable practitioners of the forensic art. In October, 1745, remote Hanover was stirred by the visit of George Whitefield, the great Methodist divine. It is most likely that Patrick heard him preach. In any case, his appearance directly affected the Henry family and must have stimulated the imagination of the young lad. Perhaps the greatest pulpit orator that England had ever produced, Whitefield had been reaching into the byways and the dens of iniquity to bring lowly miners, drunkards, and prisoners to the way of Christ. Such was the power of his oratory that he loosened the pockets of the scoffing Benjamin Franklin and even made Lord Chesterfield call out during a sermon.

In Great Britain he preached in open fields when churches were denied him and in America he reached backwoodsmen and others never stirred by the conventional churchmen. On October 10, 1745, the *Virginia Gazette* reported that Whitefield had arrived in Hanover County the previous Friday and preached several times to large audiences. The circumstances under which he happened to come to the country were curious, if not revealing. In 1743 a young Scottish gentleman then residing in Hanover County happened to obtain a volume of Whitefield's sermons preached in Glasgow and taken down in shorthand. This same volume was studied with much benefit by another man in the county who invited his neighbors to visit his house to hear them read. The feelings of many of the local people were excited "and they could not avoid bitter and violent weeping." The news spread, and others moved by curiosity or religious zeal crowded the house in which the services were conducted. "Numbers were pricked to the heart, the word became quick and powerful; 'What shall we do?' was the general cry."

"My dwelling house," said Samuel Morris, a leader in the new movement, "was at length too small to contain the people, whereupon we determined to build a meeting-house merely for *reading*. And having never been used to social prayer, none of us durst attempt it." The Morris Reading House, as it was called, was followed by others.[17] The way was soon prepared not only for Whitefield's visit but for development of the strong Presbyterian movement in Hanover.

Furthermore, the agitation led to a division in Patrick's own family which made it easier for him to come under the Dissenting influence. Morris, an obscure bricklayer but sincere and devout, became closely associated with several of Patrick's family and later in the 1760's one of his law clients.[18] Bald-headed Old Isaac Winston, Patrick's grandfather, was probably one of four gentlemen who, becoming convinced that the parish minister was not preaching the true Gospel, paid fines for non-attendance at church and built reading houses.[19] And how shocking to the Reverend Patrick and other family conformists when in October, 1745, Isaac was indicted by the General Court for permitting a Dissenting minister, John Roan, to hold services at his home! The trial, the first intimately connected with his family which Patrick was old enough to understand, was belatedly conducted before the Council, sitting as the highest court in the colony, on April 14, 1747. Besides Governor William Gooch, the members of the Council present included such influential landed gentry as William Nelson, Lewis Burwell, Thomas Lee, and John Robinson, father of Speaker and Treasurer John Robinson with whom young Patrick would later lock horns. The prosecution was represented by the Attorney-General of "our Lord the king," the defendant by his own attorney. That John Roan had held the services at Isaac Winston's without license was undeniable; but the twelve-man jury, which included Isaac's Hanover friend Peter Fontaine, held that, although the people assembled in Winston's house, they did not do so in a riotous manner. Roan preached there, they had to admit, but not contrary to the canons of the Church of England as set forth in the information. The case was continued until the next court for the matters of law arising from it to be argued, and Winston was fined twenty shillings and costs of the prosecution.[20]

When this local *cause célèbre* was being debated in the Henry family with Patrick's grandfather and Uncle Patrick in opposing camps, it is likely that his mother, although married to a devout Episcopalian, was already leaning toward unorthodox religious beliefs. Certainly when the indictment was returned against Isaac Winston in October, 1745, the way, both in and out the family circle, was prepared for the appearance that very month in Hanover of the famous Whitefield. This event was built up to the proportion of a minor religious crisis which must have left its impression on the susceptible young Patrick. And the more so since it would not be Whitefield's last visit to Hanover.

What a crop of troubles for Parson Henry, troubles that had their repercussions at Studley and elsewhere in the family entourage! First the Parson had been much oppressed with fever and ague, those common Tidewater ailments. And, before he could recover, the dangerous and alluring Mr. Whitefield had arrived in Hanover and had the temerity to request permission to preach at St. Paul's. Whitefield was an ordained Anglican minister, to be sure, but what doctrines would he preach and with what unconventional shouting and gesturing? Temporizing, the Reverend Patrick asked Whitefield to come to Mount Pleasant so that he could converse with him and decide if the request was "proper." This and subsequent events Parson Henry explained in a letter, sent through Colonel Henry, to propitiate Commissary Dawson at Williamsburg.

Whitefield did not reply to the Parson's invitation. The next day, on the way to St. Paul's, the Parson was told that Whitefield would preach either in the church or churchyard. Arriving on the spot, he found a great gathering of people. In a dilemma, he gave Whitefield permission to preach in the church upon condition that he read the common prayer, "etc." before the sermon. For, wrote the harassed Parson to the Commissary, "If I had refused him access to the Church, he would have preached in the Churchyard, or very near it and then the whole congregation would have gone over to him, this was what I plainly foresaw, as did also my Friends; for tho the number of his followers there were but few, yet all the people to a man had a great desire to hear the famous Whitfield." And as all the local New Light men were present, who "exclaim upon our Liturgy, I thought, that their great Apostle's using it, must infallibly silence them for ever on that subject. These, Sir, were my chief reasons for allowing Whitfield to preach in the Church, and I shall be extremely glad if you approve of them," wrote Mr. Henry, as if wringing his hands. On that and the following Sunday Whitefield also preached in private houses but he encouraged the local Dissenters to return to the church and some of them declared that they would do so.[21]

The visit of perhaps the greatest preacher of his age must have been the subject of talk for many years in the Hanover back country and not least in the Henry family. Patrick, already under the strong religious influence of his parents and Uncle Patrick, quite likely read if he did not hear some of Whitefield's sermons. Indeed, his most famous speech contains some lines that invite a significant comparison with the spellbinding divine. One of Whitefield's sermons printed in recent years is "on the Method of Grace," based upon his text from Jeremiah 6: 14: "They have healed also the hurt of the daughter of my people slightly, saying, Peace, peace; when there is no peace." "How many of us," exhorted Whitefield, "cry, Peace, peace, to our souls, when there is no peace. How many are there who are now settled upon their lees, that now think they are Christians . . . whereas if we come to examine their experiences we shall find that their peace is but a peace of the devil's making. . . ." [22] In the concluding paragraph of his epochal speech at St. John's Church, Richmond, in March, 1775, Henry exclaimed:

> It is in vain, sir, to extenuate the matter. Gentlemen may cry peace, peace—but there is no peace. The war is actually begun.

And so on to the oft-quoted finale.

Probably Patrick was familiar with the words beginning "Peace, peace" in the text from Jeremiah, but it seems certain that, with his retentive mind and strong power of observation, he was influenced by Whitefield's sermons which he read or heard.[23] When examined today, the sermons are not deeply moving. The effect came largely from the rude strength, the awesome impetuosity of the great pulpit orator. One needed only to have that squint eye seemingly fastened upon him, and to hear that voice, to have an abiding memory of the great evangelist. Undoubtedly, Whitefield handed down in Hanover and environs a tradition of vigorous speaking with which Henry was familiar. If he could learn to speak with Whitefield's force and dramatic power, yet add a poetic touch, he would be an orator indeed.[24]

Far more important than Whitefield was the religious movement to which he gave impetus. During the 1740's the Great Awakening, one of the most fruitful religious developments in American history, swept the colonies from New England to Georgia. It was characterized by great revivals, with thousands converted to a highly emotional and, as some conservative churchmen deemed it, undignified religious faith. In the South, especially, it was a revolt against the Anglican Church, with its complacent formalism and compulsory fees and taxes. It drew support chiefly from the backwoodsmen and lower classes and greatly helped the growth of the Presbyterians, Baptists, Methodists, and other Dissenting sects.

After Whitefield, the next leader in Virginia of the Great Awakening was Samuel Davies. No person during this period had a greater effect on Patrick's oratory than this famous Presbyterian minister. Henry, as Samuel Meredith noted, was an Episcopalian, but very friendly to all the other sects, particularly the Presbyterians.[25] It is highly probable that Davies influenced his ideals of religious liberty and helped to make him a champion of persecuted Dissenters.

Samuel Davies was one of the greatest religious leaders in colonial America. Born in New Castle County, Delaware, he first assaulted the Anglican stronghold of Hanover in 1747 when in his twenty-second year. The very same day that Isaac Winston was tried before the Council, the tall, dignified young man, pale and wasted by disease, made a successful appeal there for permission to preach. Soon Davies' carefully prepared, impassioned sermons were impelling the people to ride long hours through the forests to hear him, and he won noteworthy recognition during a trip to England and Scotland. It was some admiring Englishmen who gave Davies the gold ring and gold-headed cane later criticized by one of his frontier Presbyterian congregations as worldly symbols.

Over the opposition of Attorney-General Randolph, Davies secured a license to preach in four back-country charges, incidentally compounding the troubles of poor Parson Henry.[26]

"I need not inform you of the present distracted condition of my parish nor of the future disturbances I justly apprehend from these Itinerants," the Reverend Mr. Henry wrote Commissary Dawson in June, 1747, two years after Whitefield's disrupting appearance. He went on to explain how these preachers manage "to screw up the people to the greatest heights of religious-Phrenzy," and then leave them in that wild state for perhaps ten or twelve months until another enthusiast came among them.[27]

The merits and demerits of the young minister with the sonorous voice and burning words must have been the subject of much discussion by Patrick's elders. Mrs. Henry, who could be quietly determined, joined Davies' flock, as did her daughters Jane and Lucy.[28] In Hanover he preached at Fork Church, a simple frame building in the lower county within easy riding distance of Studley.[29] Mrs. Henry attended the church regularly in a double gig, taking with her the receptive young Patrick. From the first he showed a high appreciation of the earnest divine in the black gown, white wig, and bands. As he returned with his mother from the church, she would make him repeat the text and substance of the sermon.[30] It was invaluable experience.

Henry, who, either in Virginia or at the Continental Congress, listened to many of the best speakers in America, always said that Davies was the greatest orator he ever heard.[31] After Henry moved to Mount Brilliant, he could still conveniently hear Davies, at Providence Church in Louisa. Patrick was also located near Fork Church after his marriage. Henry was eleven years old when Davies started his crusade in Hanover, twenty-three when Davies left to assume the presidency of the College of New Jersey, now Princeton. It indeed seemed that God had given Patrick a superlative tutor and mentor in oratory during his formative years. If he could not study rhetoric in Athens and Rhodes or listen to a Marcus Antonius and Lucius Crassus, as did Cicero, still he was singularly fortunate for a backcountry lad.

Of Davies we read so much praise that we are not surprised to find him rated among his contemporaries as second only to the great Whitefield. Among the superlatives with which he was credited were a powerful voice, rich and well-modulated; an elegant diction and dramatic yet restrained delivery; a deep conviction which led him to admonish a King of England when he believed George II was interrupting his sermon.

There are obvious comparisons in subject matter and delivery between Henry and Davies. Both delivered some of their greatest speeches under the shadow of war or impending war; both were inspired by crusading zeal. For Davies the main task on this earth was to sway the masses to evangelical religion; for Henry, to lead them in the fight for liberty. Davies reinforced the tradition of vigorous speaking left in Hanover by Whitefield.

In Henry's speeches we often find a rhythm, a biblical style with crusading overtones, that assuredly bears the influence of Davies. We can illustrate with only a few excerpts from sermons which Henry must have listened to or heard discussed:

For example, there was Davies' sermon on the defeat of General Braddock, delivered at Hanover, July 20, 1755, the year after Henry was married.

> "And, O Virginia! O my country! shall I not lament for thee? Thou art a valley of vision, favoured with the light of revelation from heaven, and the gospel of Jesus: thou hast long been the region of peace and tranquillity; the land of ease, plenty and liberty. But what do I now see? What do I now hear? I see thy brazen skies, thy parched soil, thy withering fields, thy hopeless springs, and thy scanty harvests. Methinks I also hear the sound of the trumpet, and see garments rolled in blood—thy frontiers ravaged by revengeful savages; thy territories invaded by French perfidy and violence. Methinks I see slaughtered families, the hairy scalps clotted with gore; the horrid arts of Indian and popish torture. And, alas! in the midst of all these alarms, I see thy inhabitants generally asleep, and careless of thy fate. I see vice braving the skies; religion neglected and insulted; mirth and folly have still their places of rendezvous. Let our country, let religion, liberty, property, and all be lost: yet still they will have their diversions; luxury spreads her feast, and unmans her effeminate guests. In spite of laws, in spite of proclamations, in spite of the principle of self preservation, thy officers are generally inactive, thy militia neglected and undisciplined, thy inhabitants unprovided with arms; every thing in a defenceless posture: but few Abrahams to intercede for thee; but few to stand the gap, and make up the breach, to prevent the irruption of vengeance; but few mourning for the sins of the land! 'The Lord God of hosts, and every thing around thee,

call thee to weeping and mourning, and girding with sackcloth: but instead of this, behold joy and gladness, eating flesh and drinking wine; let us eat and drink, for to-morrow we die.' And shall I not weep for thee, O my country? Yes; when I forget thee, O Virginia, 'let my right hand forget her cunning, and my tongue cleave to the roof of my mouth.' " [32]

Another of Davies' sermons was that on "The Curse of Cowardice," from the text in Jeremiah 48: 10. "Cursed be he that doeth the work of the Lord deceitfully, and cursed be he that keepeth back his sword from blood." We have seen that Henry in his "Give me Liberty" speech would employ lines from Jeremiah. Davies' text from Jeremiah was used in his sermon to the militia of Hanover County when a general muster was held May 8, 1758, with the purpose of raising a company to be commanded by Captain Samuel Meredith, Henry's brother-in-law:

"But when, in this corrupt, disordered state of things, where the lusts of men are perpetually embroiling the world with wars and fightings, throwing all into confusion; when ambition and avarice would rob us of our property, for which we have toiled, and on which we subsist; when they would enslave the free-born mind, and compel us meanly to cringe to usurpation and arbitrary power; when they would tear from our eager grasp the most valuable blessing of heaven, I mean our religion; when they invade our country, formerly the region of tranquility, ravage our frontiers, butcher our fellow-subjects, or confine them in a barbarous captivity in the dens of savages; when our earthly all is ready to be seized by rapacious hands, and even our eternal all is in danger by the loss of our religion; when this is the case, what is then the will of God? Must peace then be maintained, maintained with our perfidious and cruel invaders? maintained at the expense of property, liberty, life, and every thing dear and valuable? maintained, when it is in our power to vindicate our right, and do ourselves justice? Is the work of peace then our only business? No: in such a time, even the God of Peace proclaims by his Providence, 'To arms!' Then the sword is, as it were, consecrated to God; and the art of war becomes a part of our religion. Then happy is he that shall reward our enemies as they have served us. Ps. cxxxvii. 8. Blessed is the brave soldier:

[73]

blessed is the defender of his country, and the destroyer of its enemies. Blessed are they who offer themselves willingly in this service, and who faithfully discharge it." [33]

With this compare Henry's Stamp Act and "Give me Liberty" speeches and lines such as these in his exhortation at Newcastle to the Hanover volunteers after the outbreak of the Revolution:

It was for them now to determine, whether they were worthy of this divine interference; whether they would accept the high boon now held out to them by heaven—that if they would, though it might lead them through a sea of blood, they were to remember that the same God whose power divided the Red Sea for the deliverance of Israel, still reigned in all his glory, unchanged and unchangeable—was still the enemy of the oppressor, and the friend of the oppressed—that he would cover them from their enemies by a pillar of cloud by day, and guide their feet through the night by a pillar of fire—that for his own part he was anxious that his native county should distinguish itself in this grand career of liberty and glory, and snatch the noble prize which was now offered to their grasp—that no time was to be lost. . . .[34]

In another of his Hanover sermons, Davies asked for the power of a Demosthenes that he might carry his point to his audience. Thus Henry could early hear invoked that most eloquent orator of antiquity with whom his own name would be so often linked.[35]

6

~~~

Difficult Years

Xerxes that great, wasn't free from Cupid's Dart
And all the greatest Heroes felt the Smart.
——From an acrostic written by George Washington,
age fifteen, on the name of Francis Alexander [1]

Nearly all my successes are founded on previous failures.
——LOUIS N. PARKER, *Disraeli*

BY THE time Patrick was about fifteen years old his father
had given him educational advantages exceptional for the time and
place. But John Henry now had to let him shift for himself. There
were no funds to send him over to King's College or even to near-by
William and Mary, and he placed him in a country store to learn
the mercantile business.[2]

At Hanovertown, Newcastle, crossroads, and similar vantage
points in the county there were a number of stores run by thrifty
Scots or other merchants. These stores were much like those in Bristol
or London except that they were not specialty shops but offered a
variety of goods.[3] Indeed, they would carry almost any salable article
which British merchants could ship them. The rural customers would
pay in money, tobacco, and other commodities, often on credit terms
too uncertain for the storekeeper's comfortable anticipation. Thus we
find several of Patrick's relatives and acquaintances buying from A.

Gordon, a Scotch storekeeper at Newcastle, such diverse items as snuff, shoes, "Stone Muggs," drum lines, a fine scarlet cloak, "balladin" silk, and breast buttons (the last three by the sporting young John Syme). Their grandfather Winston bought a snaffle bridle, spectacles, and numerous other articles in exchange for a hogshead and a cask of tobacco. And John Lewis, the lawyer by whom Patrick would soon be befriended, bought a looking-glass, a candle mold, and some diaper tape.[4]

After Patrick had been trained for a year in a store such as Gordon's, John Henry purchased a parcel of goods for him and his brother William. With this parcel, doubtless of the size to be expected from John's limited resources, the two lads set up a store of their own. We have no evidence that either was anxious to enter the business. They had to do something and no occupation appears to have been readily available except farming or trading. The brothers were jointly interested but Patrick, although the younger of the two, was "the principal manager." At that period of his life William appears to have been a thin reed on which to depend for business help. "I have seen an original letter from Colonel John Henry to his son William in which he remonstrates with him on his wild and dissipated course of life," Wirt wrote.[5]

The exact location of the store is uncertain but it is said to have been near the New Kent border, at the junction of the old Newcastle road and the present Old Church Road.[6] Situated there, a store would draw from travelers passing through the lower county or going across the river at Newcastle into King William. While keeping the store, Patrick, according to a persistent local tradition, lived with his half-brother, John Syme, at his large house. This mansion, supposedly on the high ground above the Pamunkey, has long since been destroyed but there are some magnificent old trees and boxwood on the grounds, and, especially in summer, an enchanting view of the countryside to the northward: the lush fields spreading to the Pamunkey where once stood the thriving colonial port, the tracing of the river as indicated by the trees alongside, and, above the farther bank, the corresponding heights in King William County gradually rising until they fade into a blue haze.[7]

For further details of Patrick's first storekeeping venture, subsequent writers have relied largely on the traditional account by William Wirt. After saying that John Henry set up his two sons in trade, Wirt declared that William's idle habits were, "if possible, still more unfortunate than Patrick's." The chief management of the business fell therefore on the younger brother, and his management seems to have been "most wretched."

"Left to himself, all the indolence" of Patrick's character returned, Wirt asserted. He found "the drudgery of retailing and of bookkeeping . . . intolerable." He was too kindhearted to disappoint any customers who asked for credit, too easily satisfied by excuses for nonpayment. The joys of the chase which echoed around him also deepened his disgust with his confining employment.[8]

As a lawyer less than a decade later, Henry had a practice which consisted mainly of routine suits—prosecutions for debt and other kinds of technical legal business. But neither in this work nor in keeping accounts for thousands of legal cases did he find the drudgery intolerable. Wirt's statement, given without citation of proof, must again be taken with a grain of salt. Kindhearted and popular though Patrick was, one wonders if he could have been quite so easily satisfied with the excuses of his laggard debtors. The suit papers for the period in Hanover, New Kent, and King William, where nearly all his customers lived, are destroyed, but about a decade later we find record of his prosecuting several small debtors for his second store in a court as far distant as Staunton.[9]

Undoubtedly, the immature Patrick was going through a somewhat formless and happy-go-lucky phase. But Wirt was again painting too much in black and white. Although he still fails to cite his authority, he was probably on surer ground when writing that while Patrick was a storekeeper he "procured a few light and elegant authors" and acquired, for the first time, a taste for reading.[10] He now had leisure time and had reached the age when he should have been more appreciative of good books. It is quite likely that he read the *Virginia Ga-*

zette and, especially perhaps, since his cousin was an editor, some issues of the *Gentleman's Magazine*.[11]

It is also highly probable that Patrick used his opportunities while a storekeeper to study the character and mental reactions of his customers. Wirt intimated that Henry resorted to arts in this study that appeared so far above his years, so much like "an afterthought, resulting from his future eminence" that he would hesitate to make the statement if it were not attested by so many reliable witnesses.[12]

Patrick took particular delight, Wirt added, in comparing the character of his customers and in ascertaining how each would react in a special instance. He would state a hypothetical case and call for their individual opinions as to the proper conduct to be followed. If they differed, he would ask for their reasons and greatly enjoy the resulting debate. He is also said to have entertained them with stories, drawn from his reading or, more often, from his own fancy.[13] By noting the reaction of his hearers, mostly plain and untutored country-folk, he was finding what would or would not appeal to a jury or popular assembly. He was learning, if unconsciously, the clear and simple style and arts of persuasion which would help to make him a great popular orator.

After about a year the Henry brothers' store failed, mostly, it appears, because of the unwise extension of credit.[14] How much this extension was Patrick's, how much that of the "wild and dissipated" William we can only surmise. It was then the general, indeed necessary, custom for many storekeepers to give credit with the understanding that payments would be made when the crops were sold. There was little ready cash, and if a crop failed or trade was interrupted by war and other untoward events, the merchants suffered with the rest.

Even within the present century tales have been told in Hanover of Patrick's unfortunate mercantile ventures. For example, he is said to have been stretched out at full length on a sack of salt "in the thick of a subtle discussion when a customer entered, saying: 'Have you any salt, sir?' 'Just sold the last peck,'" Patrick replied.[15]

We are not informed whether this purported incident occurred while Patrick was keeping his first store or the second, which he opened a few years later. No accounts survive for his first store but the numerous entries for his next brief venture,[16] with their evidence of careful bookkeeping, give us further reason to doubt if he was as careless as depicted on the earlier occasion. This is not to imply, however that he gave the first store undue attention, especially after the first unsuccessful year. He was "disgusted with the unpromising business," and we can sympathize with him when his thoughts turned elsewhere. It is significant, however, that he, not his older brother, William, liquidated the business of the partnership.[17] Patrick completed this undertaking in about two years. Then, at the age of eighteen, he was married to Sarah Shelton.[18]

It was the fall of 1754, and word had lately arrived from the western frontier that young Colonel Washington had surrendered his rude Fort Necessity to a superior French force. Not only were the times parlous, but Patrick was almost penniless and without prospect of remunerative employment. There was indeed reason for stating that he had "rounded out his embarrassments" and given "symmetry to them" by getting married.[19] His bride was a sixteen-year-old girl almost as poor as he was. We may well believe that her parents had their misgivings about the union, and in a traditional family account the opposition of John and Sarah Henry was expressed in strong terms. "Not that they objected to Sarah, for she was dear and sweet, but that they felt Patrick over young to set rocking that cradle that rocked almost continually until he was well nigh unto his grave." [20] It is too easy, however, to dismiss Sarah Shelton as the daughter of a small farmer or honest farmer [21] or even by saying that she was "an estimable woman, of most excellent parentage." [22] In accordance with the tendency to paint Patrick's early life too much in vivid contrasts, the position and influence of the Shelton family has been understated. They belonged to a sturdy clan, with considerable property and influence in both Hanover and Louisa counties. Through John Shelton's marriage to Eleanor, daughter of William Parks, Williamsburg bookseller and first publisher of the *Virginia Gazette*, the Sheltons are believed to have inherited a number of books which were available to Patrick. More important was the material help which they provided him at a critical period. The marriage was a turning point in his career.[23]

It appears to have been a love match, the very stuff of romance. Couples of their age were then usually more mature than they are today, and youthful marriages were a common occurrence. Sarah and Patrick had probably been acquainted since early childhood. The Shelton place, Rural Plains, is only a few miles from Studley, and with a number of young people in the family, Patrick must have frequently been in and out of their house. In the words of a present-day Shelton, still living in the home of his eighteenth century ancestor, the best chance for courting in Hanover used to be at houseparties.[24] It takes little imagination to see Patrick with other young people visiting at Rural Plains for days on end and not missing a chance to dance a jig or reel with Sarah or for more furtive love-making. An English ship at Hanovertown or Newcastle, a service at St. Paul's, a marriage or a funeral would draw people for miles around, and courting couples could somehow evade parental supervision.

No picture has survived of Patrick's young bride. But there is good reason to believe that she was a pretty girl, with the medium build, dark hair and eyes characteristic of her family.[25] In view of her age, the courtship could hardly have extended to tedious length. But we can dismiss the story that the marriage was an unduly hurried affair, performed without John Shelton's permission.[26] For the two minors parental consent was required by law and the ceremony was probably performed after the publication of banns three times at St. Paul's. This deterrent to hasty marriage was the preferred Anglican practice, surely to be expected of the Parson's nephew, and it was considerably cheaper than marriage by license.[27]

The definite and apparently reliable Shelton tradition is that the ceremony was performed in the front room still used as a parlor at Rural Plains.[28] And may we not also believe that the marriage was blessed by not one but two clergymen? Late that October, the very month of the nuptials, all the Anglican clergy in the colony were called to a convocation at Williamsburg. But however important the reasons as given by Commissary Dawson for the meeting—"the blind zeal of Fanaticism," the "furious malice of popery," or "the licentiousness" of those opposing "all" religion—the Reverend Patrick and the Reverend Mr. Barrett of St. Martin's were absent from the convention. It is likely that both of the reverend gentlemen were present at the ceremony back in Hanover uniting the youthful offspring of their prominent parishioners.[29] We can safely imagine Parson Henry riding up to the gambrel-roofed brick house, carrying the morocco prayerbook with his name in gilt letters, which still survives, and himself intoning some of the words by which his lovesick nephew agreed somehow to support his adolescent bride, while she, as the ceremony then prescribed, promised to love and honor him "even as Sarah obeyed Abraham calling him lord." [30]

Honeymoon trips were neither customary nor within the financial reach of most young Virginians of that period. A throng of friends and relatives usually gathered for the wedding, and for days afterward there was much eating, drinking, and rough joking at the expense of the young married couple. The last toast having been drunk ("May all your troubles be little ones" or an eighteenth century equivalent), and the last guests seen to their horses and carriages, the almost penniless couple turned to face the future.

Fortunately, the parents stepped in and did what they could to keep the wolf from the door. The financially embarrassed Colonel Henry could offer only limited assistance. But John Shelton, though he had his own troubles, gave Patrick and his bride six Negroes and Pine Slash, a tract of three hundred acres cut off from the Rural Plains estate. With this property they were to support themselves by farming.[31]

Pine Slash farm, a half-mile distant from the Rural Plains house, was connected with it by a sandy road over the gently undulating fields. It is often described as poor land, which may leave the inference that John Shelton had done shabbily by his daughter; but the farm actually contains some good sandy loam soil and is little different from the average land in Hanover, with the exception of the fertile river bottoms. Probably, however, at the time when Patrick tilled the fields several were worn down by repeated tobacco culture with inadequate fallowing and fertilization.[32]

In that day of primitive agriculture, six slaves were few enough to handle three hundred acres. The Negroes, none more than a generation or two from Africa, were hardly efficient help, and one or more, doubtless, assisted Sarah with the household. As Edmund Winston later wrote, Patrick was "oblidged to labour with his own Hands to obtain a scanty support for his family." [33] Seeing him hoeing or worming tobacco with his slaves—sunburned, sweating, roughly dressed— one would hardly have envisaged a future statesman. But he could no longer be accused of laziness, and he was again learning from personal experience the problems of the common people whom he was soon to champion.

There were difficulties enough. But both he and Sarah had been born and reared on a farm, and they were doubtless advised by John Shelton. At best they would have a hard struggle, especially since it would be a year before they could sell a tobacco crop—and that in bad times. Young people, however, were then satisfied with fewer things. There was the joy that came from starting married life with a girl whom he loved. The following year their first child was born, the daughter, Martha, on whom Patrick was to rely so much in later years.[34] And they could savor the pleasures of rural life: the Hanover fields and forests, now brown, red, and gold, seemed beautiful that fall to happy newlyweds, and in addition there were the local sports and festivities.

Even though Patrick might make a precarious livelihood as a farmer in the Hanover of the 1750's, his lot was no worse than that of many small planters in the neighborhood. One could raise one's foodstuffs and didn't need a great deal besides. In the words of Daniel Boone, all one needed for happiness was "a good gun, a good horse, and a good wife." [35] There were many attractions in the rural life, the more so since it was not necessary to work hard out of the growing season. Patrick might well have been content to bring up his family in obscurity, but in 1757 fate intervened in the form of an accidental fire at Pine Slash. The dwelling house in which the young bride and groom had begun their married life was burned along with most of their treasured if simple furniture.

The family found shelter in a former overseer's house about a hundred yards distant. Little more than a glorified cabin, this house still stands as a memorial to that ruder day.[36] The story-and-a-half structure boasts of only three connecting rooms in a line facing frontward, with three smaller ones above, under the dormer windows.[37] It was hardly the place that Sarah would have chosen to bring up her children after having been reared at dignified and substantial Rural Plains. The Shelton tradition is that the fire occurred in the spring of 1757, and that fall the Henrys moved to the inn at Hanover Courthouse, the sprawling wooden building which in altered form still stands on the highway.[38] The good host then was Sarah's father.

For Patrick, farming had been little more than a makeshift device, and after the fire he was hard pushed for cash money. While continuing to farm Pine Slash, in 1758 he opened another country store. With youthful optimism he again attempted the very trade in which he had already failed.

To repair the loss from the fire and buy a small stock of goods, he sold some of his Negroes. The sad departure of these members of the little Pine Slash establishment added to the family woes.[39]

The year 1757, when fire destroyed the home of the obscure young Virginia farmer, was a turning point in history. The Seven Years' War, begun officially the year before, had become, in its world-wide scope, in the strength of its contestants and the importance of its issues, one of the great wars of modern history. After a series of military reverses, the "Great Commoner," William Pitt, was reluctantly called to the British War Office. Here he brought a needed energy, a refreshing patriotism and passionate oratory, which would offer an inspiration and example for all Americans. In 1757 the British ally, Frederick of Prussia, eluded his Russian and Austrian opponents and soundly trounced a French army at Rossbach in central Germany.

And in that same eventful year young Robert Clive, drawing up his little force in a mango grove at Plassey, India, crushed the French hopes for exploitation of that vast country.

But such goods news of the war as trickled to Hanover through the *Virginia Gazette* or sporadic letters from overseas was viewed against a background of nearer realities. Braddock's defeat had opened the back country to raids by the French and their savage Indian allies. Even after young Wolfe's brilliant victory at Quebec in 1759 there would be four more years before the formal peace, four more years of burdensome taxation, interrupted trade, and the French-Indian menace.

The anxieties and disappointments of the Henry family circle during this difficult period may be gauged from the contemporary records. "We are now in Spirits concerning the Ohio Expedition," wrote John Syme to an English correspondent on April 24, 1755. "The Forces from Great Britain, Virginia and Maryland, 24 hundred Stout men" planned to march the following week; he was sure the French forces would be inferior.[40] But the following September Governor Dinwiddie was writing to the Lords of Trade in London of "the very great consternation" created in Virginia by "the unexpected and fatal defeat of His Majesty's Forces on The Banks of Monongahela."[41] In order to protect the frontier from the French and Indians, the Burgesses passed an act empowering a lottery for the raising of £6,000 and allowed Treasurer's notes for a total of £20,000 to pass as money. The notes were to be paid off by the next June with the aid of additional taxes.[42]

If the back-country settlers escaped scalping or torturing by the savages now loose on the warpath, they might be ruined by economic adversities. Little Mr. Maury, the harassed minister in upper Louisa whom Henry would soon confront in the Parson's Cause, wrote a jeremiad on conditions in his area: "Money is much scarcer than it has been for many years. Our spring crops of wheat and barley, oats and rye have been ruined by an early drought. . . . I fear scarce enough [corn] will be made for the sustenance of our people."[43]

Already as a result of the growing French and Indian menace an intercolonial congress had assembled in June, 1754, at Albany in New York, but Maryland, Virginia, and more southernly colonies had not been represented. Had the plan of colonial union approved by the congress not been spurned both in America and Great Britain, the American Revolution might have been postponed for generations. But, excepting wise Ben Franklin, the influential Pennsylvania delegate at Albany, there were few Americans who could see intercolonial or even many intracolonial problems in their full perspective. As plans were made for the impending conflict, Virginians, like other colonials, were eager to secure the aid of the British and to shift to them a large share of the resulting taxation.

The experience of John Syme helps us to understand the difficulties of the Virginia planters and of storekeepers like Henry, who derived their livelihood chiefly from them. It also does much to explain why many colonials were being alienated from the Mother Country. While welcoming protection of the Redcoats, Syme was becoming increasingly bound in the tentacles of the mercantilist system. By 1775 he would be indebted to a Bristol company to the sum of £25,000, an impossible burden for a Hanover planter.[44]

Syme's troubles began on June 9, 1753, when he wrote Lidderdale, Harmer and Farrell of Bristol that they had been strongly recommended to him by Colonel Peter Randolph and that he had sent them fifty hogsheads of his tobacco. Their house was the first to which he had ever shipped, and if he met with "proper encouragement" he would in turn endeavor to promote their interest. He had been obliged to draw largely on them that year as the result of setting up housekeeping with his bride, Mildred Meriwether. Syme wrote, however, that he would probably make a hundred hogsheads during the coming season, and in the meantime he enclosed an invoice of goods which he hoped they would send by the first opportunity. Not surprisingly, the "sundry" goods were numerous and expensive, leaving an initial balance in favor of the Bristol agents.[45]

Less than a year later, in May, 1754, Syme wrote the Bristol merchants that he had again been obliged to draw heavily on his crop. But his bills would be "very trifling" another year; he had increased the number of his Negroes, and his crop would be much better in quantity and quality. So much for his hopes. Was he also putting too much trust in the English factors? "I have solicited many People," he wrote, "to try you with some Tobo., but the ill Opinion, some Gent. have taken Pains to possess the Planters with, of your House, has made them shy at Present." Syme expected this ill-feeling to wear off, but the planters may have had reason for being leery of Messrs. Lidderdale, Harmer and Farrell.

Syme at any rate was still buoyant. His debt was large but £1,250 was owed him that summer with which he intended to purchase Negroes "to seat my Mountain Lands." Little did he realize that he was piling up debts which would initiate lawsuits not to be settled until more than a generation after the Revolution. How much Syme's troubles were due to fleecing by the merchants, trading at a point too distant for his supervision, how much to his own extravagance and bad business judgment, it is now difficult to determine. Syme, however, had large property holdings which he could sell at intervals.[46] But most of the planters and small farmers who bought from Henry's store were less fortunate. If their economic ships foundered, could he stay above water?

The hard times, his business failures, and increasing family burdens probably explain why Patrick chose not to volunteer for the war as did many of his friends and relatives. In May, 1756, before the formal opening of the Seven Years' War, we find the public-spirited John Syme and Patrick's former neighbor, West Dandridge, becoming officers in a volunteer cavalry company. It was a gallant and inspiring gesture, although the gentlemen proved of no great help in the irregular frontier warfare against the elusive and seemingly tireless foe.[47] Major William (Langloo) Winston, because of his backwoods experience, doubtless served more effectively, as did Samuel Meredith and Joseph Winston, who was later compensated by the House of Burgesses for many wounds.[48] From these men and especially from his uncle, Langloo, who withstood an Indian attack on his house and suffered property depredations by the militia, Patrick could learn much of the frustrations and hardships of a long war.[49]

As an able-bodied young man, he must also have attended the general musters of the militia and learned something of military drill if only as practiced by country levies and half-trained officers. It would all be worth-while experience when he served as a colonel and war governor during the Revolution.

From his second store and the slender income still added by the farm, Patrick had to make a living for his fast-growing family. To Martha, now becoming a lively little girl, there were added three boys, John, William, and Edward; and two daughters, Anne and Elizabeth. In 1759 he may already have had four mouths to feed.[50]

Patrick would have had his troubles as a colonial storekeeper even in good times. The mercantilist system was always weighted in favor of the British manufacturers and shippers. And now that French warships and privateers were interrupting the Virginia trade, there was unusual difficulty in securing a stock of goods at salable prices.[51] To cap it all, in 1758 the unseasonable summer weather produced a short crop of tobacco for which there was no adequate compensation through the increased prices.[52]

On the other hand, there were some advantages over his earlier mercantile venture. Patrick may have learned from his previous failure. His ne'er-do-well brother was no longer a partner while he himself was spurred by the needs of his growing family and the store appears to have been conveniently located at a crossroad about a mile from Hanover Courthouse.[53]

There is no discounting Patrick's happy-go-lucky disposition, not yet entirely sobered by marriage and business adversity. But, in accord with the general tendency to exaggerate his shiftlessness, he has been blamed too severely for the failure of this second venture. Thus we have this statement from William Wirt, which has influenced many later accounts:

> He soon found that he had not changed his character, by changing his pursuits. His early habits still continued to haunt him. The same want of method, the same facility of temper, soon became apparent by their ruinous effects. He resumed his violin,

[87]

his flute, his books, his curious inspection of human nature; and not unfrequently ventured to shut up his store, and indulge himself in the favourite sports of his youth.[54]

Much of this is pure conjecture.

Fortunately, the account book for this store has been preserved. There are 111 pages of entries with such quaint items as "stickshair" for hairpins and "shew-buckles." [55] These entries, clearly recorded in good ink, are not in Patrick's handwriting. He had employed a clerk but when he was not too badly needed on the farm Patrick must have sat in the store for long hours listening to the conversations of customers and adding to his knowledge of human nature. The store accounts indicate that most of the customers lived within a dozen miles, though some were from the upper end of Hanover or Louisa and more distant counties.

For the rest, the accounts throw further light on Henry's activities at the time and remove some misconceptions as to his storekeeping. Opened in the hot Virginia midsummer, the store had cash sales the first day of only two shillings sixpence. The next day, July 9, 1758, Patrick himself was charged for some "green baze" at 2/11, perhaps for a new dress for Sarah. While he could comfort her with only a dribble of small sales during the next months, he was at least able to use some of the store goods for family purposes. Thus in late July and early August he was charged with three yards of "duffil" amounting to £1/1; two papers of pins, a pair of buckles, and "stickshair" for 2/9; and a knife, four yards of "frise," two stickshair and thread for 17/11. That was on August 9, and Sarah must have given him a lengthy list when he rode to the store, for he also got a pair of buckles, six laces, "1 cuttan knife," and a pair of stockings.[56]

Fortunately, relatives and associates tried to bolster the shaky business venture. Poor Colonel Henry mustn't have his son fail again. And Patrick with so many mouths to feed! One of the first customers was Charles Crenshaw, reader at Parson Henry's "Lower Church," and among others in the next two months were Uncle Isaac Winston, though only for a few shillings' worth of "baze," and William Pollard, clerk of the court where John Henry was a justice. Pollard, a gentleman with whom Patrick would be intimately associated through his future legal practice at the courthouse, bought two pocketbooks, and there were also small purchases by the interested Colonel Henry and by a few of the Winston and Dabney relatives. Laggard debtors, however, who did not or could not pay their accounts, included Uncle Billy (Langloo) Winston, brother William Henry (now elevated to Captain), and West Dandridge, Patrick's neighbor of the Mount Brilliant days.[57]

Customers in such stores often did not pay their accounts until after they had sold their tobacco in the fall. For the three lean summer and early fall months after Patrick began business his collections totaled only about ten pounds, his outstanding accounts ten times that figure. October was a somewhat better month and in November, 1758, when the tobacco crop had been sold he listed credits of over £150 with debits of less than £50. But after that business fell off, and in 1759 the credits dropped to £77 as against debits of £134. The next year there were only twenty-six customers for over six months (including Patrick's slave Jean, buying on his account!) and the store was closed.[58]

The fault lay only partly with Patrick. It is likely that the clerk who stayed in the store was none too efficient. Also the lean war years had been climaxed by the failure of the tobacco crop in 1759: the farmers were left with little cash money or sound credit.[59] Henry had lost the capital which he had invested and was in debt, but he was not insolvent. We have his statement in later years that he was never sued for a debt of his own. He was able to salvage something by sale of his remaining goods, and the generous John Shelton let Patrick and his family live with him at the Hanover tavern.[60]

Moreover, the two storekeeping experiences had not been a complete waste. From hard experience Patrick had learned the need of efficient business methods. Also he observed at close hand how the local planters were caught in the economic vise. After witnessing the improvident methods of some plantation masters, he would probably have conceded that their troubles were partly of their own making.

Yet the people were in need of a vigorous champion, and he would soon turn to a profession which enabled him to fill this rôle.

Of Henry's private life and character during this period we get a further glimpse through his illustrious contemporary, Thomas Jefferson. Beginning in 1812, Jefferson is known to have provided several accounts of his long-time political associate. They are not only harsh in their judgment of Henry but contain a number of inaccuracies or worse. The errors in the last accounts may be largely attributed to the failing memory of an old man; but it also appears likely that the Sage of Monticello was still piqued by some earlier political differences with Henry, including the latter's indictment of Jefferson's harassed administration as wartime Governor. His comments on Henry do not show the great Mr. Jefferson at his best.

> My acquaintance with Mr. Henry commenced in the winter of 1759-1760 [Jefferson wrote]. On my way to the college I passed the Christmas holydays at Col. Dandridge's in Hanover, to whom Mr. Henry was a near neighbor. During the festivity of the season, I met him in society every day, and we became well acquainted, altho' I was much his junior, being then but in my seventeenth year, and he a married man.[61]

In a second letter to Wirt on August 5, 1815, Jefferson continued with further reminiscences of Patrick, vivid and suggestive but marred by serious inaccuracies.

> His manners had something of the coarseness of the society he had frequented; his passion was fiddling, dancing, and pleasantry. He excelled in the last and it attached everyone to him. The occasion, perhaps, as much as his idle disposition, prevented his engaging in any conversation which might give the measure either of his mind or information. Opportunity was not wanting, because Mr. John Campbell was there, who had married Mrs. Spotswood, the sister of Colonel Dandridge. He was a man of science and often introduced conversations on scientific subjects. Mr. Henry had a little before broken up his store, or rather it had broken him up; but his misfortunes were not to be traced, either in his countenance or conduct." [62]

[90]

In his first letter Jefferson added:

> Mr. Henry began his career with very little property. He acted, as I have understood, as barkeeper in the tavern at Hanover C[ourt] H[ouse] for sometime. He married very young . . . got credit for some little store of merchandize, but very soon failed. . . .[63]

Jefferson also made a statement to Daniel Webster in 1824 in which he asserted that Henry "was originally a barkeeper." [64]

Although probably accurate, the comments on his barkeeping carry an unfortunate implication. In 1805, Nathaniel Pope, Jr., seeking data for Wirt's biography, was informed by Henry's cousin, William Overton Winston of Hanover, that to his certain knowledge Henry acted as a barkeeper for his father-in-law, John Shelton, at Hanover Courthouse and that he, Winston, frequently went to see him while Henry was serving in that capacity. During this time Winston said Henry was "generally clad in a Ozna[burgh] Shirt Jump. Jacket and Trowsers of Ozna or checks, and very often Barefooted . . . he was very active and attentive to his guests and very frequently amused them with his violin on which he performed very well." [65]

Taverns were operated by some substantial gentlemen of the Piedmont, such as Colonel Boswell of Boswell's Tavern, Louisa County, and liquor was served as a matter of course. John Shelton had various interests and was apparently trying hard to maintain his own and his son-in-law's family. Patrick, a repeated failure and living with his wife and children at Shelton's tavern, would have been most ungrateful not to have helped with the guests when needed. There is a difference between lending a hand to his generous father-in-law and being "originally a barkeeper."

As for Jefferson's criticism of Henry's manners, Pope's description confirms that Patrick showed evidence of his rustic surroundings. But his conduct and social position were good enough for him to be received by West Dandridge, one of the highest-born gentlemen in the county, a first cousin of Martha Washington and son-in-law of Governor Spotswood.

Moreover, it was not true that Patrick "had a little before broken up his store, or rather it had broken him up." His account book shows that he did not close the store before July, 1760, and that he himself sold the remaining stock to Crenshaw and Grant in September, 1760, apparently for £25.1.3¾.[96] And conceding that the youthful Henry was not yet entirely over his happy-go-lucky ways, he must have formulated some serious plans to be put into operation after the relaxation of the holiday season during which he met Jefferson, for within a few months Patrick passed the bar and was soon to become established in a successful legal practice.

7

Admission to the Bar

The doctor should be old, the lawyer should be young.
———Burmese Proverb

Sometime about April 1, 1760,[1] Patrick Henry came to Williamsburg to obtain a license to practice law. Dogged by his failures and now hard-pressed even to contribute to the support of Sarah and the children, his stay at the colonial capital appears to have been only long enough to accomplish his purpose. Many accounts of the trip, however, are replete with the now-to-be expected inaccuracies as to this period of his career. Traveling when he did, his sanguine disposition had to stand—besides the quizzing of the learned bar examiners —the further trial of the dreary spring weather. For much of that season an English traveler noted a depressing series of rains and mists, capping earlier snows and downpours. Not even the most ebullient youth would have ridden the muddy Tidewater roads from choice.[2]

Yet there was a great deal at Williamsburg to interest a country lad. He called upon Tom Jefferson, a tall, red-haired, hazel-eyed youth of seventeen, who had just entered William and Mary College. He observed the college's brick buildings, one perhaps designed by the great Christopher Wren. Then down Duke of Gloucester Street, by the shops, taverns, and private residences, a few finer than any he had seen in Hanover, excepting Scotchtown. On the left, back some distance from the street, was the imposing building to which the citizens gave the still more imposing title of the Governor's Palace. And less than a mile farther eastward was a building of more immediate significance to a potential lawyer: the Capitol where met the Burgesses, the Council and its alter ego, the General Court.[4]

Absorbed in his immediate problems of dire economic necessity, Patrick probably found in Williamsburg, Capitol and all, no overweening interest. But surely here was the stuff to stir, if only in afterthought, a slumbering ambition.

On March 11 Governor Fauquier had prorogued the Assembly to meet on June 1, and the recently crowded capital had shrunk to its normal population of about a thousand persons, white and black.[5] Patrick, gawking down the muddy street, was now less likely to be spattered by the horses or carriages of proud bewigged gentlemen. Nevertheless, there were enough members of the board of examiners in town to pass favorably on his application for admission to the bar —that is, if they were so disposed. And he did get two of them to pass him, the legal minimum, after difficulties of which we get a confused picture in the contemporary accounts.

The legal profession which Patrick proposed to enter was now beginning to enjoy an influence unknown in early colonial history. Over a century before, the Virginia Assembly, irritated by the many troublesome suits caused by "the unskilfulness and covetousness" of attorneys, even took steps to exclude all lawyers from practice in the colony.[6] Many of these so-called attorneys were not trained lawyers but only jackleg traders, factors, or other laymen with clever pens and tongues.[7] Even with such charlatans in their ranks, the lawyers were so useful that the legislature soon sanctioned them again,[8] but with continued restrictions. As late as 1745 an Act of the Assembly, in force when Henry was admitted to practice, reinforced the earlier laws against exorbitant fees and malpractice.

Slowly the colonial lawyers had gained influence and prestige. The growth of population and wealth, the increasing complexity of business, the decline in early enmities and jealousies affecting their pro-

[94]

fession, all contributed to their improved position. In Virginia, as Judge Minor wrote, "for fully a century, the lawyer had seemed to fame and fortune unknown." [9] Then, during the first half of the eighteenth century, a few attorneys such as John Holloway, Edward Barradall, and Sir John Randolph won solid reputations.[10] And now in the generation before the American Revolution the lawyers came into their own. Indeed, there have been few revolutionary movements in which they exerted more influence.[11]

The hitherto unsuccessful Patrick had thus selected an ideal time to enter the legal profession. But, we must confess, this was due more to a change in his luck than to any clever design. By and large, we cannot quarrel with Judge Winston's statement that he was "a virtuous young man, unconscious of the powers of his own mind, and in very narrow circumstances, making a last effort to supply the wants of his family." [12]

In reply to a query by William Wirt in 1805, George Dabney wrote that Henry did not read law for more than six or eight months before he applied for his license,[13] and this is substantiated by Colonel Meredith.[14] On the other hand, Edmund Winston stated that Henry obtained a license to practice law "after six weeks reading of such books as he could borrow, *with other assistance*." [15] Although only fifteen years old at the time, Winston could have had the information from reliable family sources. Jefferson also, in his reminiscences a half-century later, said that Henry, when in Williamsburg for the examination, told him he had been reading law for six weeks,[16] while other witnesses set the time at a month or nine months.[17] Whatever the exact period, it was brief enough.

"Looking forward into life," Henry later wrote a young correspondent, "and to those prospects which seem to be commensurate with your talents, native and acquired, you may justly esteem those incidents fortunate which compel an exertion of mental power, maturity of which is rarely seen growing out of an uninterrupted tranquillity." He spoke of "adversity toughening mankind," and added that "the characteristic of the good or the great man, is not that he has been exempted from the evils of life, but that hc has surmounted them." [18] Perhaps he was remembering his "exertion of mental power" on this first visit to Williamsburg.

The examining board which Henry faced included some of the ablest lawyers in the colony. It was composed of Robert Nicholas, an eminent lawyer who would later become Treasurer of Virginia; John Randolph, Attorney-General of the colony; Peyton Randolph, afterwards President of the First Continental Congress; and George Wythe, later Jefferson's law tutor, the first professor of law at an American college, and a member of the Virginia Court of Appeals. Already they ranked among the outstanding lawyers in all the colonies—a formidable obstacle for a backwoods youth like Patrick, especially as he had to appear before each separately for quizzing.

Patrick possessed native wit and courage; he would overcome his other failings. For an account of his meeting with the learned examiners we turn again to Jefferson:

> Two of the Examiners . . . Peyton and John Randolph, men of great facility of temper, signed his license with as much reluctance as their dispositions would permit them to show. Mr. Wythe absolutely refused. Robert C. Nicholas refused also at first, but on repeated importunity and promises of future reading, he signed. These facts I have afterward from the gentlemen themselves, the two Randolphs acknowledging he was very ignorant of law, but that they perceived him to be a young man of genius and did not doubt he would soon qualify himself. [19]

Jefferson's account is more suggestive than literally accurate. From the records of Goochland court we learn that on "the XV day of the Month Annoque Domini MDCCLX" Patrick Henry produced a license to practice in the county and inferior courts signed by George Wythe and John Randolph and, having taken the prescribed oaths and test, was admitted to the local bar. [20] Thus Jefferson incorrectly cites Peyton Randolph and Nicholas as signing the license with the reasons therefor. On the other hand, Jefferson does confirm not only that John Randolph signed the license but also the general account of Henry's difficulties with the examiners. And Jefferson's statement is confirmed by George Dabney.

"I heard one of the Gentlemen who licensed him say that he was so Ignorant of Law at the time, that he should not have passed him if he had not discovered his great genius," Dabney recalled.[21]

Attorney-General Randolph, a witty and elegant gentleman as well as a profound lawyer, was so shocked by Henry's ungainly appearance and manners that he at first refused to examine him. But understanding that he had obtained two signatures (actually one), Randolph reluctantly began the examination. A brief time was enough to remove the erroneous impression he had obtained from Henry's appearance. With increasing surprise, doubtless produced by "the peculiar texture and strength of . . . Henry's style, and the boldness and originality of his combinations" Randolph continued his examination for several hours. He persisted with his questioning of the candidate, not only on the principles of municipal law where he apparently soon discovered Henry's deficiency, but on the laws of nature and of nations, the policy of the feudal system, and general history, which last proved to be his "stronghold."

During the very short portion of the examination which was devoted to the common law, Randolph dissented, or affected to dissent, from one of Henry's answers and called upon him to give the reasons for his opinion. This produced an argument and the experienced Randolph now employed against Henry those same arts that he so successfully used on his legal opponents. He drew him out by questions, tried to puzzle him by subtleties, assailed him with declamations, continually observing the defensive mechanism of Henry's mind.

"You defend your operations well, sir," Randolph perforce declared after considerable discussion, "but now to the law and to the testimony."

Randolph then took Henry with him to his law office where he opened his authoritative treatises. "Behold the force of natural reason," he said. "You have never seen these books, nor this principle of the law; yet you are right and I am wrong. And from the lesson which you have given me (you must excuse me for saying it) I will never trust to appearances again.

[97]

"Mr. Henry, if your industry be only half equal to your genius," Randolph concluded, "I augur that you will do well, and become an ornament and an honor to your profession." [22]

Altogether, while stories of this phase of Henry's career are exaggerated, they do contain a basic element of truth. Henry had prepared for the bar considerably less than a year. He must have had a certain familiarity with legal practices gained by watching sessions of the county court. Attending the trials was one of the favorite pastimes for visitors to Hanover Courthouse, and Colonel Henry was a gentleman justice. John Shelton's tavern, too, where Henry was now living, stood just across the road from the courthouse. When time lay idle on his hands what more natural than to join the curious onlookers there? Wirt's statement that Henry's original preparation for the bar consisted only of reading Coke on Littleton and the Virginia Laws may be too indicative of a Horatio Alger beginning.[23] Possibly Henry, already branded as a failure, would not reveal the full details of his legal study to his friends: he may well have studied more than the two books listed before braving the examiners. Yet his preparation for the bar was certainly sketchy enough.

But Henry's lack of legal training was not the extraordinary fact that it is often depicted. There was not a single law school in America at the time, and superficial preparation for the bar was the rule, not the exception. Among Henry's eminent legal contemporaries in Virginia, George Wythe, Edmund Pendleton, John Marshall, and others had had only a slender preparation for their bar examination. The broad training of John Adams and Thomas Jefferson was almost unique. Even the few colonials who were able to study at the Temple in London got only a sketchy legal background: some dinners in Hall to satisfy the residence requirements, a little reading and experience under a lawyer. If William Byrd II was at all typical, not a few devoted almost as much time to the theaters and taverns, to ladies of sorts in the city, as they did to more formal study.

With such thin knowledge as he could draw upon or improve, Patrick began practice in the county courts. Since the bulk of the Hanover records are destroyed, it is fortunate that a mass of records survive for adjoining Goochland. The courthouse in Goochland was as near to upper Hanover as was Hanover Courthouse, and there Patrick argued nearly a third of his suits during his first year of practice, with many more in subsequent years.[24]

The first Goochland Courthouse was not located at its present site, some twenty miles above Richmond on the James, but a few miles nearer at Maidens, on the James River, then called Maiden's Adventure. It was still a semi-frontier region in Henry's time, and he could hear the traditional story of the Indian maiden, in love with a white man, who swam the river there to inform the white people that Indians were planning to massacre them.[25] Only five years before Patrick began practice, in 1755, the county court had agreed to "pitch upon the land of John Payne Gent. as the most convenient place" to erect a new courthouse. This edifice, later replaced by the present building, was to be forty-two feet by twenty with partitions at the end for two jury rooms; and it was to have the usual prison, pillory, and stocks.[26] In the courthouse village, as at Hanover Courthouse, there was much on court days to divert, if not always to edify, the itinerant lawyer. There were auction sales of horses, Negroes, or other possessions; brother lawyers arguing and conferring; taverns or ordinaries thronged; slaves flogged or malefactors exposed in the stocks or pillory to the public gaze. Patrick, now a responsible if impecunious family man, was hardly to be lured by the tavern vices. But living not far away was his cousin, John Payne, and he may also have enjoyed the hospitality of the Michaux, the Huguenot family across the river from Maidens, while within a few hours' ride was Woodville, the pleasant frame house of Valentine Wood, the county clerk, and Patrick's future brother-in-law.[27]

Two of Henry's first cases, typical of the grist that then came to the mill of a fledgling colonial lawer, were *Harding* v. *Webber* and *Harding* v. *Prewitt*.[28] The first suit was heard at Goochland court in April, 1760, just after Henry had been admitted to the bar, the second at the following August court there. The declaration in *Harding* v. *Webber* written by Henry for the plaintiff is copied in the prescribed form, full of such words as "said," "whereas," and "aforesaid," the legal terminology of which Thomas Jefferson would complain after helping to rewrite the Virginia code. The gist was that Webber had failed after numerous requests to pay £30 due Harding, and that the latter had thereupon entered suit. The previous year the deputy sheriff had been ordered to levy a writ against Webber but, after what effort is not stated, had noted "not found within my Baili-wic." On a motion by Henry who took the case for what he could make of it, an attachment was ordered against the defendant's estate for thirty pounds damage returnable to the next court. The sheriff of Goochland was ordered to attach sufficient goods and chattels of Webber to satisfy the damages.

The following August, 1760, Henry appeared again in Goochland court as attorney for the same William Harding in an action against John Prewitt.[29] Prewitt was alleged to have disposed of sundry Ne-groes on Harding's account and to have kept the money for himself. And this was said to have caused Harding to have been imprisoned, doubtless for debt, and to have "undergone greivous hardships" for which Henry sought payment of £200. The machinery of the law moved slowly then as now. But in June, 1762, there was a verdict for Henry's client and motion in arrest of judgment, and finally in April, 1763, the motion was overruled and judgment was ordered in accord-ance with the verdict.

Another among Henry's early Goochland cases in which his hand-written declaration survives was *Moore v. Bolling*. The Bollings were members of a prominent family with whom Patrick would soon be associated in the Burgesses; one branch boasted of descent from the Indian princess, Pocahontas. Now Thomas Bolling, Gent., was being sued by James Moore for unlawful use of a gelding. Henry in his declaration as attorney for the plaintiff said that Moore had thereby lost his own use of the gelding and sustained "other Enor-mity & abuses on the said Gelding . . . whereby the said John saith he is the worse . . . by fifteen pounds and therefore sues."

The suit papers provide significant curiosa of an earlier day. With an unconscious humor George II is still entitled "King of France" as well as "Defender of the [Catholic] Faith." The sublime unwillingness to change on the part of the British hierarchy was to cost them dear during the coming decades. More practically, the suit papers themselves were folded longitudinally with the outer one acting as a binder and were thus conveniently filed or carried in the saddlebags of the sheriff or deputy making the summons. Notations were written on the outside of the folder for convenience in handling. From such notations on *Moore* v. *Bolling,* we learn that the case was continued in the courts during 1762 and 1763 and a nonsuit was finally declared in May, 1764.[30]

A petty case which afforded a change from the debt actions was *Winston* v. *Spencer,* a suit for slander at a time when personal defamation was taken more seriously than today. The hearing must have afforded much entertainment to the idle onlookers at Goochland court during that hot August of 1760. The Henry family connections were offering considerable help to the struggling young lawyer, and his cousin John Winston gave him this case which an established lawyer might have considered hardly worth the bother. In his declaration Henry stated that on an unnamed date in 1760 "the Said Spencer did utter, publish, and declare aloud" that John Winston was a hog stealer and "much Scandal and many & great Crimes did then & there charge the plaintiff . . . the Said pltf hath Suffer'd much in quietude and undergone much contempt & Danger and is injured & Damaged Five hundred pounds & thereon he brings Suit." This case in all its amusing pettiness dragged through the courts for several years. The records show that Spencer was summoned to appeal on the third Tuesday in August, 1760, and individual witnesses were called in September and October, 1761; March, 1762; and July, 1762. Finally, after various continuances, a judgment was given in September, 1764, in the sum of twenty pounds, far less than the amount Winston considered himself damaged when Spencer did "declare aloud" that he was a hog stealer.[31]

Perhaps one reason John Winston was proclaiming (with the help of his young lawyer-cousin) that the "hog stealer" charge injured his character to the extent of the £500 was that he was sinking into a financial morass. In any case, this unhappy circumstance also was legal grist for young Henry. While he was Winston's attorney in the slander case, he was also suing him in a debt action for £3. Whether Henry ever collected any damages is not clear, but we can make a likely surmise from this notation on the order of the Goochland court: "Above order executed and Winston carried to Prison for want of Security." [32]

Probably about 1760-1761 Henry appeared for Robert and James Donald & Co., merchants of Glasgow, in a debt action. In 1750 one Jacob Page was alleged to have agreed to pay Donald & Co. £11.-1.6½, and Henry now sued him for the amount with damages. The decade or more during which the Glasgow merchants had been held up by their debtor illustrates the difficulties of the British merchants, while the notation in Henry's declaration that the defendant subjected himself under penalty to pay £22.3.1 (double the original debt) in case of default speaks strongly of the troubles on the other side. Moreover, "you can't get blood out of a turnip." There were further difficulties with collections, Henry's own experiences only too often duplicating those of the less popular merchants. When he won a debt suit for his cousin James Dabney, the sheriff wrote on the suit papers this discouraging notation: "No effects." [33]

In order to fill the gaps of knowledge about Henry's early practice, let us now turn to his account book. Part of the first page has been lost from the book [34] but we know it contained on the debit side the account for his first clients, Coutts and Crosse, Merchants. [35] Patrick Coutts was a prosperous Scotsman in Richmond who later appeared as a witness in the Parson's Cause. He was not lacking in independence and Scotch wit, as is indicated by the following story. Coutts was a great friend of the last William Byrd of Westover who, stricken in his final illness about the same time as Coutts, sent a hurried messenger to the Scotsman to wait for him. But Coutts, although dying, had the strength to reply, "Tell William Byrd that when Patrick Coutts makes up his mind to die, he waits for no mon." [36]

After Coutts and Crosse, there appear to have been a few more entries, then John Shelton, charged £3.16.3 in six minor cases, usually at fifteen shillings each. [37] There is increasing evidence that Henry's relatives and family associates were rallying to his support as they had to a considerable extent when he was a storekeeper. That is, they were offering him cases even though they did not, or sometimes could not, pay him for his services. In addition to his father-in-law, his wife's mother, Eleanor Parks Shelton, gave him three minor suits in 1760 and duly paid him by cash the one shilling tenpence charged; his uncle William (Langloo) Winston of the Forks of Hanover gave him a suit against John Winston, the notorious debtor; Cornelius Dabney, a case described in the account book as for "fee v. Grant" with the "Tax on writ 16.3"; and William Coles, Hanover, a somewhat similar suit.[38]

Patrick's brother-in-law, William Shelton of Louisa, and his uncle Major Isaac Winston of Henrico, in 1760 or thereabouts, also gave him business carrying fees of a few pounds. Major Winston's account included this item:

"To Sundry writings Relative to y.ͬ Father's Estate   2.10."
There are also two items dated 1760 with the following annotation: "N Ballance fully settled with Isaac Winston." [39]

Patrick's grandfather, Isaac Winston, Sr., had died that year after a long and full life. His will, dated February 6, 1760, long survived in one branch of the numerous Winston family. This will,[40] clearly and precisely written and with negligible errors in spelling or punctuation, begins as follows:

"IN THE NAME OF GOD, AMEN. I, Isaac Winston, of the County of Hanover, being in good health and perfect memory, do make and ordain this my last Will and Testament, and do hereby dispose of all such worldly goods, as it hath pleased Almighty God to bestow upon me, in manner and form following. . . ."

Isaac then listed these bequests: thirty-four slaves in lots chiefly to his sons; £350, in current money, twelve silver spoons, and the following possessions for his "loving wife" Mary [Dabney] Winston: "my riding chair and harness . . . her bed and furniture; also her three gilt trunks with one jar; as also her side-saddle, and furniture." So weak was woman's position in the eyes of the colonial law that Isaac bequeathed to his wife several of "her" possessions!

The irregular life of many slaves, even of enlightened masters, is indicated by the fact that only the mother is listed for several Negro children. We also note a mulatto girl, Tamer, daughter of Kate.

There were generous bequests to three of Patrick's uncles and his first cousin (Isaac's grandson), Edmund Winston; a £5 bequest to Sarah Henry; £40 to each of Patrick's sisters, Lucy, Mary, Ann, Eliza, when they came of age or married; a Negro for a grandson, Walter Coles, and even a £80 bequest for Dr. John Walder, presumably Isaac's family physician. But Patrick and his brother, William, are not mentioned at all. Apparently, as late as February, 1760, they had not endeared themselves to their grandfather.

Isaac's will was probated in Hanover. Besides the large part of Patrick's business conducted there, with the considerable litigation in adjoining Goochland, there was already in 1760 some scattered business in a few other counties. For one account, against John McCown, Augusta, there is a credit of seventy-five pounds of butter at sixpence. And against Thomas Yuille of Chesterfield he lists seventeen debits for fees and taxes aggregating £10.10—all duly paid.

Beside Yuille, there were a few relatively large clients, with accumulated fees during the year of about £5 to £15: James Littlepage of Hanover, who also officiated as clerk of court in Louisa; Johnson and Boswell, Hanover merchants; William Harding, Goochland; Charles Crenshaw of Hanover; and Robert Hudgens, Cumberland. The great majority of the cases are minor suits with standard fees of seven shillings or fifteen shillings. No fee in an individual case was for as much as a pound except that for the work on the Isaac Winston estate, £2.10, and they were seldom as much as ten shillings. Altogether Henry handled some 176 cases—largely debt actions and administration of estates—for about seventy to seventy-five clients. Of these over thirty appear to have been from Hanover, over twenty from Goochland, and the rest chiefly in the near-by frontier counties. At the end of 1760 his accounts for civil cases stood approximately as follows: debits, £123.13.3, credits, £68.18.11.

Thus in his first year of practice Henry is known to have collected some £69 and he had a reasonable hope of securing nearly half of the balance due, or about £50. Moreover, this does not allow for a few missing pages in his account book or for his criminal cases, of which there is no surviving record. He probably collected over £100 during the eight months or thereabouts that he had practiced in 1760. It was a good start for a young lawyer of the time and place. The produce or other income from his farm was available and apparently he and his family were still living with John Shelton at the Hanover Courthouse tavern.[41]

Before the end of 1760 Patrick Henry's legal forms bore a new date—the first year of George III. On October 25 the brave but ineffectual George II had finally died and been succeeded by his grandson, George III. "Never did a King ascend the throne with a more universal applause . . . every tongue was busied in his Praise," Arthur Lee wrote from Edinburgh to his brother, Richard Henry Lee. "A perfect Harmony subsists between his Ministers, at the Head of whom Mr. Pitt still holds the foremost place in Worth & Eminence."

"The young king" had committed only "one Error since his accession," Arthur Lee continued, and this, we must agree, was a grave one.

> Instead of permitting the Ladys who come to Court, to Kiss his hand, he salutes them himself, pleased with the royal Touch they flock in such numbers to his Court, that He is like to [be] Kissed to Death . . . for who can help liking such a polite, genteel, goodnatured young King.[42]

John Adams wrote in his journal on February 9, 1761, that George III by his speech to Parliament had proved himself to be "a man of piety . . . a friend of liberty" and "a patron of merit." [43] Little did Adams then suspect that George would become the *bête noir* of the American revolutionists. Sincere and zealous as he was in his effort to end factionalism and revive the personal power of the sovereign for the well-being of the country, it was ominous that he had lived a secluded life apart from the royal court and had grown up "full of prejudices . . . fostered by women and pages." [44]

[105]

If Henry had been a somewhat negligent storekeeper, he was now a diligent lawyer. He was entrusted with much business that required prompt and meticulous attention and his account books show the names of numerous clients who continued to come back to him. His records for 1761, with a few pages missing, indicate that he had some 180 civil cases, and that his practice, instead of being confined chiefly to Hanover and Goochland, now extended over a much wider area. Of the seventy-nine clients in the slightly incomplete list, a third were from the recently created Cumberland County, a good day's ride to the westward, with a few from Louisa, Albemarle, and Chesterfield. There were only about seventeen cases each from his native Hanover and from Goochland. In Hanover he had to meet competition from such established lawyers as James Lyons and John Lewis, while across the river to the northward in Caroline was the astute Edmund Pendleton, his future political associate. But if willing to spend long days with horse and saddlebags, making the best of inns, ordinaries, or chance private hospitality—if willing to take numerous petty cases, there was opportunity for an enterprising young lawyer in the new counties spreading toward the mountains. Of course he had to spend much time away from home, especially when the more distant county courts were in session.

Henry continued to have numerous debt cases, with Scottish merchants or their agents among his principal clients.[45] The Goochland records, however, include a few cases of a different type, as when he represented John Walker in a suit against Elizabeth Napier for non-payment of medical services. The plaintiff, through his attorney, Patrick Henry, stated that he was practicing the business of a physician and surgeon during 1760 in the Parish of St. James Northam, Goochland County. At the special instance and request of the said Elizabeth "for & towards Effecting the Cure of one who did then and there labour under grievous & distressing Maladys disorders Distempers & Sickness," Dr. Walker, the plea continued, administered unto the said Elizabeth "many doses of powerfull Salubrious & Healing Medicines for Effecting" her cure and recovery. Likewise at her special request he performed on her body "many Chirurgical operations

Amputations Incisions & Scarifyings" and "travelled many miles for making a cure aforesaid," expending "much time medicine & money."

In view of the quackery of the times we may well wonder whether Elizabeth Napier recovered because of or in spite of the medicines, amputations, etc., or whether she recovered at all. In any case, Henry's plea stated that his client had often requested the said Elizabeth to pay his fee and she always refused. She was therefore sued for £12. Notations on the case show that she was ordered to appear before the court in December, 1761, and again in January, 1762, but was not found either time. Particularly in hardship cases, or where the defendant was popular and influential, it is questionable how conscientiously the sheriff endeavored to levy the judgment. He might quietly pass word that he was going to deliver the papers on a certain day and it would be easy for many defendants to slip over into the next county before he appeared. In the case of poor Elizabeth Napier, however, the practices of Dr. Walker were not all that she had to submit to, for the final notation on the papers is "Above executed on a Neagro of the within Nam⁴ Eliz⁴ Napier. Sto⁵ McCaul, S. [Sub] Sheriff." [46]

Altogether for 1761, Henry charged civil fees of about £161, nearly £40 more than the previous year. He was paid, however, only £55 as compared with £69 in 1760. This is partly explained by the hard times in the fifth year of the war; many of his clients could only pay him after making their own collections. He had made a good record.

Of interest because of the local prominence of the defendant and the underlying facts was one case during 1762, *Hicks* v. *Payne*. Henry's cousin John Payne, Jr., was a member of an influential Goochland family, several of whom were vestrymen and members of the county court. (A decade later, while he was visiting at the Quaker settlement of Guilford, North Carolina, his daughter, Dorothy, the future Dolly Madison, was born.[47])

Like those in the other colonies, the Virginia authorities now had trouble securing levies for the Seven Years' War. This was understandable considering the removal of the French and to some extent

the Indian menace after the capture of Quebec in 1759. Even in better times the colonial recruits received miserable pay for the hardships
of field service.

In his declaration for the plaintiff, Patrick Henry set forth that
Payne agreed to pay Hicks a bounty of £10 if he would serve in the
Second Virginia Regiment for one campaign. Henry then stated that
Hicks did enlist but that Payne had fraudulently refused to pay the
bounty. Suit was therefore entered for damages of £15 covering costs
and attorney's fee. The case was dragged through numerous continuances until June, 1764, when there was a verdict and judgment
for the plaintiff of £8.5.7.[48] By then Henry had championed the popular interest in the Parson's Cause and carried more weight with a
Goochland jury than he had a year before.

Other aspects of his business during the year are significant. He
had charged £311 to outstanding debts owed him and also receipts
of £300. There were a smaller number of petty cases with unpaid
fees and a number of sizable accounts, largely for merchants, but including John Hawkins, the Hanover slave dealer. In the *Virginia
Gazette* we find one of his advertisements for a slave auction to be
held at the courthouse when lawyers, traders, and countryfolk were
assembled for court week.[49] In all, Henry had some 280 civil cases
in 1762 for ninety-four clients as compared with 180 for seventy-nine
the previous year, with a comparable increase in collections. While
some thirty clients were from Hanover, there were over twice that
number from Cumberland, Goochland, Louisa, and other westerly
counties. Thus he was acquiring a large practice and influential friends
in an area spreading over a hundred miles of the Piedmont. His
name was becoming widely known in the back country.

The bond for a debtor whom Henry's father sued in 1763 was
witnessed by William and Mary Henry. Patrick's dissolute brother,
William, had married and settled down quietly on a plantation in
Fluvanna County.[50]

Although Patrick secured a conditional judgment in *Baine* v. *Barnet*, after various legal procedures, it was later dismissed. Perhaps

one explanation for Barnet's failure to pay his debts is found in the attached bill against him. Along with such items as "2yd Calico" 7/6, "1 Chamber pot" 1/6, a small knife 8d, a candlestick 1/, an ounce of indigo 1/ and various purchases of sugar and molasses, there were also numerous entries such as the following: a bottle of rum 3/3, 2 gallons of rum 14/, a pint of rum, and 2 quarts of rum.[51]

The year 1763 was marked by a further increase in the size and quality of Henry's practice despite poor collections. He had some 493 civil cases listed for 160 clients of whom half were in Hanover and the rest in adjoining counties, including forty in Cumberland, newly opened to the westward. He now charged fees of well over £600 or twice as much as during the previous years, but collections were less than £200.

The fees charged against Thomas Yuille, Merchant, Rocky Ridge were £212, the largest by far for any client to date, but there are no credits to offset the long list of debits. By now Henry was advancing considerable sums of money to his clients. Thus, of £212 charged Yuille during the year, £196 was for funds which Henry had advanced him or paid out for him.[52] Small loans in such instances were usually fees to county clerks or other minor charges paid for his clients in order to avoid the inconvenience of collection in a county of wide distances and bad roads. But the larger advances were probably in most cases funds which he was lending for merchants or other clients with money to supply at a time before there were available banks or commercial loan companies.

By now we should not be surprised that several large fees for the year and many small ones are listed as unpaid.[53] Sometimes the account book contains the names of a half-dozen or more clients in sequence with no credits in 1763. William Kerby, Hanover, had paid only two shillings on a fifteen-shilling account and Aaron Trueheart, Hanover, had paid with cash and a hat, we trust a new one which gave Henry good service.[54]

Some other items for the year are worthy of note. John Harris who paid Henry sixteen shillings for a suit is listed as "alias Fighting Jack." We presume, therefore, that he could more than hold his own

[109]

in the rough fighting, often with biting and gouging, which Henry frequently witnessed on court days. And Fighting Jack's address, appropriately called "The Slashes," Hanover, was that poor district in which Henry Clay was soon to be born. Carter Braxton, King William County, listed for £0.16.3, unpaid, was an influential burgess and future signer of the Declaration of Independence. Henry Terrell, Hanover, who paid a small account for some land is listed as "al[s] [alias] wild Harry" for reasons which we may well guess. Several clients belonged to families of jurors before whom Henry appeared that December in the Parson's Cause.[55]

The difficulty which Henry was having with collections not merely helps us to understand his work as a lawyer but further reveals a cause for the growing rift between Virginia and the Mother Country. Not that there was as yet any talk of rebellion; even assertion of the natural rights of the colonists would meet with cries of treason, as Henry was soon to learn. Yet a picture was developing to help us understand why Virginia, so different from Massachusetts in many respects, would join with her in leadership of the Revolution. Under the restrictive trade laws the colonial tobacco planters were caught in an economic squeeze. Granting that part of the trouble lay in their own wasteful agriculture and extravagant living, we must still note deeper causes not of their doing.

The point is well illustrated by a contemporary account of Robert Carter of Nomini Hall, with further correspondence of John Syme. Carter, a first cousin of Henry's client Carter Braxton, was the landed magnate and councilor whose portrait, probably by Sir Joshua Reynolds, has come down to us: a handsome young man in silk coat and high lace collar, with a mask in his hand, as if he were about to hasten away to a masquerade party. That portrait was painted when Carter was enjoying a fashionable sojourn in London; returned to Virginia, he had the ability, the wealth, and the connections needed to bargain well in his tobacco sales. In 1764 he made a shipment of ten hogsheads of tobacco to James Buchanan and Company of London. On the hogsheads, averaging over one thousand pounds each upon arrival in London, there were these charges: the "old subsidy" of £35 and other heavy duties, freight at £8, import and cocket £1, primage, cooperage, porterage, and further minor yet cumulative costs. It is not surprising that on the total sale price of about £75 Carter made "a very modest profit." [56]

The continued correspondence of Henry's half-brother with his Bristol agents throws more light on the situation. In May, 1758, John Syme wrote of the "Poor Prospect of a Crop, there being scarce any Plants," and events proved the accuracy of his prediction. Then in June, 1760, he complained more bitterly that what with "insurance, shrinkage, and interest on money borrowed prior to the sale, his tobacco shipment would not bring "near one half" what it would have sold for in Virginia. He also had lost £1,000 through the death of some male slaves but he had another scheme: if Farrell and Jones would advance him "a Sum of Money, at 3½ or 4 Pr. Ct. to be laid out in Negroes, their Crops should be Mark'd with a distinguishing mark. . . ." It will be recalled that Syme was opening up new lands in the back country which were not exhausted by cultivation. Now he would buy more Negroes and plunge still deeper.

Yet even while Syme floundered into debt, he continued to place extravagant orders with his agents. His list in 1761 included "a Suit of Best Cloath, of a Fashble Color with two pair Breeches, made very long over the knees," and a velvet waistcoat to match. "Kagley has my measure," Syme said, "& Please give him a Charge to let it be the best of its kind."

In 1760 John Syme had written Farrell and Jones that "You'll receive some Tobo. from Colo. Henry & he tells me, he Purposes to be a constant Shipper but Can't Promise for him." [57] Patrick's father was already over his head in financial troubles. His difficulties and those of some more prominent Virginians were painfully noted in a list of judgments for sterling money obtained in the Virginia General Court during 1757-1763 by persistent British creditors. Several of the judgments were for large amounts, such as John Moorey, a London merchant, against William Lightfoot and Mordecai Booth for £1,492.10.10½; Stephen Nash and others against James Littlepage, clerk of Louisa County, for £248.0.7; and Edmund Smith against

Warner Lewis, a relative of George Washington, for £580.18.5½. There were also judgments for considerable amounts against Nathaniel Harrison and Benjamin Harrison, of the influential James River family, and against Richard Lee. And coming close home, in April, 1758, Bowden and Gergulier had obtained a judgment against Henry's father-in-law, John Shelton, for £365, while Robert Donald, in October, 1759, obtained one for £99.16.9 against his brother Scot, John Henry.[58] We may be sure that Henry heard at family firesides and from clients rich and poor a full chronicle of their grievances, fancied and otherwise, against the British merchants. And proud, independent men, already in a grumbling mood, would lend a willing ear when he spoke eloquently of other British abuses in the religious and political spheres.

Writing nearly a hundred years after Henry's death, with the account books in his possession, William Wirt Henry estimated that Patrick had charged fees from the fall of 1760 to the end of 1763 in 1,185 suits, exclusive of "many fees for advice, and for preparing papers out of court." [59] A summary, not allowing for the sixteen missing pages of the account book, is as follows:

YEAR	NO. OF CASES	ACCOUNTS UNPAID	PAID
1760	176	£123.13.3	£ 48.18.11
1761	180	161.6.7	54.10.10
1762	280	310.11.6	300.7.0
1763	493	659.11.10½	225.19.5½

Henry's success is all the more creditable in view of the severe limitations imposed by the Virginia Assembly on attorney's fees. As a phase of its intermittent efforts since the early days of the colony to curb mercenary lawyers, the Assembly by a law of April 10, 1761 had stipulated the maximum fees with penalties for lawyers in the inferior courts.[60] Altogether, Henry's record for these years makes one deplore Jefferson's unfounded statement that he "kept no accounts" and that for every case a fee was an indispensable prerequisite.[61]

In 1761 Henry had sued Thomas Barnett for "Sundry goods" sold to him in January, 1760, when Henry was closing his store. He was given conditional judgment, changed at the November, 1762, Goochland court to an attachment for £20 returnable at the next court. No proper funds being found, the attachment could only be "executed on a Cloth Brysh." Finally after more court action, with Henry appearing, Barnett wrote this note "To the Most Worshipful Court of Goochland County":

GENTLEMEN,
    Please to enter Judgment against me to P. Henry Jr. for Seven pounds fifteen shillings & six pence. I am
Gent.
Yr. hble Servt
THOMAS BARNETT

This note from Barnett was dated November 26, 1763.[62] Within two weeks Henry was to deliver his famous speech at Hanover Courthouse in the Parson's Cause, an opening scene in the Revolutionary drama.

8

The Parson's Cause

Charm us, Orator, till the Lion look no larger than the cat.
————TENNYSON, *Locksley Hall Sixty Years After*

The finest eloquence is that which gets things done.
————DAVID LLOYD GEORGE

TODAY the old village of Hanover Courthouse is only a twenty-minute drive northward of Richmond, on the lower Washington highway.[1] Here, hardly noticed by many fleeting motorists, is the county seat of Patrick Henry's early years. The simple wooden tavern where Patrick and his family lived by grace of his father-in-law, John Shelton, still stands on the west side of the highway. Within, not radically changed by the sprawling additions of later years, is the former taproom where Patrick is said to have helped serve the thirsty guests. And just across the road is the old brick courthouse, built about 1737. The T-shaped building, with its stone-capped arches, its tall hip roof covering the bar of the T, its graceful cornice with hand-carved dentils, is not radically different from a number of courthouses and churches built during the period.

As the autumn of 1763 turned to winter, the little edifice, still barely a quarter of a century old, had already begun to acquire the mellow quality that is often so becoming to colonial Virginia architecture. It was young Patrick Henry, however, who that December

[114]

gave the building its historic importance. For it was here, in the courtroom with its wooden benches and raised judge's seat, that Henry first found his powers as an orator.

In the previous February, 1763, the Treaty of Paris had been finally signed. The British ministry, bumbling though well meaning, was planning a program of legislation which would radically change the relationship of Great Britain and her American colonies. But in Hanover this policy was as yet little known or understood. For the underlying events leading to the Parson's Cause we must search the earlier history of the Anglican Church—its uneasy status in Virginia and the mounting reaction against it.

In England it was the age of Chesterfield and Hogarth, of the two- and three-bottle men, so-called because of the amount of wine they could hold at one sitting. The Methodist movement had not fully exerted its leavening influence. With the Established Church at a low ebb in the Mother Country, it is not surprising that her difficulties were multiplied in the new and distant American colonies. Clergy of superior character and ability, only too difficult to recruit for English charges, were often reluctant to take their chances with the independent-minded vestries, meager salaries, and rough living conditions in Virginia.

"Certainly nothing does so great disservice to religion as the leaving of so many Parishes destitute of ministers and the Supplying so many with indifferent ones either as to their ministerial talents or good life," declared a statement sent to the Bishop of London in 1724, presumably by the aging but still vigorous James Blair. He complained that the tenure of the local ministers was so "precarious," the living so mean, as to be "an encouragement only to the lowest sized of Divines to adventure amongst us." Foreshadowing the argument in the Parson's Cause over payment of the parsons in money instead of tobacco, Blair criticized the poor quality of tobacco given them and the late payment.[2]

There were numerous examples of good men laboring for a pittance in the Lord's vineyard, as Blair himself would have been the first to affirm. Indeed, they were in a large, if not overwhelming, majority. Nevertheless, only too many instances of incompetent and immoral ministers were pointed out and exploited by Virginians already becoming restless under the restrictive Anglican Establishment for which they perforce paid taxes. Although not yet disposed to break the yoke of the State Church, they were ready, indeed often eager, to hear of the shortcomings of men supposed to set them Christian examples.

And however pious these divines may have been, they were frequently pedantic and tiresome. Their sermons were often tedious essays, more heavily loaded with classical allusions than with practical religion. Only too typical of many ministers in back-country parishes was the Reverend Mr. Mossom of St. Peter's in upper New Kent, a church which Henry probably attended occasionally when living in lower Hanover. The Reverend Devereaux Jarratt wrote that in his youth he seldom went to St. Peter's where Mr. Mossom preached entirely from a written sermon, fixing his eyes continually on the manuscript and so close that his words seemed addressed to the cushion rather than to the congregation. Small wonder that Jarratt was for a time more interested in training horses for the turf or cocks for match and main than in religion and that his later rôle as an evangelical minister was partly the result of Presbyterian influences.[3] In fact, it was not surprising that many Virginians of the upper as well as the lower class gave only lip service to the Established Church. Sir John Randolph, the Attorney-General, for example, was described by Commissary Blair as "a good friend to the College and Country, I can't say to the Church." [4]

Blair wrote thus in the year of Henry's birth. Already a situation was developing in Virginia whereby a bold opponent of the clergy might become a popular hero, and this would be especially true after opposition to the Anglican Church had been accelerated by the growth of the Dissenting movement through the Great Awakening.

A rector of Fredericksville Parish had earlier been accused of loving drink "perhaps too well." [5] About the same time that the charges against him were being noised about, in 1742, a clergyman of Richmond County in the Northern Neck was held by the Council to have been guilty of drunkenness and profane swearing.[6] When an English bishop had been admonished on a similar charge he had replied, "When I swear, I do not swear as a Bishop. I swear as Sir Jonathan Trelawney, a country gentleman and a baronet." [7] But the Richmond County minister had not been able to offer a similar excuse, nor had a brother clergyman in Isle of Wight County who was convicted not only of profane swearing but of drunkenness and lewd and debauched actions.[8]

Yet it is easy to dwell on those unfortunate stories and to overlook the great majority of the Anglican ministers who were faithful and long-suffering even if not inspiring. Moreover, after the spread of the Dissenting faiths, not all the Dissenting ministers set noble examples, as is evident from the records of the Hanover Presbytery. Within the Anglican fold Commissaries Blair and, to some extent, Dawson [9] endeavored to eliminate the worst applicants or incumbents while the Reverend Patrick Henry was among the lesser clergy who sought to strengthen the personnel.[10] But such reforming efforts were handicapped by the remote control of the Virginia Church through the Bishop of London and by jurisdictional disputes within the colony.

The complexities of the situation were illustrated by two unhappy episodes during the decade preceding the Parson's Cause. The first involved the notorious John Brunskill, pastor of a mountain parish in Fauquier County where John Marshall had just been born. In the opinion of Governor Robert Dinwiddie, Brunskill was guilty of a whole catalogue of sins. They included tying his wife to the bedpost and cutting her with knives, as well as "many indecencies" that modesty forbade Dawson from detailing in a report to the government. When urged to institute judicial proceedings against Brunskill, Commissary Thomas Dawson appeared willing enough, but said that he lacked authority to suspend or remove ministers "even in the most notorious cases." There was a long wait while a report of the affair was sent to London and meantime Brunskill, who blatantly contested the case, remained an open scandal. And to compound the difficulties, several ministers resented what they deemed unwarranted lay interference in their affairs. A rift was opening between the clergy and a large section of the Virginia populace.

It was widened by the case of the Reverend William Kay. In the judgment of the leader of the clerical party, the Reverend John Camm, professor of Divinity at William and Mary, the Kay affair was proof of the overweening power of the vestries over the ministers, which, if longer countenanced, would enable very few ministers to remain in their charges whenever "the least disgust" was aroused against them. Received at a parish in Richmond County, Kay found that he had as a leading vestryman "one great, powerful Colonel," Landon Carter, whom he was unable to please. Carter, the son of "King" Carter, was himself the owner of Sabine Hall and married first a Wormeley of Rosegill, then a Byrd of Westover. Of his good qualities Henry would find evidence during the coming Revolutionary agitation, but to Kay he was the proud aristocrat at his worst. With more courage than tact, Kay even preached a sermon on pride, a sermon which Colonel Carter naturally took unto himself. The vestry under Carter's leadership closed Kay's church; the minister instituted a suit for damages in the General Court; the Colonel losing there, appealed to England. He vowed that "he would clip the wings of the whole clergy" in the colonies, and he sulked in his tent while awaiting further opportunity to advance his none too gentle opinions.[12]

Against such a background we come to the opening events of the Parson's Cause. In 1754 a convention of the Virginia clergy, fortified by the Kay case, protested to the Governor against an order of the Council prohibiting a member of the clergy from holding the office of justice of the peace. The next year they were more seriously disturbed by the passage of a law permitting payment of their salary either in tobacco, as in the past, or in money. This started a train of events leading directly to Henry's employment as a counsel on the anti-clerical side.

The facts of the case were generally known and Henry must have heard them extensively discussed by Parson Henry, Colonel John Henry, and his own back-country clients and associates. For well over a century it had been the custom to pay Virginia ministers in tobacco, and since 1696 their salaries had been fixed at the rate of sixteen thousand pounds per annum. With tobacco usually selling for only a few cents a pound the clergyman's salary was slender enough at best, even allowing for extra fees (such as those for marriages and burials) or income from glebe property. Still payment in tobacco did mean some additional stipend when the price of the weed was high, and the system was accepted by the clergy without undue grumbling. The procedure was confirmed by an Act of the Assembly in 1748 which received the royal assent. But in the summer of 1755 there was a bad drought and a very small quantity of tobacco was raised. In October the General Assembly, intimating that it would be too burdensome for the people to pay their tobacco debts in kind, passed an act permitting payment in money at the rate of 16s. 8d. per 100 pounds. This was twopence per pound and the Act was popularly called the Two Penny Act. It was to be in force only ten months, too short a time to be completely curtailed by the slow process of royal disallowance. Indeed, the Act did not contain the usual suspending clause by which a law altering another approved by the King might be declared ineffective until it also had received the royal confirmation.[13]

The clergy now began to be seriously alarmed.[14] They began to protest in unison and sent letters and memorials to England. In one letter, signed by ten ministers, including Parson Henry, they protested the 1755 law as "a breaking in upon our establishment, an insult upon the Royal Prerogative & contrary to the liberty of the subject, as well as to natural Justice & Equity." In a new and unprecedented manner, the letter continued, the legislature had altered the law confirmed by the royal assent so as to make it optional to pay ministers either in money or in tobacco. And this was at "an under rate" of twopence per pound when the market was generally expected to be threepence if not fourpence in currency worth. When the market price of tobacco was low, as had generally been the case since 1724, the clergy had to be satisfied with depreciated [or lower] salaries, and now in justice they ought to have the benefit of the rising market. Moreover, the option law was retroactive and deprived them of property which they had already earned and which was due them before the law went into operation.

The letter then continued with a lengthy passage eloquent about their measly salaries, extensive parishes, and other onerous living conditions in the new country. Included also was a complaint against the Two Penny Law as extending only ten months and another charge, difficult to prove, that the legislature designedly favored "the rich and the great" at the expense of the clergy and the poor. The Reverend Patrick Henry was the senior minister in point of service signing the letter and there is every reason to believe that he still held to his convictions when his nephew was employed to uphold the contrary opinion.[15]

There is said to have been considerable sympathy for the clergy. Despite the growing sentiments against paying taxes for an Established Church, the Two Penny Law might have been repealed by the legislature if several of the extremists among the clerical party had not played into the hands of the opposition. In one such instance, shortly before the vote on the Two Penny Act, the House heard that the Reverend Mr. Rowe, a William and Mary professor, had asked publicly how many of the burgesses ought to be hung. Everyone who would vote to settle the parsons' salaries in money was "a scoundrel." And if they applied to him for the sacrament [communion], he would refuse them. Censured by the House and faced with imprisonment, Rowe hurriedly presented a petition of apology and was discharged from custody.[16] But details of the explosive affair with its lingering resentments must have been repeated to Patrick Henry by burgesses such as John Syme, West Dandridge, or Thomas Johnson, his client in the Parson's Cause.

Then the 1758 Assembly, anticipating that there would not be enough tobacco grown to meet the "common needs of the country," passed the second Two Penny Act. It contained the same provisions as that of 1755 except that it was limited to twelve months instead of ten. Again there was no clause providing for suspension until royal approval, although the King had specifically instructed the Governor to require its inclusion in such laws. Like Governor Dinwiddie, the newly appointed Governor Fauquier refused to heed requests from the clergy that he veto the measure. Besides the crop failures, the people were being taxed more and more heavily for the war and Fauquier was anxious not to incur their ill-will.

The patience of the more belligerent parsons, already worn thin, was now exhausted. The clergy held a convention at Williamsburg in early 1759, of which Henry could hear much from his uncle, and they sent the Reverend John Camm of Williamsburg to present their case in London before the Privy Council and Lords of Trade. Camm was able and courageous, but none too prudent; and he had not yet played his rôle in a Miles Standish-Priscilla Alden affair which would give him a measure of popularity among the gossip-hungry provincials. Asked by a much younger man to court a girl for him, Camm was referred by her to a biblical text (II Samuel 12:7). He found this to read, "Thou art the man," and they were duly married.[17]

An appeal to the King over the heads of the Assembly and Governor was an extreme and inflammatory procedure. The clergy well knew that the assertion of the royal prerogative in what the people considered local matters had more than once provoked deep resentment. Only six years before, in 1753, the Burgesses had sternly protested the levying by Governor Dinwiddie of a pistole fee for attaching his signature to land patents. His action was "illegal and arbitrary," it contended, and contrary both to the charters of the colony and the royal instructions. It was "an Infringement of the Rights of the People, and a greivance highly to be complained of." [18] In the resolutions passed by the Burgesses after Henry's Stamp Act speech in 1765 there would be references to the violation by the British government of the colonial charters and to Virginians who supported the Stamp Act as enemies of the colony.

But it was lean, studious Richard Bland who did the most to build up the theoretical argument which Henry would have the genius and courage to advance to its ultimate conclusion. Bland, now in his mid-fifties, was an alumnus of William and Mary College which, despite some temporary difficulties between the faculty and student body, was then doing its full part toward making the Virginia of that period a mother of statesmen. By the 1750's Bland was recognized as Virginia's most learned student and exponent of the colonial laws. In a contemporary letter on the Pistole Case, printed in pamphlet form, Bland had written—fruitful thoughts!—that "the Rights of the Subjects are so secured by Law that they cannot be deprived of the least part of their property without their own consent. . . . For if it is against Law, the same Power which imposes one Pistole may impose an Hundred." Bland was apparently the principal author of the Two Penny Act of 1755 and the sole author of that of 1758.[19]

Reinforcing his earlier arguments, Bland also engaged in a pamphlet war with the Reverend John Camm. In "A Letter to the Clergy of Virginia," printed at Williamsburg in 1760 and apparently reaching leaders of opinion in the colony, Bland argued that the royal instructions certainly ought to be obeyed and that only the most pressing necessity would justify any person in disregarding them.

But Bland then added this explosive statement which Henry would do so much to popularize: "As *salus populi est suprema lex* where this Necessity prevails, every consideration must give Place to it, and even these Instructions must be deviated from with Impunity." This point was "so evident to reason, and so clear and fundamental a Rule in the *English* Constitution, that it would be losing of time to produce Instances of it," Bland continued.[20]

Yet learned and convincing as Bland was, he would be at the most a conservative revolutionist. He was not yet ready to carry his thought to a radical conclusion; he would oppose Henry's Stamp Act resolution in the close and bitter debate during the next year. Jefferson, with his usual frankness and perception, praised Bland for writing the first pamphlet on the connection of the colony with the Mother Country which had any pretense to accuracy. But he added this note on Bland's mental struggles:

> He would set out on sound principles, pursue them logically till he found them leading to the precipice which he had to leap, start back alarmed, then resume his ground, go over it in another direction, be led again by the correctness of his reasoning

to the same place, and again back about, and try other processes to reconcile right and wrong, but finally left his reader and himself bewildered between the steady index of the compass in their hand, and the phantasm to which it seemed to point.[21]

We may well sympathize with the plight of the clergy under the second Two Penny Act. Yet by the appeal to the King the strength of their cause became lost in a far more important question of whether in a purely local matter—involving local taxation—"any other will than that of the Assembly should prevail." [22]

In London a Virginia agent and the solicitor for Mr. Camm now presented their arguments before the Privy Council. Upon their recommendation to the failing George II, he disallowed the two tobacco Acts and rebuked the Assembly and Governor Fauquier. Because of slow-moving bureaucrats and sailing vessels, Camm did not return to Virginia until June, 1760. The usually genial Fauquier had had his patience tried enough when Camm successfully appealed over his head, and the minister was hardly tactful in the delayed session which he had with the Governor at Williamsburg. In fact the angry Fauquier turned at last to some Negro servants and told them to look at Mr. Camm so that they might know him again.

"If ever he should come to ask for me, suffer him not to enter my doors," he declared. [23]

Lines were now beginning to be drawn for the Revolutionary struggle. Camm, who would become a leading Virginia Tory, entered a suit for damages in the General Court and planned, if he failed, to seek further aid in England. The Assembly, aware not merely of their side of the case but of the general background of resentment against the clergy, appropriated a fund for defense. Not willing, under the circumstances, to risk everything in one suit, the ministers brought actions for damages in several counties.

The first suit was instituted by the Reverend Thomas Warrington of York County, friend and confederate of the pertinacious Camm. The jury awarded considerable damages and, according to Commissary William Robinson, did not give more because two of the jurors had a private quarrel with the minister.[24] Many difficulties of the clergy in these suits arose from the resentment against them which had developed for other reasons. The extent of the popular feeling was further indicated by the next suit, brought by the Reverend Alexander White who had been associated with Parson Henry in the appeal to the Bishop of London. The case was tried at King William Courthouse in the adjoining county to Hanover, and Patrick Henry, even if not present, must have been familiar with the proceedings. For understandable reasons, the King William justices refused to interfere in the suit and left it to the jury which delivered the bare verdict "we bring for the Defendant." [25]

The third suit was brought in Hanover by the Reverend James Maury. Born of Huguenot refugees in 1718, Maury had attended William and Mary and had gone to England to take holy orders. In 1763 he was living in Louisa County near the border of Albemarle and, apart from the Parson's Cause, he is best known for teaching at his classical school there such Virginians as Thomas Jefferson and Bishop Madison. No sketch of Mr. Maury's career is complete, however, without some personal data from his family Bible, where we learn that he and his "dear Molly" had been married in late 1743 and that, by the year of the Parson's Cause, she had blessed him with eleven children.[26]

Despite his boarding pupils and clerical labors, he was hard put to make ends meet; when Jefferson entered his school in 1758 he was "a harassed if not unhappy man" and inveighing against the Two Penny Act. It was not until the second Act had been passed and annulled, however, that he took legal action.

Maury first attempted to get the back pay which he considered due him from his Louisa vestry. Then he applied to Thomas Johnson and Tarleton Brown, collectors of the parish levies. Rebuffed in both instances, he felt it useless to appeal to the county court, which was under the influence of the vestry, in large part composed of the same men, including not a few of the influential Johnson's friends or relatives. Maury, therefore, entered suit on April 1, 1762, in neighboring Hanover against the collectors and their securities. He was represented by Peter Lyons, the able King's attorney for the county, while John Lewis, another competent Hanover lawyer, was secured for the defense.

If the wheels of justice now seem to move slowly in the United States, they were even more lethargic in colonial Virginia. The defendants pleaded the Act of September 14, 1758, and their strict compliance therewith. The plaintiff filed a demurrer to the plea and it was argued on November 5, 1763, some thirty-one months after Maury had first entered his claim against the Louisa vestry. The Hanover court upheld Maury's demurrer, and John Lewis withdrew from what appeared a hopeless case. It only remained to call a petty jury to consider the amount of the damages.[27]

At this desperate stage Patrick Henry was employed to replace John Lewis as attorney for the defendants. Although Patrick had been practicing such a brief time, Johnson had already recognized his competence by employing him in two previous cases during the year. Moreover, Johnson, an experienced hand in county politics, was not unaware that Patrick's father was presiding justice of the county court and that the Henry-Winston-Dabney connections had long been entrenched in the court and would weigh heavily with a Hanover jury.

Obviously, Patrick had little time to prepare the case, though the facts were generally known. But on the hopeful side he had the support of the Johnsons, a leading Piedmont family, with their entourage, and he was backed by the growing Presbyterian element in Louisa as well as in Hanover. Providence Church, the wooden Presbyterian meeting house in lower Louisa, had been established on the land of Joseph Shelton, Henry's relative by marriage. The Reverend John Todd was preaching here to some fifteen or twenty sturdy pioneer families, sure to welcome any opposition to the State Church.[28] There is, indeed, reason to believe that when the Reverend Maury opposed the vested political interests of the county, he likewise aroused the opposition of the poor farmers generally who were complaining of the clergy for causes financial or otherwise. And although Maury was a conscientious and morally irreproachable if somewhat dogmatic

clergyman, he had to bear much of the odium for numerous ministerial misfits in the colony during recent years.

In Patrick Henry's legal records there is the following account
for 1763 with "Thomas Johnson formerly Deputy Sher. Louisa":

```
1763 To Fee & Tax v Ingle's 16/3
            Sci. fac v.D.  15/                     1.11.3
      To fee ad⁵. Maury  15/
      To fee for mo. in Hudson's affair            15.–
      To fee ad⁵. Daniel  15/                      1.10
```

Note the item "To fee ad⁵ Maury 15/," obviously for the Maury
suit. In the Parson's Cause, one of the most important legal cases in
American history, Henry charged Johnson only fifteen shillings. The
legal limit, it was no more than he received for hundreds of routine
cases, and it was not paid for nearly five years.[29]

When the case had first been heard at Hanover Courthouse in
November, 1763, the county justices had ruled that the Two Penny
Act was "no law." The trial for damages was set for the following
month and a select jury chosen under conditions which, Maury asserted, indicated rank favoritism for the defendants.

"How far they, who gave the order [for selecting the jury],
wished or intended it should be regarded," Maury wrote Camm,
the clerical leader, "you may judge from the Sequel." [30] The Hanover sheriff who made the selections first went into a public room full
of gentlemen and informed them of his errand. One of the gentlemen excused himself as having given his opinion in a similar case.
The sheriff then left the room without summoning any of the other
gentlemen present. He afterwards met, on the courthouse green, another gentleman, R. Squire Taylor of King William, whom he excused after Taylor said that he was a churchwarden and not fit to
serve. The sheriff, so far as Maury could hear, made no further attempt to summon gentlemen.

"These, you'll say, were but feeble Endeavours to comply with the
Directions of the Court in that Particular," Maury declared.

Then the sheriff "went among the vulgar Herd," the little parson continued. After he had selected and set down upon his list some eight or ten of these, Maury met him with it in his hand.

"They are not such jurors as the court directed you to get," Maury complained after looking over the list. "I have never before [heard] of but one of them. And as one of the collector's securities, he is a party in the cause and not fit for a juror on this occasion."

"Yet this Man's Name was not erased," Maury bitterly wrote. "He was even called in Court, &, had he not excused himself, would, probably, have been admitted." Indeed, Maury, writing a few days after the trial, could not recall that the partial members of the court expressed either surprise or dislike that a more proper jury had not been summoned.

Maury objected to the personnel of the jury, but Patrick Henry insisted that they were honest men and therefore unexceptionable. They were immediately called to the Bible and took the oath. "Three of them, as I was afterwards told, nay, some said four, were Dissenters of that Denomination called New Lights, which the Sheriff, as they were all his Acquaintance, might have known," Maury concluded.[31]

Maury's understandable indignation at the plight of the clergy, accentuated by his own family struggle, hardly made him an impartial witness. He was not likely to evaluate judicially tales about the case which reached him and largely came from his own sympathizers. Several of the jurors were indeed Dissenters and the court, sympathetic to Patrick and his clients, hardly exercised itself to select an impartial jury. But the parson's statement that the sheriff immediately left the public room is based merely on what someone present told him; nor did he actually see the sheriff make the subsequent selections in the manner charged.

Again, was the jury selected from "the vulgar Herd"? Patrick's friend and relative, George Dabney, might well have been disqualified for the jury service. As one of the fast-growing group of Hanover Dissenters, he was sincerely opposed to the Anglican Establishment; but he was also a gentleman of high and independent character.[32] John Wingfield was a landowner and land processioner;

and either he or another John Wingfield, apparently a son or near relative, was later clerk of the upper church in St. Paul's Parish, under the Reverend Patrick Henry.[33] John Thornton was a member of a substantial family from Gloucester County and was the owner of Mayfair, a Hanover estate.[34] Benjamin Anderson had just been selected as a processioner; he was appointed the next year to collect a parish levy, and in 1767 he attained the eminence of vestryman.[35]

As for the other eight jurors, none belonged to a family as prominent as the Dabneys and several were only small landowners, in one instance hardly that.[36] And yet as a group they did not deserve Maury's low social classification. In this and other respects he was at least unconsciously prejudiced.

Early winter had now come to Hanover, but it did not prevent the people from crowding to attend the final hearing in the bitterly controversial case. When, on December 1, John Henry and the other gentlemen justices took their seats and the case was called, the courtroom was filled to overflowing. The clergy attended in a large body to show their solidarity in the proceedings and to enjoy the legal triumph, now apparently assured.[37] Present, too, we surmise, were a few members of the Burgesses [38] and several of the Johnson clan with their Louisa following, as well as many people from Hanover and other adjoining counties. For young Patrick there was a fighting chance to win a victory which might be of great significance in his career. It would prove that his mounting if unspectacular success as a lawyer during the past three years was no flash in the pan.

Among the ministers coming to Hanover Courthouse for the trial was the Reverend Patrick Henry. Seeing his uncle approach, Patrick, according to the usual version, walked up to his carriage, accompanied by Samuel Meredith, and expressed his regret at seeing him there.

"Why so?" the Reverend Patrick Henry asked.

"Because, sir," Henry replied, "you know that I have never yet spoken in public, and I fear that I shall be too much overawed by your presence to be able to do my duty to my clients; besides, sir,

[128]

I shall be obliged to say some hard things of the clergy, and I am very unwilling to give pain to your feelings."

Parson Henry then reproved his nephew for having taken the case. But Patrick defended himself by declaring that the clergy had not thought him worthy of being retained on their side and he knew of no moral principle which obliged him to refuse a fee from their opponents.[39]

Allowing full latitude for the legal ethics of the day, that seems a calculating approach. The story fits Henry's motives as later criticized by the Reverend Maury, and has been commonly repeated.

Seldom quoted is another detail of the story which shows Patrick in a far more favorable light. "Besides," he added to his uncle, ". . . in this controversy, both my heart and judgment, as well as my professional duty, are on the side of the people."

Henry is also said to have requested the Reverend Patrick to "do him the favor to leave the ground."

"Why, Patrick," his uncle replied, or so the story goes, "as to your saying hard things of the clergy, I advise you to let that alone: take my word for it, you will do more harm to yourself than to them. As to my leaving the ground, I fear, my boy, that my presence could neither do you harm nor good in such a cause. However, since you seem to think otherwise, and desire it of me so earnestly, you shall be gratified." Whereupon, he climbed back into his carriage and returned home.[40]

Patrick now entered the courtroom for the trial. Although actually he must have spoken often in public, it was true that this was his first important case, and that his oratorical talents were still unrevealed.[41]

Before him on the justice's bench sat Colonel Henry, awaiting this critical trial for the son in whom he must now have rested so many of his hopes and ambitions; with him were the other justices and some opposing clergymen, including several of the more prominent and learned men in the colony.

The Irish-born Peter Lyons [42] was still opposing counsel. Considering it only a routine case, he introduced proof of obvious facts: the bond of the defendants as collectors for Louisa County, the order of the Louisa vestry directing that a levy be made for Maury's salary for 1759, and the testimony of two witnesses, Gist and McDowell, the largest tobacco dealers in Hanover County, through whom he established that the price of tobacco in the county in 1759 was fifty shillings per hundred pounds. Lyons, a lawyer whose ability would attain notable recognition, now rested the evidence for the plaintiff.

Patrick Henry then introduced Maury's receipt for £144, the value of the tobacco due him in accordance with the Act of the Assembly, and concluded the evidence for the defendants.

Rising again, Lyons made what under different circumstances might have been an effective argument for the plaintiff. The jury was sworn to decide the case in accordance with the law and the evidence, and Lyons made it clear that—the law of 1758 having been disallowed—the parsons had to be paid in accordance with the old law of 1748. It only remained therefore, for the jury to fix the amount of damages due Maury.[43] And in actual fact this was the only duty left them after the decision of the Hanover court the previous month. In view of the popular feeling against the clergy, however, Lyons also attempted to mollify the jury by a "highly wrought" eulogy of the ministers' benevolence.

Henry now rose to reply to Lyons. Many of the people had never heard Patrick speak. They were obviously disheartened, as we have seen, by his faltering commencement, whereas the clergy exchanged "sly looks" as if already anticipating their victory.[44]

But these sentiments of the audience soon underwent a marvelous change. For now the oratorical powers which Henry possessed found expression. Now the Virginians first witnessed the transformation which the outpouring of his oratorical genius affected in him. Now he displayed that ability to lose himself in an occasion or an opportunity which has been displayed by the great masters of art throughout history.[45]

As his words rolled forth and his mind began to glow from its own action his posture became erect and lofty, according to Wirt's account. The spirit of his genius awakened all his features. His coun-

[130]

tenance became fired with the spirit of his words, his eyes seemed to pierce the spectators. In his varying tones and especially in his emphasis there was "a peculiar charm, a magic," of which everyone who had heard him later spoke but of which they could give no adequate description. They could only say that it struck upon the ear and upon the heart, in a manner which language could not depict.

The scene might seem fantastic if it were not attested by numerous witnesses; if it did not fit in with later manifestations of Henry's genius.

The people, who had been discouraged by Henry's introduction, were now caught in the spell of his words, his appearance and manner. In less than twenty minutes, they could be seen in every part of the courtroom, on every bench, in every window, leaning forward in "deathlike silence." Their attention was all fixed upon Henry to a degree that seems almost unbelievable until we realize that they were hearing the first oratorical outburst of one of the greatest orators in history.

Wirt also wrote that the attitude of the clergy was changed from mockery into alarm and despair and "at one burst of his rapid and overwhelming invective, they fled from the bench in precipitation and terror." If this seems exaggerated, we may well believe Wirt's assertion that John Henry was so surprised and enraptured that he forgot his assigned rôle as impartial presiding officer. "Tears of ecstacy" which he was unable to repress streamed down his face.[46]

Even though Wirt's imaginative treatment is only partially accurate in detail, the general impression is correct. Some forty years after the event he was able to get in touch with several old men who had heard Henry's speech. They seemed, he wrote, "to have been bereft of their senses." They could only repeat in general that they followed implicitly wherever Henry led them: "that, at his bidding, their tears flowed from pity, and their cheeks flushed with indignation: that when it was over, they felt as if they had just awakened from some ecstatic dream, of which they were unable to recall or connect the particulars." It was a speech such as they believed "to have never before fallen from the lips of man." To that day, the old people of Hanover could conceive of no higher compliment to a speaker, than to say of him: *"He is almost equal to Patrick, when he plead against the parsons."* [47]

We have noted that it was the appeal to England which had created the greatest opposition to the clergy. The only topic of Henry's speech for which Wirt could secure an authentic account related to the order of the King in council voiding the 1758 law passed by the Assembly. Actually, this question had been passed on in the hearing on the demurrer and should have been ruled out as irrelevant. But the Hanover justices, not excluding John Henry whose emotions were intimately involved, were lax in their procedure. They gave Patrick as much latitude as he wanted and, leaving the technical legal points, he soon moved boldly and vigorously into a discussion of the compact theory of government and of natural rights.

Henry insisted on the relationship and reciprocal duties of the King and his subjects. Advancing the doctrine of John Locke as popularized by Richard Bland and other colonial leaders, he contended that government was a conditional compact, composed of mutual dependent agreements "of which a violation by one party discharged the other." He bravely argued that the disregard of the pressing wants of the colony was "an instance of royal misrule, which had thus far dissolved the political compact, and left the people at liberty to consult their own safety." Despite the dissent of the King and his Council, the Two Penny Act "ought to be considered as the law of the land, and the only legitimate measure of the claims of the clergy." [48]

The account by Parson Maury, written the day after the trial, was not utilized by Wirt. It is naturally critical of Henry but confirms the revolutionary tenor of his argument. Instead of mentioning that Henry rose to oratorical heights as is generally accepted, Maury said that he "harangued the Jury for near an Hour." And this harangue, he added, turned upon points as much beyond Henry's depth and that of the jury as they were "foreign" to the purpose.

"The Act of 1758 had every characteristic of a good law. It was a law of general utility, and could not, consistently with the original

[132]

compact between king and people, stipulating protection on one hand and obedience on the other, be annulled," Henry declared.

. . . "The only use of an established church and clergy in society is to enforce obedience to civil sanction, and the observance of those which are called duties of imperfect obligation." When the clergy ceases to meet these ends, "the community has no further need of their ministry, and may justly strip them of their appointment," Maury quoted Henry as asserting.

And then he continued with the boldness of a true revolutionary tribune, a boldness shocking to conservatives. The clergy of Virginia, by "refusing to acquiesce in the law in question, have been so far from answering, that they have most notoriously counteracted, those great ends of their institution. Instead of useful members of the state, they ought to be considered as enemies of the community. In the case now before them, Mr. Maury, instead of countenance and protection and recovery of damages, very justly deserved to be punished with signal severity."

Unless the jurors were disposed "to rivet the chains of bondage on their own necks, I hope they will not let slip the opportunity now offered of making such an example of the plaintiff as will hereafter be a warning to himself and his brethren not to have the temerity for the future to dispute the validity of laws, authenticated by the only authority which could give force to them for the government of this colony: the authority of a legal representative, of a Council, and of a kind, benevolent and patriot governor." [49]

Strong words these, putting a finger on the action of the clergy which did the most to anger the people.

"A king by annulling or disallowing laws of this salutary nature, from being the father of his people degenerates into a tyrant and forfeits all right to his subject's obedience," Henry added to the "horror" of the "more sober and virtuous part of the audience."

It was at this point that there was the murmur of "Treason, treason, treason," which foreshadowed the cry from the opposition two years later during Henry's speech against the Stamp Act.

"Yet Mr. Henry went on in the same treasonable & licentious

Strain without Interruption from the Bench, nay even without receiving, the least exterior Token of their Disapprobation," Maury noted. "One of the Jury too was so highly pleased with these Doctrines, that, as I was afterwards told, he every now and then gave the traiterous Declaimer a Nod of Approbation." [50]

Henry had grown up in the countryside and had benefited from three years of personal experience with the local juries. In the latter part of his speech he resorted to an emotional appeal, not without a touch of demagoguery, in which he accused the clergy of failing to practice benevolent Christian precepts.

Again we cannot pretend to quote Henry with literal accuracy.[51] But his bold, swift phrases were those of a young man warmed up with his argument and not stopping to weigh words. He ended by urging the jurors to make an example of the plaintiff. Under the ruling of the court, they would have to find for Mr. Maury—but it need be for only one farthing.[52]

Henry had now stirred the jurors to such a degree that Mr. Lyons in his concluding remarks could not change them. In less than five minutes they returned a verdict of one penny damages for the plaintiff. The court, itself too moved for any impartial decision, denied Lyons' motion that the verdict was contrary to the evidence and that the case should be returned to the jury. It also refused a motion for a new trial, although it did allow an appeal to the General Court.

As for the excited people, their enthusiasm was now out of bounds. Wild with joy, they seized Henry and bore him on their shoulders around the courtyard.[53] He had proved himself a master of the art of swaying a popular audience. And in attacking the tyranny of Church and State he had said, boldly and forcefully, what most of the people felt, yet had never heard expressed, at least in a public assembly.

Henry's essential argument, based on the compact theory of government, was not original, as we have noted. It had been developed notably by the Englishman John Locke, intellectual defender of the British Revolution of 1688, who drew on ideas that lay deep in history. Locke's books and principles were widely circulated in Virginia. The quick-minded Henry could have learned of them from his studious father, from books which Sarah's family had inherited from John Parks, her bookselling grandfather, or through his own resources, including contacts with lawyers and legislators in county courts—this in addition to what he must have absorbed directly or indirectly from Richard Bland.

When Henry made his meteoric appearance in the Parson's Cause, the public was somewhat more prepared for revolutionary thought than when Bland had published his early pamphlets. The boldness or worldliness of a vociferous minority in the clergy and the growth of Dissenting sects had led to a growing independence of thought on religious issues. And the broader the revolution, the broader the base. The distance from the Mother Country, the influence of the frontier and of non-English immigrants were combining to give a sharp edge to liberal thought, whether originating at home or in Europe. In 1759, when the religious issue was already being connected with the political in the expression of popular rights, another pamphleteer had built on the framework of Richard Bland. Colonel Landon Carter, who had been nursing his wrath since the Kay controversy, entered the field with his pamphlet, "A Letter to the Right Reverend Father in God." [54] The aggrieved Carter, powerful lord of many lowland acres, laid on with economic and constitutional arguments much like the veteran Bland's. It is not surprising that both gentlemen were avidly read by a small group of planters and professional men, who did much to determine public opinion.[55]

Yet the opposition was still extremely formidable; the cautious and conservative had ample reason for hesitation. Carter lost some influence through his obvious bias, but he also knew where in prudence to draw the line. And even if the more influential Bland had been willing to move to his logical conclusion—to advance his doctrine of popular rights to the point where the government might brand it as treasonable, he still lacked Henry's gifts of oratory, not to say popular leadership. For the sad fact was that the learned Bland was "a most ungraceful speaker." Indeed, Mr. Jefferson, who later candidly noted this, said that it was also true to a remarkable extent of Peyton Randolph and John Robinson. Henry thus had an opportunity equal to his courage and imagination.[56]

There remain only a few more notes to be added to the account of this Virginia *cause célèbre*. Some two months before Henry had appeared in the Parson's Cause, the persistent Mr. Camm had been unable to get a printer in Virginia for a strongly worded broadside against his opponents. He had therefore gone to Maryland to publish the pamphlet, about mid-October, 1763. This was followed later in the month by an interchange of letters in the *Virginia Gazette* between Bland and Camm; Henry would doubtless have been reminded of Bland's constitutional arguments even if he were not soon to be casting about for arguments to use at the December term of Hanover Court.[57]

The next April, 1764, in the wake of Henry's victory, Camm published a second pamphlet in which he fired shots not merely at Colonel Bland but at Patrick:

> If so old and deep a Politician as the Colonel, so able a Writer, a Man so acute at Demonstration, can express himself in this unguarded Manner in Print on the Subject of the Prerogative, pronouncing the Freedom he takes with the Power of the Crown as an expression of Regard to his Sovereign, no Wonder that an obscure Lawyer, the other day, when a Court had previously adjudged the Two penny Act to be no Law, and a Jury was summoned on a Writ of Inquiry to settle the Damages the Plaintiff had sustained by the said Act, adjudged no law, should tell the Jury that the King by disallowing the said Act, had forfeited *the Allegiance of the People of Virginia;* and that the Parsons, for opposing the said Act by *legal Means,* instead of obtaining Damages, deserved to be *severely punished.*[58]

But the "obscure Lawyer" had already turned the tide, had turned it so completely that any further efforts on the part of the clergy were only sound and fury. Maury and Camm in particular were angry and determined enough to continue the fight. Parson Maury, bitter against Henry, wrote that, after the court was adjourned, Patrick apologized to him, declaring that he had engaged in the cause solely "to render himself popular." Henry, who was notably good-natured, very likely did make some propitiatory remarks after the trial, as lawyers often do. But whether this was all he said or implied to Maury may be doubted in view of Henry's explanation to his uncle and other evidence as to his convictions in the matter.

"I would have given a considerable sum out of my own pocket, rather than that my friend Patrick should have been guilty of a crime but little, if anything, inferior to that which brought Simon, Lord Lovatt to the block. He exceeded the most seditious and inflammatory harangues of the tribunes of old Rome," Henry's first client, Patrick Coutts, said after the trial.[59]

We may well believe that the clergy, angry with Henry as they were, "more than hinted" that he should be prosecuted for treason, and furnished the King's officials in the colony with a list of witnesses. The affair even had unpleasant reverberations in his family circle. The next year, 1764, his uncle, the Reverend Patrick, instituted suit in Hanover for the tobacco due him for the year 1759, and young Patrick was attorney for the defendant. But this suit was continued while awaiting the result of the suit brought by Mr. Camm and then dismissed.[60]

That same year, while the ministry in England was planning a Stamp Act, Camm's case was tried by the General Court. It was decided against him on the ground that the Two Penny Act was in force until disallowed by the King.[61] This was a dubious decision in view of the understanding that the Privy Council had declared it void *ab initio*, and the vote was five to four. But Henry had drawn support from the leading planters as well as the common people. With diehard determination, Camm appealed to the Privy Council in London. That august body finally heard the case in 1767 and upheld the Virginia court on questionable grounds.[62] After Henry's argument and certain subsequent events, the government was apparently glad to end the case.

The clergy, and not least the harassed Mr. Maury, needed larger salaries. But the actions of their vociferous minority had not increased their popularity, and many Virginians were even turning to the Dissenting sects. There were numerous petitions to the Assembly at about this time for abandonment of parishes, the majority of the church members having removed or joined the Dissenters.[63] The Anglican ministers were entitled to a decent living, to be sure, but should it have been within a state-supported church?

Strangely, Patrick Henry, who would be known as a devout member of the Episcopal Church, contributed largely to the undermining of its State Establishment. In so doing, he advanced principles—both political and religious—which at a critical period united most Virginians of high and low degree, the lordly Landon Carters and poor backwoodsmen. And, more than that, he helped to loosen a chain of events leading to the Revolution. His achievement is all the more remarkable in that his oratorical triumph was apparently so unstudied. When several Hanover men who had heard him, and others with intimate knowledge, were queried by William Wirt, they all stated that Henry's talent had been "not so much as suspected." [64]

It was not merely coincidence that in a list of the Hanover Committee of Safety on November 8, 1775, we find two names identical with those of jurors in the Parson's Cause while another member had testified in the case.[65] But we are anticipating. Henry, impregnated with liberal principles and fired with a genius, perhaps as unsuspected by himself as by others, would next raise his voice against the Stamp Act.

9

A Backwoods Leader

With the triumph of Wolfe on the Heights of Abraham began
the history of the United States.
——GREEN, *A Short History of the English People*

In the House of Burgesses, one could tell by his apparel, and
deportment, no less than by his sentiments a member from . . .
anywhere above the fall line of the river.
——BEVERIDGE, *John Marshall*

At the Capitol in Williamsburg, now restored with noteworthy vision and verisimilitude, is the Hall of the House of Burgesses. In one end of the rectangular room is the original speaker's
chair. Here when Henry entered the Burgesses in 1765 was en-
throned the Honorable John Robinson, master parliamentarian, generous and, as events proved, too generous creditor of the lowland
aristocracy. Seated in front of him on two oval-shaped benches were
the Burgesses, the highest elective body in His Majesty's largest
American colony. Today the shiny benches and elegant cushions, rep-
licas of the originals as they were when new—with no nicks, scars, or
tobacco stains—seem appropriate to the representatives of the "Tucka-
hoes," the Tidewater oligarchs, dressed in silks, linens, and laces. But
what of the "Cohees," the back-country and mountain men? In that
critical decade they were to play a determining rôle. It was of little
importance that Patrick Henry, their most influential leader in the

impending legislative battles, was plainly garbed, with unpowdered hair, and that some of his followers from the frontier appeared in homespun with buckskin shirts and coonskin caps. They represented a new and vital force, a force that not only would help spearhead the assault against the entrenched Tidewater aristocracy but even against King and Parliament.

In Hanover Patrick had breathed the spirit of the back-country men, and he would do so all the more when he moved in 1765 to Louisa, the semi-frontier county just to the westward. A generation later a traveler passing into Louisa from another county still had to ride for twenty miles through a lonely pine forest. One traveler lost his way and not until midnight did he find a tavern, which unwillingly admitted him.[1] On the frontier it often mattered little who one's ancestors had been in the older country. What counted most was courage, hardihood, and enterprise. Crude and even lawless as it was in many respects, the back country was a leveling force for democracy, a force that reacted on more settled and conservative areas. And it was not until Henry's time that America began to feel its strongest impact. Many backwoodsmen, of that restless type which the Anglo-Saxon race in particular has bred, were moving through Louisa into even more westerly Virginia counties and the Carolinas. Before Henry made his "Give me Liberty" speech in 1775 the tide would have started rolling into Tennessee and Kentucky.[2]

Patrick Henry was now undergoing experiences which enabled him to catch the spirit of this movement. It had a profound effect upon him, and through him and other leaders of his breed on the new America.

This influence was especially strong during the years just after the Parson's Cause. In 1764 Henry went to Williamsburg to represent his friend, Captain West Dandridge, in a disputed election. Already, Henry had been mentioned as a possible burgess from Hanover. The following year he would be back in the capital to represent Louisa County, and among its independent-minded citizens he would find a congenial home. During the next few years numerous legal cases and land interests would require him also to be often in Augusta County, another frontier region where a number of his relatives were settling.

The election cases give a vivid impression of Hanover politics in its more earthy phase. There, as elsewhere in the colonies, rum, cider and other spiritous liquors played a rôle in elections. The suffrage in Virginia was then extended to freeholders who owned fifty acres of unimproved land or twenty-five acres with a house.[3] This meant that the privilege was given to the majority of males who were free, white, and twenty-one. And since many were poor and uneducated, signing their rude mark to legal papers, it is not surprising that they were susceptible to various pressures from candidates for office. Treating or serving liquor to the voters was a common practice; indeed, almost necessary for election. Even Colonel George Washington found that his high character and military renown alone could not win him a seat in the Burgesses. During a second and victorious campaign in 1758, his political managers totted up a bill of £39 for punch, beer, rum, wine, brandy, and "Dinner for your friends." [4]

Not long afterwards, the Assembly enacted a law with strict provisions against the direct or indirect use of "money, meat, drink, entertainment or provision," to obtain one of the coveted seats in their august body.[5] This law Henry now invoked on behalf of his client (and future father-in-law), Captain Dandridge.

Nathaniel West Dandridge, Henry's hospitable neighbor of his upper Hanover days, had served in the Burgesses for several years. But the hard times and his ill management were fast getting him in financial straits. For these reasons he was probably glad to accept an appointment as coroner for Hanover. The Governor issued a writ for election of a new member, and James Littlepage was chosen. But Dandridge, who had apparently decided to run again for the Burgesses, accused Littlepage of getting elected by undue influence. Littlepage, a large landowner in the county, had also for the past two decades been clerk of Louisa County, which office he was tolerantly allowed to hold through a deputy. His election to the Burgesses appears to have been largely the result of his opposition to the rigorous inspection of tobacco offered for shipping. There was also at least a strong suspicion of truth in the charge that Littlepage had exerted undue influence on the voters. The electors had to travel to the courthouse, often many miles distant, and voting was *viva voce*, usually with the candidate or his manager standing by. Littlepage, or at any rate his friends, offered some of the freeholders liquor to ease the pains of the trip to the courthouse, though whether this might be construed as no worse than generous hospitality was a moot point.

The case was argued in late November, 1764, before the Committee of Privileges and Elections.[6] Thus Henry had the opportunity to display his talent before some of the leading men in the colony. The chairman of the committee was Richard Bland, and the members included Peyton Randolph, George Wythe, Richard Henry Lee, Edmund Pendleton, George Johnston, and other gentlemen with whom Henry was to be closely associated in the next critical decade.

From a letter which was read to the committee and from other evidence we clearly learn Littlepage's announced purpose "to serve the People that's now so injured by the damned Inspecting Law," which, he asserted, gave the Merchants "a View or a Review, on the Tobacco, after it has past [inspection] that has so great influence on the Men called Inspectors."[7] He also seems to have had his own personal reasons for being angry at the prevailing trade restrictions, for in October, 1759, Stephen Nash and others of Great Britain had obtained a judgment against him in the General Court for £248.0.7 sterling.[8] Now, at a time when almost all the local officials were appointed, he wanted the tobacco inspectors to be elected annually by the freeholders. His opinions, strongly expressed in churchyards, private homes, and elsewhere, were clear enough to the Hanover electorate.

There was also considerable evidence on the treating of voters, which Henry could muster against Littlepage. At one party given by a Littlepage supporter during the campaign, the assembled freeholders were supplied with four gallons of rum punch. And this being exhausted, Littlepage ordered two more gallons, assertedly on his friend's account. Some upper Hanover freeholders whom he solicited to vote said it was too cold to go the more than twenty-five miles to the polls. He thereupon invited them to call at his house en route, where they were hospitably entertained, though no more, it was asserted, than was Littlepage's custom. Considering the weather and the free-drinking habits of the time, it is not surprising that several electors had partaken freely before they came to the house and, since further refreshment was provided there, that quite a number "went merry to the Court House." By way of rebuttal, however, it was argued that Littlepage had left early in the morning and that a friend of Captain Dandridge's had attempted to treat a voter. A thirsty freeholder named Grubbs had come to the courthouse offering to vote "for any one who would get him a Dram." When a Dandridge supporter had failed to satisfy him, a friend of Littlepage's, allegedly without the latter's knowledge, had procured him the drink. The worthy Grubbs then duly voted for Littlepage.[9]

As a whole, the testimony provided a clever lawyer like Henry with some evidence of undue influence in the election, but the law, however strictly worded, had been lightly regarded. When the hearing assumed extraordinary interest, it was for entirely unexpected reasons.

A day or two beforehand, a poorly dressed young man had been observed sauntering in the lobby of the Capitol. He seemed to be a stranger to everyone and the burgess recalling the incident had lacked the curiosity to inquire his name. But when the hearing was called, how astonished he was to find the same young man appear as counsel for one of the contestants, and still more by what he said!

Williamsburg was then filled with great gentlemen and their families present for the Assembly, and there were the usual social activities centering around the Royal Governor. It was all very different from the simple society in which Henry lived. At the Capitol the proud bearing of the aristocrats and the dignified procedures of the House of Burgesses were enough to deter any young man of less courage and independence. Henry, dressed in "very coarse apparel," was ushered into the committee room. His practice had been confined to the back country and it was said none of the members knew anything of him. This statement, however, was somewhat exaggerated, in view of his argument in the Parson's Cause.[10]

[143]

At first none of the committee, save the chairman, treated him with "decent respect." Only Richard Bland could not depart, even on this occasion, from the instincts of a gentleman. But the learned Bland, looking somewhat like the "musty old Parch[ment] w'ch he handleth & studieth much," would hardly be swayed by a shoddy argument.[11] Nor would the other able lawyers on the committee.

Soon Henry changed the attitude of his hearers. He launched forth into a full and brilliant declamation on the rights of suffrage, superior to anything ever heard before within those walls. Coming from a man of such unprepossessing appearance, it filled the committee with amazement. Again, as during portions of his argument in the Parson's Cause, there was a deep silence while he spoke, not a sound being heard except from his lips.[12]

But Henry was not dealing with Hanover justices and jurors. Despite his stirring plea, the committee held that Dandridge's petition was "frivolous and vexatious." Littlepage was declared to be duly elected, and Dandridge was ordered to pay his opponent's costs as a result of the petition.[13]

Many of the burgesses were doubtless more guilty of treating than Littlepage, and they wanted the law to remain a dead letter. The next June, 1765, we hear of a candidate swilling the planters with punch and having "every man of the least distinction in the county ... in his interest." [14] Henry was personally abstemious, but there is no record of his endeavoring to uproot the established custom. Indeed, his account book [15] shows the following credits for a Hanover client on May 17, 1765, apparently just after Henry was elected to the Burgesses from Louisa:

By waggoning punch etc. to Louisa	£1. 0. 0
By 1 Loaf Sugar 15/	.15
By 28 gall^s Rum @ 5/	

Although Henry's trip to the capital had failed of its immediate purpose, his ability had impressed influential burgesses. He was also in a position to hear strong arguments against the hated stamp tax whose passage by Parliament the Burgesses were then seeking to prevent. This agitation was in full force when he was in Williamsburg for the election case.

Little did complacent British ministers realize that the Stamp Act was, in its ultimate results, one of "the most momentous legislative Acts in the history of mankind." [16] With the acquisition of Canada and the removal of the French menace there, the colonials felt far less need for British protection, yet a clumsy, bludgeoning effort was made to tighten controls and increase revenues in America at a time when her people, growing powerful and cocky, were chafing under the limited controls that already existed.

Such ineptitude is not surprising if we examine closely the life of the period. The past few decades had hardly been among the most enlightened in British history. The drunkenness, prostitution, callousness, and corruption that characterized the age had only begun to be relieved by the moral fervor of a Whitefield or Wesley, the flaming patriotism of a Pitt. The mass of English, Scots, and Welsh could hardly be expected to grow excited over governmental injustice in distant America when they themselves were worse governed. No one could rightly claim that the Parliament which passed the Stamp Act truly represented the people. In England the rotten and pocket boroughs made a travesty of equal representation, and there were less than three thousand voters for all Scotland.[17] George III had now set about to dispel the enveloping political apathy and corruption by a vigorous personal rule. With the government in the hands of a small, profligate class, many of them in financial need, it was not too hard for him to manipulate them by bribes, pensions, and offices. But if George was firm in controlling ministers for what he deemed a worthy purpose, he was also muddleheaded, with a weak mind finally giving away under stress. And, "blindly complacent," he saw in "Radicalism, industrial strife, or American rebellion nothing but wanton attack on the most perfect of governments." [18]

At a time when a high order of statesmanship was needed in dealing with the American problem, little could be expected of the King and his compliant ministers. With regard to the Stamp Act, perhaps it is remarkable that the American *bête noir*, George Grenville, made as much effort as he did to conciliate the colonies.

In addition to Virginia, numerous American colonies were already suffering from the British commercial restrictions. But the situation was at its worst in New England. She had little more than a subsistence agriculture and her prosperity largely depended upon the exchange of fish, lumber, grain, and provisions for the sugar, molasses, and money of the foreign West Indies and the Spanish Main.[19] The commerce was needed to meet the unfavorable balance of trade with Great Britain from whom New England was forced to buy most of her manufactured goods. There was a virtually prohibitory duty on sugar and molasses in the interest of the British West Indies, but these small islands could not possibly meet the demand. The trade with the French Islands continued through a system of flagrant and almost open smuggling.

Moreover, this took an unpatriotic turn during the Seven Years' War. Neither the Middle nor the Southern colonies had equaled New England in her contributions of men and supplies to the French War, but the illegal Yankee trade with Canada as well as the French Islands had flourished unblushingly.[20] And if the British were to enforce the customs laws, they would stop an important outlet of American trade.

Even before the end of the war, writs of assistance—general warrants to permit searching of private dwellings on suspicion of smuggled goods—were issued in America. At the superior court at Boston in early 1761, James Otis opposed the writs with a fiery eloquence. They were a violation of all the rights of nature, of the English constitution and of all the charters and compacts with the colonies, he asserted.[21]

It was an opening signal of the coming Revolution. Otis' bold words sound much like those of Henry nearly three years later in the Parson's Cause, although there is no proof that Henry was influenced by the Massachusetts firebrand. Otis, grievously injured a few years afterward during a political affray, lost his early dominance of the Massachusetts Revolutionary scene. His brilliant mind under an eclipse, he was supplanted by that master agitator, Sam Adams, and his clever cousin John Adams.

While condemning the British ineptitude in arousing the opposition of such colonial stalwarts, we must appreciate the difficulties of the London government. By the Treaty of Paris, Great Britain had acquired all of Canada and the disputed territory stretching to the Mississippi. Pontiac's Indian uprising soon thereafter, perforce crushed by British troops, pointed to the need of expensive imperial protection. But the British national debt had been doubled by the French war, and country gentlemen were paying in taxes about twenty per cent of their income from land.[22] To landowners, strongly represented in Parliament, it seemed only fair that Americans should bear a larger burden of the imperial defense. The impatient members gave little thought to the fact that the colonials, considering their resources, had already been taxed heavily for the war; that they had little ready cash, and had been allowed to build up a tradition of taxation only through their chosen representatives. Moreover, life in new, rugged America did not encourage subservience. And by 1763 over a third of the Americans were of non-English stock—Scotch-Irish, Germans, Huguenots, and Welsh; not to speak of proud Southerners, jealously independent New Englanders, and others of British blood quick to resent oppression.

In 1763 George Grenville, "a dry precise man of great knowledge and industry, almost always right in little matters," was appointed Chancellor of the Exchequer. Courageous and honest, he faced a baffling problem of balancing liberty and order.[23] It was a question which has continued to perplex abler political leaders and which the Americans themselves were to solve only partly by the Revolutionary War. Henry himself would later offer solutions for it not acceptable to many of his compeers.

The vast territorial acquisitions of the British by the Seven Years' War had produced in the minds of their ruling class a "subtle transition" from the idea of governing colonies primarily with a view to their trade to that of governing them with a view to their manpower and revenue. And if this policy were adopted it meant, in the frank words of the conservative Massachusetts Governor, Thomas Hutchinson, that there must be "an abridgement of so-called English Liberties in America." [24]

At various meetings of Parliament during the autumn of 1763 and the spring of 1764, Grenville developed his fateful policy. During the previous May Pontiac and his braves had gone on the warpath, capturing every fort between Lake Erie and the Ohio, and even laying siege to Detroit and Pittsburgh. In order to control the Indians and purportedly to allow time for working out a permanent policy for land cessions and the fur trade, George III drew a line along the crest of the Alleghenies, west of which all colonists who had "either wilfully or inadvertently seated themselves" were required to vacate. What was intended to be a temporary program was labeled as a permanent policy of exclusion and it had much more effect on Americans than appears on the surface.

Among Henry's friends and clients in the back country were many men who, in the words of Lord Dunmore, had "no attachment to Place" but were forever imagining that the lands "further off" were better than those upon which they had settled. Dunmore, then Governor of Virginia, alluded to the various proclamations issued to restrain such frontiersmen. But he added that they were "impressed from their earliest infancy with Sentiments and habits, very different from those acquired by persons of a Similar condition in England." They did not believe that the government had any right to prohibit them from such a vast area, uninhabited save for a few scattered tribes of Indians. [25]

It was still too early to perceive the effect of the Proclamation Line upon aggressive American elements, whether backwoodsmen, merchants, or land speculators. [26] But a tempest was stirred up soon enough by other British legislation. That same memorable year of 1763, George III assured Grenville, through the now expected favors and perquisites, of a parliamentary majority. Conscientious and well-meaning, Grenville envisaged the need of large funds to administer the newly augmented empire, and he outlined a threefold plan to secure them. "Grenville lost America because he read the American dispatches, which none of his predecessors had done," [27] quipped a contemporary treasury official. To add a touch of irony, Grenville was the brother-in-law of the great Pitt the Elder!

First in the well-intentioned program, the navigation and customs laws were to be strictly enforced in America. The old policy of salutary neglect was discarded. Measures were taken to break up smuggling, and another Sugar Act was passed which not only seriously curtailed trade but, it appeared, would add grievously to the debts owed in America for British merchandise. Second, an army of ten thousand men was to be maintained in America. The British asserted that it was needed to protect the colonials, and they could call up fresh memories of wars in which the Americans might well have been overwhelmed if they had depended only upon their own resources.

But with the French menace in Canada now removed, the colonials saw even less need for Redcoats than before. The British, they suspected, were planning to overawe them while enforcing the new trade regulations. In any case, the revenue from the Sugar Act was expected to pay only a third of the costs for the troops. It seemed to the ministry only fair that the Americans should pay a share of the remainder; Grenville, therefore, proposed a second revenue measure.

This was the famous, or infamous, Stamp Act. Grenville well knew that even the bold Pitt had refused to "burn his fingers" with such a tax, and both his secretary, Jackson, and the Earl of Hillsborough advised him to drop the scheme. Nevertheless, he told the Commons in March, 1764, that he might pursue it, and the House agreed that he had the right to do so. This action, when published in America, caused much alarm. There were meetings and protests throughout the colonies. Massachusetts took a lead in the opposition, and a committee of her House of Representatives on June 25 sent a letter seeking co-operation to the Speaker of the House of Burgesses. [28]

It was not until October 30, however, that Governor Fauquier convened the Virginia Assembly. Two weeks later the Burgesses appointed a committee to draw up addresses to the King, Lords, and Commons in opposition to the proposed tax. Little did the committee dream that one of their number would be the first President of the Continental Congress and three others signers of the Declaration of Independence. It included influential conservatives such as the chairman, Peyton Randolph, the Attorney-General, and Edmund Pendleton, but also George Wythe, Richard Bland, Richard Henry Lee, and John Fleming.[29] Lee and Fleming were soon to be associated with Henry in the liberal opposition. Lee, a member of a family comparable in influence to the Randolphs, is reported to have introduced the resolutions for the declaration of protest against the Stamp Act. He is also said to have shared with the learned and incorruptible Wythe in the authorship of the resolutions although they must have been influenced by Bland and others.[30] Bland had published *The Colonel Dismounted* on the day the Burgesses met, and the wording of the subsequent resolutions indicates his influence.[31]

From a letter of Governor Fauquier to the Board of Trade we get an impression of the fight that was going on behind the scenes at the very time Henry appeared in Williamsburg for the Dandridge-Littlepage hearing. The terms of the resolutions drawn up by the committee were "very warm and indecent as Your Lordships will observe in their Journals," Fauquier wrote. But some of the members told him that their whole study had been to endeavor to soften the terms, and they had reason to hope that there was nothing in them to give the least offense.[32]

The majority of the committee were moderates or liberals, too much so, it seems, for the House. At the committee meetings and informally, no doubt, in taverns and private residences, the discussions on the resolutions continued for several weeks. From John Syme, John Fleming, a committee member whom he had already met on many a court day, or other burgesses, Henry could hear much of the issue. He doubtless deplored that the resolutions were toned down somewhat but rejoiced that they still retained much of their original spirit.

As finally phrased, the memorial to George III began with the conventional expressions of their "firm and inviolable Attachment" to his "sacred Person and Government" (in the Declaration of Independence he would not be regarded as so sacred). Next they proceeded to recall what they termed their "ready Compliance" to the royal requisitions during the Seven Years' War and the "heavy and oppressive Debt of near Half a Million" which the colony had incurred. And then in language reminiscent of Richard Bland they entreated the King to protect them "in the Enjoyment of their ancient and inestimable Right of being governed by such Laws respecting their internal Polity and Taxation" as were derived from their own consent with the approval of the sovereign or his substitute.[33]

The wording of the memorial to the House of Commons [34] is especially significant because Henry obviously drew on it for his later Stamp Act resolutions. The remonstrance stated that

> ... it is essential to British Liberty that Laws imposing Taxes on the People ought not to be made without the Consent of Representatives chosen by themselves; who, at the same Time that they are acquainted with the Circumstances of their Constituents, sustain a Proportion of the Burthen laid on them. This Privilege, inherent in the Persons who discovered and settled these Regions, could not be renounced or forfeited by their Removal hither, not as Vagabonds or Fugitives, but licensed and encouraged by their Prince and animated with a laudable Desire of enlarging the British Dominion, and extending its Commerce. . . .

To the contrary, the privilege was

> . . . secured to them and their Descendents, with all other Rights and Immunities of British Subjects, by a Royal Charter, which hath been invariably recognised and confirmed by his Majesty and his Predecessors . . . in prescribing a Form of Legislation. . . .

In accordance with this charter, laws for the administration of justice and the welfare of the colony had been hitherto enacted by the Governor, Council, and Burgesses. To them requisitions for supplies had been directed by the Crown.

It was also argued that a Stamp Act would be "ruinous" to a colony which was already taxed for several years ahead to redeem the money spent for the war and was still put to large expense to defend her frontiers against the restless Indians. An increase in the tax burden would be "intolerable," especially since the people were greatly distressed already by the scarcity of circulating cash amongst them, and by the small value of tobacco in the British markets.

There was likewise a significant reference, as events proved, to the losses that the intended acts would cause to Great Britain. The plantation trade, "confined as it is to the Mother Country, hath been a principal Means of multiplying and enriching her Inhabitants: and, if not too much discouraged, may prove an inexhaustible Source of Treasure to the Nation." [35]

But the memorials were disregarded. In February, 1765, the Stamp Act was passed by the Commons with opposition on the floor only from Colonel Isaac Barré,[36] who had served in America during the late war, and from a few other members. "In fact, the affair passed with so very, very little noise, that in town they scarcely knew the nature of what you were doing," [37] wrote Edmund Burke, who was in the gallery of the Commons. Grenville, conscientious as ever, had seriously considered a proposal for American representation in Parliament. But even if enough narrow placemen could have been lined up for passage of the measure, there was little hope of its success. Against practical operation of the representative principle, there was always the wide ocean barrier. And while many districts in Great Britain also lacked direct representation,[38] as was pointed out by advocates of the stamp tax, they were all close enough to Westminster to exert strong pressure.

Despite the British constitutional theory, it was absurd to argue that North Carolina or New York were adequately represented by members from Bristol or Essex. Americans were guilty of much constitutional quibbling, but they could validly contend that the Stamp Act was a flagrant case of taxation without *effective* representation. To Samuel Adams or Patrick Henry the point would be obvious. They could hardly prove by the letter of the law that there was "any generical distinction between taxing and other legislative Acts" [39] for which Parliament had authority. Yet in English constitutional tradition there was a definite distinction, and, as Edmund Burke later declaimed, "the greatest contests for freedom in this country were from the earliest times chiefly on the question of taxing." [40] The English had avoided regular imposition of taxes on Wales until Welsh members sat in Parliament and they had been similarly mindful of Irish opinion, little as they regarded it in other respects. It was a perceptive Irishman, however, who later wrote that no free people would ever admit

> that persons distant from them 1,000 leagues are to tax them to what amount they please, without their consent, without knowing them or their concerns, without any sympathy of affection or interest, without even sharing themselves in the taxes they impose—on the contrary, diminishing their own burdens exactly in the degree they increase theirs. [41]

Passed so lightly that February, the Stamp Act was approved without debate or division by the Lords, and on March 22 received the royal assent. [42]

In the colonies the passage of the Act was anticipated. Henry could now find the full text printed in the *Virginia Gazette*. "Whereas, by an Act made in the last session of Parliament, several duties were granted, continued, and appropriated towards defraying the expenses of defending . . . the British colonies . . . in America . . . from . . . the first day of November . . . [1765] there shall be raised . . ."

> 1. For every skin or piece of vellum or parchment, or sheet . . . of paper, on which shall be engrossed, written, or printed any declaration, plea, replication, rejoinder, demurrer, or other pleading, or any copy thereof in any court of law within the British colonies and plantations in America, a stamp duty of three pence.

> 2. For every skin or piece of vellum or parchment, or sheet or piece of paper, on which shall be engrossed, written, or printed any special bail . . . in any such court, a stamp duty of two shillings.

And so on for fifty-five provisions, couched in the sprawling, repetitive language beloved of the hair-splitting lawyer. Above all, Patrick was affected by the numerous provisions relating to attorneys. Stamps, printed by the government and sold by duly appointed officers, were to be affixed to nearly all legal documents. This was a hardship on the general public and especially on the lawyers, already restricted in Virginia as to the size of their fees. And lawyers were a vocal lot, influential in county courts and the Burgesses.

The taxes were not only numerous but diverse. They were also to be collected on newspapers, pamphlets, advertisements, land grants, almanacs and calendars, privileges and franchises issued by the legislatures, almost all customs papers, appointments to public office (other than military, naval, or judicial) for a year or less and with salaries and fees or perquisites of £20 or more, and so on for hundreds of items embracing almost every phase of workaday life.

Considering the special American conditions one finds doubtful validity in the argument that there was a heavy stamp tax in England. Most of the duties were only from threepence to a few shillings, it is true, but they were to be paid in currency. And of that there was little enough, what with hard times, the unfavorable balance of trade, and British prohibitions against coinage and paper money. On college diplomas the tax was two pounds, on the appointments for office ten shillings, on the licenses for retailing liquors three pounds. Tavern keepers too could be prime agitators: Henry's friend, Thomas Johnson, as we shall see, and probably John Shelton. And further irritating the people in lighter as well as serious moments, there were Number 43 "For every pack of cards, one shilling," and Number 44 "For every pair of . . . dice, ten shillings." [43] Gaming had become more popular of late years in Virginia and the government had thus found still another way to aggravate mettlesome gentlemen.

Owing largely to the chain of events released by Henry's Stamp Act resolutions, the law was never put into operation as planned. One needs little imagination, however, to envisage the crippling effect it would have had upon colonial business. Moreover, the penalties for violation could be imposed at the option of the informer or prosecutor in any court of record or admiralty which had jurisdiction in the colony where the offense was committed.[44]

The duty "will fall particularly hard on us lawyers and printers," Benjamin Franklin had said. The day after the passage of the Act, however, he wrote home from London, that "we might as well have hindered the sun's setting. . . . Frugality and industry will go a great way toward indemnifying us." [45] The governors of Massachusetts, New York, and Maryland all sent assurances that the Act would be peacefully executed despite the opposition. Even the fiery Otis wrote that it was the duty of everyone to humbly acquiesce in all the decisions of the supreme legislature. "Nine hundred and ninety-nine in a thousand of the colonists will never once entertain a thought but of submission to our sovereign, and to the authority of parliament in all possible contingencies. . . ." [46]

In Pennsylvania the Assembly had been in session when the news of the Act was received in Philadelphia. But it had adjourned without taking public notice of its passage.[47] In Virginia the Assembly met in early May.[48] Its leaders, after their resolutions the previous December, seemed indisposed to protest further. American liberties appeared to be slipping away when late in the month a raw young burgess from Louisa—Patrick Henry—first took his seat in the House.

During the past seven months since the Dandridge-Littlepage case Henry had continued to increase his legal practice, not only in Hanover but in Louisa and other westerly counties. In 1764 he had credited his mulatto farmer with drawing 650 boards at 1/6 per hundred, and from March 1, 1765, he employed a Louisa carpenter for £12.5.[49] Evidently, Henry was building the house on Roundabout Creek in Louisa into which he and his family would soon move.

Before they could settle on Roundabout plantation Henry was elected to the House of Burgesses from Louisa. The Dandridge-Littlepage election case, added to his brilliant argument in the Parson's Cause, had won him great prestige in the county. Above all, he had the backing of the Johnson family, influential land proprietors

[155]

and officeholders, and bold champions of popular rights. It was Thomas Johnson who a few years before had bearded Thomas Walker, a fellow burgess, and the Tidewater aristocrats in a manner that led him to be arraigned by a committee of the House.

"You little know of the plots and schemes and contrivances that are carried on there . . . one holds the lamb while the other skins," Johnson asserted. "Many of the members are in places of trust and profit and others want to get in, and they are willing to assist one another in passing their accounts, and it would surprise any man to see how the Country's Money is squandered away, which he had used his endeavors to prevent, and could never succeed but once, and that in a trifling amount." [50]

When the clerk's salary was proposed, he (John Randolph) walked through the Burgesses, according to Johnson, and nodded to his "creatures and Partisans" on each side of the aisle who followed him out of the House. Johnson also received a nod which he disregarded. But afterwards, being "particularly beckoned to," he went out and was solicited by Randolph and many members to favor the largest sum proposed for the clerk's salary. This Johnson refused to do, but most of the members voted for the highest salary.

He likewise accused Walker of cheating the county out of eleven hundred pounds when a wartime contractor of provisions.

Johnson's remarks were an affront to the powerful Tidewater leaders then controlling the House. But a resolution that his words were "false, scandalous, and malicious, and reflect highly on the Honor of the House" was carried by only 32 votes to 22.[51]

A considerable minority of the Burgesses concentrated among the newer back-country members was restive under the control of the Eastern oligarchy. It gained further strength during the agitation in connection with the Parson's Cause and the Speaker Robinson affair. If the back-country men could catch their opponents napping and secure an eloquent popular tribune to lead them, they might carry the day in the Burgesses. At least Johnson had a man in mind who might eloquently present the liberal viewpoint.

In 1764 Louisa had been represented in the Burgesses by Thomas

Johnson and his brother William. About May 2, 1765, however, a new writ was ordered for election of a burgess in place of William, who had accepted the office of coroner, though viewing dead bodies could hardly be a pleasing pursuit. Nathaniel West Dandridge the year before and now Johnson, when resigning from the Burgesses in order to accept the office, were doubtless attracted by the opportunity to make some needed money in return for light duties. It is not surprising, moreover, to read that the Johnsons were disgusted with the machinations, if not "the delays and sophistries" of the reigning oligarchies, and William is said to have resigned so as to bring his friend and attorney, the bold and eloquent Henry, into the House.[52]

Such facts may seem enough to have assured Henry's election, even though he had not yet established residence in Louisa. But his admiring friends and neighbors in Hanover were not taking any chances. When the election was held, forty-one residents of Hanover with freeholds in Louisa went up to vote for him.[53]

In Henry's account book, next to some items for 1764, there is the following notation:

> Patrick Henry Esquire the
> greatest orator of Nature

The notation is not in Henry's handwriting, and had been scratched over, probably, in modesty, by Patrick. Doubtless it was written by some rustic admirer, perhaps moved to do so after the Parson's Cause. Soon there would be even more cogent excuse for the ecstatic tribute.

10

The Stamp Act Speech

> Two facts of supreme importance summarize the colonial
> period of our history: England established an empire in Amer-
> ica and England lost an empire in America.
> ———MUZZEY AND KROUT, *American History for Colleges*

> "Possibly this step of the mother country, though intended to
> oppress and keep us low, in order to secure our dependence,
> may be subversive of this end."———RICHARD HENRY LEE

O N WEDNESDAY, May 29, 1765, the Houses of Burgesses
met for what in the prosaic words of the *Journal* might seem a routine
proceedings. The Clerk, John Randolph, one of the powerful Randolph clan, chronicled some minor business; then penned an innocu-
ously worded statement "relative to the charging certain Stamp
Duties in the Colonies and Plantations in America." The Burgesses
had met in the Committee of the Whole House to consider the duties
levied by Parliament, the *Journal* noted. The next day the members
were reported as having passed several resolutions which were twice
read and agreed to with some amendments. Including the text of the
amended resolutions, not as much space was given to the Stamp Act
debate as to the proceedings on the previous Saturday in connection
with the petition of William O'Bryan Goff, "Branch Pilot on Potow-
mack River." [1]

The *Journal* was not designed to be a medium for colorful literary expression, nor indeed to give a full account of the legislative business. Randolph, a staunch conservative, could be counted on not to make more of Henry's epochal speech and the violent debate connected therewith than was necessary. There was also the disturbing fact that the proceedings would be reported in England. Nevertheless, it does seem surprising that the most momentous debate in the Burgesses since its inception in 1619 should be given such short shrift. A true impression of the event can be obtained only by piecing together all the odd bits of supplementary information.

It is usually younger men who start radical movements, older men who join hands against them. Martin Luther was in his thirties when he posted his Ninety-five Theses on the church door at Wittenberg, Oliver Cromwell only forty-one at the convening of the Long Parliament; and Alexander the Great, hardly a defender of the *status quo,* was dead at thirty-three. The point was even more apt in the new America where "ability, prowess, and initiative were not sacrificed to mediocrity and inertia entrenched in aged authority." [2] By an unusual coincidence Patrick Henry introduced his Stamp Act resolutions on May 29, 1765—his twenty-ninth birthday. And what is still more remarkable, he had been a member of the Burgesses for only about nine days.

He had been admitted after taking the outmoded oaths still required of the new burgesses. The Puritan and Glorious revolutions, the development of Parliament and of the trading class had done much to change old England, but it would take the impending Industrial Revolution to effect a peaceful transformation of the country. Meantime, Henry, before being admitted into the House of Burgesses of distant Virginia in 1765, had to comply with the Test Act passed by Parliament in 1673 to exclude Roman Catholics and Dissenters from public office and the Abjuration Act of 1702 requiring renunciation of the Jacobite Pretender.[3] To these formalities Henry subscribed, apparently on May 20.[4]

The House of Burgesses was now the most influential legislative body in the colony. Membership there was comparable to being in the House of Commons, on which the Burgesses modeled its procedure.

With the Speaker and clerk in robes and many of the Tidewater aristocrats in silks and satins, Henry—thin, sallow-faced, and still careless of dress—hardly cut an impressive figure. But, apart from the acquired influence of the reigning oligarchy, the House was "an assemblage of equals."[5] It convened in the old Capitol at the east end of Duke of Gloucester Street, and the members sat on long benches facing each other and in front of the Speaker, as in the House of Commons. There was little to restrict them during the session; they spoke chiefly to sway their colleagues, not their constituents. There was no great pressure of business, and oratory was often the order of the day. "Long speeches replete with classical allusions, elaborate imagery, and glowing periods, that closed with sonorous perorations delivered with measured phrase and gestures *actually did* change votes."[6]

Further similarities to the House of Commons, though with changes brought about by New World conditions, are indicated by an examination of the roll of burgesses for the session beginning May 1, 1765. There were nominally 114 members, though little over a third were in their seats when Henry introduced his revolutionary Stamp Act resolutions. Besides two members from each of the fifty-five counties or a total of 110, the statutes provided for four from the college and boroughs: one from William and Mary, in accord with English precedent; one from Williamsburg; one from Norfolk Borough, now a center for close-fisted Scotch merchants; and one from flat, swampy and mosquito-ridden Jamestown Island.[7] No longer the colonial capital, Jamestown was a rotton borough, a Virginia Old Sarum controlled by its two remaining families of substance, the Travises and Amblers. Even the great counties of Hampshire and Augusta, spreading for hundreds of miles along the frontier, had no more representatives than little Charles City or Isle of Wight. The back country, especially in certain sections, suffered from under-representation for its area and population.

With the economic and political system so balanced in their favor, the House was under the control of the reigning oligarchy[8] which included not merely the Tidewater aristocrats but in a sense their relatives who had left the depleted tobacco lands of the East for the virgin soil of the Piedmont. But would these more adventurous scions, now seeking with their gangs of slaves to clear the forests and build new if less ducal Westovers and Sabine Halls be content with the conservative Eastern leadership? Would their frontier or near-frontier environment make them more likely to hearken to the leadership of a Henry or a Lee?

Most important were the burgesses who would share with Henry the leadership in the coming Revolution. The membership of the 1765 House included a remarkably high proportion of Virginian (and indeed American) statesmen of the coming decades: a President of the Continental Congress, a President of the United States, governors, eminent jurists. There were six of the seven Virginia signers of the Declaration of Independence, and the seventh, Jefferson, would leave his lawbooks to hear the memorable debate.[9] Masters of large and complex plantation communities, whose numerous Negroes must needs be controlled by humor and tolerance as well as firmness; vestrymen and burgesses; often lawyers or county justices—nurtured in classics which bred traditions of liberty and personal responsibility as well as a mellowing culture—such gentlemen would not find it too difficult to step into greater rôles. And country life under not too onerous conditions had given them the sturdiness and heartiness to bear the strain.

John Robinson, genial Speaker of the House, was leader of the dominant conservative political group. The astute Edmund Pendleton of Caroline, an able and experienced lawyer and leading legislator, was likewise a conservative. So to a lesser degree were George Wythe, Richard Bland, and the majority of the lesser members. They were propertied men, privileged gentlemen who would not disturb the *status quo* without due consideration. Yet they were proud and independent, not likely to brook too much interference with their way of life, even from King and Parliament. They were more like the British aristocrats who would accept the Reform Bill of 1832 than the French nobles who were exiled with the Bourbons. Nearly all of them followed Patrick Henry, Richard Henry Lee, and their

[161]

associates into the Revolution, followed them cautiously at times, as became men with responsibilities, but intelligently and heroically.

The Burgesses having met for an adjourned session, the same committees were retained except for filling vacancies.[10] Henry was appointed to fill one of the more important, in the Committee on Courts of Justice. This committee consisted of some twenty members; most of them were obscure burgesses but the chairman was Edmund Pendleton, and one of the members was another eminent lawyer, the idealistic George Wythe, under whom Thomas Jefferson studied law.[11] The committee rooms were in the Capitol, "a very good building, in the form of an Each [H]," in the words of a contemporary traveler. The General Court met in one wing on the first floor, the Assembly on the other, while on the second floor were the Council and committee chambers. With the court convening on April 10 for twenty-four days, this traveler, probably a French agent, reported on the twenty-eighth that some five or six hundred people had gathered from all parts of the colony and from adjoining provinces for transacting business and settling matters with correspondents.[12] There were also those gathering for the meeting of the Burgesses.

Never was there a more disagreeable place than Williamsburg at that time, according to the traveler. "In the Day time people hurying back and forwards from the Capitoll to the taverns, and at night, Carousing and Drinking In one Chamber and box and Dice in another, which Continues til morning Commonly." [13] The traveler's report gave more indirect evidence—if any were needed!—that the planter's economic miseries were not altogether British-inflicted.

"There is not a publick house in virginia," he wrote, "but have their tables all batered with the [dice] boxes, which shews the Extravagant Disposition of the planters." Many of them possess "very great Estates, but are mostly at loss for Cash. they live very well haveing all the necessaries on their Estates in great plenty." Their chief drinks were madeira wine and punch made with Jamaica rum.[14]

It is remarkable that Henry escaped so many vices of the time and place, yet was apparently not disliked as prudish. With his simple tastes, he probably preferred to stay in one of the relatively quiet and less expensive taverns. But if for some reason he roomed at Mrs. Vobe's hostelry "where all the best people resorted," he certainly would have run a good chance of having his pockets emptied. While at Mrs. Vobe's the French traveler became acquainted with several of these "best people," particularly Colonel William Byrd, III, Captain Russell, Sir Peyton Skipwith, and Captain Le Forêt—acquaintances of whom he soon "was like to have had reason to repent, for they are all professed Gamesters, Especially Colonel Burd, who is never happy but when he has the box and Dices in hand." [15] Gambling reduced few planters to as serious straits as it did this last Colonel Byrd of Westover (an admirable gentleman in some respects), but it was becoming an increasing vice among them, and Henry needed to avoid temptation. Fortunately, it took no great effort on his part. He was there for a serious purpose; this accomplished, he would hurry home.

Taking his seat on May 20 or thereabouts, Henry found the House busy with a number of minor bills. It passed an engrossed bill to prevent hogs from being allowed to run at large in the new town of Richmond. A member was ordered to carry the bill upstairs to the Council for their concurrence. It considered an amendment proposed by the Council to a bill for amending an act regarding the trial of slaves for capital crimes and the more effective punishment of conspiracies and insurrections by them. The amendment passed and the Attorney-General, Peyton Randolph, was ordered to inform the Council. After disposing of a few other matters, the House adjourned until Tuesday morning. The remainder of that week through Saturday, May 25, was devoted to routine business—except for action on Friday in connection with the proposal to establish a public loan office.[16]

It was during the debate on this plan, so important to Speaker Robinson and his dominant coterie, that the House first listened to Henry's oratory. Robinson had now been Speaker of the House and Treasurer of the colony since 1735 and was the most influential planter in Virginia. An "excellent man, liberal, friendly, and rich," as Jefferson stated, his very generosity proved his undoing. While in office he had lent to hard-pressed friends and associates large sums in Virginia paper money which had been redeemed and which he was legally bound to destroy. This was indeed a breach of trust but Robinson felt that it was important to save his friends (including influential members of the Assembly) from financial ruin. It appears that he planned to return the money either by payments of his creditors or if necessary from his own large estate.

Much-married like many of the gentry, Robinson had taken in 1759 his third wife, Susannah, daughter of Colonel John Chiswell of upper Hanover. Henry may, therefore, have met the eminent Speaker-Treasurer at one of the lingering social sessions after service at the upper Fork Church or when Robinson came over from King and Queen for Hanover court; if so Henry would have had a gracious salutation. His opposition to the Treasurer which now developed was based on general grounds rather than any detailed knowledge of his mismanagement. Shortly before Henry appeared in the Burgesses, Robinson "became sensible that his deficit to the public was become so enormous as that a discovery must soon take place." With his influential friends in the Assembly he devised a plan for a public loan office from which money would be lent to individuals at good landed security. The colony was to borrow £240,000 sterling in Great Britain, secured and paid through a tobacco tax. Of this, £100,000 was to be used to redeem and burn the paper money issued to meet the expenses of the recent war. The balance of £140,000 was to be lent out on "permanent Security" at interest of five per cent. In Royle's *Virginia Gazette* for May 17, 1765, there was a detailed explanation and defense of the proposal, written probably by an interested member of the House to prepare for its introduction. The motion for the land office was, therefore, offered to the Burgesses and, in Jefferson's opinion, if it had passed, the debts due to the Treasurer on the loans would have been transferred to the public and the deficit completely covered. Other evidence, however, is now offered to show that Robinson's motives were less reprehensible.

Henry attacked the scheme on some general grounds "in that style

[164]

of bold grand, and overwhelming eloquence, for which he became so justly celebrated afterward," recalled Thomas Jefferson, a spectator. Jefferson had been "intimate" with Henry since 1759-60 and had a special interest in him. "I can never forget a particular exclamation of his in the debate, which electrified his hearers," Jefferson wrote Wirt. "It had been urged, that from certain unhappy circumstances of the colony men of substantial property had contracted debts, which, if exacted suddenly, must ruin them and their families, but with a little indulgence of time, might be paid with ease.

" 'What sir,' exclaimed Henry, 'is it proposed, then to reclaim the spendthrift from his dissipation and extravagance, by filling his pockets with money?'

"These expressions," Jefferson added, were "indelibly impressed on my memory." Henry "laid open with so much energy the spirit of favoritism, on which the proposition was founded, and the abuses to which it would lead that it was crushed in its birth."

The young, inexperienced member from Hanover carried with him all the members of the upper counties, leaving a minority composed merely of the aristocracy, Jefferson concluded. From that time his popularity swelled apace.[17]

Jefferson's memory was again faulty; the loan office proposal was passed by the House despite Henry's spirited opposition. A committee was appointed to confer with the Council on the matter, but it was defeated there.[18] Henry had not gained an immediate victory, and he was making powerful enemies. But he was winning still more valuable support, especially from the back-country members.

In a surviving portrait by Wollaston [19] we get an impression of Robinson, Henry's most formidable opponent at this period. His hands emerge from the fashionable turned-back cuffs, doubtless of ruffled lace imported from England. And the face is that of a masterful gentleman with whom life has not gone too hard. But his equanimity was now disturbed by Henry's assault on his pet land office bill; soon in the Stamp Act debate, Henry would give the honorable Speaker the shock of his life.

It was Robinson, incidentally, an alumnus of William and Mary and a skillful parliamentary leader, who had been the urbane Speaker of the House in 1758 when George Washington, returning after his exploits in the war, had been given his vote of thanks by the Assembly. Robinson was not an arch-conservative and had opposed the royal governors on a number of occasions—always, however, within prescribed bounds.[20] If he had lived, his great influence might well have been enough to make the Revolution in Virginia take a more moderate course.[21]

Only five days, including the weekend, separated the loan office debate from Henry's Stamp Act speech. On Monday, May 27, the House passed an Act for appointing a colonial agent in Great Britain, and a number of minor bills. A petition from Peter Pelham, organist of Bruton Parish Church, Williamsburg, showed the legislature having a power over the Church not dreamed of in present-day Virginia. Pelham prayed for relief from the "great Labour and Expense" he had incurred when repairing the organ and was eventually paid £50.[22] Again, on May 28, messages were received from the Council listing bills in which they had concurred,[23] and there was a little more routine before the House adjourned until the next day when the Stamp Act was scheduled for consideration.

During the four-week session, the Burgesses had disposed of pressing business. If debate on the Stamp Act should now lead to their dissolution, they would be as prepared as practicable. When meeting on May 1, they had appeared uncertain as to what action to take concerning the hated measure.[24] No answer from England had been received to their protests of the previous session. Their respectful, at times almost suppliant, tone [25] was hardly such as to move the British ministry. In the colony powerful forces of timidity or self-interest were favoring delay. Much depended upon whether those Virginians desiring strong measures would have effective leadership.

As the closing date drew near, with the necessary business transacted, it was natural for some members to be starting home.[26] A four-week session in the midst of the growing season had involved enough personal sacrifice already, and there was a long journey ahead for members from the more remote counties. Perhaps also there was truth in the report of a contemporary writer that many of the members had retired, knowing, he supposed, what was to come up.[27] But while many of the absent members may have expected a debate or other embarrassing action on the Stamp Act, they could hardly have anticipated the stirring events which took place during the closing days of the session. And for these they would praise or revile the young member from Louisa.

As a result of the Parson's Cause, Henry had been recognized in his native county as the boldest advocate of colonial rights.[28] His reputation had been spreading throughout the colony, and he was not wholly unknown even in England.[29] In his first important speech in the House, that on the Treasurer's case, he had shown another flash of his courage and oratorical brilliance. Conservatives were coming to dislike, doubtless even to dread, his developing leadership; liberals and the rising yeomanry were "filled with admiration and delight." [30]

In many respects Henry was a singularly modest man, and he was none too careful to preserve his papers for posterity. Nevertheless, he left for his executors, along with his will, a copy of his Stamp Act resolutions and an account of the events of their passage.[31] This account, written in Henry's handwriting on the back of the paper containing the resolutions, begins as follows:

"The within resolutions passed the House of Burgesses in May, 1765. They formed the first Opposition to the Stamp Act & the scheme of taxing America by the British Parliament. All the colonies, either thro fear, or want of Opportunity to form an opposition, or from influence of some kind or other, had remained silent.

"I had been for the first time elected a Burgess a few days before, was young, inexperienced, unacquainted with the Forms of the House, and the members that composed it," Henry continued. "Finding the men of Weight averse to Opposition, and the Commencement of the Tax at Hand, and that no person was likely to step forth, I determined to venture, & alone, unadvised, & unassisted, on a blank Leaf of an old Law Book, wrote the within."

Now Henry must speak thoughts that were burning for expression. The session must not end in feeble inaction. In other colonies the opposition appeared to be sputtering out. Now he must speak out against the Stamp Act, else all protests would prove to have been in vain!

Certainly he would have the backing of his upcountry constituents. Discriminatory laws, bad crops, the burdensome war and aftermath had not put them into a tractable frame of mind, and the Stamp Act added insult to injury.[32]

A few days after the passage of Patrick's resolutions, John Syme wrote that "we have been very much alarm'd of late" by the Act. "One hardship (among many others) of that Tax is that 'tis to be paid in Silver, of which there is scarce any in the colony." [33] But, as Patrick readily perceived, this was only one phase of the aggravated situation. Unlike the Two Penny Act, the Stamp Act affected influential classes throughout the colonies. Whatever the legal niceties, it was a long step toward crushing hard-earned American liberties. In the words of two later historians, "If the principle of Parliamentary taxation were established, the colonial assemblies would lose control of the purse, and Parliament would then be able to make the governors and judges independent of colonial control." [34] If the Act were not successfully resisted, the very framework of colonial rights would be destroyed.

On the blank sheet of an old lawbook, by report a volume of Coke's *Institutes*,[35] Henry—afire with zeal—set down some resolutions for consideration of the Assembly. Coke, who had argued the authority of the law so learnedly against the Stuarts, would nevertheless have been surprised at this use of his famous text. In ideas and even wording the resolutions bear a strong similarity to the writings of Richard Bland and, above all, to the resolutions passed by the Burgesses in the previous December.[36]

But there was none of the courtier's language for Henry, no respectful appeal to be dropped if the opposition was obdurate. Just as in the Parson's Cause, his was the language of action, of the young man ready to move ahead whatever the obstacles. And these would be great. For it was one thing to write deferential memorials to King and Parliament before the Act was passed, but a very different thing to oppose it after it became the law of the realm. He might skirt the very border of treason. It was a matter on which he should at least seek the advice of more experienced hands.

Before offering the resolutions, Henry is said to have showed them to only two people, John Fleming of Cumberland and George Johnston of Fairfax.[37] Judging from their later action, they must have encouraged him, if not promised definite support. Indeed, Paul Carrington, a surviving member of the House, wrote in 1815 that resolutions "were expected to be offer'd by Mr. P. Henry, respecting the Stamp Act, and that some . . . to wit" Henry, Johnston, Fleming, Robert Munford and perhaps others were "in Conclave, at Lewis, Consulting & preparing resolutions upon that Subject, but who held the pen I never knew or heard." [38] Upon close examination of the copy of the resolutions—as distinguished from his personally written explanation on the back—they appear not to have been penned by Henry and bear considerable resemblance to the handwriting of John Fleming. A likely theory is that Henry turned in his original resolutions to the Clerk of the Burgesses and that they were subsequently lost or destroyed. The copy Henry retained was probably made by Fleming during their "Conclave." [39] In his explanation Henry does not specifically state that he prepared the copy in his possession.[40]

What seems to have happened is that Henry wrote five resolutions and showed them to Fleming and Johnston, probably at the meeting recalled by Carrington. There it seems likely that two other resolutions were prepared [41] and were kept separate from Henry's five. If his were accepted, including the drastic fifth resolution, then one or more of his associates might propose the other resolutions.

Wednesday the twenty-ninth of May, 1765—a late spring morning in the Tidewater, and only important business could keep the mind of many burgesses on the subjects at hand. The House, meeting at ten o'clock, passed the Treasurer's report and attended to some minor matters.

Then George Johnston proposed that the House meet in the Committee of the Whole and Henry seconded the motion.[42] It was carried; the Clerk placed the mace under the table and Peyton Randolph, the Attorney-General, took the place of Speaker Robinson as the presiding officer. Not a handsome man, with a certain heaviness of features often noticeable in his family, Randolph was nevertheless tall and dignified, with a grave manner.[43] With this elegant and accomplished gentleman in the chair, Henry proposed a series of five resolutions and Johnston seconded them. These resolutions as contained in Henry's personal copy are as follows:

Resolved

That the first Adventurers and Settlers of this his Majesties Colony and Dominion brought with them and transmitted to their Posterity and all other his Majesties Subjects since inhabiting in this his Majestie's said Colony all the Priviledges, Franchises & Immunities that have at any Time been held, enjoyed, & possessed by the People of Great Britain.

[defaced]

That by two royal Charters granted by King James the first the Colonists aforesaid are declared intituled to all the Priviledges, Liberties & Immunities of Denizens and natural-born Subjects to all Intents and Purposes as if they had been abiding and born within the Realm of England.

Resolved

That the Taxation of the People by themselves or by Persons chosen by themselves to represent them who can only know what Taxes the People are able to bear and the easiest Mode of raising them and are equally affected by such Taxes themselves is the distinguishing Characteristick of British Freedom and without which the ancient Constitution cannot subsist.

Resolved

That his Majestie's liege People of this most ancient Colony have uninteruptedly enjoyed the Right of being thus governed by their own assembly in the article of their Taxes and internal Police, and that the same hath never been forfeited or any other way given up but hath been constantly recognized by the Kings & People of Great Britain.

[170]

Resolved

Therefore that the General Assembly of this Colony have the *only and sole exclusive* Right & Power to lay Taxes & Impositions upon the Inhabitants of this Colony and that every Attempt to vest such Power in any Person or Persons whatsoever other than the General Assembly Aforesaid has a manifest Tendency to destroy British as well as American Freedom." [44]

The resolutions listed in Henry's copy are with a few minor changes those which actually passed the Committee of the Whole. The preamble and purported sixth and seventh resolutions are listed below:

Whereas, the honorable house of Commons in England have of late drawn into question how far the general assembly of this colony hath power to enact laws for laying of taxes and imposing duties, payable by the people of this, his majesty's most ancient colony: for settling and ascertaining the same to all future times, the house of burgesses of this present general assembly have come to the following resolves:—

6 Resolved, That his majesty's liege people, the inhabitants of this colony, are not bound to yield obedience to any law or ordinance whatever, designed to impose any taxation whatsoever upon them, other than the laws or ordinances of the general assembly aforesaid.

7 Resolved, That any person who shall, by speaking or writing, assert or maintain that any person or persons, other than the general assembly of this colony, have any right or power to impose or lay any taxation on the people here, shall be deemed an enemy to his majesty's colony. [45]

The *Boston Gazette* for July 1, 1765, also printed a preamble, with a sixth and seventh resolution. It may well be that they were passed in the Committee of the Whole and later rescinded but that copies had meantime been hurriedly dispatched out of the colony. [46] Otherwise it seems difficult to explain how they got into circulation. On the other hand, Governor Fauquier was informed that the gentlemen had two more resolutions in their pockets, but finding the difficulty they had in carrying the fifth, which was by a single voice, and knowing the others to be more virulent and inflammatory, they did not produce them.[47]

The first four resolutions were a clear, incisive statement with Henry's historical justification of a policy directly opposed to that held and now specifically advanced by King and Parliament. But the sixth and seventh resolutions went still further; they were a call to open rebellion. The Virginians were not "bound to yield obedience" to any tax laws not passed by their own Assembly. Any person speaking, writing, or maintaining to the contrary "shall be deemed an enemy to his majesty's colony." Even if the last two resolutions did not reach the floor, Henry's fifth was left with its bold assertions—the Assembly had "the sole exclusive right" of taxation and every attempt to fix the power elsewhere had "a manifest tendency to destroy British as well as American freedom."

Small wonder that, in Henry's words, "violent Debates ensued. Many Threats were uttered, & much abuse cast on me by the party for submission. After a long & warm contest the Resolutions passed by a very small Majority, perhaps of one or two only." [48] This and nothing more on the actual debate! The brief descriptions of the proceedings given by Jefferson, Paul Carrington, and Governor Fauquier also contain a tantalizing lack of detail, but from them we can recapture at least some of the drama.

Jefferson, ever inquisitive and active-minded, was standing at the lobby door, and long afterwards the scene was still imprinted on his consciousness. Henry and Johnston were opposed, he declared, by Peyton Randolph, Bland, and Wythe,[49] and all the old members of the House. To which Governor Fauquier added in his report to the English government that the most strenuous opposers of the "rash heat" were Speaker Robinson, Peyton Randolph, and Wythe. The influence of the conservatives in the House was as yet little diminished. They opposed Henry's resolutions, not on any question of colonial rights, but on the ground that the same idea had been expressed in a more conciliatory manner in the memorials of the previous session to which no reply had yet been received.[50]

But in the words of Jefferson, "torrents of sublime eloquence from

[172]

Henry, backed by the solid reasoning of Johnston," carried the day.[51] What group or groups of burgesses did they sway? Fauquier indicates that the conservative opposition was "overpowered by the young hot and giddy members." [52] More precisely, we know that Henry's support came chiefly if not entirely from the back country and northern Virginia—in general, the newer counties more remote from Williamsburg. There the democratic influence of the frontier and near-frontier was deeper impressed, there the opposition to entrenched privileges was stronger, whether against the Tidewater aristocracy or the London government.[53]

The closest and most dramatic debate was on Henry's fifth resolution. It was then that he rose to the heights which rank his Stamp Act speech among the world's great orations. His first four resolutions, according to Carrington, passed "without violent opposition," though by a close vote. But on the fifth and strongest the debate was "most bloody."

"Tarquin and Caesar had each his Brutus, Charles the First his Cromwell, and George the Third—" Henry exclaimed in words that have become a part of the American heritage. He paused dramatically.

"Treason," shouted Speaker Robinson, and "Treason, Treason" was echoed from various parts of the House.

Then, if we may accept later evidence, Henry uncowed and with great presence of mind, finished his sentence with deliberate emphasis—"may profit by their example. If *this* be treason, make the most of it." [54]

Paul Carrington could only state that Henry's arguments on his resolutions were "beyond my powers of description" and that in the debate on the fifth his "manly eloquence" surpassed anything Carrington had ever heard before.[55] But Jefferson, writing at a time when he was disposed to depreciate Henry, nevertheless spoke of hearing "the splendid display of Mr. Henry's talents as a popular orator. They were great indeed; such as I have never heard from any other man. He appeared to me to speak as Homer wrote." [56]

Jefferson, within easy hearing distance during the entire debate and vote, told how he afterwards saw the agitated Peyton Randolph come out of the House.

"By God, I would have given one hundred guineas for a single vote!" Randolph exclaimed. For a single vote would have divided the House and then the vote of Speaker Robinson would have defeated the resolution.[57]

Just how close was the division on the resolutions and how moving was Henry's oratory is indicated by the figures on the voting given by Governor Fauquier. A copy of the Stamp Act had "crept into the House," he reported, and a motion was made to consider it at the end of the session, when most of the members had left town. On May 29 in the Committee of the Whole five resolutions were proposed and accepted, all by very small majorities. They were reported and agreed to by the House the next day, "the members being as before in the Committee." The greatest majority for any of the resolutions was 22 to 17; for the fifth resolution a bare 20 to 19.[58]

The following day, May 31, after Henry had left for home, his fifth and strongest resolution was rescinded by the House. Some of "the more timid" members had, according to Jefferson's account, become "alarmed" and changed their vote on this resolution. Yet a fuller set of resolves, including the inflammatory fifth, had already been disseminated as if all had been passed by the Burgesses. The final results were little affected by the later expunging of the fifth resolution from the *Journal*.

And now we find Henry censured in an official report to the royal government.

"In the course of the debates," Fauquier continued, "I have heard that very indecent language was used by a Mr. Henry a young lawyer who had not been a month a Member of the House; who carried all the young Members with him; so that I hope I am authorized in saying there is cause at least to doubt whether this would have been the sense of the Colony if more of their Representatives had done their duty by attending to the end of the Session." [59]

So much for the views of the urbane but now perturbed Royal Governor. In the countryside there was probably more opposition to the Stamp Act than in the Burgesses with its restricted membership. But the resolutions would doubtless not have been introduced, much less passed, if it had not been for Patrick Henry. And what to Fauquier was "very indecent language" became in the eyes of the world magnificent eloquence establishing Henry's place among the great orators of all time.

This account of Henry's Stamp Act speech, in similar or nearly similar detail, was commonly accepted for over a hundred and fifty years. To be sure, the erudite Henry Cabot Lodge in his biography of Daniel Webster, published in 1883, dismissed Henry's claim to be ranked among the great orators as based "wholly on tradition." [60] But it was not until a generation later, in 1921, that the *American Historical Review* published—and properly so—the eyewitness account which laid open the text of Henry's Stamp Act speech for further criticism or reconstruction.[61] Taken from the journal of a presumed French agent, the narrative was discovered in the archives of the Service Hydrographique de la Marine at Paris. The journal is an authentic document, and there seems no question as to the honesty of the author. Numerous historical writers and lecturers have since contended that the new version has to be accepted, at least in part, in place of the traditional accounts based substantially on recollections of nearly fifty years later. That is an apparently tenable assertion, and it must now be evaluated on the basis of the full evidence.

Let us begin with the traveler's diary for May 30, 1765. On that day he set out early in his carriage, had breakfast at present Yorktown and arrived at Williamsburg, the colonial capital, at noon. There he went immediately to the Assembly where he was entertained by "very strong" debates (now in their second day) on the Stamp Act, recently enacted by the British Parliament.

"Shortly after I Came in," he continued, "one of the members stood up and said he had read that in former times tarquin and Julus had their Brutus, Charles had his Cromwell, and he Did not Doubt but some good american would stand up, in favour of his Country."

This Burgess was just starting to continue in "a more moderate manner" when the Speaker of the House rose and declared that the last member had spoken treason. The Speaker was "sorey to see that not one of the members of the house was loyal Enough to stop him, before he had gone so far."

Then we come to the report which allegedly takes so much of the force from Henry's speech. After Speaker Robinson had interpolated as stated, the traveler wrote that "the Same member stood up again (his name is henery) and said that if he had afronted the speaker, or the house, he was ready to ask pardon, and he would shew his loyalty to his majesty King G. the third, at the Expence of the last Drop of his blood, but what he had said must be atributed to the Interest of his Countrys Dying liberty which he had at heart, and the heat of passion might have lead him to have said something more than he intended, but, again, if he said anything wrong, he beged the speaker and the houses pardon. some other Members stood up and backed him, on which that afaire was droped."

This is the portion of the journal that is usually quoted by historians questioning the traditional version of Henry's speech. But if we read the "Frenchman's" journal for the very next day, May 31, we find the affair was not dropped in one sense, for the writer adds, "I returned to the assembly today, and heard very hot Debates stil about the Stamp Dutys." He also makes the doubtful statement—in view of the close vote and other contrary evidence—that the whole House favored entering resolves on the record.

Then on June 6 the traveler made another significant entry. Stopping at a tavern in Newcastle, Virginia, he talked with two influential citizens who had had ample opportunity to get an accurate impression as to the tenor of Henry's speech. The rain detained him for twenty-four hours at the tavern but he still heard nothing discussed but the stamp duties.

"I'll sooner die than pay a farthing and I am sure that all my countrymen will do the same," one of the back-country men freely declared.

There was "a great deal said about the Noble Patriot Mr. henery,

[176]

who lives in this County," the traveler continued, "the whole Inhabitants say publicly that if the least Injury was ofered to him they'd stand by him to the last Drop of their blood. some of them muter betwixt their teeth, let the worst Come to the worst we'l Call the french to our sucour; and if they were in Canada the British parlem't would as soon be Dd. as to offer to do what they do now."

Moreover, when in Annapolis, Maryland, only a week later, the writer visited a tavern where the large company was toasting the Virginia Assembly and "Damnation to the Stamp Act," and on July 9 he quoted a traveler from Philadelphia as saying that the people of Boston were highly inflamed against the Mother Country and that their first toast after dinner was the Virginia Assembly. There was nothing to indicate that the daring of the principal promoter of the Virginia action was deflated.

A full examination of the traveler's own journal thus reveals that he did not later find Henry's speech was considered as weak as indicated in the entry of May 30. The English is imperfect, and the editor of the journal states that while it is in the same handwriting throughout, the manuscript appears not to have been the first one, but the result of subsequent copying. There are also errors in fact, not only the amusing notation that "admiral Bradock" had taken his whole fleet up the "Potowmak" to Alexandria after his defeat in Canada, but some other misstatements that cannot be so easily laughed away. Thus the traveler in two instances gives information based on partial knowledge and later contradicts himself. When stopping in eastern North Carolina he speaks of the entire colony as being situated "very low," but afterwards refers to mountains there. He gives the names of the twenty-five Virginia counties (actually there were over fifty), and a few days later refers to Hanover and Louisa counties, not given in his earlier list. He erroneously asserts that there were only two Presbyterian "meetings" in the entire colony and that Fredericksburg had all the trade of the back settlements. Yet the traveler's account is one of the few eyewitness descriptions we have of Henry's Stamp Act speech. What substantial evidence is there to

[177]

bolster the traditional version, until late years always accepted by the historians?

There are other descriptions, though presumably not by eyewitnesses, which were written not long after the event. The *London Gazeteer and New Daily Advertiser* for August 13, 1765, contains an account written by an anonymous correspondent from Virginia on June 21. This correspondent speaks of a member of the Burgesses as having "lately blazed out" in the Assembly where he made the references to Tarquin, Caesar, and Charles the First and threatened an unnamed person, obviously George III, with a Brutus or a Cromwell. The account added that the member was not sent to the Tower but after getting some "ridiculous violent Resolves passed" rode off in triumph.[62]

On the following August 12 the respectable Commissary William Robinson, head of the Anglican Church in Virginia and a cousin of Speaker Robinson, wrote a somewhat similar description of the speech to the Bishop of London.[63] Both of these letters emphasized the violence and treasonable nature of Henry's speech; they contain no references whatsoever to any apology. This is also true of the accounts by the British writer William Gordon writing in 1788 [64] and those within the next few decades by Edmund Randolph [65] and by the Virginia historian, John Daly Burk.[66] All of these men had excellent opportunities to obtain information from Henry's contemporaries.

Other references to the proceedings of the Burgesses were found in letters sent within the next few months by the Virginia Royal Governor, Fauquier, and by correspondents of a Bristol and of a Glasgow newspaper. Fauquier, who had good reason not to magnify the disturbance, nevertheless wrote the Board of Trade in London, "In the course of the debates I have heard that very indecent language was used by a Mr Henry a young lawyer"; the Governor says nothing of any apology.[67] While sketchy, the newspaper reports tend to confirm that the tone of the debate was as usually described. The Bristol dispatch, written from Virginia on June 5, 1765, speaks of "the shackles" being forged by the Stamp Act as mentioned "with freedom" in the House of Burgesses.[68]

William Wirt, when collecting data for his biography, was able to find several witnesses of the Stamp Act speech. From the respected John Tyler, a Governor of Virginia, he got confirmation of the traditional account of Henry's speech with the emphatic ending. Wirt heard frequently that there had been the cry of treason after Henry's flaming words, but there were variations at the end, though none in the form of an apology. He, therefore, submitted Tyler's version to Jefferson for approval.

"I well remember the cry of treason, the pause of Mr. Henry at the name of George III, and the presence of mind with which he closed his sentence, and baffled the charge vociferated," Jefferson answered positively.[69] His statement is all the more significant in view of the fact that he and Henry had by then become political enemies and he did not hesitate to give Wirt some information on Henry which was hardly complimentary.

Roger Atkinson of Mansfield, near Petersburg, was an esteemed Virginian who doubtless knew Henry as well as several burgesses who heard him deliver his Stamp Act speech. In a letter to his brother-in-law familiarly describing the Virginia delegates to the Continental Congress of 1774 at Philadelphia, Atkinson wrote of Henry: ". . . a real half Quaker, Patrick Henry, your Brother's man—moderate & mild, & in religious matters a Saint but ye very Devil in Politicks—a son of Thunder. . . . He will shake ye Senate & some years ago had liked to have talked Treason in ye House, in these times a very useful man, a notable American, very stern & steady in his country's cause & at ye same time such a fool that I verily believe it w'd puzzle even a king to buy him off. . . ."[70]

We can further reconstruct the scene at Williamsburg with the help of the reminiscences given Wirt in 1815 by Paul Carrington. Carrington was then a distinguished judge with a lawyer's appreciation of exact testimony. He realized the tricks that the years could play with his memory. But he noted that he could recall more distinctly events which happened fifty years before than those which occurred within the past few months. He was stating nothing that was not "Clearly within my knowledge," and he had some pertinent documents before him.

Henry's first four resolutions were agreed to without violent opposition, Carrington recalled. But when the fifth and last came to be considered, "meaning that which Mr. Jefferson [called] the strongest and most Bloody, Mr Henrys Manly eloquence Surpass'd everything of the kind I had ever heard Before, it was that which brot forward Speaker [Robinson] Crying out 'Treason, Treason' and Mr Henrys presence of mind in reply, of which you must have Read or heard."

Carrington had searched his memory and, like all of Henry's contemporaries who left recollections of the Stamp Act speech, he did not recall a hint of an apology. There were not even any stories of extenuating remarks by Henry which they felt it necessary to rebut.[71]

Possibly Henry, after skirting the edge of treason, did make some conciliatory remarks. But the evidence is overwhelming that these remarks, if actually made, were not a weak apology. It was an age when gentlemen would bow politely even before attempting to run each other through in a duel. Obsequious words, as we have noted, were customary when referring to King and Parliament, and even when drawing up the Association of 1769 to severely curtail trade with Great Britain the Burgesses began: "We his Majesty's most dutiful Subjects . . . avowing our inviolable and unshaken Fidelity and Loyalty to our most gracious Sovereign." If Henry did speak any apologetic words, they were doubtless uttered almost tongue in cheek to give him some legal protection. His apology to Mr. Maury after his speech in the Parson's Cause was not taken too seriously. Perhaps the "French" traveler misunderstood Henry; there were no comparable assemblies then meeting in France and the traveler's knowledge of the Virginia language and customs was faulty, as intimated.

Moreover, in skirting the edge of treason, Henry was not out of character. Only eighteen months before at Hanover Courthouse he had declared that a king by annulling a law so salutary as the Two

Penny Act of the Virginia Assembly had degenerated into a tyrant and forfeited "all Right to his Subjects obedience." And at Hanover too Henry had shocked the "more sober" part of his audience and provoked a murmur of "Treason, Treason, Treason." From the Parson's Cause it was a logical step to the House of Burgesses and the Stamp Act speech.

Late in the afternoon following Henry's climactic argument, a roughly dressed young man in leather breeches was seen walking up a Williamsburg street. On his arm he was carrying his saddlebags, and he was leading a lean horse and chatting with a sympathetic burgess. The young man was Patrick Henry, en route to his home in the back country.[72] A guinea for his thoughts as he left the stage! Certainly he left on a note of high achievement, and there is no valid reason adduced now to argue that it did not ring true.

"How could you have ventured to lift your voice against so terrible a junto?" Henry's friend, John Tyler, later asked him. His reply indicated that he had already built within himself the resources of character and religious faith which would sustain him in even greater trials:

"I was convinced of the rectitude of the cause and my own views, and that although I well knew that many a just cause had been lost, and for wise purposes Providence might not interfere with its safety, yet I was well acquainted with the extent of our back country, which would always afford me a safe retreat from tyranny," he replied.

In the back country where he would be aided by hardy and resourceful frontiersmen, Henry felt that he could escape the long arm of the King's justice. But he did not anticipate that danger.

"I was always satisfied," he added, "That a united sentiment and sound patriotism would carry us safely to the wished for port, and if the people would not die or be free, it was no consequence what sort of government they lived under." [73]

Henry was not as saturated with the philosophic writings that bred revolution as was John Adams. But he could at least subconsciously appreciate something of what Adams wrote that very year of the Stamp Act debate:

"I always consider the settlement of America with reverence and wonder, as the opening of a grand scheme and design in Providence for the illumination and emancipation of the slavish part of mankind all over the earth." [74]

As Henry had sensed, God helps those who help themselves. Already the Stamp Act resolutions, in stronger form than that which finally passed the Burgesses, were being carried to other colonies. And the results would be more far-reaching than even the optimistic young Patrick could have imagined.

11

The Road to Revolution

Things had been working up for trouble during many years—
only a good cry, a common grievance which united all mal-
contents, was needed.
——SIR CHARLES OMAN, *The Great Revolt of 1381.*[1]

Let these truths be indelibly impressed on our minds—that
we cannot be HAPPY without being FREE—that we cannot
be free, without being secure in our property—that we cannot be secure in our property, if, without our consent, others
may as by right, take it away. . . .
——JOHN DICKINSON, *Letters from a Farmer in Pennsylvania.*[2]

Henry had sowed his seeds. To what extent would he
and other Virginians help with the reaping? To what degree would
this be the work of other colonies, especially those to the northward?
Our "French" traveler, detained at the Newcastle tavern a few days
after the passage of Henry's resolutions, had heard nothing talked
of but the Stamp Act; the local people would stand by "the noble
Patriot . . . to the last Drop of their blood." [3] The extent to which
this back-country sentiment expressed the general opinion is indicated
in a letter sent at this time by a Virginian to a Bristol correspondent.

The consequences of the Stamp Act and of other "acts of power,
equally destructive of the rights of the people in the plantations,"
the writer could not then determine. But Virginia and the other

[183]

American colonies were in a ferment. Full of resentment against their Mother Country, they looked upon her no longer as a parent, but as "a hard and cruel task master." If the same spirit grew, as this Virginian anticipated, His Majesty would find it difficult, if not impossible, to execute his arbitrary schemes. Already, the "soldiery" had been turned out in Williamsburg to prevent the burning in effigy of the Chancellor of the Exchequer and another unpopular member of Parliament.[4]

Mild and agreeable as travelers found the Virginians, they were a formidable people when aroused. Shades of Bacon's Rebellion! Would the authorities be able to quell the agitation if it continued to grow apace? By July 11, the stamp tax was said to have filled the entire colony with "the utmost Consternation and Astonishment." At the next election, so it was reported, every man voting for the Stamp Act resolutions would be re-elected and none on the other side. The statement did not reckon with the entrenched strength of the Eastern conservatives or how much they would bend with the wind. But it was asserted that an assurance of "strenuous opposition" to the Stamp Act by all lawful means would be a condition required of every member.[5]

By November 5—was it ominous that this was Guy Fawkes Day?— Governor Fauquier was writing Secretary Conway in London that he was extremely concerned. The amiable Governor, who liked his peace, his cards, his philosophic breakfast table and conversation there with Wythe, Professor Small and the precocious young Jefferson, now found himself in a situation too difficult for him to overcome.

"The Flame is spread thru' all the Continent, and one Colony supports another in their Disobedience to superior powers," Fauquier wailed.[6]

Meantime, what of the young lawyer who, in the words of a hostile critic, had succeeded in getting passed "some ridiculous violent resolves"? Would Henry take a strong hand in the developments of the following months? His critic noted that he had not been sent to the Tower and had ridden off in triumph.[7] But would he continue

[184]

to be so fortunate and so influential and would his actions continue in the public interest?

Above all, in the coming months, would he let his oratorical powers tempt him into demagoguery? The Virginians would soon hear of Whig mobs running amok in other colonies. Here, too, there were men ready enough to guzzle liquor pillaged from the cellars of conservative leaders, to wreck buildings, and tar and feather. Yet there is nothing to indicate that Henry would encourage them to erase the distinction between boldness and lawlessness. The details that we have of his life during the year after the Stamp Act include no evidence of violent political activities: only building the new house at Roundabout, other plantation and domestic matters, and his county law practice.

A letter written in early 1764 to a local merchant shows him corresponding for his wife on petty business which women today would personally transact:

> The Shoes wch my Wife took up for Molly Goodwin, when tried on, were found not to be Fellows; the small Shoe fits, the other being too large. If you have black Callimancoe Shoes of the size of the smallest of these returned, please to send her a Pair of them and one pair of white Kid Gloves.[8]

Henry's account book indicates that he continued to use overseers but kept a careful record of their farming operations despite all his suits and other scattered legal business. No one could any longer rightly accuse him of neglecting personal business.

Was success arousing in him undue pretensions for himself and his family? Certainly not if clothes made the man. We do not know how long Henry used the leather breeches in which he had left Williamsburg. But two years later when he was a recognized leader of the liberal party in the Burgesses he was willing enough to have his overseer, David Melton, not only make five pair of shoes for the Henry Negroes but a pair for his wife, two pairs for Patsy, and four for John and William. And Patrick himself seemed glad to take pot luck with his family in such clothing as he acquired in part payment of legal fees. He credited clients about this time for several pairs of shoes, twelve yards of "coarsest white linen" and five handkerchiefs, "very coarse." He was not too proud for a swap of coats, and when silk stockings displaying a neat expanse of legs were a mark of the gentleman, he accepted two pairs of worsted ones for a fifteen-shilling credit.[9] Henry still had the common touch, apparently without affectation. Returned to his little world of crowded family life, of plantation seasons and jogging off for court days, he could not have foreseen the flaming events which he had incited. Like Martin Luther, when he posted his theses at Wittenberg, Henry had set a train of powder which would explode across his own country, and beyond.

On August 17, the *Bristol Journal* published an ominous letter dated June 6 from Annapolis, Maryland. After noting that the Stamp Act was to take effect in America on November 1, the correspondent had continued, so the *Journal* noted, with this "strange" remark which it italicized: "In the year 1755, on the first of November, happened that dreadful and memorable earthquake, which destroyed the city of Lisbon." By June 6 word of the Virginia resolves could have reached the Maryland capital, and the correspondent was possibly hinting at another form of earthquake. Certainly, it was not long afterwards that a copy of the unrevised resolutions reached Philadelphia and was being forwarded northward with astonishing results.

The resolutions are said to have been dispatched from Williamsburg immediately after their initial passage, and they bear earmarks of having been hastily copied as if for a departing mail. The third resolution is omitted, probably through error, but the copy included Henry's fifth resolution, which was rescinded, and the inflammatory sixth and seventh, which are known only to have been proposed in the Committee of the Whole.[10] There is strong evidence that the Williamsburg correspondent did not wait to ascertain whether any resolutions proposed in the committee would secure final approval of the House. When published in the *Glasgow* (Scotland) *Journal* for October 31 as plantation news from "Wilmington in Virginia," the resolutions included a note from the correspondent that the sixth and seventh were not passed but only drawn up by the Committee.[11] But no such explanation has been found in any contemporary American newspaper.

The resolutions as dispatched to the North were so bold that some cautious souls were afraid to be caught reading, much less publishing them. After reaching Philadelphia, they were forwarded on June 17 to New York. Here, in this commercial city with its powerful Tory element, they were handed about "with great privacy." They were regarded as so treasonable that their possessor refused to print them in the city. An Irish gentleman inquired about them, and, so this version continues, was permitted with due precaution to have a copy which he carried to New England. Here in radical Rhode Island they were printed in the *Newport Mercury* of June 24, along with a statement that they were enclosed in a letter of the previous Tuesday from a gentleman in Philadelphia to his friend in Newport.[12] Since the resolves were of "an extraordinary nature," the editor thought they "might not be disagreeable." A classic understatement!

Now the ball was set rolling. On July 1 the resolutions were reprinted in the *Boston Gazette* with a similar explanatory note, followed on the fourth by the *Massachusetts Gazette*.[13] There was no mention in these newspapers of Patrick Henry, but by July 8 the *Boston Gazette* was enboldened to write, "The People of Virginia have spoken very sensibly, and the frozen Politicians of a more northern Government say they have spoken treason." Their spirited resolves were cited as a perfect contrast to a tame and insipid address lately sent from that side of the water to placate the "Tools of Corruption."

"Oh! Those Virginians are men: they are noble spirits," declared Otis' associate, Oxenbridge Thacher, as he lay on his deathbed.[14] And General Gage, the British commander at New York, wrote home that the resolves gave the signal for a general outcry over the continent.[15]

By a coincidence, the Massachusetts legislature had met on May 29, the very day that Henry proposed his resolutions. Apparently at the suggestion of James Otis, their House of Representatives passed on June 8 a resolution that a circular be sent to all the assemblies calling for an intercolonial congress to consider the Stamp Act. The meeting, in New York on the first Tuesday in October, was to be attended by committees appointed by all the assemblies on the continent. They were to ponder their present difficulties owing to the Stamp Act and to consider a united appeal for relief to King and Parliament. It was not the first time that the Massachusetts House had caught the vision of what might be accomplished by co-operation of all the American colonies.[16]

But the Massachusetts plan bade fair to go the way of Ben Franklin's Albany Union and earlier proposals for intercolonial organization. The Stamp Act Congress was not scheduled to meet until so late that any protest it made could hardly reach England in time to prevent the law from going into effect.[17] Furthermore, the loyalist party in the Massachusetts House, though unable to defeat the resolution for the congress, succeeded in electing as delegates, besides James Otis, two "fast friends of Government,—prudent and discreet men," calculated to do their part to hamper the proceedings of the congress.[18] The first response from other colonies, too, was pleasing to the loyalists. The Speaker of the New Jersey Assembly reported on June 20 that its members were unanimously opposed to uniting on the present occasion.[19] The New Hampshire Assembly, after seeming to favor the meeting, failed to appoint delegates.[20]

"Nothing will be done in consequence of this intended congress," wrote Governor Bernard of Massachusetts in July. Even the liberal Governor of Maryland thought that the resentment would probably die down despite the violent outcries by the lawyers.[21]

Then the influence of the Virginia resolves began to be felt. It was seen, on the one hand, in the lawful protests of legislative bodies and of the Stamp Act Congress; on the other, in the action of violent men often working with torch and club. At times the two methods of redress were interchangeable, the one reacting on the other. "Contention, like a horse full of high feeding, madly hath broke loose," [22] and it would have no end until powerful Britain deemed it expedient to bend before the storm.

[188]

To the uninformed it might seem strange that distant, semi-tropical South Carolina was the first colony to accept the Massachusetts invitation. On August 2, her House of Commons appointed three delegates to the congress, and passed resolutions against the Stamp Act as having "a manifest tendency to subvert the rights and liberties of this province." Playing a lone hand as they would often do in their history, the South Carolinians had not waited to learn whether they would be supported by other colonies. And yet their courageous action was not startling to those who knew this province's long record of encroachment upon executive power, whether of King or Royal Governor. Undoubtedly it had been affected by news from New England, but the influence of the Virginia resolves was also felt, either directly or indirectly.[23]

It is not surprising that the next formal action was in Rhode Island. With her local self-government, her valuable if sometimes disorderly political leadership, this little colony was in a position to give loud voice to the popular opinion. Often regarding herself "as the ally, rather than the subject of Great Britain," [24] she had been a leading opponent of the Sugar Act as destructive to her vital molasses trade with the French West Indian islands and her interrelated rum distilling and African slave trade.[25] The Stamp Act added insult to injury. By August, Henry probably knew that the Newport newspaper had been the first to publish the Stamp Act resolves; on the thirteenth, Providence instructed her delegates in the Rhode Island General Assembly to use their utmost endeavors to have delegates appointed to the Stamp Act Congress, and also to work for the passage of a series of resolves incorporating those of Virginia.[26] The completed resolutions against the Stamp Act were published not only in Rhode Island [27] but on August 19 in the radical *Boston Gazette*. Beginning almost exactly as did Henry's, they continued in much the same vein:

1. That the first Adventurers, Settlers of this His Majesty's Colony and Dominion of Rhode Island and Providence Plantations, brought with them and transmitted to their Posterity . . .

Many printers faced ruin if they had to pay in sterling such taxes as a penny on each full sheet of their newspapers and two shillings per sheet for pamphlets. We find a personal interest in their now emboldened protests, as, for instance, in the *Boston Post Boy*, which reported on the twenty-second [28] that several thousand persons had subscribed to associations in Virginia, New Hampshire, and Massachusetts to work in conjunction with other colonies to oppose the Stamp Act "by all lawful Means." [29]

By all lawful means! Already the words were becoming a travesty. Under the rough, semi-independent conditions in America, the people were developing a habit of taking the law into their own hands, which would lead to some not too admirable chapters in our history.

Publication of the Virginia resolves had thrown Boston "into a flame," and in Connecticut "the peoples Spirits took fire and burst forth into a blaze." [30] The agitation, fanned by the weekly newspapers, was comparable to the Great Awakening when Jonathan Edwards and George Whitefield were arousing the multitude. At Boston even the ignorant slaves were affected. Sent on an errand one evening, a slave refused with tears in his eyes. "Me, 'fraid, Massah, Tamp Act he catch me," he explained.[31] The Virginia resolutions, widely distributed in the press, steeled the opposition, especially since in the disseminated version it was declared that the people were not bound to obey the law and that those so doing were enemies of the colony.[32]

The substance of the Virginia resolutions was incorporated in whole or in part in those adopted by various colonies. Like the Providence resolutions,[33] the Rhode Island resolutions, as reprinted in the *Pennsylvania Gazette* on September 26, began almost as if Henry had taken his quill in hand: "That the first Adventurers, Settlers," etc. How surprised and thrilled he must have been to learn that his resolutions also influenced those passed by the Pennsylvania, Maryland, Massachusetts, and Connecticut assemblies and elsewhere.[34]

Even the distant British were now being stirred from their complacency.[35] They probably were not unduly disturbed by the agreement of the Providence girls to permit no addresses from youths favoring the Stamp Act. But it was a rather different matter when "Ploughjogger" wrote in the *Boston Gazette* for October 14, "I don't believe our young folks would love to dance together at husking frolics and to kiss one another a bit the less if they wore woolen skirts and shifts of their own making," [36] and the New England women began spinning from dawn to dark to avoid buying British cloth.[37] These events were part of an economic boycott which, spreading throughout the colonies, would soon reach grave proportions. By the summer of 1766 colonial orders for British goods had been cut £600,000 and the movement was fast gaining strength.[38]

Precisely how fast all this news reached Virginia we do not know. For some months, however, there had been a movement to avoid purchase of British goods, and in late August there was an ominous disturbance in neighboring Maryland. By July the *Maryland Gazette* had received several manuscript copies of the Virginia resolves along with requests for publication. They were published on July 4 with a group of seven resolves received from a Virginia gentleman and, with other incendiary news, led to a serious public outbreak late the next month. In order to express their aversion to the attacks on liberty and more particularly their anger against the newly arrived stamp collector for Maryland, a turbulent Annapolis crowd paraded the collector's effigy through the streets of the capital, gave it the "Mosaic Law" at the whipping post, then pilloried and burned it. It is not surprising that the Maryland stamp collector was one of several who fled to save their lives.[39]

As the news of the rioting and boycotting in other colonies spread into Virginia, Henry began to realize what might be accomplished by a man with his popularity and oratorical powers. Several of the leading agitators, such as zealous Sam Adams of Massachusetts, worked largely behind the scenes. But Henry saw something of what might be accomplished by a few determined, outspoken, leaders.

At Williamsburg he had spoken nobly. The outcome God would determine and, meantime, Henry must pick up the threads of his personal affairs. Corn and tobacco must be tended; even if his overseer and slaves worked as hard as could be expected in the langorous weather, they needed his supervision. Though master carpenters of the period were versatile, he and Sarah must keep sharp eyes on the Roundabout construction. A number of lawsuits were set for the summer and fall dockets, and there were other pressing cases. He was getting ahead, to be sure, but the law is a jealous mistress, no less so when one must depend on volume of business.

Yet at county seats on crowded, often turbulent court days, on the long rides over the alternately muddy or dusty Piedmont roads, it was good to be with sturdy countryfolk who stood resolutely behind you. Rough, weather-beaten, even illiterate as many were, they saw causes in terms of simple equations. In the case of the Stamp Act, they would hardly weigh niceties of right and wrong even if there were not other things to arouse their antipathies to Great Britain. In his native Hanover, in Goochland, Louisa, or other Virginia counties, Henry seems to have met with little or nothing to make him regret his actions or plot a more moderate course. And this included contacts with friends and relations. When off guard in familiar circles he had to endure little of that petty, nagging opposition which has weakened many a bold advocate of popular rights.

Colonel Johnson, proprietor of the Newcastle tavern, was related to the powerful Louisa County Johnsons, and his brother-in-law, Major John Boswell, ran a tavern in the western part of the county where Patrick must often have sojourned.[40] Business and neighborly associations likewise threw him much with the fiery Sheriff Thomas Johnson of Roundabout Castle, his old Louisa client in the Parson's Cause. On July 1, 1766—a month after he rode his lean horse back from Williamsburg—we find Henry charging Johnson for twenty-five gallons of rum at 4/6 per gallon, which Patrick's man had carted to Louisa Courthouse. So the health of "the noble Patriot" could now be toasted in bumpers of what had been his own liquor! In addition, there were some two dozen debits against Johnson for legal work. The Major was not credited as being able to pay his friend, Patrick, any cash during the year—only a barrel of corn to his overseer.[41] The blunt-speaking Major Thomas Johnson now found himself owing Patrick £28.18.9 at the end of the year;[42] it may be doubted that his debts made him speak less violently to Patrick against the Stamp Act with its onerous duties levied by a distant government.

At the beginning of 1765 the Virginia debt to Great Britain had been computed at a million pounds, with no prospect of "a mite" being raised toward its discharge, wrote one correspondent to England.

"Our provincial debt amounts to £750,000. The new duties and stamps will complete our bankruptcy," he continued. If the colony issued paper money, it would not be accepted as legal tender. "But you [presumably the British merchants] will not be the only sufferers. The public will lose more in revenue on tobacco, than it will gain by stamps. We cultivate that commodity to exchange for your manufactures, which we shall soon convince you, we have no need of." [43]

Of course, Henry was able to make some collections, as, for instance, when in Cumberland on July 22 he received £4 on a debt owed Spiers and Company, the British merchants.[44] But most Virginians, among them Colonel John Henry, were hard put to muster even such petty sums. With his tutoring and surveying perhaps still added to his plantation revenues, Colonel Henry had not found it necessary to draw much on Patrick during 1763-1764.[45] But in 1765 the worthy Colonel was largely supported by his successful son. On May 16, a few days before Patrick took the oath as burgess, we find that he paid out to or for his father over £28, including £8.1.1 for a judgment against the Colonel as garnisher of one Weetley. Later, from October 5 through October 26, at a time when business was being disrupted by the Stamp Act, he advanced his father nearly £100 for a merchant's account against him, sheriff's fees in Goochland, and so on. The whole account for the three years is meticulously noted with total debits of £131.7.4 and some tobacco, against which poor Colonel Henry had been able to pay back only £45 and a tub of butter in 1763.[46] John Henry, who had backed his son's violent speech in the Parson's Cause, now had the stamp tax to add to his inherited Scotch antipathies to the English. John Syme, too, had been suing a debtor in Goochland and petitioning the Burgesses to break an entail on some of his Hanover lands; the records give hints of similar diffi-

[193]

culties and consequent hard feelings against British creditors on the part of others in the family connection.[47]

Yet they were nearly all luckier than Cousin John Winston. On April 25, 1766, Henry's brother-in-law Valentine Wood [48] issued an order in *Fossic et c.* v. *Winston*: "George the Third . . . To the Sheriff of Goochland County . . . take John Winston . . . before our Justices . . ." And John, being unable to pay the judgment, was listed as in prison with the execution to be discharged upon the payment of £5.18.4 and interest at five per cent from January 1, 1766.[49]

Even members of the most influential Piedmont families were now usually debt ridden. In conversations with Patrick they were hardly likely to view the causes with sweet reasonableness: their own improvidence in many instances; the British merchants' commissions and other charges and dues, consuming some three-fourths the value of the crop; the long war; and now the Stamp Act. To Patrick's brother-in-law, Captain Meredith, and his uncle Major William Winston, the stamp tax must have seemed a poor reward for their sacrifices in the war. Talking to some of his Shelton in-laws, to his mother, and to his sister Lucy, now allied with the influential Woods, Patrick could also get the viewpoint of Presbyterians lately under the spell of the great Parson Davies. Had not John Knox, the granite fountain-head, said that "if princes exceed their bounds, they may be resisted by force"? [50] It was an explosive doctrine, not yet put fully to the test in Virginia. Yet we know that these Dissenters had imbibed from Davies and his successors the Presbyterian doctrine of individual responsibility. When the Revolution began, one would be hard put to find many Tories among the Hanover and Louisa Presbyterians.[51]

In Virginia the agitation given such a fiery impetus by Patrick Henry had met with two powerful stumbling-blocks. First, the usually mild and friendly Fauquier had been too alarmed to call another session of the Assembly, and it would not be allowed to meet until late the next year. Also, the restriction on the Assembly was supported by a subservient press. At a time when the newspapers were so vocal in many colonies, we find one Virginia writer turning to the

Maryland Gazette when unable to publish in his provincial paper a reply to the local Stamp Act propaganda.[52] It was well known, he wrote, that "we are in this Colony deprived of that great SUPPORT OF FREEDOM, THE LIBERTY OF THE PRESS." The only newspaper in Virginia "is totally engrossed for the vile Purpose of ministerial Craft."

Besides spreading the Virginia letter with a bold explanation from the author on the front page, the *Maryland Gazette* published in its October 17 issue two other items ominously indicative of the rebellious spirit of the Virginia populace. The first was a letter of September 24 from the county justices of Westmoreland—home of the Lees, Masons, and Washingtons—to the Governor and Council. Beginning on November 1, when the Stamp Act would go into operation, the justices stated that they would no longer perform their official functions, since by doing so they would "become instrumental in the Destruction of our Country's most essential Rights and Liberties." There was also a front-page item about the public hanging in Westmoreland of the effigies of George Grenville and of Colonel Mercer, designated to be the chief Virginia stamp distributor.

By late October the editor of the *Virginia Gazette* had screwed up his courage, or shifted enough with the wind, to publish an account of the mounting agitation. True, he gave considerable space to the usual gossipy news from abroad, so beloved by eighteenth century readers. But even Court news was eclipsed by that of the Stamp Act. The front page of the *Gazette* was now mostly devoted to a long address by conservative Governor Bernard of Massachusetts, seeking to frighten the opponents of the Stamp Act.[53] If stamps were not used, all the public offices would be shut down. And Bernard foresaw a critical situation when, the law enforcement being crippled, nobody's property or person would be safe, and the dependents on trade would be brought to want. More encouraging from Henry's viewpoint was the news from North Carolina that their stamp distributor had resigned his office rather than face the popular wrath.

It would become just as disagreeable for the stamp distributor in Virginia. As in North Carolina, the failure of the Governor to call the

Assembly had made it difficult to organize a concerted protest. But there was a demonstration in Williamsburg which showed evidence of careful and formidable preparation; since a number of leading people from the back country were in the town at the time, it would not be surprising if Henry or his associates were parties to the conspiracy. In late October the Virginia stamp distributor, Colonel George Mercer, arrived from London. After a rough reception in Hampton by the local mob, he proceeded to Williamsburg.

As luck would have it, the General Court was in session and the capital was filled with visitors. Mercer went to the coffeehouse at the Exchange, but he did not find the good fellowship of less troublous times. He was accosted by a crowd of grim Virginians and only by resigning his stamp collector's post saved himself from personal danger.

Was Henry, or, more likely, were some of his principal supporters in the crowd of people who at the significant words "one and all" pushed up near Mercer at the coffeehouse? We have a clue in Fauquier's statement that he would have called the gathering a mob had it not been composed chiefly of propertied gentlemen, some of them leaders of their counties. Rumors had been spread that, at the time of the General Court, parties would come down from most parts of the colony to seize and destroy the stamped papers. The Stamp Act was to go into effect the next day. The crowd demanded the collector's resignation in no uncertain terms. Only the presence of the respected Governor and his firm courage prevented a bloody scene. Mercer, no martyr for a hopeless cause, promptly gave up his position. He ate humble pie, and he ate it so graciously that he was borne out of the Capitol gate amid acclamations and treated at a public house.[54]

That same October the Stamp Act Congress had convened. The results were published too late to help inflame public opinion in Virginia before the Mercer incident but, as in the other colonies, they strengthened the hand of the patriot forces. Twenty-seven delegates had attended the New York meeting representing nine colonies;

Henry could only deplore the fact that Virginia was among the four absent colonies. After much debate the delegates adopted a declaration of rights and grievances, and memorials to the King, Lords, and Commons. The influence of Henry's resolutions upon those adopted by the congress was seen in such statements as that His Majesty's liege subjects in the colonies were entitled to "all the inherent rights and liberties of his natural born subjects" within the kingdom of Great Britain, and that it was essential to the freedom of a people and the undoubted right of Englishmen that no taxes be imposed on the colonists except with their own consent, given personally or through their representatives. The eighth resolution, declaring that the Stamp Act had "a manifest tendency to subvert the rights and liberties of the colonists," was an obvious rephrasing of the statement in Henry's own fifth resolution that every attempt to place the power of taxation elsewhere than in the General Assembly "had a manifest tendency to destroy British as well as American freedom." [55]

Before the Stamp Act Congress few colonial leaders had even met those of other colonies. The formation of an intercolonial Whig party was only in embryo; the sentimental and practical ties with Great Britain were very strong. Even had a Henry been present to spur the cautious members, they could hardly have been expected not to acknowledge "all due subordination" to Parliament.[56] But in the petition to the Commons they did stress the distinction in reason and sound policy between the necessary exercise of parliamentary jurisdiction in general acts such as the regulation of trade throughout the whole empire and the exercise of this jurisdiction by imposing taxes on the colonies. Repeal of the Stamp Act was declared to be advantageous to Great Britain as well as to her colonies.

The Stamp Act Congress, an expression of unity forced by a heedless Parliament, was an important step in the development of the American nation. The first intercolonial congress ever to represent the majority of the American people, it set forth, tactfully yet clearly, some of the essential principles upon which a new American republic would soon be formed. "We should stand upon the broad common ground of those natural rights that we all feel and know as men, and as descendants of Englishmen," Christopher Gadsden, radical South Carolina delegate, had prophetically written soon after the adjournment of the New York sessions. "I wish the charters may not ensnare us at last by drawing different colonies to act differently in this great cause. Whenever that is the case, all will be over with the whole. There ought to be no New-England man, no New-Yorker, known on the Continent, but all of us Americans." [57] At the next intercolonial congress, in 1774, Virginia would be represented by a notable delegation including Henry, who would reiterate Gadsden's last sentiment in much the same words.

Before November 1, when the Stamp Act would take effect, the rioting had spread through many of the colonies. Already nearly all the stamp distributors had resigned—some with mobs snapping at their heels.

From Richard Bland and other authorities Henry could get still more learned arguments to confirm the right of resistance. Surviving account books of the *Virginia Gazette* for 1764, record Henry as a subscriber to that essential source of domestic and foreign news, and John Syme as the purchaser of *Rousseau on Education* and Bland's *The Colonel Dismounted*,[58] the last of his pamphleteering attacks on the clerical position in the Parson's Cause. In that age when books and even pamphlets were few and precious, Bland's final blast against the clergy must have been fully discussed in the Henry family circle, and for more than its superficial implications. Never unduly diverted from his studies even by his three wives and twelve children (better than average, as one historian notes, for "learned, bookish men"),[59] Bland was by now the oracle of the colony on matters of constitutional rights and privileges. When publishing *The Colonel Dismounted* back in 1763, he had so far overcome his caution as to state that "any tax respecting our INTERNAL polity, which may hereafter be imposed on us by Act of Parliament, is arbitrary, as depriving us of our Rights, and may be opposed." Bold orating of such ideas in simple popular phrases was inimical to Bland's temperament; he had opposed Henry's Stamp Act resolutions. Yet, moved by the logic of events, he published the next year his *Inquiry into the Rights of the*

British Colonies,[60] in which he developed further his Whig doctrine of the natural right to resist unlawful exercise of power by statute or prerogative. "If a man invades my Property, he becomes an Aggressor," Bland declared, "and puts himself into a State of War with me; I have a right to oppose this invader." [61]

With even the cautious Bland now fitting his words to his logic and erudition, it is not surprising that radicals throughout the colonies were now flouting British authority. And what made the situation doubly dangerous, leading citizens in many areas were encouraging or participating in the agitation. The colonies, they felt, would not be restored to peace and quiet until the British repealed the Stamp Act. It was not too surprising that Henry Laurens of Charleston recognized some disguised members of the mob which invaded his house as gentlemen of his acquaintance.[62] In Virginia Henry found a strong ally in the aristocratic Richard Henry Lee. Not realizing that the Stamp Act would raise a storm, Lee had applied for a collector's post. But on further consideration he became one of its foremost opponents, not without bitter jibes from the conservative faction. Knowing his aristocratic background and political influence, one venomous critic castigated him in the *Gazette* as a hypocrite, a wolf in sheep's clothing:

> Richard stand forth, I dare thee to be try'd
> In that great court where conscience must preside. . . .[63]

Politics in its bolder and more dedicated form is no career for the timid and thin-skinned. Fortunately, Lee, like Henry, was not to be deterred by political vilification. Early in 1766 he drafted the "Articles of Association by the Citizens of Westmoreland," the first of those potent organizations binding the subscribers to import no British goods until the Stamp Act was repealed. Signed at the top by Richard Henry Lee, and with five other Lees, three brothers of George Washington, Thomson Mason, and other leading gentlemen of the county among its 125 bold signatories, the Westmoreland Association indicates how many Americans even of property and position were willing to venture their lives and fortunes.[64] In the wording of this document—as in so many of the colonial protests—we find the influence of Henry's Stamp Act resolutions. In fact, the Associators were even ready to implement the violent seventh resolution, never passed by the Burgesses. Whereas this resolution had declared that any person asserting the right of taxation except by the Assembly was to be deemed an enemy of the colony, the Westmoreland Association asserted that such an offender would be immediately regarded as "the most dangerous enemy of the community" and that they would go "to any extremity" to stigmatize and punish him.

In the case of Tory Archibald Ritchie, they proved their sincerity. Ritchie, a prominent merchant and shipowner of Hobbs Hole, the present Tappahannock, flatly declared that he planned to use stamped paper in clearing his ships and that he knew where he could obtain the stamps. If such merchants could defy the popular will, then the whole fight for self-taxation might collapse. In accordance with plans drawn up by the new Associators, four hundred Sons of Liberty gathered within a few days at Ritchie's home on the Rappahannock. Faced with threats of the pillory, or worse punishment if need be, Ritchie capitulated. Swallowing his pride, he signed a humiliating retraction later published for the edification of the colony in Rind's *Virginia Gazette*:

> Sensible now of the high insult I offered this County . . . and being convinced, such Proceedings would establish a Precedent, by which the hateful Stamp-Act might be introduced into this Colony, to the utter Destruction of the public Liberty; I do most submissively, in Presence of the Public, sign the Paper, meaning to show my deep Remorse for having formed so execrable a design; and I do hereby solemnly promise, and swear on the Holy Evangelist, that no vessel of mine shall sail clear on Stamp'd Paper, and that I never will, on any Pretence, make use of, or cause to be made use of Stamp'd Paper unless the Use of such Paper shall be authorized by the General Assembly of this Colony.[65]

A month later in March, 1766, the Sons of Liberty at Norfolk passed resolutions against the Stamp Act, reminiscent of Henry's, and they declared that they would sacrifice their lives and fortunes, in co-operation with the other Sons of Liberty in American provinces, to defend and preserve "those invaluable blessings" transmitted by their ancestors.[66] Virginians from Tidewater to the back country, gentlemen and plainer folk, were now united against the Stamp Act —nearly all of Henry's late opponents moving willingly or otherwise with the popular tide.

As in Virginia and Massachusetts, so in numerous other colonies, the lawlessness could be controlled only by force, and there were lamentably few British troops in America. To be sure, such officers as Colonel James in New York, who wore his hat at the "damn my eyes cock," would "cram the Stamps" down the throats of the New York patriots with his sword; the local mob replied with a furious riot. The workmen, sailors, and Negro slaves ganged together that early November night, did not care to assault British cannon and fortifications with small arms; after many threats and sinister implications they contented themselves with burning Colonel James' library, wrecking his furniture, and drinking up his cellar. Yet it was becoming apparent that enforcement of the Stamp Act might provoke armed rebellion.[67]

In the end, it was combined opposition to the Act both in the colonies and Great Britain that led to repeal. On November 25, 1765, it was reported from New York that vessels arriving from London or Bristol were only half loaded. Letters from England stated that more than half the workmen at various English factories were discharged. They were beginning to be contentious and said they would be inevitably ruined unless restraints were removed from American trade.[68] Fearing bankruptcy, merchants in numerous British cities and towns petitioned Parliament for repeal of the Stamp Act. Glasgow complained that she was faced with absolute ruin; her merchants were owed more than a half million pounds by Virginians and Marylanders alone. By early December, countermanded American orders were reported to amount to £700,000 sterling.[69]

Henry must by now have perceived that his was no common destiny. Yet even he could hardly have comprehended his influence on events in high political circles at distant London. In October the

[201]

Privy Council reported to George III that the Stamp Act question was of "too high a nature" for its determination, and "proper only for the consideration of parliament." [70] And by December 5 the King was writing Conway:

> I am more and more grieved at the accounts of America. Where this spirit will end is not to be said. It is undoubtedly the most serious matter that ever came before parliament; it requires more deliberation, candour, and temper than I fear it will meet with.[71]

Not long before, the Grenville ministry had fallen for reasons not related to America. The new Prime Minister, the Marquis of Rockingham, "a decent, plain man," set about to effect a compromise which would end American opposition without destroying legal authority.[72] George III and several ministers sought only to amend the Stamp Act, but pressure by the merchants and the eloquent outbursts of Pitt carried the day. Pitt had not won a great empire for England in the late war to see it lost by a "short-sighted financier"; he rejoiced openly in American resistance.[73] On March 18, 1766, the King signed a bill for total repeal, thus ending one of the most important battles in parliamentary history. To salve its pride, Parliament also passed a Declaratory Act stating that it had power to make laws for America "in all cases whatsoever." This was temporarily overlooked, however, by the colonists in their general rejoicing.

The glorious conclusion of the fight to which Henry had given such spirited impetus must have been known to him by late April.[74] Shortly before, the *Virginia Gazette* [75] had reported that the Sons of Liberty in Maryland were assembling deputies from every county at Annapolis to consider how to prevent the execution of the Stamp Act if it were not repealed. Of any similar plans by Henry and his associates in Virginia, we have no knowledge. But the turbulent spirit of the colony several months after the repeal of the Act was indicated by an event which occurred in June at Cumberland Courthouse, with a tragic sequel in Williamsburg and upper Hanover. Relatively it seemed a little thing when a grandee like Colonel John Chiswell was said to have killed himself in his Williamsburg house. But when we consider that he did so rather than trust the colonial authorities not to sacrifice him to the popular clamor after he had killed a lower class opponent in an affray, we see glimmerings of a sentiment somewhat like that which rent the colony during Bacon's Rebellion. The last grim phase of the Chiswell affair, as we shall soon explain, occurred during the Colonel's burial at Scotchtown, where Henry would soon live.

12

A Maturing Statesman

History does not more clearly point out, any fact than this, that nations which have lapsed from liberty, to a state of slavish subjection, have been brought to this unhappy condition, by gradual paces.————RICHARD HENRY LEE [1]

Your Mother Country has . . . acted with . . . the greatest Kindness and Affection towards you her Children; and as an indulgent Parent has a Right to expect a Return of Duty, Obedience, and Gratitude.————GOVERNOR FAUQUIER [2]

IT IS easy to oversimplify the popular movement in Virginia of which Henry was now a leader. It was not merely a protest against the Established Church or British misrule as symbolized in the Stamp Act. There was also a ground swell of opposition to the entire aristocratic regime in the colony. For although class lines in the Virginia of the 1760's were not as closely drawn as some would have us believe, they nevertheless smacked of England of the Georges and Lord Chesterfield. In numerous instances, to be sure, families of poor immigrants would, by fortunate planting, trading, and marrying, rise quickly into the aristocracy. Class distinctions, however, were still sharply drawn, and they aroused increasing resentment among a people who were moving out to the new country partly to break these very restrictions. The snobbishness at times was almost unconscious, as in the case of William Byrd II, who lost his wonted tolerance

[204]

when telling "the tragical story" of an aristocratic girl who had married an overseer.

"Had she run away with a gentleman or a pretty fellow, there might have been some excuse for her, though he were of inferior fortune," Byrd smugly noted, "but to stoop to a dirty plebeian, without any kind of merit, is the lowest prostitution. I found the family justly enraged by it." [3] The Reverend Devereux Jarratt, son of a carpenter in New Kent County, wrote that in his youth "we were accustomed to look upon what were called gentle folks as beings of a superior order." [4]

Colonel John Chiswell of Scotchtown was to fall victim to the popular feeling now inflamed by the agitation against the Stamp Act. Owner of Scotchtown, the feudal estate near Mount Brilliant, vestryman, county justice, burgess, connected by marriage with the Randolphs and the Robinsons (his daughter, Susannah, was third wife of Speaker John), Colonel Chiswell was a typical member of the reigning aristocracy in its best and worst aspects. Like that of numerous Virginia aristocrats, his family position had been only recently attained. Nevertheless, it was secure. He was courageous and public-spirited, but proud and haughty. While attending a party at a Cumberland Courthouse tavern on June 3, 1766, Chiswell had been insulted by one Robert Routledge, a merchant and, we are told, quondam Scotch rebel. Routledge, who had been drinking heavily, allegedly assailed Chiswell with the most "insolent" abuse, even throwing a glass of wine in his face. The evidence conflicts, and a recent account of the affray shows Routledge less culpable than was formerly believed. But although the Colonel had exchanged some unpleasant words with Routledge, there was not sufficient provocation for such an insult. Chiswell, in a fury, ran the so-called plebeian fellow through with his sword.

He was arrested and jailed. After the Cumberland court refused to give him bail, three aristocratic judges of the General Court went on his bond and secured his release, which gave rise to further criticism. Chiswell became convinced that the Virginia authorities would give in to popular demand and sentence him to die shamefully on the gallows.

Returning to his home at Williamsburg, he was undoubtedly further depressed by finding his daughter, Susannah, mourning the recent death of her husband, Speaker-Treasurer Robinson, at a time when there was a grave shortage in his accounts. On October 14, 1766, Colonel Chiswell killed himself in his home on Francis Street.

Chiswell's remains were brought to Scotchtown to be buried. It is quite possible that Henry was present at the terrible scene during the funeral; if not, he got full details from his cousin William Dabney, or other eyewitnesses.

A report had been spread that the story of Chiswell's suicide was actually a stratagem to facilitate his escape from what many of the populace believed to be his merited punishment.

An "immense" crowd assembled at Scotchtown at the time set for the funeral, Dabney's son wrote, insisting that the coffin be opened. They were certain that it was either empty or occupied by some substitute for the body of the lordly Colonel. Prepossessed with this belief, they could not be persuaded that in "the blackened and distorted features of the corpse before them they beheld the genuine relics of that proud man whose execution they had so lately demanded as an expiation due to the offended majesty of justice." The controversy ran so high that the funeral was suspended, and the people declared they would not permit the body to be buried until it was identified by a respected gentleman present—William Dabney. They knew that he was Chiswell's cousin and intimately acquainted with him. Dabney inspected the corpse and pronounced it that of Chiswell. The commotion then ceased.[5]

But such popular clamor could break out in new forms. It might lead to useless excesses or be channeled into public service in bravest form. Again we must stress the divergent parts that could now be played in the colony by a popular leader, and turn to an examination of Henry's rôle in the impending sessions of the Assembly.

Upon the excuse that a session was not urgently needed, Governor

Fauquier four times postponed the meeting of the Assembly. He was not taking any unnecessary chance with the terrible young member from Louisa and his bold associates. He feared that the members might break loose and pass more "offensive or Seditious" resolutions, and he explained to Secretary Conway that he thought too highly of them to have them cut their own throats and lose all their friends. It was not until early November, 1766, that the House was finally convened [6]—seventeen months after the passage of the Stamp Act resolutions. In the Declaration of Independence, one of the long list of "injuries and usurpations" dramatically catalogued and attributed to George III was that he had "dissolved representative houses repeatedly, for opposing, with manly firmness, his invasions on the rights of the people."

With the trading season now on in Williamsburg and the Assembly convening, Henry was probably there in time to enjoy in his modest way not merely the festivities but perhaps the public demonstrations (seven shillings the series) of "that wonderful element"—electricity —lately discovered by Ben Franklin. Lest good religious people be disturbed by this manifestation of natural philosophy, it was explained that such knowledge tended to enlarge the human mind and to give "more exalted ideas of the GOD OF NATURE." [7] Although Henry never received the cultural stimulus at Williamsburg comparable to that enjoyed by Jefferson, life there was a broadening experience.

From his work in the Burgesses particularly, Henry got practical experience, rigorous competition, and inspiration. When the House convened on Thursday, November 6, it was found that nearly a third of the previous members had not been returned, including some who had opposed the Stamp Act resolutions. A number who had been absent at the time were not re-elected, and it is likely that in certain instances, at least, the voters had thus showed their displeasure. Altogether, there were 108 members reported present—more than double the number at the previous opening session. [8] Henry's epochal speech, with the accompanying resolutions, had contributed to a notable increase in attendance as well as to more significant results.

Henry had been again elected from Louisa County, along with Richard Anderson, a prominent landowner and one of his more remunerative clients.[9] His account book shows him as crediting a Louisa client with seven shillings sixpence for taking the poll at the election, that is, counting the men for Henry in the *viva voce* voting. With his speeches against the parsons and the Stamp Act fresh in the popular mind and with the Johnsons foursquare behind him, he must have had little trouble getting enough freeholders to go to the courthouse and call out his name. Probably his popularity also contributed to the re-election of John Syme and the election for a first term of their cousin Walter Coles of Halifax. The recent death of Speaker Robinson was a grave loss for the conservatives, though Edmund Pendleton and their other leaders in the Burgesses were re-elected. Henry personally deplored the death of George Johnston, who had spoken so forcefully in behalf of the Stamp Act resolutions. On the other hand, Richard Henry Lee, John Fleming, and Robert Munford were all back in their seats along with many vigorous though less vocal representatives of the upcountry.

On May 16, 1766, the *Gazette* had announced, with extravagant eulogy, the death of Speaker Robinson. Examination of his records soon revealed the extent of his illegal loans. What action would be taken by the Assembly now that Patrick Henry, Richard Henry Lee, and their lieutenants could muster such strength? Upon it would depend not merely the financial stability of the colony but the growth of the liberal party.

The first test came when the Assembly had to fill Robinson's two positions—Speaker and Treasurer. The power wielded by John Robinson when fortified in the two posts had made not only liberals but some conservatives anxious to sever them, and the movement gained strength from the rumors now current as to the depleted if not bankrupt condition in which Robinson had left the treasury.[10] For some time there had been talk of the family connections, private friendships, and other indirect methods through which he had retained much of his power. With taverns so accessible and many legislators not loath to enjoy the flowing bowl, the imagination is also pricked by a rhymester's hint as to "wine burgessian, potent to deceive." [11] Of such subtle influences exerted by the forces of privilege, Henry, Lee, and their allies would get a stomachful during the next decades.

Light is thrown on the opposition to the Henry-Lee party forces by a letter of Governor Fauquier. Soon after Robinson's death, Fauquier wrote to the Lords of Trade that Richard Henry Lee and Attorney-General Randolph were candidates for the Speaker's post. Fauquier then endorsed Randolph as possessing "the good qualities of his late most intimate friend" (Robinson), and as being one of the foremost promoters of all requisitions of the Crown. He also stated that in event of a vacancy in the attorney-generalship he would nominate George Wythe, who likewise had exerted himself in support of the government and particularly in opposition "to the late hot and virulent resolutions which brought on the dissolution."

"Such men my Lords," Fauquier added, ". . . merit the favorable eye of the Government, and I hope your Lordships will think it for the service of the Crown to let it be cast on them." [12]

Undoubtedly, the favors of the Crown were being thrown to the conservatives. But how far the tide had moved in the opposite direction was indicated in October, 1766, by an address by James City freeholders to Lewis Burwell, their representative in the Burgesses. Signed by a majority of freeholders in the county and published on the front page of the *Gazette* just before the opening of the Assembly, the address urged Burwell to work for a separation of the speaker's and treasurer's offices. "If enjoyed by one person, it would lay a foundation for such undue influence as is inconsistent with the liberty of a free people." [13] So even the Tidewater, stronghold of privilege, was now affected by the radical movement. Poor Fauquier had little reason to change his opinion of the previous month that the people were "sour"; everything had become "a Matter of heat and Party Faction; everything was contested." [14]

On Thursday, November 6, the opening day of the Burgesses, the House proceeded to the choice of a Speaker. Peyton Randolph, favored by the government party, was nominated by Archibald Cary, and elected over Richard Bland, proposed by Richard Henry Lee. [15]

[209]

A major battle developed soon afterwards over the motion, offered by Lee and seconded by Henry, to prevent the union of the speaker's and treasurer's posts. Of Lee's speech to the aroused Burgesse~ we have a surviving fragment. After supporting his arguments with historical examples, Lee exclaimed:

> "If, then, wise and good men in all ages have deemed it for the security of liberty to divide places of power and profit; if this maxim has not been departed from without either injury or destroying freedom—as happened to Rome with her decemvirs and her dictator—why should Virginia so early quit the paths of wisdom, and seal her own ruin, as far as she can do it, by uniting in one person the only two great places in the power of her assembly to bestow?" [16]

The cool, resourceful Pendleton led the party favoring the *status quo,* but Lee received powerful support from Henry who, so George Dabney recalled, by his eloquence prevented the retention of "the dangerous system." [17] Actually, while there was a warm debate, Henry's arguments do not appear to have been spectacularly decisive, for the vote of the House on the motion that the two offices should not be united in the same person was 68 to 29.[18] Perhaps Henry had the reluctant support of Governor Fauquier who had instructions from London to separate the two offices. Although arousing further jealousies and enmities among the conservatives, Henry had strengthened his position with the rising moderates and liberals and especially with Richard Henry Lee, with whom he had become joined in important legislative battles.

A lifelong friendship and alliance, based on congenial ambitions and ideals, was now being formed between Henry and Lee, the slim, beak-nosed young aristocrat from Westmoreland. The "patriot Romans thought that every good Citizen should serve his Country seven years," Lee wrote approvingly about this time,[19] and he himself was to serve over thrice that number during a strenuous and critical period. Unfortunately absent when Henry presented his Stamp Act resolutions, Lee was now fighting alongside him with all the force of his family influence, his learning, and his flaming patriotism.

The road to democracy in Virginia would be long and hard. Liberal leaders of Lee's background and ability were few enough then or later, yet vital to the popular cause. Conscious of how strongly the opposition was still entrenched, Lee wrote his brother Arthur in December pointing out some explanations for their political power. A few years before, Lee declared, the Assembly had passed a law calling for more frequent convocation of the Burgesses, but the measure had never secured the royal approval. Moreover, in Virginia the legislative power was lodged in the Governor, Council, and Burgesses, of which the first two were appointed by the Crown. "The same persons who compose our Council during pleasure, with the Governor, at their head, are the Judges of our General Courts (and only so long as they continue of the Council), where all causes ecclesiastical and civil, both common law and Chancery business is determined." This combination gave the executive branch in Virginia more power than existed under the British constitution as it operated in the Mother Country. It was also in direct contradiction to the injunction of the great French writer, Montesquieu, whom the studious Lee quoted in point.[20]

In his conciliatory opening message to the Burgesses, the Governor did not allude to the one matter that was now agitating the entire colony. This was the plight of the public treasury as revealed after the death of John Robinson. The resulting events did much to consolidate the strength which Henry and his supporters had gained in the Stamp Act fight. They would continue to move forward, if at times almost imperceptibly, until they were in a position where—if they so desired—they could risk a final break.

In May, 1765, when Lee had audaciously proposed in the Burgesses that a committee be appointed to examine into the state of the treasury, Speaker Robinson had "fixt his eyes [upon him] with a dark and terrible frown," and a number of Robinson's powerful supporters had turned from the Westmoreland member with "haughty and disdainful airs." Lee had fought strenuously to carry his motion,[21] and

[211]

had been supported by the eloquence of Henry, but they could then accomplish little. By November, 1766, much water had flowed under the bridge. A committee appointed to report the condition of the treasury included Henry, Lee, and others from the liberals or moderates.[22] A thorough investigation was assured.

On December 12, Richard Bland, chairman, handed in the committee report to the Burgesses. One never knows when any experience in life will be useful. Henry's knowledge of bookkeeping, obtained during his unlucky storekeeping episodes, helped him when the committee examined "with the utmost Precision they were able" Robinson's involved accounts.[23] To add to the difficulties, many county officials were found to be greatly in arrears with their collections due the Treasurer. It appeared advisable for the committee to await the separate accounting being made by Robinson's executors. His estate, as the executors detailed it, included some twenty thousand acres of land, four hundred slaves, and a considerable personal estate.[24] This property, which would have been envied by many a European nobleman, was available for liquidation, along with all the Treasurer's bonds and securities for loans.

But these variegated holdings appeared to be none too large when the amount and nature of the debts were revealed. Edmund Pendleton and his fellow executors, poring over ledgers and odd pieces of paper, found that the total indebtedness to the Robinson estate was over £130,000, of which more than £100,000 had been from the treasury.[25] The list of debtors read like a roll of the great and privileged in eastern Virginia. The members of the Council owed nearly £15,600, those of the Burgesses more than £37,000.[26] Henry could now find another explanation for the late Treasurer's hold upon the House. The conservative gentlemen from the Tidewater would most likely have voted against his Stamp Act resolutions in any event, but it is probable that at least a few were influenced by debts to the Speaker-Treasurer which would have been awkward or even ruinous if called.[27]

On the other hand, the debts were not too embarrassing to Henry and his allies. Probably John Syme, already heavily involved, was disturbed by the £332 he owed Robinson, but relatively small amounts were owed by Samuel Meredith, Jr., and by Dr. Thomas Hinde, a Henry family physician. Patrick Henry himself owed only £11, and Henry Lee, Richard Lee, and Richard Henry Lee other small amounts, no more than might be expected as taxes due the treasury.[28] John Robinson, always generous, might have lent any one of them considerable sums of money whether or not he was in the opposition, but it was fortunate for their cause that Henry and Richard Henry Lee in particular were not financially involved in the scandal.

Although there were several executors of the Speaker-Treasurer's great estate, with all its intricate and embarrassing accounts, the largest share of the burden fell on Edmund Pendleton. Always competent and painstaking, he now set forth on a task which would absorb the best years of his career and make him "shoulder multiple burdens that no fiduciary had faced before in Virginia." [29] In a memorial to the Burgesses he and his fellow executors held out the encouraging view that they could ultimately pay Robinson's debts to the colony. Because of the distressed situation of the country, however, the great scarcity of money, and the danger of involving many families in ruin so that they could not meet obligations, the executors asked to pay the debt over a period of three years.[30] This memorial was ordered to be laid on the table,[31] and was considered at the next session of the Assembly; the investigating committee meantime continued its work and doubtless required much of Henry's time.

The death of Speaker Robinson and subsequent events had added materially to the strength of the liberal party. But Edmund Pendleton was now becoming recognized as the ablest and most influential leader of the moderate conservatives. As chief administrator of the Robinson estate, he was in a position to save or ruin many members of the Burgesses, and he was sincere in believing that he should not deal harshly with these floundering debtors. At the same time, it was important that Henry and his allies should in the public interest— that of the poor farmer and frontiersman as well as the Tidewater

magnate—keep a tight check on Pendleton's policy as chief administrator of Robinson's tangled public and private affairs.

Henry was becoming—thanks mostly to his bold eloquence—one
of the most influential members of the Burgesses. He was made a
member, in junior ranking to be sure, of the important Committee of
Privileges and Elections which included Pendleton as chairman,
Bland, Wythe, Washington, and Richard Henry Lee. He was also
appointed to the Committee of Propositions and Grievances, of which
Bland was chairman, and the members ranking ahead of Henry in-
cluded Pendleton, Wythe, John Syme, and Peyton Randolph.[32]
Repercussions continued from the Stamp Act controversy,[33] and
Henry was made a member of the committee to erect a statue to
George III in "grateful Acknowledgment" of the repeal of the
Stamp Act and to bring in a bill to erect an obelisk "to perpetuate the
Glorious Repeal of the late unconstitutional act." If details of this
action reached London, it would be entertaining to know what the
ministry thought of Patrick Henry and Richard Henry Lee serving
on this committee, even though it also included some leading conservatives.[34] But legislative bodies do not always pursue an undeviating course, and neither the statue nor the obelisk was ever erected.[35]
Probably one reason was the joker, virtually overlooked at the time,
by which Parliament coupled with the Stamp Act repeal a declaratory
act asserting that it had the right to tax the colonies.[36]

On November 12, 1766, Henry was given leave of absence from
the House until December 1. He was, therefore, probably absent
during some of the action on a memorial from his father seeking aid
for his proposed maps of Virginia. During the past few years, Colonel John Henry's estate had been much reduced by poor management and inadequate knowledge of plantation affairs, and with the
aid of a brother Scotsman he had started a school for some ten or
twelve boys. A year or two later, the pupils were increased to about
twenty, which number he continued to teach until his death.[37] But
teaching has never been one of the more remunerative professions,
and, utilizing his experience as a surveyor, John Henry tried with

the maps another scheme to eke out a living for his family. He could by the same means render a further public service.[38]

The proposed map of Virginia was to be five feet by three, and those for the individual counties fifteen inches by twelve. Each was to contain much statistical information and thus provide valuable data on a colony still largely uncharted and with resources only vaguely surmised. Copies of the colony and county maps were to be neatly printed in London. But the Burgesses ordered the memorial referred to the Committee of Propositions and Grievances, and on December 5 it was rejected by the House. Might Patrick's political enemies have been responsible for the refusal of the Burgesses to aid this estimable project? Colonel Henry was finally able to complete the state map through private subscription, but his hopes for its success were never realized.[39]

This Assembly dealt with a number of matters which were more significant than appeared on the surface. It was symptomatic of the changing times that on December 10—five weeks after the opening of the session—Henry was named first in a committee to wait on the Governor in regard to the various bonds given by the late John Robinson. The other members were Thomson Mason and Richard Henry Lee.[40] Mason, recently returned from study at the Middle Temple, shared the liberal ideas (and the chronic gout) of his brother, George Mason, future author of the Virginia Bill of Rights.[41] Again, near the end of the session Henry was named first in a committee, including Thomson Mason and George Wythe, to wait on the Governor with the address of the House to order suits against Robinson and his securities.[42] Henry was advancing fast from the new, inexperienced member of the previous year.

The power which Henry was securing in the colony as a whole was reflected within his resident county. He was now allied with the Johnsons, Andersons, and a few other leading planters in the clique that ruled Louisa. The previous year he had followed in his father's footsteps by being made a member of the vestry, which, as we have seen, was then a powerful body exercising many functions now reserved for non-ecclesiastical authorities.

Once again Henry swore that he would bear true allegiance to George III, and testified on his conscience "before God and the world" that the person pretending to be the King of England under the name of James the Third of England or the Eighth of Scotland "hath not any right whatsoever to the crown." [43] So much for the claims once upheld by any Jacobite Henrys in Aberdeenshire. But how long would Patrick feel bound in good conscience to support George III?

It was about this time, or within a few years after he entered the Burgesses, that Henry prepared a manuscript giving his views on the subject of needed changes in Virginia. The first part of the manuscript seems to be lost, but the remaining portion (or Henry's copy of it) deals primarily with the need for religious toleration. In this connection, Henry comments on such topics as disestablishment of the Anglican Church in Virginia, slavery, home manufactures, and the best method of opening up the trans-Allegheny region. Written apparently in response to a query, the manuscript (as printed by William Wirt Henry), is the earliest surviving production of Patrick Henry's pen, aside from business papers.

In the first paragraph, Henry argues that the morals of the clergy would be advanced by toleration. A minister seldom needs to condemn a parishioner ("A good life," says Henry, "is the best lecture.") but there comes a time when wickedness is so notoriously offensive that it is the duty of a minister to condemn the offender. A minister of the Established Church, dependent on the favors of powerful persons in the community, might be ousted for his courage. Perhaps Henry was thinking of Mr. Kay, evicted after he presumed to preach against pride in Landon Carter's parish. If such an ouster should occur, however, where toleration exists, "the unprejudiced everywhere" would revere the minister "as a victim to wicked intrigues, and heap their deserved benefactions upon him." Thus, "toleration . . . is the surest method to give us a virtuous clergy. It is the business of a virtuous clergyman to censure vice in every appearance of it. Therefore under a general toleration this duty will be commonly attended to."

In the second paragraph of the surviving fragment, Henry recognized that the proposal of toleration might be condemned as a foreign innovation. "Will anyone censure me as an innovator? I care not," he asserts defiantly. " 'Tis prudent to adopt the policy of other countrys, when experience shows it to be wiser than our own in anything." There follows a somewhat rambling digression on the value of borrowing useful ideas. ("Most nations have learned from abroad those sciences and arts that embellish and sweeten human life. This is the greatest advantage arising from a social intercourse among nations, and keeps the civilized world cemented together like one great family." As proof, Henry cites several examples.) Then why not borrow the idea of toleration? The era of religious intolerance does not constitute a heritage of which we can be proud. Other colonies—and it is obvious from later passages that Quaker Pennsylvania is one he has in mind—have followed a wiser policy, which we might do well to copy: "Colonys on the continent have experienced a more enlarged system; and their growth and real prosperity, are the just encomiums of that policy from which those countrys received their happy constitutions."

There follows a poorly organized but illuminating third paragraph. After protesting that he cannot "do justice to a subject so copious and important in a few pages" and that he abridges everything, Henry goes further than mere toleration and makes clear that he favors partial disestablishment of the Church in Virginia. "Much learning," he declares, "hath been displayed to show the necessity of establishing one church in England in the present form. But these reasonings do not reach the case of this colony. . . ."

Henry refuses, however, to pursue the arguments as "I have neither leisure nor abilitys to write a volume on the subject"—an understandable remark in view of his heavy law practice and increasing range of interests. "It is out of my province to attempt a reformation in the church," Henry continued. "Nor should I have meddled with it. . . ." He notes that he should not have brought up the question in this discussion, but the observation makes the reader wonder if he regretted, at least, temporarily, his part in the Parson's Cause. Nevertheless, he insists, "I see clearly the evils we feel can only be redressed by the proposed alteration."

In the remainder of the manuscript, and its most interesting and revealing portion, Henry exposes some of the evils which beset Virginia and points clearly to their remedies. The evils lie in the system of slavery and large plantations; the remedy in an influx of thrifty and industrious free farmers and artisans—the type of people who would be attracted to Virginia by religious toleration. He specifically recommends the Scotch-Irish and German Dissenters who had been attracted to Pennsylvania in such numbers. Many of these immigrants had lately moved to the Valley of Virginia, and he was coming into personal contact with them through his law practice and family connections in Augusta County.

It is clear that Henry really favored democracy and a society in which free farmers and artisans predominated. "The disadvantage from the great number of slaves," he wrote, "may perhaps wear off when the present stock and their descendants are scattered through the immense desserts in the West." As a plantation master living in a county and state where slavery was now deeply entrenched, Henry knew how futile it would be even to talk of returning the Negroes to Africa. "To re-export them is now impracticable, and sorry I am for it," he declares with admirable candor. He comments with vivid detail on the great economic potentialities of the western country,[44] and makes some pointed remarks on the growth of sections with religious toleration and few slaves. Written in some later periods of American history, these comments would have ruined his political career, and, as it was, must have galled any of his conservative opponents who perchance read them.

> How come it that the lands in Pennsylvania are five times the value of ours? [Henry pointedly inquired.] Pennsylvania is the country of the most extensive privileges with few slaves. A

[218]

Dutch, Irish, or Scotch emigrant finds there his religion, his priest, his language, his manners, and everything, but that poverty and oppression he left at home. Take an instance nearer to us. The country beyond the mountains is settled on a plan of economy very different from ours. Europeans, instead of Africans, till the lands, and manufacture. The tax to the established Church is scarcely felt. The people brought their priests with them. The lands in some parts there are almost as dear as at Williamsburgh, and notwithstanding the many disadvantages arising from situation, they are the most flourishing parts of Virginia, and this in a few years. . . .[45]

He continued with some trenchant paragraphs emphasizing the threefold plan of home manufactures, religious toleration, and free soil.

I agree entirely with those who insist on the necessity of home manufactures. We differ in the means of procuring them. To what purpose do we offer premiums, when experience tells us no one will obtain them? Common sense informs us that the first thing to be thought of is manufacturers. The present inhabitants of the colony must manufacture under great disadvantage, for the countrys with whom we are connected send continual supplies to our doors, offering to take in Barter those commoditys, the culture of which we understand. If attempts are made, we find the many difficulties attending them too great to be conquered. It must ever be so till we have procured numbers of skilful artists.

Henry saw no need to prove the usefulness of importing good artisans. A general religious toleration appeared to him the best means of peopling the American colonies and of enabling the people "to procure those necessarys among themselves, the purchase of which from abroad has so nearly ruined a colony, enjoying, from nature and time, the means of becoming the most prosperous on the continent."

Our country will be peopled. The question is, shall it be with Europeans or Africans? To do it with the latter will take many years; with the former 'tis quickly done. Is there a man so degenerate as to wish to see his country the gloomy retreat of slaves? No; while we may, let us people our lands with men who secure our internal peace, and make us respectable abroad; who will contribute . . . influence and stablish in posterity the benefit of the British Constitution.

Tell me no more of ideal wealth. Away with the schemes of paper money and loan offices, calculated to feed extravagance, and revive expiring luxury.

He concludes with a clinching argument for religious toleration:

To many the observations above will seem of small weight. When I say that the article of religion is deemed a trifle by our people in the general, I assert a known truth. But when we suppose that the poorer sort of European emigrants set as light by it, we are greatly mistaken. The free exercise of religion hath stocked the Northern part of the continent with inhabitants; and altho' Europe hath in great measure adopted a more moderate policy, yet the profession of Protestantism is extremely inconvenient in many places there. A Calvinist, a Lutheran, or Quaker, who hath felt these inconveniences in Europe, sails not to Virginia, where they are felt perhaps in a [greater degree]. . . .[46]

Although Patrick was still a young man, he was already providing an answer to Jefferson's assertion that "he could not write." [47] Lines such as, "Is there a man so degenerate as to wish to see his country the gloomy retreat of slaves?" bespeak the great orator, whose style, not yet entirely formed, would flower in the deathless "Give me Liberty" speech at St. John's Church. The literary style in the narrow sense and the organization of the material show a lack of experience. But the paper reveals evidence of considerable education and power of expression along with a notable breadth of viewpoint.

The reference to "schemes of paper money and loan offices" indicates that Henry was still mindful of the recent discussion of these topics in the Burgesses. Proceedings there, along with his own practical experience, help to explain his preoccupation with the problems of the West. Certainly there was much happening in and out of the Burgesses to keep the question of western settlements—and the unhappily related one of slavery—before him during the next few years.

When the Burgesses next met in March, 1767, Henry was again present from Louisa, along with his half-brother; his brother-in-law, Samuel Meredith; and his cousin Walter Coles, representing other back-country counties. Fortunately, in view of numerous absentees at the difficult March season, there were few important matters under consideration.[48] Like its model, the House of Commons, the House of Burgesses was determined to uphold its dignity. James Pride, convicted of writing a scandalous letter to the clerk of the Committee of Privileges in excuse for non-attendance upon it, was ordered to be put in close confinement in the public jail without the use of pen, ink, or paper; to be fed on bread alone and allowed no strong liquor whatsoever. The *Journal* has little more to say on the subject, but undoubtedly Pride had a fall.[49]

Much of the time of the House was consumed with the case of the late Treasurer Robinson. In early April the House resolved that five per cent interest be charged upon his estate for the public money which he had "received and misapplied." [50] A week later the committee—including Henry—appointed to examine the accounts, reported that Robinson's estate still owed the public £102,019.5.7.[51] The Assembly passed a bill to empower the administrators to sell portions of his real and personal estate for payments of his debts. This included the great Scotchtown plantation which Henry himself would soon buy.[52] And, meantime, as a member of the House committee, Henry continued to observe the persistent though conservative methods by which the administrators, particularly the hard-working Pendleton, sought to collect the heavy debts still owed the estate —this without upsetting the Virginia economy or, indeed, unnecessarily bankrupting any of the delinquent landowners.

On April 7, 1767, the House resolved itself into a Committee of the Whole to consider the state of the colony, as it had on the opening day of the fateful Stamp Act debates. It thereupon agreed that an address be presented to the King representing the great distress of the colony because of the lack of a sufficient circulating medium of exchange. "Under our present Circumstances trade must necessarily be greatly obstructed, . . . the Poor liable to very dangerous oppressions . . . , and . . . we shall be rendered unable to pay the great Balance due to Great Britain."

An eleven-man committee was appointed to draw up the address, including John Blair, chairman, Bland, Nicholas, and Henry. It was also ordered that the committee prepare a scheme for issuing paper money to be transmitted to the colonial agent in England. The address was duly prepared and accepted by the House, as was an ambitious plan for the emission of £200,000 in paper money, redeemable in 1783. Only about £71,000, however, was issued during the next few years, and the lack of sufficient currency continued to be a cause of discontent among the debtor classes of which Henry was a champion.[53] Thus when his father, Colonel Henry, and an associate had to make a part payment due on a bond in 1771, they were given a receipt for ten pistoles in foreign coin, difficult to secure and sold at a premium.[54]

In the plan for issuance of the paper money Henry's committee alluded to the necessity of securing permission from his Majesty "which 'tis hoped may be by April 1768." They hoped to get approval from England within a year! Yet, from a letter in November, 1767, of Governor Fauquier to the Earl of Shelburne, Secretary of State, we learn that the Governor had just received from Shelburne the King's Order in Council repealing and annulling three Acts passed by the Assembly in 1765 and confirming five other Acts passed in the same session.[55] Not until two and a half years after their passage did the Burgesses know whether these acts would receive the approval of the government.

Small wonder that many laws were passed by the colonial assemblies for a year or some other limited period, as in the case of the Two Penny Act. Before slow-moving officialdom in London could disallow the laws, they would have served their purpose. The difficulties in administering the now large and complex American colonies from London was becoming obvious in many ways.

13

Frontier Lands and Connections

Stand at Cumberland Gap and watch the procession of civilization, marching single file—the buffalo following the trail to the salt-springs, the Indian, the fur-trader and hunter, the cattle-raiser, the pioneer farmer—and the frontier had passed by. Stand at South Pass in the Rockies a century later and see the same procession with wider intervals between.

————FREDERICK JACKSON TURNER
The Frontier in American History

As THE westerly regions were opened up there developed in the colonies an indigenous type—the American frontiersman. With his buckskins, moccasins, and long rifle, he would be immortalized by James Fenimore Cooper and a host of later writers. Patrick Henry was no Daniel Boone or Davy Crockett but he lived intimately with many of their breed and largely shared their aims and ideas. When the frontiersman had moved westward and someone settled within "two whoops and a holler" or sound of a rifle shot, then he felt that it was time to move again. Henry's motives for his peregrinations were more complex, dictated partly by family interest and a chance for a good bargain. But he never lost his love for the free country life. Every few years he would pick up his family and move, and often it would be westward to a less settled region. Severing old ties caused him little pain or regret. It was somewhat like a soldier breaking camp, a shepherd moving to new pastures.

[223]

Before Henry was thirty years old, he had lived at Studley, Mount Brilliant, the two houses at Pine Slash, and Hanover tavern. His next move, in the year of his Stamp Act speech was to Louisa County. The semi-frontier life there was hardly likely to form him in a more conservative mold. Rather, during his Louisa residence, he came still more under the influence of back-country thought and readily plunged into speculation in back-country or western lands. When buying seventeen hundred acres on Roundabout Creek from his father in late October, 1765, he had been described as living in St. Martin's Parish in western Hanover,[1] but by December his account book showed no more payments to the Louisa carpenter for completing the rough work on his new house.[2] Apparently before the end of the year Sarah, the ten-year-old Martha or Patsy, the younger boys, and the simple family possessions were moved to the new home clinging to the hill over the little branch of the South Anna. And it was here that Patrick's and Sarah's second daughter, Anne, must have been born on July 19, 1767.[3]

What sort of house was Roundabout, the first that Henry ever built and the family home for some three years? A few of the plantation masters in the neighborhood were erecting mansions worthy of the Tidewater; he might have attempted to imitate them. Thomas Johnson, of the dark-haired, dark-eyed family with which Patrick was now so closely associated, had built at adjacent Roundabout Castle a spacious frame, dormer-windowed house, resembling Wakefield, Washington's birthplace. There was a central hall, great side chimneys, and ten rooms, four of very large size. Perched on a near-by hill was another pretentious Johnson home, inherited through the rich Meriwethers.[4] But Roundabout, the new Henry house, was a simple story-and-a-half structure more typical of the rude period that had not yet passed. There were three rooms downstairs and one above; and these, with their hand-hewn lumber and rough finish, were more sturdy than comfortable. Henry employed a local mason, one John Anderson, to make various additions and improvements after they had moved to the house, including lathing, plastering, and whitewashing. John was paid in cash, corn, fodder, and rum. On

December 26, 1766, he rode his mare to Roundabout, and, after a cheery greeting to all the Henrys, got his quart of Christmas rum. But Patrick did not settle with Anderson for finishing work on the building until late November, 1767.[5]

At Roundabout Henry proved his eye for a good house site. From the hillside on which the new house sat there was a pleasant view of the rock-encrusted hill sloping down to Polecat Branch and, beyond, the quiet valley of the Roundabout, then the rolling fields and forests. There was also some good tobacco and grain land, and distances to court and market were not great, at least according to back-country standards.

Louisa County, named for a daughter of ineffectual George II, had not been cut off from Hanover until 1745. By the 1760's a new gentry was rising there, as elsewhere in the Piedmont, a gentry based on unexploited land, tobacco, grain, and slaves. A few of these families, like the Johnsons, had a tradition of culture and leadership. Not debilitated or mentally ossified by wealth and leisure, and with the peculiar vigor of a new country, the Piedmont leaders were beginning to contest the supremacy of the aristocratic Tidewater families of which they were, indeed, sometimes offshoots.

But while there were now a considerable number of large landholders in Louisa, it was essentially a county of small freeholders with few slaves. Their virtues lay more in sturdiness and independent thinking than in knowledge of the classics. "No overfed voluptaries could hew in the forest and dig in the fields with them." [6] At the county seat Henry would meet an occasional gentleman attending court or stopping at the tavern for his rum or brandy, but more often men in hunting shirts and leather breeches, including an occasional Indian trader! [7] Accentuating the diversity of thought were the large number of Dissenters settled in the county, the Quakers and the Presbyterians with their zeal for education. Only about a dozen miles southeast of Roundabout, near the Three Chopt Road, lived the Presbyterian divine John Todd. There at Providence Church, a plain wooden building which some of Sarah's Shelton kin had helped establish, he ministered to a new but influential congregation, and his classical academy was one of the earliest in the colony under Presbyterian control. The Todds were venturesome folk like many of the early Louisa settlers. Several of the Louisa County Todds or near-relatives of the name were among the frontiersmen, who, again pushing westward, settled in Kentucky; one was the grandfather of Mrs. Abraham Lincoln.[8]

With the center of population and economic power moving westward a great leader might soon tip the scales against the conservative oligarchy. Henry, while living at Roundabout continued, it seemed almost casually or accidentally, to add to his fame and influence. Roundabout was only nine miles south of Louisa Courthouse where he had now acquired a considerable practice.[9] He took his gun with him to court, hunting along the way the deer, pheasants, partridges and other game which abounded.[10] Often he would hunt for several days at a time, carrying his provisions and camping at night in the woods. After the hunt, he would go to Louisa court without bothering to change his coarse cloth coat, stained with the trophies of the chase, or his greasy leather breeches and leggings. His saddlebags on his arm, he would enter the courtroom and take up the first of his cases that happened to be called. And if there were any opportunity for his peculiar talent, he would eclipse his opponent and astonish the court and jury by the powerful outburst of his eloquence.[11]

He would captivate his audience even when speaking on trivial subjects. A rival lawyer, Peter Lyons, when practicing at court could write a letter and draw up a declaration or plea at the bar as accurately as he could in his own office. That is, in all circumstances except one—when Henry rose to speak. But when he spoke even on such a trifling subject as a summons and petition for twenty shillings, Lyons confessed that he was obliged to lay down his pen and could not write another word until Henry had finished.[12]

Roundabout, with its clearings in the still encroaching forest, was warming to Henry's pioneer blood. And it was fairly convenient to the new Richmond market as well as to several Piedmont county seats where he carried on most of his growing law practice. Adjoining his plantation to the northward was the Mountain Road, doubtless the muddy yet passable route by which he sent cattle and produce to market, a few years later, receiving in exchange cloth, spices, saltpeter, rhubarb, pipes, and so forth.[13] But he also spent many an hour jogging over the Three Chopt Road which meandered through ruts and holes a few miles southward along the Goochland county border. A recent outgrowth of a forest trail, the Three Chopt Road was named for the triple axe marks on trees alongside pointing the way westward to a great empire hardly touched by the white man. Virginia was bounded by the Atlantic Ocean to the east and "the South Sea to the West, including California," Thomas Lee had written the Board of Trade in 1750, blithely ignoring French and Spanish claims.[14] But even after the definite British territorial accessions by the Treaty of Paris, the Old Dominion alone embraced an empire three times the size of the British Isles.[15] There were opportunities to challenge the vision of a Cecil Rhodes, and possibilities for wealth which a Rhodes would not have scorned. By the late 1760's Henry was to be counted among the illustrious Virginians who were sniffing after land profits, despite the obstacle set up by the Proclamation Line. He was also one of the few political leaders who saw the advantages of encouraging religious toleration in the projected settlements and of an economy not based on slavery.

Among significant, though imperfectly understood, causes of the impending Revolution, we have noted the creation in 1763 of the imaginary line restricting settlement beyond the crest of the Alleghenies. Three years later, in July, 1766, Governor Fauquier felt duty bound to issue a proclamation warning bold colonials trespassing in the forbidden area to evacuate. Whoever failed to obey could expect no protection, Fauquier threatened, and would be exposed to the revenge of the exasperated Indians.[16] But Fauquier's gesture, for it could be little more, almost immediately encountered implacable opposition. Small frontier farmers in restless search for new lands, venial Indian traders, seaboard colonies with charter or other claims to territory beyond the crest of the Alleghenies, were all determined not to stop at a hypothetical line.

[227]

The issue of the Proclamation Line was brought directly to Henry's attention at the November, 1766, Assembly by a petition from the frontier county of Augusta. This petition protested the impediments to western settlement offered by the line and by lands to the westward held under claims "never complied with." Many Virginians and German emigrants wanted to settle in this fertile country little used except as an Indian hunting ground. As a result of the petition, the Burgesses ordered a memorial to be sent to the King requesting that the territory be opened to the land-hungry people.[17]

And now the frontiersmen eager to move westward were buttressed—or at times, incited—by a new crop of land speculators. They were more aggressive and powerful than any America had yet known, and Henry was in the vanguard. Even before the French War, some six or seven million acres of western lands in Virginia had been granted or petitioned for—an area larger than many European states. The roll of the speculators was studded with the names of Washington, Lee, Mason, Nelson, Blair, Pendleton, and other Virginia families influential in the Council and Burgesses.[18] Several of Henry's Winston relatives were granted fifty thousand acres in 1749,[19] and there were, as well, the land schemes of John Henry and his brother, the Parson: from early childhood Patrick had heard talk of wealth to be made from such speculation. The prospects for fat profits were especially alluring in a debt-ridden plantation country where the economy provided inadequate opportunity in other fields.

The French and Indian and Pontiac's wars put a damper on the western land companies, but soon afterward they were revived and invigorated. The old Ohio Company, the Loyal Company, and the Mississippi Company, represented in London or Virginia by such men as Colonel Hugh Mercer, Arthur Lee, John Lewis, and Dr. Thomas Walker, were soon pushing their rival claims. The versatile Dr. Walker, master of the vast Castle Hill estate in neighboring Albemarle County, was a noted Kentucky explorer, a surveyor and a land speculator. He was serving in the Burgesses with Henry, and there was a closer family tie. John Syme's first wife, Mildred Meriwether, the bride of his youth, was the daughter of Dr. Walker's wife

[228]

by her earlier marriage. It was for John Syme's daughters by that union that he was ordering from England about this time some shoes, stockings, a bundle of old silk, and brocade for stays and coats.[20] Dr. Walker, strengthened by his wealthy Meriwether connection, encouraged Henry's interest in land speculation, which had already been whetted by an equity which Henry had acquired in John Shelton's lands in Southwest Virginia.

Some years earlier, Henry's father-in-law had acquired thirty-four hundred acres near the farther end of Southwest Virginia, close to the present Tennessee border. This land included fourteen hundred acres on Moccasin Creek, a bold mountain stream joining the North Fork of the Holston River near the spot where Gate City, Virginia, now stands, with nearly two thousand more virgin acres on the Holston or tributaries. Early in 1766 Shelton authorized Henry to sell those tracts. He thereupon advertised them in the frontier village of Staunton (the Augusta county seat though a week's ride from the Holston) and secured the assistance of Captain William Fleming, who lived in the newly opened part of Augusta. But there were difficulties in obtaining a decent price for land so distant from settlements and open to Indian attack. In the meantime, Shelton, against whom some British merchants had got a judgment for £365 during the late war,[21] found that his estate was, in Henry's words, "like to be sold for a trifle." [22]

Shelton still owed Henry sizable accounts, several dating back to his storekeeping days, and during the hard years immediately after the war, Henry had made him some large cash advances. Finally, to save his father-in-law from bankruptcy, he purchased the Moccasin Creek and Holston lands. Patrick's friend, Jefferson, was a witness to the mortgage in which Shelton later lost his equity of redemption, and Henry also assessed Shelton the small charge for Jefferson's legal service in connection with the land.[23]

Certain details as given by Henry in his account book help to indicate how vague and undefinable were some of the land claims in the western country. On the other hand, they show that Henry was developing a meticulousness in money matters that might possibly shade into avarice. In the accounts against the hard-pressed Shelton, he states that Sarah's father had promised to give Patrick upon the marriage ten Negroes and four hundred acres adjoining the Shelton place in Hanover. But Shelton had delivered only six Negroes and three hundred acres. "The deficiency will greatly over ballance any claim against me," Henry wrote.[24]

There seems to be a hint of a difficulty with his father-in-law, though such practical discussion of dowries was then common. In truth, it was so practical in certain instances that one might almost have expected the bride to be returned if her father fell behind in his payments! And yet the generous Shelton had provided much of the support for Patrick and Sarah during their early years, including not merely the land and slaves but for some time the very roof over their heads. Henry might reasonably have been expected to lean over backwards in favor of Shelton when figuring the "over Ballance" noted against his father-in-law unless some circumstances, now unknown, tipped the scales the other way.

With his brother William, young William Christian of Augusta, and other companions, Henry set out on the long trip to examine the Shelton grants. From Dr. Walker he could get much information about the western country, including Walker's valuable log or descriptive journal of his explorations through Southwest Virginia into Kentucky in 1749-1750. On that trip the Walker expedition had killed thirteen buffaloes, eight elk, fifty-three bears, twenty deer, four wild geese, and about one hundred and fifty turkeys "besides small game."[25] When the Henry party rode forth, settlement of Southwest Virginia had been set back by the Indian raids during the late French and Pontiac's wars. There were still only a few settlements in the new country, largely along the Wilderness Trail, celebrated in history through the travels of Daniel Boone and other notable pioneers. This trail the Henry party had to utilize for at least part of their trip. Like the Walker expedition, they doubtless rode horseback, employing other horses to carry their packs, and took advantage of gaps and fords to cross the rugged mountains and deep streams.

After leaving Louisa, the Henry brothers and their companions needed about a week to cross the outer Piedmont and eastern ranges of the Blue Ridge. Big Lick, now Roanoke, was a likely spot to enter the Wilderness Road. Once a game path and Indian trail, this road was now the principal route westward to Cumberland Gap and the vast unsettled stretches of Kentucky. At Dunkard's Bottom on the New River, Henry, sensitive to new people and forces in Virginia, could stop at the settlement opened up by the Dunkards, an energetic though outlandish German Protestant sect. The Virginians in this far frontier were not all cut in one pattern. The Dunkards were, in the opinion of Dr. Walker, an "odd set of people." They "make it a matter of religion not to shave their Beards, ly on beds, or eat Flesh, though at present, in the last they transgress, being constrained to it, as they say, by want of a sufficiency of Grain and Roots, they having not long been seated here." [26]

In Philadelphia at Independence Square may still be seen a human scalp, dried and stretched, the relic of an early Indian raid.[27] Passing along the Wilderness Road in the vicinity of present Blacksburg, Henry entered a community where, only about a decade before, cabins had been left smoldering by the redskins; a baby had been brained against a log, the head of a man put in a bag and left with a neighboring woman. If the woman looked inside the bag she would find an acquaintance, the Indians told her.[28] In that dangerous frontier area, now in an uneasy peace with a savage foe who resented the loss of their hunting grounds, several of Henry's sisters and other relatives were already settling.[29] Probably after visiting some of these venturesome kinfolk, he stopped at the line of forts which had given Colonel George Washington such concern when in command of the long frontier during the French war.[30] Moving southwestward in the direction of modern Bristol, Henry reached, near present Seven Mile Ford on the Holston, the great land grant of Colonel James Patton who had been scalped in the recent war.[31] Beyond, in the wild Clinch River country near Cumberland Gap, Captain William Russell and his family, including little Willie, the smallest boy in John

[231]

Henry's school at Mount Brilliant, would soon make a precarious settlement.[32]

Henry found mountain scenery that proved the bounty of the Almighty, and fertile valley land watered by limpid streams and with natural blue grass. But he was disappointed in locating only one of the Shelton tracts. He was forced to allow for rival Cherokee Indian claims which, as recognized by the Treaty of Hard Labour in 1768, gave them the Clinch and Holston lands.[33] But soon afterwards he bought full rights in the thirty-four-hundred-acre Shelton property, hoping that the treaty line would be altered. Eventually, after controversies involving the Indians, settlers, and government, he would acquire nearly all of the property.[34]

But that is a later story. When Henry returned from the Holston country about 1767 he had some claims which were dubious not merely because of the Proclamation Line but because of rival Indian rights. Yet some of the new land on the sparkling creek and rivers was among the best in the colony. True, there were the little matters of getting the wild country cleared and made accessible to the remote eastern market. But Henry, with the vision of a real Western speculator, was not deterred by such obstacles, especially since he had no large capital involved.

After his return from the Holston, he directed his interest to a larger venture on the great Mississippi. In 1767 he acquired from John Shelton a mortgage on six tracts or one share in a new land venture with "Walker, Patton and others," lying, as Henry noted in his account book "on the waters of the Mississippi." A vague description for land along one of the vast expanses of the Father of Waters and its tributaries! Elsewhere we learn that the land was in western Kentucky near the junction of the Mississippi and the Ohio. Apparently at the request of Captain Fleming, Henry discussed with Dr. Thomas Walker plans for Fleming to reconnoiter the distant country. Walker, so Henry wrote Fleming in June, 1767, was satisfied with his "prudence & Veracity in viewing that country & in fixing on some such spot as would be proper for the first company of adventurers to begin the execution of the scheme" which Henry had hinted to him. The details had not been arranged, but it was obvious that Henry and Walker were planning for settlement in this area. Far more practical than Colonel John Henry had ever been, Patrick added that he thought some knowledge of the country was "obviously necessary" before any real progress could be made.

"Pardon me if I recommend to you a diary," Henry continued in a realistic vein. "Even the trees, herbs grass stones hills etc. I think ou[gh]t to be described. The reason I wish you to be so particular is that a succint account of your Journal may be printed in order to invite our countrymen to become settlers.

"The Task is arduous," he added, "to view that vast forest, describe the face of the Country & such of the rivers Creeks etc. as present themselves to view is a work of much Trouble, hazard & fatigue & will in my Judgement intitle you to the favourable notice of every gentleman engaged in the Scheme." He hoped that it was convenient for Fleming to start on his expedition sooner than originally planned, and he wished for him "Success which those who labor for prosperity deserve. . . ." [35]

If Henry's interest in the West and its problems needed further stimulus, it was provided by the marriage of several of his sisters to rising young leaders of frontier Augusta County. Already one of his wife's sisters had married a Scotch McClanahan, of a prominent Augusta family,[36] and Henry was probably responsible for a romance that blossomed between the scion of another, William Christian, and his favorite sister, Anne. William was the son of Patrick's client, Captain Israel Christian, a prominent Staunton merchant and burgess. Of fighting stock like his sturdy sire, young William had served before he was twenty as a gallant captain in the French and Indian War.[37] When he later studied law under Henry, he greatly endeared himself to Patrick by his manliness and intelligence. Henry was delighted to learn that the dowry for Anne's marriage to his pupil was being arranged, as witness this letter in early 1768 from Colonel Henry to Israel Christian:

Your son has for some time been making his addresses to one of my daughters. I find the match is as good as concluded. It seems to depend chiefly on you—for as I can at present do nothing worth mentioning, and he has not much in possession. . . I should be pleased to know what you can do for him. At my wife's death, and mine, there will be some considerable estate to be divided among my daughters; but it is of such a nature that it must be kept together for our support. . . .[38]

John Henry also had special reasons for being pleased when Anne married the promising representative of the substantial Valley family, for a judgment of £100 against the Colonel by a British merchant had now been added to his financial woes. True, he was in good company: besides the large claim against John Shelton, Benjamin Harrison was posted for £470 and £83 in two judgments, and Richard Lee for £113.[39] But this did not make John Henry's burden more tolerable, nor could he have enjoyed leaning upon Patrick. It was comforting for the Colonel to feel that he had reared such splendid daughters and that they were getting worthy husbands. Before very long, Anne Christian and her fast-growing family were settled in newly established Botetourt County, where William was a leading citizen, and near by lived her sister Susannah, wife of Thomas Madison, son of the long-time clerk of Augusta and relative of the future President.[40] A sturdy and attractive brood, these Henry sisters, worthy of their distinguished brother. And like attracting like, they had a penchant for dashing young frontiersmen. They were quite willing to go with their husbands into semi-wilderness country still under the threat of war whoop and scalping knife. Mary Henry also married an Augusta frontiersman of a prominent family, Luke Bowyer, who studied or practiced law with Patrick.[41] With their relatives by marriage, the Flemings, settled at Bellomont in Botetourt, Henry had a bevy of relatives in that developing area.[42] The rich grain fields and pasture lands spreading from the upper James River into the Alleghenies still testify to the sound judgment of these early settlers. Late in 1773 Henry wrote that he himself had bought five thousand acres in this area which he prayed his correspondent to help William Christian locate for him.[43]

With the opening up of the large area in southwest Virginia, new counties were created. In 1769 Botetourt had been formed from Augusta, and the first meeting of the county court was held the next year with Henry's first cousin, Edmund Winston, as one of the King's attorneys. The county seat, the present town of Fincastle, and Christiansburg were established by Captain Israel Christian, who settled in Botetourt.[44]

Many ties, personal, political, and economic, were connecting Henry with the fast-developing western counties. Their representatives in the Burgesses had been among his most ardent supporters during the Stamp Act debate; they continued to turn to him, and he to them. And while visiting his own Botetourt lands and his numerous relatives settled near each other there, he need not lose contact with cultured people. William Fleming, for instance, was a Scotsman of aristocratic connections who had studied medicine at the University of Edinburgh. A dignified, courteous gentleman, he could command the respect of rough frontiersmen while retaining a love of good books which caused him to collect one of the finest libraries in western Virginia.[45]

As an influential burgess, Henry was in a strategic position to promote western land development. When the House passed a bill in April, 1767, to encourage settlement in the newer parts of Augusta County, Henry was selected to carry the bill to the Council for their concurrence.[46] And, two years afterwards, he was one of several burgesses ordered to present a petition to the Governor requesting that he inform the House whether "the Faith of Government" was then found to confirm any Orders of Council for land grants between the Alleghenies and a line run from the western termination of North Carolina to the junction of the Ohio and the Mississippi.[47] He was a member of a strong committee, including Bland, Pendleton, and Treasurer Nicholas, appointed by the House a week later to present a memorial to the Governor calling attention to the valuable territory which would be lost to the colony if its western line were run from the Holston to the mouth of the Kanawha. That Henry's own land claims as well as the general welfare were affected, is seen in a provision of the memorial, which he doubtless influenced, in regard to the proposed severance from the colony of land previously granted under "the known and fixed" rules of the government.[48]

Not only did Henry have good reason to fear that part of his Holston lands would be abandoned to the Cherokees,[49] but he was associated in a petition for fifty thousand acres on the Ohio below the New River. There still survives a draft copy in his handwriting of a set of propositions for this Ohio Company to offer the proper authorities. The company would give a yearly acknowledgment to the Crown in lieu of quitrents and would purchase the lands from the Indians and promise to help them settle elsewhere. Moreover, they would contract to place five hundred families on the grant within seven years.[50] The propositions and the petition, filed about 1769,[51] show that Henry, through his own study and exploration and his father's map-making, had acquired a knowledge of the western country not evident in the Ohio patent petitioned for by his Winston relatives a generation before.[52] The new petition was much more precisely defined; it was also loaded with the names of Henry's relatives and associates. Beside John Blair, Jr., Thomas Nelson, Senior and Junior, and Thomas Jefferson, all identified with the old aristocracy,[53] the petitioners included Gabriel Jones, the prominent Augusta lawyer, a Preston and two McDowells of influential Augusta families, Patrick Henry, William Henry, John Madison, William Christian, and Samuel Meredith.[54]

By the Treaty of Fort Stanwix in 1768 the Iroquois Indians surrendered to the English whatever rights they had claimed to the trans-Allegheny portion of present West Virginia and to the lands lying between the Ohio and Tennessee rivers. The English title to part of this territory was further confirmed by an agreement with the Cherokees.[55] Lord Dunmore, the new Governor of Virginia, had grandiose plans for land speculation along the Ohio River or its tributaries. From Henry, interested in private purchase of land from the Cherokees, Dunmore got the legal opinion that the sale of land by the Indians to Pennsylvania traders at Fort Stanwix was valid; such purchase by private individuals from the Indians gave satisfactory title.[56] There is suggestive evidence that Dunmore may have helped to foment the Indian war of 1774 in order to promote his land schemes.[57] In any event, Henry had some pointed comments on Dunmore's action when he met Samuel Wharton at Philadelphia in September. Henry, in Philadelphia as a delegate to the Continental Congress, had been invited to breakfast with the influential Quaker merchant and land speculator, and Wharton quoted him as stating:

> that he was at Williamsburg with Ld.D when Dr. Conolly first came there, that Conolly is a chatty, sensible man, and informed Ld. Dunmore of the extreme richness of the lands which lay on both sides of the Ohio; that the prohibitory orders which had been sent him relative to the land on the hither side (or Vandalia) had caused him to turn his thoughts to the opposite shore, and that as his Lordship was determined to settle his family in America he was really pursueing this war, in order to obtain by purchase or treaty from the natives a tract of territory on that side . . . .

Henry then added:

> that he was convinced from every authority that the law knew, that a purchase from the natives was as full and ample a title as could be obtained, that they had Lord Camden and Mr. York's opinion on that head, which opinion with some others that Ld. Dunmore had consulted, and with the knowledge Conolly had given him of the quality of the country and his determined resolution to settle his family on this continent, were the real motives or springs of the present expedition.

Henry, mindful of his plans for purchase of Indian lands, asked Wharton where he could buy Indian goods.

"It's not possible you mean to enter the Indian trade at this period," Wharton inquired.

"The wish-world is my hobby horse," Henry laughingly replied.[58]

[237]

This interchange would take place in September, 1774, only two weeks before the battle with the Indians at Point Pleasant, a prelude to the Revolution. Meanwhile, Henry was developing a large stake in the new western country spreading to the Mississippi and beyond, which was adding to his dissatisfaction with static British policy.

14

⟨∼✦∼⟩

A Man of Varied Interests

From this time the English government of America is little
more than a series of deplorable blunders.———Lecky [1]

T HE seven years from the end of the 1767 session of the Burgesses until the convocation of the Continental Congress in 1774 were
for Henry another full and rewarding period. It was less strenuous
and spectacular than the era of the Stamp Act debates and their violent aftermath but full of solid accomplishment. The conflict with
England, advancing by well-defined steps out of the realm of political theory, fell for a time into the doldrums, Henry being one of a
small band of patriots—radical demagogues, as the Tories would
have it—who kept aloft the banner of colonial rights and made an
imperishable contribution to American liberty.

At the same time his amiability, his virtual freedom from bitter-
ness and violent enmity, helped him not only to push his political
program but to engage successfully in other activities. It would be
too much to say that he now realized the eighteenth century ideal of
the "compleat gentleman." His cultural interests, although commend-
able, were nowhere near equal to those of Fauquier or Jefferson. In
dress and even in manners he had evolved considerably from the
gauche young man who had represented West Dandridge at the com-

mittee hearing a few years before. But we still cannot picture him in silk and satin, dancing the minuet at the Governor's ball or languidly disputing a Latin construction. And certainly he would never risk his fortune on the turn of the dice as did William Byrd III.

Yet in a number of ways Henry was approaching the contemporary ideal of the well-rounded life—the "nothing overmuch" of the classical tradition. From the conservative viewpoint he was overdoing matters in becoming the most influential leader of the popular party in the Burgesses; he was a champion of the oppressed Dissenters and he even spoke a courageous word for the lowly slaves. Admitted to practice before the General Court, he no longer found it necessary to ride the courthouse circuit for so many petty suits. His family was increased by two more daughters, suggesting already a motif for the verse by his witty great-grandson:

> The cradle in your house was never still:
> It was the Rock of Ages, so to speak,
> And whilst you rocked, were dreams of freedom spun,
> Midst infants' cries, distracting, piercing, shrill.[2]

Henry had now heard such orators as Richard Henry Lee, Samuel Davies, and perhaps George Whitefield. But for further inspiration on a high level he turned perforce to the printed page and especially to the accounts of English political luminaries in the indispensable *Virginia Gazette*. During the decade following repeal of the Stamp Act, the *Gazette* carried copious notices of Edmund Burke. By 1769 the speeches of that eloquent Anglo-Irishman on behalf of the colonial cause had made him a toast of the Sons of Liberty. The *Gazette* was even more loaded with references to William Pitt, the American idol.

In his practice of beginning his speeches quietly, then gradually rising to a crescendo, Henry was possibly influenced by Pitt's example.[3] But could Henry employ such oratorical periods as did Pitt, or should he, speaking to less educated audiences than Pitt's, merely develop his simpler style? [4]

In any event, how thrilling to read Pitt's famous phrases!

[240]

PATRICK HENRY
From the portrait by Thomas Sully

Aberdeen at the end of the seventeenth century. From
a copy of an illustration in John Slezer's *Theatrum Scotiae*.

King's College, Aberdeen. The
Crown Tower, completed in 1700.

Judge Peter Lyons, President of the Supreme Court of Appeals of Virginia, the King's Attorney in the "Parson's Cause." From Thomas Sully's painting in the courtroom at Richmond.

Hanover Courthouse, built in 1735.

To the King's most excellent Majesty.

The humble Address of the House of Burgesses of Virginia.

Most Gracious Sovereign,

We your Majesty's dutiful and loyal Subjects the Burgesses of Virginia, now met in General Assembly, beg Leave with all Humility to approach your Royal Presence.

The many Instances of your Majesty's benevolent Intentions and most gracious Disposition to promote the Prosperity and Happiness of your Subjects in the Colonies, encourage us to look up to the Throne, and implore your Majesty's paternal Assistance in averting a Calamity of a most alarming Nature.

The Importation of Slaves into the Colonies from the Coast of Africa hath long been considered as a Trade of great Inhumanity, and, under its present Encouragement, we have too much reason to fear will endanger the very — — Existence of your Majesty's American Dominions.

We are sensible that some of your Majesty's Subjects in Great Britain may reap Emoluments from this Sort of Traffick, but when we consider that it greatly retards the Settlement of the Colonies with more useful Inhabitants, and may, in Time, have the most destructive Influence, we presume to hope that the Interest of a few will be — disregarded when placed in Competition with the Security and Happiness of such — Numbers of your Majesty's dutiful and loyal Subjects.

Deeply impressed with these Sentiments, we most humbly beseech your Majesty to remove all those Restraints on your Majesty's Governors of this Colony which inhibit their assenting to such Laws, as might check so very pernicious a — Commerce.

Your Majesty's ancient Colony and Dominion of Virginia hath at all Times and upon every Occasion been entirely devoted to your Majesty's sacred Person and Government, and we cannot forego this Opportunity of renewing those Assurances of the truest Loyalty and warmest Affection, which we have so often, with the greatest Sincerity, given to the best of Kings, whose Wisdom and Goodness we esteem the surest Pledges of the Happiness of all his People.

Petition of the House of Burgesses of Virginia to George III. From the document in the Public Record Office (Colonial Office Papers) London.

Fork Episcopal Church in upper Hanover County where Henry worshipped at least part of the time when he lived at near-by Scotchtown.

Rural Plains, Hanover County, where Henry was married in 1754.

The Raleigh Tavern,
Williamsburg.
From an old print.

The Apollo Room
in The Raleigh Tavern.
From an old print.

The Old Capitol, Williamsburg, built 1701-1705;
burned 1746; rebuilt and
again burned 1832.
From an old print.

Virginia State Library

Pine Slash, overseer's house, Hanover County, where Henry
and his family lived briefly after their house was burned in 1757.

Scotchtown, northwest of Ashland, Hanover County.

Virginia State Chamber of Commerce Photograph by Flournoy

Letter from Patrick Henry to Mr. George Thomas, February 18, 1764. The first known letter by Henry.

I rejoice that America has resisted. Three millions of people, so dead to all the feelings of liberty, as voluntarily to consent to be slaves, would have been fit instruments to make slaves of the rest.[5]

On the practical side, he would also applaud the argument of expediency as advanced by Pitt in the Commons and duly reported in the *Gazette*:

The profits from America are two million [pounds] a year. That is what carried you successfully through the last war. You have prohibited where you ought to have encouraged. . . . You have but two nations to trade with America; would you had twenty. . . .

Will you quarrel with yourselves now the whole House of Bourbon is united against you?[6]

Even the statesmanlike vision of Pitt could not entirely pierce the future. He could not foresee the British Commonwealth today with its self-governing dominions. But the only hope of keeping America satisfied after she had developed a large and complex economy was to give her an increasing home rule. That would have pulled the teeth from any protests by Sam Adams and Patrick Henry against British tyranny.

But Pitt's arguments also included a strong conservative plea. In contending for more rather than fewer commercial restrictions on America, he stood by the thesis that Parliament had a right to bind her. The Stamp Act should be repealed absolutely, but the sovereign authority of Great Britain over the colonies should be asserted in as strong terms as could be devised.[7]

How would Henry answer that argument, especially since it would be blunderingly developed in concrete parliamentary legislation during the coming years? Under the influence of Richard Bland and others, he had stated in his fourth Stamp Act resolution that the Virginia people had "uninterruptedly enjoyed the right" of being governed by their Assembly in the matter of their taxes and internal police. And in his fifth resolution he had added that the General Assembly had the sole right to levy taxes upon the people of the colony.

The fifth resolution, to be sure, had not passed the Assembly and the fourth had been slightly amended. No matter! In amended form Henry's resolutions were still in strong opposition to the prevailing constitutional argument advanced by the British political leaders. Indeed, there had been only the feeblest opposition in Parliament to the Declaratory Act. Let us follow the constitutional debate as it was developed during the next few years through specific legislation in England and counter-measures in the Burgesses and elsewhere.

Although George III and several of his ministers had wished only to amend the Stamp Act, the House of Commons, already under severe pressure for total repeal, had succumbed to the eloquence of Pitt. The Declaratory Act, however, should have made it clear that the British government would not yield on the basic question of parliamentary supremacy, and its stand was certainly obvious after the passage in 1767 of the Townshend Acts. The Rockingham ministry was succeeded by a hodgepodge ministry under the leadership of Pitt. But, his faculties weakened by ill-health and mental depression, the Great Commoner soon entered upon a dark period of retirement from the political world.[8]

Into the vacuum created by Pitt's absence, there moved the forceful and calculating figure of Charles Townshend, the Champagne Charley of "melancholy eminence in imperial history."[9] As Chancellor of Exchequer, Townshend proposed to reduce the land tax, always a popular measure with the country squires, and to make up part of the deficit by increasing the revenue from the colonies. Complacent and narrowly expedient, he argued that if it were internal taxes against which the Americans were howling, then he would give them external taxes, collected at the ports. And in May, 1767, the House lightly adopted his revenue bills.[10] Duties were imposed on lead, paper, English paints, glass, and tea; above all, in the light of later developments, *tea*. Writs of assistance, against which James Otis had argued with courage and eloquence rivaling Henry's, were specifically authorized and other measures taken to strengthen the custom collections. The money so obtained was to be used to create a colonial civil list, thus making both governors and judges independent of the colonial assemblies.

Instead of being outwitted by Townshend's plan of external taxation, the advance guard of American leaders moved forward to meet the new foe. Their cry was now changing from "no representation, no taxation" to "no representation, no legislation." [11] Henry could read in the *Gazette* the most influential expression of the new popular sentiment. In *The Farmer's Letters*, written by John Dickinson of Pennsylvania and published in the *Gazette* and other newspapers throughout the colonies, Dickinson urged a policy of peaceful but firm opposition to the British policy. Remembering the Stamp Act riots, he declared that liberty's cause is "of too much dignity, to be sullied by turbulence and tumult." But he also warned that if the colonies admitted that Great Britain could lay duties upon exports to them for the purpose of levying money only, she then would have nothing to do but to lay those duties on the articles which she prohibited them from manufacturing. The tragedy of American liberty would then be finished.[12] Implicit in Henry's Stamp Act resolutions had been the doctrine that the power of taxation was being used to destroy American rights. "The power to tax involves the power to destroy" is the cogent phrasing of the proposition by a great chief justice whose father had heard Henry in 1765.[13]

From his own reading, in addition to the *Gazette*, Henry got further ammunition to strengthen his position as a leader of the liberal forces. In 1764 he had bought a copy of Samuel Pufendorf's *De Jure Naturae et Gentium*.[14] Although this ponderous treatise was hardly written for a busy peripatetic lawyer, Henry with his quick mind must by now have absorbed a cardinal point of the profound German jurist—that the will of the state is merely the sum of the wills of the individuals composing it. Henry also had available (a copy had been bought by John Syme) the latest of Richard Bland's learned defenses of the colonial position.[15]

"The colonies are distinct states, independent as to their internal government of the original Kingdom," Bland wrote in this 1766 pamphlet, "but united with her as to their external policy in the closest and most intimate league and amity, under the common allegiance." [16]

But where draw the line between internal and external government, especially when the British government had taken advantage of the colonial position to impose the Townshend duties? There is every reason to believe that Henry, impatient with timid word-play, agreed with the advanced cry of "no representation, no legislation." He would doubtless have approved the clear-minded Ben Franklin's criticism of Dickinson's distinction between duties for regulation of trade and duties for revenue, beyond the power of Parliament to levy. [17]

But even Henry had been careful to avoid overt treason and Franklin's remarks were not broadcast. How could the House of Burgesses maintain a firm position yet not be outmaneuvered by the terms of the Townshend Acts? The answer, of vital importance because of British efforts to suppress opposition in other states while placating Virginia, was given at the next two sessions of the Assembly. And, meantime, through a number of his activities both in and out of the Burgesses, Henry had strengthened his position as a liberal leader.

First in this connection were his activities as a dedicated champion of persecuted religious Dissenters.

In March, 1769, Rachel Wilson, a Quaker and grandmother of the English statesman, John Bright, was traveling in Virginia. There in Williamsburg at the end of the month she met Henry.

"We returned that night to Francis Clark's," she wrote in her diary. "Called by the way to see one of the Assemblymen, who was a man of great moderation and had appeared in Friends' favour; his name was Patrick Henry. He received us with great civility, and made some sensible remarks. We had an open time in the family." [18]

Just how Henry had appeared as the advocate of the Friends cannot be precisely determined. But when the Quakers had petitioned the Assembly two years before for exemption from the penalties for failure to perform military service, he had been appointed a member of the committee to draw up a bill to this effect. [19]

In his earlier statement on religious liberty Henry had praised toleration not only as the surest method to obtain a virtuous clergy but, especially, to attract emigrants. So far, he felt, this policy had been carried out to a much greater degree in the North and notably Pennsylvania, and it had lured to that fast developing colony many Quakers, Calvinists, and Lutherans.[20]

In Hanover, Louisa, and elsewhere in the back country Henry's religious views met with the approval of a large and influential body of Dissenters. But they would face determined opposition, social and political, from the established order. Indeed, as an Episcopalian, son of a vestryman and nephew of an Anglican minister, he could be accused of fouling his own nest. He had said that he did not care if he was censured as an "innovator." [21] Bold words again! But how much would he sacrifice for his principles, especially when some of his opposition was of that peculiarly wearing kind found within a family circle?

In his youth Henry had heard the strong opinions voiced by Parson Henry against George Whitefield and the Methodist movement. By the late 1760's the Quakers also had acquired a considerable following in Hanover and Louisa, not without the ill-concealed aversion of the conventional and well-placed. The Friends offended by their unusual dress and speech and, especially, by their opposition to war and slavery. There is an amusing story of how Henry's cousin Charles Dabney somewhat reluctantly attended a Quaker meeting, then had to linger on the scene while his excessively gallant companion stood at the horse block and helped every lady into the saddle. The Quaker meeting visited by Dabney was near his home in Hanover, and the large congregation was part of an influential element among Henry's supporters.[22] In Louisa the Quakers were among the earliest Dissenters and congregated there in considerable number.[23] Later, in 1773, we shall have occasion to note Henry's reaction to a letter written him by a Quaker correspondent seeking his views on the explosive subject of slavery.

Meantime, Henry was engaged in a successful effort to promote toleration for the persecuted Baptists. By the late 1760's the revival started by such religious giants as Whitefield and Samuel Davies had lost much of its impetus. But the Dissenters now found a powerful voice in the Baptists; and again, as in the case of the New Light and Presbyterian movement, the genesis of the revival was centered to a large degree in Hanover and adjoining counties. Samuel Harris of Hanover was converted to the Baptist faith by a minister who, in New England, had come under the influence of Whitefield and the New Lights. Harris in turn converted John Waller and John Craig, noted Baptist ministers who suffered in the propagation of their faith.

The first Baptist church north of the James River in Virginia had not been formed until 1767. Three years later there were less than half a dozen in the entire colony, but on the eve of the Revolution, in 1774, the number of their churches had increased tenfold. The Baptists were now nurturing realistic hopes not only of securing liberty of conscience throughout Virginia but even of overthrowing the Anglican Establishment.[24]

How explain the vastly increasing influence of the Baptists within so short a period? With a few exceptions, their preachers were, according to their own historian, unlearned, impecunious, plainly garbed, awkward in manners and address.[25] They were given to an unbridled emotionalism, offensive to adherents of the dignified, though often stiff, Anglican service. "While speaking of the dealings of God many would be affected and weep, some faint, till all the neighborhood was alarmed and very many became good Xians."[26] As advocates of congregational government and religious liberty they held unorthodox views which they extended into the political field.[27] Nor were they hesitant about denouncing the faults of other churches and naming individual transgressors according to their sectarian standards. It was not surprising that around 1768 a systematic persecution of the Baptists was begun in several counties near Hanover[28] and that two of Henry's strong political opponents, Edmund Pendleton and Archibald Cary, were active in the movement.

For the growth of the Baptists due credit must be given those obscure ministers who did not hesitate to risk life or limb in an unpopular movement. It was hard to stop men who were dragged from the pulpit, or cruelly beaten and threatened with death, yet continued to preach regularly even from the windows of a jail.[29]

In Hanover where George Whitefield and especially Samuel Davies had earlier won so many followers, such persecution might not have been expected. Yet when the noted Baptist minister, John Waller, attempted to preach there, Henry was doubtless perturbed to learn that a man "had thrown himself upon him, pulled him down and dragged him about by the hair." [30]

The simple service of the Baptists, their emotional approach and democratic government, held a particular appeal for the lower classes. But the Baptists were in grave need of influential advocates with the colonial government. Semple, the historian of the Virginia Baptists, wrote in fulsome terms of how their preachers, seeking liberty of speech from hostile county magistrates, obtained powerful support from Patrick Henry.

Always a friend of liberty, so Semple declared, Henry needed only to be informed of the ministers' persecution to step forward to their relief. "From that time, until the day of their complete emancipation from the shackles of tyranny, the Baptists found in Patrick Henry an unwavering friend. May his name descend to posterity with unsullied honor." [31]

That Henry was not helping the Baptists merely to strengthen his influence with the back-country Dissenters is shown by an episode involving one Baptist minister, the Reverend John Weatherford. For five months Weatherford was the enforced but by no means cowed resident of Chesterfield jail on a charge of disturbing the peace by his unlicensed preaching. Henry then succeeded in obtaining an order for Weatherford's release but the jailer refused to liberate the minister until he paid his jail fees—a sum much beyond the means of the impecunious divine. Soon, however, Weatherford was informed that the charges had been paid by an unnamed party, and he was released. Not until over twenty years later, when he was a neighbor of Henry's in Charlotte County, did he learn that Henry himself had paid the fees. Needless to say, Weatherford always thereafter spoke of him with a "glow of affection." [32]

[247]

Weatherford's pleasure in his release from forbidding Chesterfield jail was not shared by the handsome and imperious Colonel Archibald Cary, presiding justice of Chesterfield court and traditional leader in the local persecution of the Baptist evangelists.[33] Henry also bearded Edmund Pendleton in his own lair by defending several Baptist preachers arraigned in Caroline County court of which Pendleton was presiding justice.

"I have heard Mr. Henry say that Mr. Pendleton was too much devoted to the aristocracy of former times," wrote Spencer Roane, and that on the bench of Caroline court he "justified imprisonment of several Baptist preachers, who were defended by Mr. Henry, on the heinous charge of worshipping God according to the dictates of their own consciences." [34]

Actually, the issue was more complex. When strong feeling was aroused in Caroline against several ministers who were arrested for preaching without a license, the justices imprisoned them but soon offered release on small bonds. The preachers, however, preferred continued imprisonment and martyrdom.[35] On the other hand, Pendleton, a self-made man, was doubtless influenced by the landed aristocrats of whom he had become a leader. In the past these magnates had, with occasional lapses, been fairly tolerant of religious dissent. However, they now feared with good reason that toleration would strengthen the power of the liberals, and in their persecution of the Baptists they had little opposition from John Blair, Acting Governor after the death in 1768 of the philosophic Fauquier. In Caroline the liberals had a formidable supporter in Francis Coleman, an ardent admirer of Henry, who successfully organized a rising element of the middle class. Coleman, elected in 1769 to the Burgesses, topped Pendleton in the poll and eliminated his conservative colleague from Caroline; his death a few months later removed from the Henry party a promising young lieutenant.[36]

On November 15, 1770, Patrick Henry qualified to practice law in Spotsylvania County.[37] This was probably in connection with the defense of John Waller or other Baptists imprisoned there. But the eloquent speech attributed to Henry at Spotsylvania court is based

[248]

on doubtful traditions.[38] Other Baptist preachers whom he is reported to have defended successfully were John Williams and Jeremiah Walker.[39] The Baptist persecution at its height is described in a letter written by John Waller from Urbanna prison in Middlesex County, August 12, 1771. A local magistrate, Captain Jack Montague, the Anglican parson, and others had descended "in a most furious rage" upon a Baptist meeting in Middlesex. One of the brethren had been "severely scourged" and several were with Waller in the Urbanna jail, while he cited six others as imprisoned in Caroline. "The most dreadful threatenings are raised in the neighboring counties against the Lord's faithful and humble followers," Waller added.[40]

As public opinion began to react against the violent treatment of the Baptists, reigning gentlemen of the county courts were not above subtler methods of suppression. Thus, in Caroline, when the rector of St. Margaret's failed to list his chaise for taxation he was excused from a fine, but not so a humbler citizen who had let the Reverend Lewis Craig hold a Baptist service in his home.[41]

In his efforts to aid the cause of religious freedom, Henry had to wage an uphill fight even as he did in the political field. Some of the difficulties which he encountered in the House of Burgesses are indicated by the disposition of petitions presented to the Committee on Religion, of which he was a member—along with Colonel Cary and a preponderant number of other landlords of the Anglican persuasion. The committee was ordered at two sessions of the Burgesses in 1769 to bring in bills for relief of Protestant Dissenters, but there is no evidence to indicate they were introduced that year on the floor.[42] In the following May a petition from several Baptists complained of the difficulties their ministers encountered in securing licenses to preach except in meeting houses specifically stipulated. Whatever Henry's arguments may have been in the committee room or on the floor, the petition was unavailing.[43] Another petition from Caroline County in 1772, complaining that the Baptists were denied benefit of the English Toleration Act extended to other Protestant Dissenters, was not even sent to the Committee on Religion. The

[249]

short shrift it was given is thus indicated in the *Journal*: "Ordered, That the said petition do lie upon the Table." [44]

But "neither mobs, nor prison walls, nor threats, nor hunger, nor insults could silence the imprisoned preachers" [45] or check the growing popularity of the Baptist doctrines. It is significant that counties where the Baptists suffered the worst persecution became strongholds of their faith. Some of the initial opposition to the sect was on social and economic grounds. The perfervid Colonel Cary explained, for example, that he did not prosecute Eleazer Clay, a Baptist minister (and relative of the future Henry Clay) who had a "livelihood," but that some other Baptists in Chesterfield were arrested under the vagrancy law. As the Baptists began, however, to attract men of some wealth and influence, they gained more prestige.

When they threw their rising political strength behind the Henry party, they advanced their ideal of religious freedom. It "was intolerable," as they stated, "for one set of men to make application to another set of men (cap in hand) and in the most humble posture, ask their consent and allowance, to worship the God that made them." [46]

In 1772 the Committee on Religion resolved that several Baptist petitions for toleration were reasonable. [47] The committee was ordered to draw up a bill pursuant to their resolution, and it was duly presented by a respected member, Treasurer Nicholas, Henry's friend and admirer. [48] But the bill, a none too liberal digest of various English acts of religious toleration, aroused further protests. The Baptists objected particularly to the prohibition on meetings at the "night season" when their members could sometimes "be better spared . . . from the necessary duties of their callings." The Committee on Religion was asked to bring in another bill in 1774 [49] when the strength of the Henry party had been greatly augmented. From such seeds would soon come the separation of Church and State, the principle with which Jefferson and Madison are indissolubly connected.

Henry's influence as an advocate of religious liberty had been further increased by his admission in 1769 to practice before the Gen-

[250]

eral Court.[50] This was the supreme legal tribunal of the colony, and for most Virginians the court of last resort, since appeals to England were slow and expensive. In fact, such appeals were not permitted save in exceptional instances. The General Court was composed of the Governor and his Council sitting as a judicial body. Gentlemen chosen for their wealth, their ability and influence on behalf of the established order were competent to judge important cases argued by the leading lawyers of the colony. When the House of Lords served as a supreme court in England, there were always a few peers of sufficient training and ability to perform the necessary duties. Similarly, the ruling Virginians, with their English gift of improvisation, managed to have on the Council several members with legal training or at least the requisite experience and ability in other respects.

In a typical petition to the General Court during the fall of 1772 Henry wrote that his client, John Richmond, had been unable because of infirmity of mind and body to defend himself against a common capias in Louisa court. He had, therefore, been unlawfully ordered to pay a judgment of £19.19.6, and Henry asked for a writ of supersedeas and annulment of the judgment.[51] At the bottom of the petition is written, "Let Supersedeas issue," and it is signed by Lord Dunmore, the incumbent Governor, and by William and Thomas Nelson, members of the wealthy trading and planting family still commemorated in the stately Nelson house at Yorktown.

The jurisdiction of the General Court extended to all cases, whether on original process or appeal, involving not less than £10 or two thousand pounds of tobacco. Recognizing the difficulty in obtaining judgments against those local nabobs, the vestrymen and justices of the county court, the law also gave the General Court original jurisdiction in such cases regardless of the amounts involved. The General Court held two sessions, in April and October, so that Henry could frequently argue his causes, then remain in Williamsburg for the meeting of the Assembly. There were also court sessions in June and December for the trial of criminal cases;[52] in view of his continuing interest in this field, he must have been frequently in attendance.

Because of the number of frivolous appeals, a statute had been passed prohibiting lawyers from practicing in both the General Court and county courts; [53] Henry could now concentrate his practice and not spend so much time jogging over the bad roads of the county circuits. While restricted from trying cases in the county courts, he continued to draw up papers, give legal advice and lend money to local clients.[54] There were a number of resident lawyers, men of culture and ability, who practiced at the court in newly formed Pittsylvania County. But Henry's exceptional powers were widely recognized—his legal opinions being considered in the back country "like a court of last appeal"—and a Pittsylvania planter wrote in 1770 urging his brother-in-law to get the opinion from Henry which had been "long expected"; if he would only send it, the fee would be returned next month by Charles Lynch, the Bedford burgess.[55]

At the bar of the General Court, Henry was associated with such outstanding Virginia lawyers as Attorney-General Randolph, Treasurer Nicholas, and Thomson Mason. But the erudite George Wythe and Edmund Pendleton were the colonial giants. Although none of his contemporaries was more conscientious than Wythe in selecting and preparing his cases, Pendleton was the more adaptable trial lawyer and won more cases in court. Tall and personable, he was a man to have with you when business was to be done or afterwards "in discreet enjoyment of the convivial cup," and he retained a host of friends.[56]

Henry never had an open break with Pendleton during these years. They met at frequent sessions of the General Court and of the Burgesses besides less formal occasions, such as when they served together as managers of a lottery. It was an age when even colleges and churches held lotteries to secure needed funds, and the enterprising Sheriff Harry Tompkins of Hanover used this means to discharge a considerable debt to the treasury incurred by indulging too many hard-pressed debtors. Owing to the great scarcity of cash, Tompkins did not believe that he could secure enough returns from sale of his property by the usual means and therefore advertised the lottery, with top prizes of valuable tracts of land; a young male slave, Virginia-born, valued at £70; two female slaves, aged eighteen and fifteen respectively, each "big with her second child," and lesser awards of a slave, cattle, and household furnishings. Henry, Pendleton, and John Syme, as directors of the lottery and in charge of the tickets, were expected to be present for the drawings at Hanover Courthouse on New Year's Day, 1768.[57]

There was no better trial lawyer than Pendleton for civil cases at the General Court, just as there was no better debater in the Assembly. Moreover, his position as a conservative leader did not lessen his influence with the judges. This was illustrated by an incident a few years before the Revolution when the reactionary Lord Dunmore was presiding over the court.

On one occasion Thomson Mason, Pendleton's associate in a case before the court, was unable to be present. But George Wythe and Treasurer Nicholas, the opposing lawyers, were ready and pressed for immediate trial.

"Go on, sir," Lord Dunmore urged Pendleton, "for you'll be a match for both of them."

Wythe, like Henry and many Virginians, was no admirer of the Royal Governor, and he rankled from earlier defeats by Pendleton. Rising and bowing low, he replied, "With your Lordship's assistance." [58]

How could Henry have acquired enough legal knowledge and experience to appear successfully before the General Court? Judge Edmund Winston, his law student and long-time associate, argued that in reasoning on general principles Henry "did not lose in comparison with any man, and I never heard that he betrayed a want of legal knowledge." Winston said that it would naturally be asked, "How was this possible?" To which he could only reply that Henry acquired without much labor information which in the case of other men was the result of painful research.[59]

Judge Winston further recorded that he was told in Henry's family that Henry employed a considerable portion of his time in reading. Henry's son-in-law, Judge Roane, spoke of his library as consisting of "odd volumes, etc. but of good books." [60] The quality of the legal and classical volumes is evident from the inventory made after his death. The preponderant evidence is that, when he was a member of the General Court, Henry read a few good books and with his quick mind was able to assimilate much information from them which he supplemented by practical experience.

Successful as was Pendleton in trial work, there was one notable instance when Henry won greater plaudits than did his arch-opponent. This was in an Admiralty case involving the captain of a Spanish vessel which, with its cargo, had been libeled under the Navigation Act. Henry was employed as counsel for the defendant. After the trial the elderly William Nelson of Yorktown, a great merchant and long a member of the Council, said that he had never heard a more eloquent or argumentative speech than Henry's and that he considered him greatly superior to Pendleton, Mason, or any other counsel who argued the case. Nelson did not think that Henry had previously given any attention to maritime law and was astonished to find him so familiar with the subject. [61]

Yet, in the general opinion of his contemporaries, Henry was most distinguished in jury trials. We may well accept the statement of William Wirt, [62] which is substantiated by the testimony of eyewitnesses to Henry's criminal trials in later years. Wirt states:

> The defence of criminal causes was his [Henry's] great professional forte. . . . These causes brought him into direct collision with Mr. John Randolph, who had now succeeded Peyton as the attorney-general.
>
> Mr. Randolph was, in person and manners, among the most elegant gentlemen in the colony, and in his profession one of the most splendid ornaments of the bar. He was a polite scholar, as well as a profound lawyer, and his eloquence also was of a high order. His voice, action, style, were stately, and uncommonly impressive; but gigantic as he was in relation to other men, he was but a pigmy, when opposed in a criminal trial to the arch magician, Henry. In those cases Mr. Henry was perfectly irresistible. He adapted himself, without effort, to the character of the cause; seized, with the quickness of intuition, its defensible point, and never permitted the jury to lose sight of it. Sir

Joshua Reynolds has said of Titian, that, by a few strokes of his pencil, he knew how to mark the image and character of whatever object he attempted; and produced by this means a truer representation than any of his predecessors, who finished every hair. In like manner, Mr. Henry, by a few master-strokes upon the evidence, could in general stamp upon the cause whatever image or character he pleased; and convert it into tragedy or comedy, at his sovereign will, and with a power which no efforts of his adversary could counteract. He never wearied the jury by a dry and minute analysis of the evidence; he did not expend his strength in finishing the hairs; he produced all his high effect by those rare master-touches, and by the resistless skill with which, in a very few words, he could mould and color the prominent facts of a cause to his purpose. Hence he was, beyond doubt, the ablest defender of criminals in Virginia. . . .

The criminal cases were heard in the second week of the court term. The trials were usually short, and Henry used his quick wit, his knowledge of human nature and forensic gifts to avert or ameliorate the harsh punishments of the day. If his persuasive arts had been unavailing, the client would perhaps be branded or whipped or even left swinging on the gibbet before his lawyer was long returned to Hanover. Lengthy prison terms were not the vogue in colonial Virginia.

Henry never lost his simple tastes, but he now adjusted his attire to meet the requirements of a dignified appeal court and wore the customary black suit and tie wig. His appearance, at best more impressive than handsome, was greatly improved by his new attire. We derive some sharply etched details from the recollections of a young law student, St. George Tucker,[63] who first observed Henry in 1772 while Tucker was attending sessions of the high court.

Henry's face was long, thin, and dark. Although, like other rural Virginians, he spent much time out of doors his skin was not ruddy but somewhat inclined to sallowness. His profile was of the Roman type, although his nose was rather long than high. His forehead was high and straight; his eyebrows, long and full. His eyes, if we may

[255]

accept Tucker's description, were a dark gray which, crowned by dark eyebrows, appeared almost black. On the other hand, later descriptions of his eyes had them blue like the sky.

His eyes were indeed noteworthy, but the most vivid impression generally left of Henry's appearance—and confirmed by his portraits —is one of thinness and to some extent even of angularity. This is further indicated by Tucker's description of his hollow cheeks and his long, though well rounded, chin.

Of Henry's mouth Tucker saw nothing worthy of description except when he was skillfully employing his lawyer's arts. When about to express a modest dissent from some opinion on which he was commenting, Tucker continued, Henry "had a half sort of smile, in which the want of conviction was, perhaps, more strongly expressed than that cynical or satirical emotion which probably prompted it. His manner and address to the court and jury might be deemed the excess of humility, diffidence, and modesty. If, as rarely happened, he had occasion to answer any remark from the bench, it was impossible for meekness herself to assume a manner less presumptuous; but in the smile, of which I have been speaking, you might anticipate the want of conviction expressed in his answers, at the moment that he submitted to the 'superior wisdom' of the court, with a grace that would have done honour to the most polished courtier in Westminster Hall." [64]

When replying to counsel, Henry, in his remarks on the evidence and conduct of the litigants, preserved the same deference and politeness. But they were still accompanied by the skeptical smile when he felt the occasion demanded it.

In general, Henry's manner was solemn and impressive. But the voice, so often a vital factor in great oratory, was not so remarkable, Tucker recalled, for pleasing tones or variety. If never melodious, as he was inclined to think, it was never harsh, not even when raised. "It was clear, distinct, and capable of that emphasis which was one of Henry's greatest charms."

Henry had the gift, as was later exemplified in several of his famous cases, of making solemn-faced statements which would be extremely amusing to his audience. This was noted by Tucker, who stated that Henry's countenance was grave even when clothed with the half-smile to which he had alluded. His face was marked with lines of deep reflection and he looked older than his years.

> When speaking in public, he never (even on occasions when he excited it in others) had anything like pleasantry in his countenance, his manner, or the tone of his voice [Tucker concluded]. "You would swear he had never uttered or laughed at a joke. In short, in debate either at the bar or elsewhere, his manner was so earnest and impressive, united with a contraction or knitting of his brows which appeared habitual, as to give to his countenance a severity sometimes bordering upon the appearance of anger or contempt suppressed, while his language and gesture exhibited nothing but what was perfectly decorous. He was emphatic, without vehemence or declamation; animated, but never boisterous; nervous, without recourse to intemperate language; and clear, though not always methodical.

From his account books we can gather some further impressions of Henry's legal activities. In one of his more remunerative cases he charged Captain John Lawrence of Hanover a £24 fee in 1772 for fee and allowances.[65] In other instances picked at random we find him disbursing some £100 at five per cent commission as attorney for a woman and her children; representing several merchants, partly, it appears, in debt cases; charging a Lunenburg client £5 for his injunction against Jefferson and Garland and another £5 for dissolving an injunction respecting eleven other debts.[66]

Although Henry still had numerous clients in Hanover and Louisa, we now find him handling appeals for clients at such widely scattered points as the Shenandoah Valley, Charles City County on the James river below Richmond, Amherst on the upper James, Essex on the Rappahannock, Richmond City (an appeal of James Galt, the goldsmith, against the Henrico sheriff), Norfolk, and Charleston, South Carolina.[67] As a lawyer, he saw much of the seamy side of life; he knew criminals and sharp traders, spendthrifts and chronic debtors from personal contacts in and out of the courtroom. Hard experience taught him to mix his idealism with a dash of practicality.

When selling a gelding for £22 in 1772 to a Newcastle merchant, he was at pains to record that the transaction was in the presence of a witness, his brother-in-law Valentine Wood.[68]

It was remarkable how many men Henry fought in the courtroom without incurring their personal enmity. His wit and humor, his persuasive appeals to the judges, the opposing litigants could usually recognize as tools of the trade, not used with personal rancor. By the early 1770's his opponents were including a larger smattering of Virginians with influential positions or connections. Thus, a tall, taciturn frontiersman, Andrew Lewis of Augusta, whom he sued in a debt case for another Scotch-Irish litigant, was the future Revolutionary general; John Augustine Washington, another opposing litigant, was the nephew of Colonel George. In the political arena, Henry's devastating oratory, his revolutionary ideas, left scars not erased by his geniality and simplicity in private life. But there is no available evidence indicating that Andrew Lewis, Augustine Washington, or indeed any of Henry's numerous opponents in unpleasant litigation during these years ever nursed resulting grievances against him.

Financial dealings, with his own family, however, involved a special problem. Henry continued to keep detailed accounts of monetary transactions with immediate relatives such as his father, father-in-law, half-brother, and other relatives. We have noted some hint of a difficulty with John Shelton over an unfulfilled provision of Sarah's dowry and later transactions. The accounts for 1771-1772 with that poor manager, though public-spirited citizen, John Syme, may help to explain a later unpleasantness with his half-brother. Henry now charged him £12 for six days' "close work" and £107 for sundry work in connection with some land transactions and other legal services—on which nothing had been paid.[69]

Among other troublesome debtors besides Syme about this time were William Donald, the Hanover merchant who in 1771 owed Henry over £175 plus the value of two hogsheads of his tobacco.[70] But Henry's collections were still large enough to greatly offset such deficits and his reputation as a lawyer was steadily increasing. Further

[258]

evidence of this is found in the confidence shown him by the respected Robert Carter Nicholas. In May, 1771, Nicholas paid Henry £10 for suits brought by the colonial government against the securities of the John Robinson estate.[71] Then, finding that his duties as Treasurer allowed no time for his law practice, he turned it over to Henry.[72] First, however, he had offered the business to another rising lawyer, Thomas Jefferson. Young Jefferson had acquired an impressive clientele within a few years, not merely in the back country but also among some Eastern aristocrats.[73] If Jefferson's attention to the law had not become overshadowed by public duties and other interests of a versatile genius, he would have become a formidable rival of Henry's in the courtroom, despite Jefferson's lack of oratorical gifts.

In 1764-1768, the last five years before Henry began practice in the General Court, he had served in some twenty-two hundred cases, and his collections had totalled over £2,500. With the legal limitations on his county practice after he began the appeal work in Williamsburg, it is not surprising that the number of his cases was greatly reduced. It declined from 647 in 1767 and 479 in 1768 to slightly over two hundred in each of the following years. But his collections remained at the comfortable figures of £538 in 1769 and £957 the next year.

The following year—1771—was the high point of Henry's financial success as a lawyer before the Revolution. Although recording only 102 cases, he had collections of £1,300, at least $13,000 in current exchange.[74] And this was in addition to the income from his large land holdings, including the newly acquired Scotchtown estate, and from the unrecorded cash payments for criminal cases. But the next year he charged aggregate fees of only £242 and his collections dropped to £78—one-seventeenth that of the previous year.[75]

An immediate cause was the flood of 1771. At Turkey Island, below Richmond on the James, a monument still commemorates the great flood of May in that year when the large rivers of Virginia overflowed their banks rising to heights the colonists had never before known. William Nelson wrote Lord Hillsborough that four thousand hogsheads of tobacco were destroyed on the James and Rappahannock alone, and that this was trifling in comparison with the loss in human lives, homes, crops, and livestock. The elderly Nelson, now Acting Governor, dolefully depicted the flood as the most dreadful catastrophe since the first settlement.[76] Of immediate concern to Henry was the ruin of many merchants and the general loss of credit. Even before this, Treasurer Nicholas had been threatening rigorous methods to collect back taxes,[77] while in Hanover it was not surprising to find that a storekeeper, having closed his shop, was advertising that his overdue accounts would be turned over to an attorney.[78]

Many of the country folk could not afford to pay the petty fees in local litigation, much less the larger, though still moderate, charges which Henry was permitted to charge for appeals to the General Court. His precipitate loss in charges and collections was partly explained, to be sure, by the time he was now giving to his Scotchtown plantation. But there was a more serious difficulty. In May, 1773, he and five other lawyers practicing at the General Court—Pendleton, Jefferson, John Randolph, James Mercer, and Gustavus Scott—published a statement saying that they could no longer continue their practice on the present basis. Even the "confessedly moderate" fees permitted them by the law for practice in the General Court were withheld in great proportion by the unworthy part of their clientele. Some regulation had become absolutely necessary, and after October 10, 1773, the lawyers agreed not to give any opinions on cases for the General Court except on payment of the whole fee. No suit or motion would be prosecuted or defended unless the tax and half the fee had already been advanced.[79] Henry and his associates were at pains, however, to express their hopes that the "worthy part" of their clients would not disapprove of the announcement.[80]

Whatever prospects Henry had of increasing his collections were dissipated by immediate events preceding the Revolutionary War. In September, 1774, while he and Pendleton were serving as delegates to the First Continental Congress in Philadelphia, a Virginian wrote a London correspondent that the General Court could not carry on business "for want of two of our Principal Co[u]nsels, (to wit Mr. Pendleton and Mr. Henry) . . . and the other Lawyers out of respect to them & the Errand they were on refused to come to the Bar." [81] Actually, these lawyers did not want the court to meet then, for reasons which overshadow any individual personalities and require later amplification. When the General Court went into oblivion with the Revolution, Henry was recognized as one of its leading attorneys.

As a lawyer he had acquired more learning and versatility than is generally appreciated. But the genius, the oratorical gifts and knowledge of human nature that he brought to many of his cases cannot be surmised from the bare records of his account book or scattered data. In 1771, for example, Henry listed this charge against his brother-in-law Colonel Valentine Wood of Goochland: "To fee in y.r appeal v Doct.r Simeon Harris—£2.10." Wood was accused by Dr. Harris of saying false and defamatory words against him, to wit that Harris was a deserter from the King's service and "nothing more than a Surgeons boy in some Regiment to the Northward." Colonel Wood bore a good reputation; it is unlikely that Dr. Harris' medical qualifications were of the highest. Doubtless in exposing his quackery Henry had an opportunity to display his peculiar talents, solemn-faced humor along with the rest. But we only know that, after various delays, the case was appealed and his argument convinced the councillors sitting in their august splendor.[82]

More definite proof of Henry's talents was given by Joseph Scott, the Marshal of Virginia. He had been summoned, at much inconvenience to his private business, to serve as a witness in a distant court where Henry practiced. His case having been concluded, Scott was further inconvenienced by being ordered to serve on a jury. There were several speakers and his patience was almost exhausted. When Henry arose, Scott thought that he would be kept for the evening, if not the night. Much to his surprise Henry appeared to have taken no more than fifteen minutes for his reply. Scott could scarcely believe his own watch or those of other jurors when he found that Henry had been speaking for upward of two hours.[83]

Such spellbinding, and indeed all the positive qualities that Henry could master, would be needed when he became a leader in the forth-coming Revolution. Before drawing the curtain upon this critical era it is necessary to trace a few preparatory events with which he was concerned in Williamsburg and elsewhere, including a crisis in his private affairs.

15

Mounting Political
and Personal Problems

The notion of a virtual Representation hath been so often
and fully refuted, that it surely is unnecessary to multiply
Words on that Head: if the Property, the Liberties, the Lives
of Millions of his Majesty's most dutiful Subjects are merely
ideal, how deplorable must be their Condition.
——*Journal of Burgesses, 1766-1769*

I saw nothing there [in London] but the ruins of Loo,
Lady Hertford's cribbage, and Lord Botetourt, like patience
on a monument, smiling in grief.
——*Letters of Horace Walpole*

O N MARCH 3, 1768, the amiable and versatile Governor
Fauquier died at the Palace in Williamsburg after a tedious illness
borne with fortitude.[1] The meeting of the Assembly had already been
twice postponed, and elderly John Blair, President of the Council
and Acting Governor, finally called it to meet on March 31.[2] Usually punctilious in his attendance, Henry was absent from the brief
session, presumably for personal reasons.[3] For some weeks that spring
we find no evidence of legal work, and this may have been the time
when he made his trip to the Holston lands. He was disappointed
not to take a hand when the quarrel with England was revived in

the Burgesses, especially in view of the ominous county petitions.

Under the Rockingham ministry, Parliament had renewed the billeting or mutiny act, and the colonial assemblies were required to make provision for quartering British troops stationed within their jurisdiction. When the Assembly in New York, headquarters of the British forces, complied only in part, it was suspended upon order of Lord Shelburne, the Secretary of State.[4] A storm of protest rose. In Virginia the hand of the Henry-Lee party, or of their frequent ally, Richard Bland, was seen in anti-billeting petitions from numerous freeholders of counties near Louisa[5] and from residents of Westmoreland and Prince William.[6] The influence of Henry's Stamp Act resolutions is evident in the wording both of these petitions and subsequent memorials sent by the Burgesses to the King, Lords, and Commons, protesting the new Townshend duties and the suspension of the New York Assembly. The memorials, drawn up by a committee headed by Richard Bland, show the definite result of his constitutional arguments, now popularized by Henry and other advanced patriots.[7] After conceding the right of Parliament to make laws regulating colonial trade, the Burgesses declared that the Townshend duties embodied an import tax levied upon a large part of the British exports that were necessaries of life. The duties were levied without "the most distant view to the Interests of Commerce, but merely to raise a Revenue." Their real purpose was to force the colonists to part with their money against their inclinations, and therefore they constituted a tax "internal to all Intents and Purposes."[8]

Even the duties collected at the ports on lead, glass, painters' colors, and tea were thus declared internal taxes. It was true that internal taxes had seldom been collected from the colonies. And undoubtedly they were inexpedient and inequitable, especially since the colonies could not be fairly represented in a parliament at distant Westminster.[9] On the other hand, to declare that Parliament did not have the right to levy them was certainly to enter upon doubtful constitutional ground.[10] In the discriminating words of H. J. Eckenrode, the Americans of that day "were too English to be much disturbed by inconsistencies." They had been so aroused by the menace of the Stamp Act that they were determined not to submit to any more taxes imposed by Parliament.

"It is not for us to blame them," Eckenrode concludes. "Liberty cannot be made strictly dependent on a series of constitutional precedents; law seldom measures the real issues at stake in history. However defective the fathers may have been in logic,—and that they were sometimes defective we must admit,—nevertheless, they stood for the principle of self-government against the world-old system of arbitrary rule." [11]

Henry, still in his early thirties and with the impatience of the backwoodsman at all onerous restrictions, undoubtedly agreed with this extension of the colonial position. His viewpoint was strengthened by developments at the next session of the Burgesses and by other stirring events in the following years.

To a considerable degree the history of Virginia from 1768 until the Revolution turned upon the character of the colonial governors. There had been a riot in Boston as the result of the seizure by customs officials of the sloop *Liberty* which belonged to that popular merchant and genteel smuggler John Hancock. After the disorders it was decided to send two regiments of the line there; at the same time an effort was made to propitiate Virginia. General Amherst, Pitt's protégé, was dismissed from the governorship, the fat sinecure which he had been enjoying *in absentia* while Lieutenant-Governor Fauquier shouldered the work and responsibility. The plum was then given to Norborne Berkeley, Baron de Botetourt, a Court favorite impoverished by gambling,[12] who was sent personally to Virginia, thus ending a long-standing grievance of the Virginians, who had been without a resident governor since the late seventeenth century.

It was especially important to propitiate the Old Dominion. For, as Horace Walpole noted, while not the most mutinous of the colonies, she contained "the best heads and the principle boutes-feux." [13]

"Virginia aristocrats dearly loved a lord." [14] Would Botetourt be able to undermine the influence of the patriot party? A polished bachelor, amiable and eager to please, he quieted forebodings and

[265]

aroused hopes not confined to widows and virgins of the local aristocracy. His arrival in a seventy-four-gun ship, specially assigned by
the Royal Navy, his journey to Williamsburg in the coach of state,
and his reception there were all calculated to flatter the Virginians
and to strengthen the loyalist faction.[15] It might well seem that the
Stamp Act agitation and the succeeding events were only a fading
dream! But the people were not to be judged too strictly by outward
appearances. Loyal they were and loyal they intended to remain, yet
the liberal leaders had ideas of government far different from those
which the ingratiating Botetourt was expected to encourage. Even "a
friend to Decency and Moderation" like Treasurer Nicholas remained attached to the "main Principle," as events would soon
prove.[16]

After various delays, Lord Botetourt finally summoned a new
assembly to meet on the second Monday in May, 1769.[17] Patrick
Henry and William Macon, Jr., were elected to the Burgesses from
Hanover.[18] How highly the electors of his native county thought of
Henry is shown by the fact that this time he did not solicit the position or even appear at the polls.[19] Now that the quarrel with England
had entered a new stage, the Hanover people were the more eager
to have Henry rather than the less able John Syme or Samuel Meredith represent them in the Burgesses. "It was to him [Henry] that
we were indebted for the unanimity that prevailed among us," Jefferson would later recall.[20]

Due to the running difficulties with England and, above all, the
arrival of the new governor, there was an unusually large crowd at
the opening of the Assembly on May 8. They witnessed a greater
display than ever before put on by a Virginia governor. Nothing if
not a good showman, Lord Botetourt emerged from the Palace wearing a rich and handsome dress with a coat of gold thread. He entered
the elegant coach, reportedly given him by George III, and was
pulled by six white horses down the street to the Capitol.[21] On the
following day he entertained fifty-two guests at dinner,[22] among
them, probably, Henry as a leading member of the Assembly, though

with his simple frontier tastes Patrick was possibly annoyed rather than dazzled by all the opening ceremonial.

Although it was an important season for the crops, there were only two Burgesses absent throughout the session, a notable contrast to the previous meeting. There was also a sizable sprinkling of new faces, among them a tall, raw-boned, freckled-faced young man from Albemarle with whom Henry's political career was now becoming inextricably connected. After returning to his plantation and becoming established as a lawyer, Thomas Jefferson had been elected a member of the Burgesses. It was "the most dignified body of men ever assembled to legislate," the gratified Jefferson later commented.[23]

After the usual preliminaries and an exchange of compliments with Lord Botetourt, the House took another step along the road to revolution. The Speaker, Peyton Randolph, informed the Burgesses that, in accordance with its directions at the last session, he had written to the various speakers of the assemblies in America regarding certain Acts of Parliament and announced that he had several replies available for the members.

As in the case of the Stamp Act debates, Virginia was a key province. Since June, 1768, the Massachusetts Assembly had been meeting under the shadow of British guns,[24] and in New York and other colonies the situation was becoming more alarming.

"Virginia, sir, has maintained the common cause, with such attention, spirit, and temper as has gained her the highest degree of reputation among the other colonies. It is as much in her power to dishearten them, as to encourage them," John Dickinson wrote Richard Henry Lee in a letter of January 16, 1769,[25] which Lee probably discussed with Henry.

The Old Dominion was then the largest and most populous of the colonies. The other colonies watched her action with great anxiety, none the less so since some of her local leaders were taking counsel of their caution,[26] as had happened in the Stamp Act debate. The key to the situation lay in the positive action or lack of it taken by the liberal chieftains. Fortunately, they again believed that silence

would be deemed a tacit surrender of the colonial rights and acknowl-
edgement that Parliament could at pleasure tax the unrepresented
Americans.[27]

Henry was in attendance at all the subsequent meetings of the
Assembly until elected a delegate to the Continental Congress in
1774. "He was as well suited to the times as any man ever was, and
it is not now easy to say what we should have done without Patrick
Henry," Jefferson recalled. "He was far above all in maintaining
the spirit of the Revolution. His influence was most extensive with
the members from the upper counties, and his boldness and their
votes overawed and controlled the more timid aristocratic gentlemen of the lower part of the State. His eloquence was peculiar, if
indeed it should be called eloquence; for it was impressive and sublime, beyond what can be imagined."

Although it was difficult after Henry spoke to tell what he had
said, Jefferson continued, "yet, while he was speaking, it always
seemed directly to the point. When he had spoken in opposition to
my opinion, had produced a great effect, and I myself been highly
delighted and moved, I have asked myself when he ceased what the
d——l has he said?" And Jefferson added that he could never answer his query.[28]

It is unlikely that Henry and Jefferson were opposed on any important measures when Jefferson was a fledgling burgess at the May,
1769, session. In fact, he recalled that after he entered the House,
"the exact conformity of our political opinions strengthened our
friendship, and indeed, the old leaders of the house being substantially firm, we had not after this any differences of opn [opinion]
in the H. of B. [House of Burgesses] on matters of principles, tho
sometimes on matters of form." [29]

The Burgesses, to be sure, had their share of cautious and vacillat-
ing members. But if Henry and the other liberal leaders had any
difficulty in securing action from the House, all obstacles were removed by receipt of the joint address of the Lords and Commons
to the King, with its open attack upon the rights of the individual and
of jury trial. On May 16 (that warm spring month seemed a favorite

time for momentous action), the House met in the Committee of the Whole and, after a noteworthy discussion, adopted unanimously a series of four resolutions.

The first resolution upheld the right of self-taxation, much as did Henry's Stamp Act resolutions. Two of the others, which covered new ground, boldly affirmed "the undoubted privilege" of petitioning the King for redress of grievances and declared that the trial of colonials beyond the seas for crimes committed in America was "highly derogatory of the rights of British subjects, as thereby the inestimable privilege of being tried by a jury from their vicinage, as well as the liberty of summoning and producing witnesses in such trial, will be taken away from the party accused."

British justice was then severe and uncertain enough even for citizens of England, tried by their neighbors. Little mercy could be expected by any American rioter tried overseas, much less a Henry or an Adams. Although there is little or no reason to believe that Henry was disturbed by his own personal danger, yet the address to the King which the Burgesses ordered to be prepared did contain personal implications for certain of its leaders. Realizing the advantage of a united stand, the Assembly ordered copies of the resolution to be sent to the speakers of the other colonial assemblies and requested their concurrence.[30]

A committee was appointed to draw up the address to George III, consisting of the chairman, John Blair, Jr., Henry's associate in the land company, Henry, Richard Henry Lee, Treasurer Nicholas, Thompson Mason, and Benjamin Harrison. With the exception of Harrison, a landed magnate from the lower James and brother-in-law of Speaker Randolph, all the members were liberals or moderates. The address presented and adopted the next day is in such finished literary form—is such a model composition of its kind—that the committee members must have stayed up late completing it.[31] Blair, Lee, and Mason all had some literary skill and it is likely that they contributed more to the final wording of the address than did Henry.[32] Yet, behind all the polite forms, the references to the burgesses' loyalty and affection for George III, their pious wish that

[269]

even after death he "may taste the fullest Fruition of eternal Bliss," there is a firmness and boldness that bespeak Henry and his Westmoreland colleague. In branding the British action as illegal and unconstitutional, Henry and his colleagues were on doubtful ground. Nevertheless, it was another case where a narrow legalistic interpretation of the British law did not cover fundamental human rights.

What was the effect of the address upon Lord Botetourt? Friendly as he was to the colonists, Lord Botetourt was mindful of his obligation to the British government. The House, meeting behind closed doors on Wednesday morning, May 17, 1769, passed unanimously the resolution offered by Henry and his associates. But the vote had hardly been taken when the Burgesses were called upstairs to the council chamber to meet the Governor. "I have heard of your Resolves and augur ill of their Effect," he said, and ordered the House to be forthwith dissolved.[33]

But the members were ready to stand by their guns. Without pausing for refreshment and by obvious prearrangement, they proceeded up Duke of Gloucester Street to the Raleigh Tavern. Henry, a lover of music and of conviviality within moderate bounds, must have already enjoyed many associations with this popular hostelry. Here in the wainscoted Apollo Room the gentlemen gathered for what was in effect an adjourned session of the Burgesses. With an efficiency which indicates that the leaders had the situation well in hand, the state of the colony was examined and a committee appointed to offer the next day some regulations for an association to curb British trade.

What part Henry took in the deliberations we can only surmise. The Association is known to have been based largely on resolutions prepared by the masterly hand of George Mason of Gunston Hall, who was not present at the meeting, and offered by his friend and neighbor, George Washington.[34] That Henry favored the agreement wholeheartedly, we may be sure; his name is near the top of the long list of signers in the *Journal*, following that of Speaker Randolph and grouped with Nicholas, Bland, Richard Henry Lee, Washington and Jefferson, and even the conservative Archibald Cary.[35]

[270]

With such leadership and unanimity, it is not surprising that the Association not only condemned the late trade regulations of Parliament and especially the "unconstitutional" Townshend Act, but also agreed not to import, or to purchase after September 1, goods taxed by Parliament to raise a revenue in America. Only a few exceptions were listed and provisions were made for a later ban on the importation of slaves and wines unless the obnoxious Acts were repealed.[36]

After the business was finished, the Associators proceeded to celebrate. Drinking toasts was then a popular custom and used throughout the colonies as a propaganda device. There were the customary libations to the Royal Family and the Governor, and (to further soothe the conservative or moderate members) to the late Speaker Robinson and the Treasurer. But the concluding toasts—to such subjects as constitutional British liberty and its supporters, Colonel Barré, and "The Farmer" and "The Monitor"—were unmistakable in their radical Whig implications.

Altogether, eleven toasts were gulped down not long after midday, testing the capacity of even the most experienced topers. Perhaps it was just as well that the gentlemen then "retired." [37] Even when they were at home, too many planters accepted the agreeable supposition that alcohol would protect them against the rigors of the climate:

> The cordial drop, the morning dram I sing,
> The midday toddy, and the evening sling.[38]

What was Henry's aim at this time? Richard Henry Lee, writing the Earl of Shelburne soon after the dissolution of the Burgesses, declared that its "proceedings . . . may, to some, appear the overflowings of a seditious and disloyal madness: but your lordship's just, and generous attachment to the proper rights and liberties of mankind, will discover in them, nothing more than a necessary and manly assertion, of social privileges founded in reason, guaranteed by the British constitution, and rendered sacred by a possession of near two hundred years." [39] We have no record as yet of any stronger statement by Henry. But there is no evidence that he suffered from

[271]

any misgivings or failed to push any measures for which he felt he could muster adequate support.

The power that Henry had gained even in a conservative eastern county is indicated by the recollections of Judge Spencer Roane. His father, who served in the Burgesses for about a decade after 1768, came home "in raptures" over Henry.

"That a plain man, of ordinary though respected family, should beard their aristocracy by whom we were then cursed and ruled, and overthrow them in the cause of independence," was gratifying to a man of his father's Whig principles, Roane declared. The elder Roane regarded Henry as the organ of the great body of people, "an instrument by whom the bigwigs were to be thrown down, and liberty and independence established."

Among his earliest recollections, Judge Roane continued, was that of his father paying the expenses of one Bradfute, a learned Scottish teacher residing in their family, to accompany him to Williamsburg to hear Henry speak. Upon his return, the elder Roane laughed at Bradfute for having been so much enchanted with Henry's eloquence as to have unconsciously squirted tobacco juice from the gallery on the heads of the burgesses. In his excitement, Bradfute almost fell down to the House floor.[40]

Although Henry had gained a powerful influence, there were also signs that he would be stubbornly opposed. When the Speaker made the appointments for important standing committees at the November, 1769, session, they continued to consist largely of such conservative members as Edmund Pendleton, Carter Braxton, Archibald Cary, and Charles Carter. But Henry was on the key committees of Privileges and Elections, and Propositions and Grievances, and the newly constituted Committee on Religion.[41] He would continue to hold important committee posts until the Revolution.

The Association justified the hopes of Henry and other leading subscribers. In Virginia and some of her sister colonies the agreement was in large measure enforced; in others, at least it served as a threat to arbitrary ministers. At the end of July, 1769, Henry could read in the *Gazette* that the Association was meeting with the greatest encouragement in every county from which the paper had reports.[42] There was some opposition to the Spartan program of non-importation, but within a few months Virginia cloth was widely used and at least one lady, "a little incommoded with corns," even wore moccasins.[43] Flax and wool were then produced on the Henry plantation or were easily available. He had acquired a loom and flax sickle and in both March of 1768 and 1769 planted a half-bushel of flax seed.[44] He was doubtless among the burgesses appearing in Virginia cloth at a ball given by them in December to the Governor, Council, and ladies and gentlemen of Williamsburg.[45]

The Association, like the Stamp Act resolutions, offered a needed fillip to the opposition in other colonies. "Don't you think the Virginians have behaved like men?" wrote an Edenton, North Carolina, gentleman to a Philadelphia friend. "I fancy Lord [Botetourt] . . . must by this time know that Titles, Burgundy and a gilt coach will not be sufficient Inducements to bribe men out of their Liberties." [46] The *Essex Gazette* declared that the resolves had inspirited the other colonies. It saw in them "the same Sense of Justice and Value for the Constitutional Rights of America, the same Vigour and Boldness, that breath'd thro' the first Resolves of that truly honourable House, and greatly contributed to form the free and generous Spirit in which the Colonies are now one." [47]

Colonial assemblies in North Carolina, Rhode Island, and New York adopted the Virginia resolves in entirety while others, including Massachusetts and Maryland, copied them in substance. "The whole continent from New England to Georgia seems firmly fixed: like a strong, well-constructed arch, the more weight there is laid upon it the firmer it stands," boasted the *Massachusetts Gazette*.[48] The Virginia Association met with opposition from the Tories in other colonies and some of the Whigs were either slow to subscribe or guilty of backsliding.[49] On the whole, however, the Association helped to stimulate palliative measures by the government.

In London the ministry was encompassed with difficulties comparable to those at the height of the Stamp Act agitation. The opposition to the government in Virginia and other colonies coincided with a violent agitation at home. Not much was to be expected of a venial, servile Parliament, labeled by a later historian as perhaps the worst that ever sat.[50] But the vocal minority favoring the American colonies drew strength from the able leadership of Burke and from the pressure on the trading interests by the colonial non-importation agreements. To this was added the dangerous discontent following the repeated expulsions of John Wilkes from Parliament, and the deadly letters by Junius, the anonymous political satirist. Whatever Wilkes' failings, Henry, Lee, and most Virginians could only conclude that he was deprived of the seat in Parliament to which the Middlesex electors had legally returned him.[51] The bitter animosity of King and ministers to him was a gross flaunting of the popular will. While Wilkes, with the support of the turbulent London populace, resumed his agitation (duly depicted with anti-ministerial coloring in the *Virginia Gazette*), Junius continued with unerring knowledge and even literary distinction to expose the weaknesses of many exalted personages.

Henry owned a copy of the letters of this anonymous political writer and, so far as his knowledge extended, probably agreed with George Mason that they were "certainly superior to anything of the kind that ever appeared" in the English language.[52] The volume was reinforced by dozens of articles quoting or referring to Junius in the *Virginia Gazette*, giving Henry a full opportunity to reflect on Junius' bold ideas, no less appealing for their revelation of personal frailties and scandals.

Prudence and imbedded respect for authority had led Henry and other liberal leaders to avoid open attack on the character of the King and ministers. Above all, there had been an effort to indicate that obnoxious measures were the work of bad ministers; George III was uninformed or ill-advised. But what could Henry and his associates, already becoming weaned from the Mother Country, think of such diatribes by Junius as the following:

On the Earl of Hillsborough, Secretary for the Colonies:

[274]

When he entered into office, the most refractory of the colonies were still disposed to proceed by the Constitutional methods of petition and remonstrance. Since that period they have been driven into excesses little short of rebellion. . . . [53]

On the Duke of Grafton, then head of the ministry:

> What can enoble slaves, or fools, or cowards?
> Alas! not all the blood of all the Howards.

Junius continued with another obvious reference to Grafton's descent from the Duchess of Cleveland, mistress of Charles II, and repeated as applicable to Grafton the famous saying that Charles "never said a foolish thing, nor ever did a wise one." [54]

Two months later, on March 8, 1770, the first two pages of the supplement to the *Gazette* were filled with another incendiary letter by Junius. And he was now attacking not only ministers and their policies, but His Majesty George III:

It is the misfortune of your life, and originally the cause of every reproach and distress, which has attended your government, that you should never be acquainted with the language of truth, until you heard it in the complaints of your people. It is not, however, too late to correct the error of your education.

The disturbance of the colonies would make it impossible for them to take an active concern in your affairs, as they once pretended to be to your person. They were ready enough to distinguish between you and your Ministers. They complained of an act of the legislature but traced the origin of it no higher than to the servants of the C—— [Crown]. They pleased themselves with the hope, that their S—o—n [Sovereign] if not favorable to their cause, at least was impartial. The decisive, personal part you took [against] them, has effectually banished that first distinction from their minds. They consider you as united with your servants against America, and know how to distinguish the S—r—n and a venal P——t [Parliament] on one side, from sentiments of the English people on the other.

The people of England are loyal to the House of Hanover, not from a vain preference of one family to another, but from a conviction, that the establishment of that family was necessary to the support of their civil and religious liberties. . . .

[275]

The name of Steward of itself, is only contemptible;—armed with the Sovereign authority, their principles were formidable. The Prince, who imitates their conduct, should be warned by their example; and while he plumes himself upon the security of his Title to the Crown, should remember, that as it was acquired by one revolution, it may be lost in another.[55]

In 1770 accumulating political ills, intensified by the savage attacks of Junius, led to the resignation of the Duke of Grafton. He was succeeded as Prime Minister by Lord North, and before the end of the year Henry could enjoy finding the new minister lampooned in the *Gazette* through another reprint from Junius.[56] The attacks would increase until North became the most hated of all the King's ministers. Actually, he was an amiable and humorous gentleman who would nap pleasantly during attacks from the opposition speakers, then awake to come out with a *bon mot*. Yet he would become known as the obsequious servant of a misguided King.

In 1769, Henry charged Treasurer Nicholas for forty-nine days' attendance and sixteen days' traveling as a burgess. For each round trip to Williamsburg he required eight days! And for each day of attendance or travel he was paid only ten shillings,[57] far less than he was making as a lawyer. Allowing for the increase in his business as a result of his Stamp Act speech or other achievements as a burgess, the fact remains that his public service was now given at a personal sacrifice. Nevertheless, with the produce from his farm and slave labor added to his large legal practice,[58] he and Sarah had as comfortable a living as they could ever have hoped for.

Not that there wasn't considerable use for the money in the family coffers. Besides Patrick and his wife, there were by the early 1770's, six children to support, three boys and three girls. The boys, if worthy, should have the college education which Henry's father and uncle had enjoyed and which he had been denied. The girls should have a basic education, with some polite finishing, then dowries to help them make suitable marriages. How much the Henry household was concerned with dressing and preening women and girls, especially daughters of marriageable age, is indicated by a merchant's account against Patrick in late 1770. There were three yards of crimson flannel (for a petticoat?), twenty-five yards of Irish linen, nun's thread, silk, crimson shalloon, buckram, etc., for a total of over £7.[59] And a year earlier Henry had been charged for the transport of four women's saddles.[60] That his daughters were gallivanting about the countryside to a purpose is further indicated by the marriage about this time of Martha (Patsy) and her near-cousin, young John Fontaine of Hanover.[61] Surely the parental eyes beamed at the union of the Henrys and the cultured Huguenot family with whom Patrick already had personal and business ties.[62]

Among that band of French Protestants willing to sacrifice home and possessions for religious principles, the Fontaines were a superior family. Descended from the noble de la Fontaines, they included among the last generations in Europe an M.A. from the college at Guienne, France, and two bachelors of art from Trinity College, Dublin. Before they came to Virginia, one of the Fontaines had married a Maury, ancestor of Henry's old opponent in the Parson's Cause, and they were forming other influential connections. It was characteristic that the Reverend Peter Fontaine provided in his will that no liquor be supplied to make any of the company drunk at his funeral. And his son, Colonel Peter, not only deplored the preoccupation of the Virginians with tobacco at the expense of other trades and occupations, but also wrote a moving condemnation of Negro slavery. With the Fontaines, Henry's family already had numerous ties of blood or friendship; his grandfather, Isaac Winston, had requested his "trusty friend," Colonel Peter, to be one of his executors. Unquestionably, Patsy Henry had made a good match. As in the case of his sisters' marriages, it would strengthen Patrick's political influence as well as give him further contacts with a family of liberal Christian ideals.[63]

It seems likely that Patsy, Henry's eldest and favorite daughter, was married at Scotchtown.[64] The Virginia gentlemen of the eighteenth century—the ruling class with which he was now identified—

[277]

found no better way to enjoy and discreetly display their position than by being masters of fine country establishments. For Henry the realization of this ideal came when he acquired part of the great plantation which Charles Chiswell had developed in upper Hanover. Henry had been seeking a suitable home for several years, and in 1771 he bought the Scotchtown mansion, with the house tract of about 960 acres. The well-established Hanover tradition is that Henry purchased the estate from the Quaker John Payne, father of Dolly Madison. Dolly, the famous White House hostess, lived briefly at Scotchtown as a young girl.

Sometime before his death, Colonel John Chiswell had sold Scotchtown to his son-in-law, John Robinson. After Robinson's death, the great estate was cut up and sold by his executors to John Payne and a few other purchasers. Even after the subdivision, the house tract, acquired by Henry from Payne, was one of the notable Piedmont plantations. In the size of the mansion, the expanse of field, forest, and stream, it was comparable to some of the ducal Tidewater estates.

Scotchtown, eight miles northeast of the present town of Ashland, is near Negrofoot, a crossroads hamlet whose name recalls a grim incident of colonial history.[66] It was a section where there had been large land grants to a few prominent families, and in the 1770's it was still thinly settled. Here Henry could live quietly with his family, yet be within easy riding distance of the upper Fork Church and Mount Brilliant. The hilly country had a salubrious climate which might help his ailing wife, and the plantation was a bargain, picked up for £600.[67] His brother-in-law William Christian, besides sending the good news that Henry's recently purchased land on the upper James had not suffered in the recent flood, congratulated him on the acquisition of the Scotchtown estate.[68] Here Henry might have enjoyed the amenities of life on a large plantation with a number of slaves while continuing his legal and political activities. But again fate intervened. Did the tragic death of Colonel Chiswell cast a shadow over Scotchtown? Family illness of a most distressing sort and the outbreak of the Revolution soon blasted Henry's hopes for happiness on the plantation.

[278]

During 1725-1726 Charles Chiswell had been granted some seven thousand acres along the Newfound, Little, and North rivers of upper Hanover or near by.[69] He seems to have completed the great house by 1732, when William Byrd spoke of being handsomely entertained there although a light-fingered white servant, attached to the household, did ransack his baggage and drink up his brandy. Byrd also referred to the mill a half-mile from the house and to the haunch of well-cased venison which he enjoyed.[70] The new mansion, rectangular with tall chimneys at each end and stone steps, bore a resemblance to Tuckahoe, the Randolph seat in adjoining Goochland County. Charles Chiswell's son, Colonel John Chiswell, had intermarried with that influential family and continued to carry on in the grand tradition until the tragic June day in 1766 when Routlidge found the sharp point of his sword.

Patrick Henry was simpler, less sporting in his tastes than the Chiswells. Nevertheless, he was now owner of a lordly estate: a mansion with sixteen rooms, numerous other buildings, and nearly a thousand spreading acres. When Henry purchased it, the Scotchtown house, some ninety-four by thirty-six feet, was one of the largest in the colony.[71]

In its heyday the mansion was surrounded by a white paling fence, with boxwood, oak, and other trees and shrubbery. The main floor, approached by the stone steps, was conceived on a dignified plan, with eight rooms opening into a wide central hall extending the width of the building. There were several rooms paneled in solid mahogany or walnut, and Dolly Madison would recall the large black mantelpieces supported by white figures.[72]

At the back of the hall is a hidden stairway, entered by a door with a large lock. Climbing the rough stairs, one is surprised to find an enormous attic covering the entire floor. Without any fireplaces or even partitions, it could house a swarm of merry and none too finicky guests, congregated for one of the numerous colonial dances or house-parties. With several of Henry's children at the courting age and he himself a lover of music and frolic, it might be assumed that Scotchtown was a center of gaiety.

[279]

But this could not have been true of the latter years of his owner-ship. For a shadow lay over the household, a living pall over the mind of Sarah, the bride of his youth. As the tragic facts are un-folded, we may well wonder how even Henry could be tough and courageous enough to rise above the darkness to the achievements of the next few years.

Sarah's breakdown may have been due to an illness which followed the birth of her last child. The first of her six children had been born about 1755, when she was seventeen; the last two, Elizabeth and Edward, were born in 1769 and 1771 (*circa*) respectively, the last when she was about thirty-four.[73] Meantime, she had spent many lonely periods on remote plantations while her husband was absent on legal or political business. We first learn of her sickness about the time of Edward's birth. Perhaps she had an innate tendency to break under strain; the wife of a statesman often has to pay an even more onerous price for greatness than does her husband. Yet Patrick was home-loving; there is little evidence to indicate that he was away from the fireside more often than was dictated by duty and ambition.

One of the Shelton clan is said not to have approved of Patrick's conduct toward his wife. Her younger first cousin, Elizabeth Shelton Watson, thought that Patrick was hard on Sarah. He was interested in outside projects, not in his wife, she asserted. "The cradle was rocking soon after he was married when eighteen, and rocking when he died." However, Elizabeth Watson was a lady of Tory sympa-thies and none too sweet tempered.[74] In fact, it was Henry's second wife who did much of the cradle rocking for her own children.

Colonel Meredith referred to Sarah as "a woman of some fortune and much respectability."[75] In family accounts there is a singular absence of information about Sarah's Scotchtown years. But Patrick's sister Annie, in a letter from Scotchtown on October 15, 1774, said, "my brother Pat is not returned from Philadelphia yet his wife is extremely ill."[76] Just what was the malady now apparently so ag-gravated?

We have poignant testimony about Sarah's illness from Patrick Henry's family physician, which is reinforced by cumulative evidence.

[280]

In Dr. Hinde's indirect account, written and published by his son in 1843, the younger Hinde stated:

> Here (at Scotchtown) resided the illustrious patriot and states-
> man at the breaking out of the American Revolution. Here his
> family resided, whilst Henry had to encounter many mental and
> personal afflictions known only to his family physician. Whilst
> his towering and master-spirit was arousing a nation to arms, his
> soul was bowed down and bleeding under the heaviest sorrows
> and personal distresses. His beloved companion had lost her rea-
> son, and could only be restrained from self-destruction by a
> strait-dress. I cannot reflect on my venerable deceased father's
> rehearsal of the particulars, without feeling myself almost a
> bleeding heart. It was such men that Almighty God raised up to
> assert and maintain our rights.[77]

Living in 1945 at Glen Cairn, adjoining Scotchtown, was a remarkable old lady, Miss Sally Campbell. Born ninety years before,
she still had an accurate memory of many events in the neighborhood.
She had much data on Scotchtown which came directly from her
grandmother, Harriet Sheppard, who had lived at the former Henry
estate when it belonged to the Sheppard family. Miss Campbell was
told by her grandmother that Henry's wife was insane. She was confined in a basement room, so the story ran, and there was a trapdoor
in the hall, near the entrance, where Henry went downstairs to feed
her. As a child, Miss Campbell was always afraid to go to Scotchtown because of this story. "Colored people especially were scared
because of this. . . . I have always heard that Patrick Henry's wife
was crazy," Miss Campbell reported.[78]

In the basement of Scotchtown there are eight rooms, one of which
may have been put to such sad usage. An insane asylum had just
been established at Williamsburg, but it was hardly a place where
Henry would have confined his wife. It does seem that she was kept
in the basement with a Negro woman attendant—probably the kind-
est fate for the unhappy woman, considering the horrors in store for
the mentally ill in the eighteenth century, whose families were unable to care for them. The story, at least in outline, has been handed

down in the neighborhood by persons with exceptional opportunity to learn the salient facts.[79]

This was the crushing sorrow which Henry must bear during the years just ahead when he was already burdened with the responsibilities of a leader in the developing Revolution.

16

~~~

Would Colonialism Suffice?

History is neither more nor less than biography on a large scale.———LAMARTINE

"ON THE whole Virginia is much the richest [of the North American colonies] as well as of the greatest Importance to Great Britain and therefore well deserves its Encouragement and Protection," John Henry wrote early in 1770. This statement appeared in some statistical data printed on Henry's map of Virginia which the hard-pressed Colonel had finally been able to publish that year, after Patrick had bought the publication rights.

Colonel Henry estimated that there were then about 450,000 people in Virginia. Of these, 188,000 were Negro slaves, valued at over £6,000,000 in Virginia currency. Enough corn was being raised to provide a supply for all the inhabitants, but tobacco was the principal money crop, some fifty thousand to sixty thousand hogsheads being exported yearly. And yet, as John Henry—and Patrick—duly noted, tobacco was not bringing a high enough price to the planters, and the balance of trade had for many years been against Virginia. A moderate estimate of her debt to British merchants alone was £1,500,-000.

The colony was weaving cotton cloth to the amount of £250,000 per year,[1] and it was to her advantage to manufacture far more of this and other articles, as Henry clearly understood. The balance of trade continued to pile up against the American colonies. Not a month passed that Patrick did not see further abuses of the debtor-creditor relationship; an appreciable share of the blame still lay with the colonists themselves. In 1769 his uncle Anthony Winston, having been "too indulgent" to his "ungenerous" creditors, was offering his fine Bosworth estate in Hanover for sale at what he termed less than half its real value. Apparently doubtful that the large orchard, excellent wheat land, mill and other assets were sufficiently attractive, he brought forth another and wonderful selling point: there was, he believed, no other place on the continent where people had lived to so great an age as in that neighborhood; forty of the first settlers had lived to an average of eighty years.[2] But, despite any possessions that he disposed of, in 1774 the court records showed that Anthony owed British merchants £914.4 sterling with a backbreaking interest of ten per cent.[3]

With all due allowance for the extravagance and mismanagement of the planters, the British commercial system was still too restrictive for a colony of Virginia's size and complexity. This story of adverse trade balances and mounting debts to British creditors was repeated in numerous other colonies. The American colonies as a whole were not getting the "Encouragement and Protection" to which John Henry alluded. Few men were more aware of this lack than his son, Patrick, or in a better position to take counter-measures.

As an influential and hard-working member of the Burgesses, we find him in 1769-1770 promoting numerous bills in committee and on the floor. No doctrinaire, he could do prosaic spadework, could work with members not disposed to rise above the mundane. There continued to be a tantalizing lack of detail in the *Journal*, as on December 7 when the Burgesses ordered a "humble Address" to Lord Botetourt on the subject of western lands.[4] But Henry's influence is later indicated by his appointment as one of the burgesses to present the address to the Governor and to arrange for him to meet with the House.[5] In this and subsequent sessions we find him aiding bills for a speedier administration of justice in the colony, for settling damages at tobacco warehouses from the great flood of 1771, for reimbursing Hanover and King William counties for their expenses in clearing the Pamunkey.[6]

The bills for improving navigation in the river were passed in 1770-1772 at a time when the Burgesses was making a noteworthy effort to improve communications with the back country. There were hopeful projects to extend the navigational facilities of the James and the Potomac and for opening roads in the western counties as well as for cutting a navigable canal between two creeks in the Williamsburg area so as to connect the James and York rivers.[7] Henry and his associates were displaying an appreciation of the growing needs of the colony as a whole, distant Piedmont and mountain counties as well as the hitherto favored East. There was even proof of an enlarging American vision.

This vision was evidenced in 1770 by the appointment of Henry and Richard Bland to attend an intercolonial conference in New York for regulation of the Indian trade. The trade had expanded so greatly and was in such obvious need of regulation that the British government proposed a congress of the various colonies to arrange an effective system of control.[8]

Here was another movement that fitted into Henry's vision of a greater America moving toward the setting sun. He appears to have been the most active burgess in preparing a bill to appoint commissioners from Virginia to meet with those from the Northern provinces. He and Richard Bland were appointed delegates from Virginia and some money was later appropriated for their expenses. It was Henry's first extended journey away from the colony.[9] During the long rides ahead he could again absorb from Bland scholarly ideas of governmental theory and practice. Bland's son and a few other gentlemen completed the party and added interest and variety.[10]

Presumably they traveled by the established route through Annapolis, Philadelphia, and the New Jersey farms and villages.[11] Annapolis, a day's ride from the Potomac, was a small neat town of some 150 houses spread along the Severn River near the Chesapeake

Bay.[12] From there they went northward by the Elk River, Brandy-wine Ferry, Chester and Philadelphia. Ripening orchards spread out from the dusty roads, and the Maryland fields showed evidence of better husbandry than Henry usually saw in Virginia. Obviously, these farmers got higher yields per acre than did the Virginia planters, wedded to the slavery system.

"How comes it that the lands in Pennsylvania are five times the value of ours?" Henry had written in his (*circa*) 1766 memorandum,[13] going on to comment favorably on Pennsylvania's tolerance and freedom of enterprise. The British traveler Burnaby, en route from Newcastle, Delaware, to Philadelphia, noted that the land was better cultivated than any he had hitherto seen in America,[14] and at Philadelphia Henry could find further proof of what European immigrants were able to accomplish in a new country with a beneficent government and opportunity for individual enterprise. Less than a century ago, the site of Philadelphia had been a wilderness where wild Indians and savage beasts roamed; now it was a settled city of some twenty thousand people, well lighted and patrolled, with crowded streets and harbor, and even garbage collection.[15]

On Tuesday, July 10, the Virginia party finally arrived in New York only to learn that the government had canceled the congress when in the initial stage. The British were growing fearful of any meetings that might promote intercolonial unity. Just a few months earlier some soldiers of the unwanted British garrison at Boston had killed several members of a threatening mob—the Boston Massacre, which inflamed American opinion; the Whig propagandists were again busily at work throughout the colonies. From local Whig leaders such as John Lamb and Alexander McDougall, the latter of whom was proclaimed by the Sons of Liberty as "the Wilkes of America," Henry could learn how the Whigs had incited New York artisans, sailors, and laborers to none too gentle demonstrations against the entrenched conservatives.[16]

Henry and the Blands turned their faces homeward from New York, but even a brief visit to the thriving city left its influence on men seeking to rise above the provincial level. At a church on Nassau

Street the Virginians could hear services in Dutch; and, wandering to the Albany Pier, they could find Dutch goods, Dutch manners, lads and lassies.[17] Comfortable houses and new buildings indicated the presence of numerous English merchants and officials, while there were also German Lutheran churches, a Presbyterian church for the lately immigrated Scots, enough recent Irish to celebrate noticeably on St. Patrick's Day, and Jews in sufficient numbers to have their own synagogue and cemetery.[18] Although nearly as large as Philadelphia, New York had not yet entered upon its greatest period of development. How powerful would be this burgeoning port and the America to which she was a gateway if only the Northern and Southern colonies would join hands!

An immediate obstacle to the dream of unity was the violation by calculating New Yorkers of the Association to curb British trade. "Shall the year 1770 brand . . . with Infamy, and disgrace our vigorous Exertion in the Cause of our Country, in the year 1765 and 1766," wrote Fabius in the *New York Journal* for July 12. In December the Acting Governor of Virginia, old William Nelson, was to write that "the spirit of Association" seemed to be cooling there every day; he placed the blame too categorically on the defection of some Northern provinces.[19]

On July 19, 1770, the *Virginia Gazette* reported that Bland and Henry had arrived in Williamsburg from New York the previous evening. Apparently on their authority, the *Gazette* added that the commissioners from Pennsylvania and Quebec were not present at the conference and "very little business" was accomplished.[20] In any event, the trip had been a broadening experience for Henry, and it had increased his stature as an intercolonial figure. A month later, John Adams of Massachusetts wrote in his diary that he had dined in Cambridge with a Virginian, Colonel Severn Ayers [Eyre], whom he asserted to be an intimate friend of Patrick Henry, "the first mover of the Virginia Resolves in 1765." [21] In November, 1770, Henry was admitted to practice in Spotsylvania County, apparently in connection with his defense of one or more of the persecuted Baptist ministers.[22] This and a variety of business connected with his legal and plantation affairs kept him occupied until the next meeting of the Assembly early the next year.[23]

The tactless hand of the Royal Governor of New York, John Murray, Earl of Dunmore, had been felt in the disruption of the trade conference. It was the irony of fate that the popular Governor Botetourt died in November, 1770, a few months after Henry's return to the colony, to be succeeded by the coarse and mediocre Dunmore.[24] British officialdom was slow as usual; there was an interregnum with William Nelson as Acting Governor and Dunmore did not arrive in Williamsburg until late in 1771. He overcame some initial suspicions, and on the surface life in Virginia seemed to be moving quietly. But, symptomatic of the growing American independence, William Nelson wrote a London correspondent that he was wearing a good suit, made in Albemarle County of his son's wool. His shoes, hose, buckles, wig, and hat were all made in "our own Country, and in these we improve every year in Quantity as well as Quality." [25]

At a time when a tolerant governor was vitally needed, Dunmore indicated his aversion to popular assemblies by proroguing the legislature several times. After the session in early 1772, which passed some internal improvement bills and other legislation of interest to Henry, the supercilious Scottish-born Governor was reported to have refused for a time even to hold office hours for popular consultation. When a lawyer representing the provoked Virginians called upon him, he "stormed" in the best style of his royal Stuart ancestors before finally agreeing to be regularly accessible to the public.[26] He did not call the Assembly again until March, 1773, and then only because a band of clever counterfeiters threatened to undermine the credit of the colony.

Representing Hanover, along with an obscure John Smith, Henry came down to Williamsburg from Scotchtown dressed in a manner not unworthy of his position, wearing a peachblossom-colored coat—a happy if coincidental spring motif—and a dark wig tied behind. Yet when Henry was pointed out to St. George Tucker as the orator of

[288]

the Assembly, Tucker did not find his appearance particularly striking. Tucker, still a William and Mary student, had never heard a public speech except from the pulpit. He had formed the idea that an orator should have the handsome appearance of a Pendleton, the pleasing voice and polished language of a Lee, and the dramatic gestures listed by Demosthenes among the qualifications of an orator. But to Tucker's surprise he found none of these qualifications in Henry—neither in his appearance nor in the few remarks that he heard him deliver during the session. Tucker was not present when Dabney Carr made his celebrated motion to appoint the standing Committee of Correspondence. Some of his collegemates, however, told him that on this occasion Henry had far exceeded Lee whose speech Tucker heard the next day.

"Never before had I heard what I thought oratory; if his [Lee's] speech was excelled by Mr. Henry's, the latter must have been excellent indeed," he recalled.[27]

As Henry declaimed against King and ministry, the spectators rushed out of the gallery. The House was not on fire as was first supposed. These onlookers had been so aroused by Henry that some of the most prominent among them had run up into the cupola of the Capitol and pulled down the royal flag.[28]

The motion by Dabney Carr for the intercolonial Committee of Correspondence followed a series of actions on the part of the British government which Henry found deeply disturbing. When he was appointed a delegate to the New York conference, the people were still aroused by the Boston Massacre. Before he had left for New York, the *Virginia Gazette* reported that the bill for partial repeal of the Townshend Act had passed a third reading in Parliament. There had been rumors of the repeal throughout the past year, and Lord North's ministry, disturbed by the alarming drop in revenue as the result of American boycotting, had finally agreed to remove most of the Townshend duties. The proud British, however, had retained the duty on tea in order to preserve the principle of parliamentary taxation: Henry, with some of Sam Adams' ability "to scent tyranny from afar," had wondered what this exception portended.

[289]

Certainly, the British were not slackening their campaign against smuggling. Lieutenant William Dudingston, commander of the schooner *Gaspee*, had been notoriously officious and arbitrary in searching ships on the Rhode Island coast, seizing goods illegally and even firing on market boats as they entered Newport harbor. When the *Gaspee* grounded on a sandspit in June, 1772, a mob overpowered the crew and burned the vessel.

The lull in the anti-British agitation had been broken. The admiralty set up a special court of inquiry to apprehend the offenders and, when so desired, to send them to England for trial. There had also been a report that the salary of the colonial judges was to be paid by the English with revenue taken from American customs.[29] Sam Adams and his Massachusetts cohorts were now provided with fuel for fresh agitation, but the strongest protest came from Virginia.

Some liberals in the Burgesses at the March, 1773, session felt that the court of inquiry demanded the attention of the House. But, according to an account later given by Jefferson, these liberals feared that the old leaders of the Burgesses were not zealous and forward enough to meet the new conditions. Henry, Richard Henry Lee, Francis Lightfoot Lee, Dabney Carr, and Jefferson agreed, therefore, to meet in a private room at the Raleigh Tavern to consult on the state of affairs.[30]

The conferees were aware that the most urgent need was to reach an understanding with the other colonies so that the British encroachments on their liberty would prompt them to take action in the common cause. They proposed that Committees of Correspondence be set up in the colonies and—another fateful step—that their first measure should be to propose a meeting of the representatives from each colony at some central place. These representatives would be charged with the direction of measures to be undertaken by all the colonies. Thus the way was being prepared for the Continental Congress which Henry would attend next year.

The liberal group proposed that Jefferson present the resolutions in the Burgesses, but he generously suggested instead that they be offered by his young brother-in-law, Dabney Carr. This was agreed to by the conferees, and Carr proposed the resolutions which were adopted.[31] Carr, a new member from Louisa, had ties with Henry both of kinship and association. He was possessed of brilliant potentialities, and when he died two months later, Henry, Lee, and Jefferson lost a powerful supporter.[32]

The formation of the Committee of Correspondence, with liberals and conservatives co-operating, presented a striking evidence of the unity now prevailing among the Burgesses. St. George Tucker, able to recall only the one instance of Henry's eloquence at the 1773 session, explained that there was "too much unanimity" to require all the strength of any member.[33]

Another evidence of the unity in the common cause was the action in connection with counterfeiting of paper money. Forgeries had been made of all the Virginia currency then in circulation, Dunmore informed the Assembly, and that in the cleverest manner. The authorities succeeded in arresting several of the counterfeiters, including a member of the Burgesses. Dunmore immediately had them all thrown in jail without first bringing them before an examining magistrate.

Again Henry took the lead in vigorous action by the popular party in the House. He was made chairman of a committee appointed to present Lord Dunmore with a resolution which, while condemning the criminal action of their fellow burgess, Paschal Greenhill, was zealous in its guardianship of colonial rights.[34] Dunmore was entreated to arrange for every legal action needed to bring Greenhill or other forgers to justice, but at the same time the House took careful note of the action of the Governor in arresting and trying certain alleged offenders without first bringing them before an examining court as the law specifically required:

> . . . The proceedings in this Case, My Lord, though rendered necessary by the particular nature of it, are nevertheless different from the usual Mode. . . . The duty we owe our Constituents obliges us, My Lord, to be as attentive to the safety of the innocent, as we are desirous of punishing the Guilty; and we apprehend that a doubtful construction and various execution of Criminal Law, does greatly endanger the safety of innocent Men.[35]

A few days later, on March 15, 1773, Dunmore prorogued the Assembly on the thin excuse that the members had finished their current business. It had met only about ten days, and he did not convene it again until May, 1774. Earlier that day, he told the members that he had acted cautiously, on what he thought wise advice, with regard to the counterfeiters. And he added these stubborn words, indicative of the widening gulf between him and the Burgesses: "If I have done amiss the same method will not be repeated; but if it should be determined to be regular, I shall continue to exercise the Powers I am invested with, whensoever the exigencies of Government, and the good of the Country require such exertion. . . ." The next day the Committee of Correspondence prepared a circular letter to the speakers of the various colonies, enclosing a copy of the resolutions of the Burgesses inviting interchange of information. This letter Peyton Randolph was ordered to forward by express, and the replies foreshadowed the graver events of the next year.[36]

Unless Henry remained for a session of the General Court, he was probably not back in Williamsburg for some months; he doubtless missed this notable event advertised in the *Gazette* during late April, 1773:

> The Great
> COCK MATCH
> Between the
> Upland and Lowland Gentlemen,
> Will be fought in Williamsburg
> On Tuesday the 25th of May.[37]

In the statistics attached to his map of Virginia, John Henry estimated that a Negro man or woman between sixteen and forty years old was valued at five pounds, only half the price of a few years before. The planters were disturbed by the drop in the price of slaves as result of the large importation, and by the danger of filling the country so quickly with half-civilized people, many just removed from the African jungle. Since his boyhood Henry had read advertisements in the *Virginia Gazette* for Negroes with great scars on

[292]

their faces—their African "country mark"—and unable to speak English. There is no record of his owning any of the new Negroes described as Eboes (from Benin in West Africa), from Gambia and elsewhere on the Slave Coast, but a number must have been owned by his relatives and friends. Hardly any of the Virginia slaves were sprung from stock that had been in the country for more than a few generations.

It was manifestly impossible to give these Negroes the full rights of citizenship, and it was asking too much of human foresight and generosity to expect the average burgess of the time to devise some system of peonage which might gradually bring about an increase in the personal rights of the Negroes. The problem, in all its complexities, was brought closer to Henry by discussion in the House, especially of the petition of 1772 against the slave trade, and by a letter from a Quaker Abolitionist inviting an expression of Henry's opinions on the subject.

We have already noted his frank statement of about 1766 against slavery, a conviction in which he had been supported by Richard Henry Lee. When a new member of the Burgesses, Lee had so far overcome his diffidence as to make a memorable attack on the slave trade. In words strikingly similar to those later used by Henry, Lee had inquired why some of the neighboring colonies, settled much later than Virginia, were so far ahead of her in "improvements." The explanation for this strange and unhappy truth seemed to be "that with their whites they import arts and agriculture, whilst we, with our blacks, exclude both." [38]

Within the family circle, Henry's opinion was reinforced by that of one or more of the Fontaines, and perhaps his Quaker cousin, John Payne, as well as by the humane injunctions of his Uncle Patrick.[39]

Now that Henry had become a political leader, dependent on the whims and prejudices of voters, there were many reasons for avoiding the explosive Negro issue. From his boyhood he had seen the great value of slaves in opening up a new country, even though they were less efficient than free labor. And as the number of slaves greatly increased in the eighteenth century, so did the danger of insurrection. Cases were brought close to home of slaves convicted of assault, murder, and other serious crimes. A few months after Henry returned home following his Stamp Act speech, John Fleming prosecuted in Goochland court the case of the *King* v. *Taffy*, convicted of poisoning his master and sentenced to be hanged on the gallows. There were several small slave insurrections in Virginia, and in late 1769 Henry's Propositions and Grievances Committee was considering amendments of an Act dealing with such conspiracies and insurrections and with runaway Negroes who could not be reclaimed by the ordinary methods of punishment. Returning to Hanover for the Christmas season, he was disturbed to hear of a deadly affray at Bowler Cocke's plantation in which a number of whites and blacks had been killed or wounded, one man having had his head nearly cut off by a broad sword.[40]

Such grim events counseled delay in measures for improving the status of the slaves, as did the very cantankerousness of any forced labor. Henry was well acquainted with Negroes not unlike Sandy, a mulatto owned by the humanitarian Jefferson. When Sandy ran away in 1769, Jefferson could only advertise him "as greatly addicted to drink" and at such times "insolent . . . artful and knavish." [41]

On the other hand, there was much that Henry could not overlook in good conscience. Slave ships were still docking in the York and James rivers, and the Propositions and Grievances Committee favorably reported a bill for quarantining Negroes who arrived from Africa with smallpox and "gaol fever." Thus he could learn more about the long voyages from the Slave Coast to America during which the Negroes were chained naked below deck and many in despair attempted to jump overboard or to commit suicide. The name of a hamlet near Scotchtown carried an ominous significance. It was called Negro Foot, and the name probably stems from an incident such as is noted in the Goochland records for 1733. Two Negroes found guilty of felonious murder were ordered to be hanged and their "heads and quarters" set up in several parts of the country, in accordance with a gentle practice inherited from England.[42]

For such a complicated problem there was no happy solution, and meantime Henry had to take life as it was. He bought a male slave, Ben, in 1767 for £35 from William Johnson, sheriff of Louisa. John Hawkins, the Hanover slave dealer, was listed in Henry's account book for money owed since 1762, as well as a few later items such as a charge on overpayment of cash to him and "To 6½ Ells rolls for the wenches bed @ 1/6.6." [43]

From details of a Hawkins auction as well as from newspaper items and journals of the Burgesses, we get a further appreciation of why Henry had developed qualms about the slavery system. Among the Negroes sold by Hawkins and Francis Jerdone on December 4, 1766, with the prices listed, were Isaac, "with a broken back," £5; Nell and Rachael, "2 very old Women," £2; Betty and her two children, £100.15, and Black Betty and her child, Molly, £100, the mothers' value being enhanced by their childbearing qualities. There was no mention of husbands (or much bother, we may be sure, as to whether they ever had any). Sukey, a young girl, sold for only £35, as compared with £58.5 for "Peg a Young Wench" who had evidently reached puberty. [44]

Henry could not have hoped for any early eradication of the deeply entrenched institution. But his work in the Burgesses kept the matter fresh in his mind, especially through the frequent petitions, often referred to the Propositions and Grievances Committee, seeking compensation for runaway slaves who had lost life or limb when being captured or imprisoned.

There was the typical case of Lucy, slave of Junior Turner in James City County. Lucy had been delivered of a child that was found dead and on suspicion of murder was committed to cold and forbidding Williamsburg gaol, whose replica complete with pillory and whipping post tourists now find so quaintly amusing. While incarcerated, she was said to have "catched a violent cold which occasioned her Death." Her master petitioned the House in March, 1767, for compensation, and after some discussion as to the actual facts was allotted £60. [45] Again, during the same month, Fortunatus Crutchfield petitioned and was compensated by £40 for a male slave "who happened, by Mistake, not to be outlawed, but was shot with other slaves who were outlawed." [46] A few decades later, Judge St. George Tucker of Williamsburg, in a widely read dissertation favoring the gradual abolition of slavery, would deplore a cruel provision of the law in regard to fugitive slaves. If they were outlawed by proclamation of two justices, the runaway Negroes might thereafter be killed, as Tucker vigorously put it, "by any person whatsoever, by such ways and means as he may think it fit, without accusation or impeachment of any crime for so doing." [47] The eighteenth century was developing a definite humanitarian trend by no means confined to Voltaire, Rousseau and Beccaria, or the Wesleys and Whitefield. But in many ways it was still curiously insensitive: Patrick Henry would find posted on church doors the grim proclamations of outlawry.

Since early in the century, the Virginians had made repeated efforts to reduce the importation of slaves. In 1671 there had been only two thousand slaves in the colony; in 1715 only twenty-three thousand or about a third as many as whites. But the number of slaves jumped by 1770 to 188,000 and, in view of their continued importation and high birth rate, they might soon outnumber the white population. [48] In the North, slavery was not so profitable as in the South, and there was some Yankee opposition on moral grounds. But many New Englanders made large profits from the slave trade, among them Peter Faneuil, the donor of Faneuil Hall in Boston where many patriotic meetings were held. There was an unpleasant element of truth in the statement that "the Cradle of Liberty rocks on the bones of the Middle Passage." [49] However, most of the slave ships coming to the Virginia colony were English, and in Bristol we find that there was this illuminating disbursement by an African trading company as early as 1724: twenty guineas paid to Mr. Mereweather in London, "being part of the charges in repealing an Act of the Virginian Assembly imposing a duty on negroes and rum." [50] Another record of funds apparently used in London to bribe or unduly influence members of Parliament and other government officials, is found a generation later. [51] This was in 1755, during the French war, when Henry's friend Colonel Peter Fontaine, wrote his brother, Moses, "all our Taxes are now laid upon slaves and shippers of tobacco which they [the British] wink at while we are in danger of being torn from them, but we durst not do it in time of peace, it being looked upon as the highest presumption to lay any burden upon trade." [52]

Most of the opposition in the plantation colonies to the slave trade continued to be on utilitarian grounds: the heavy taxes which their legislatures put or attempted to put on imported slaves were for such practical motives as to secure revenue, to forestall Negro insurrection, to prevent depreciation in value of the slaves, and to encourage the immigration of white persons.[53] Yet a small but vocal group of sensitive Virginians were beginning to appreciate the moral dilemma created by the slavery system.

"It is a hard task to do our duty toward them [the slaves] as we ought," the Reverend Peter Fontaine complained to his brother John, "for we run the hazard of temporal ruin if they are not compelled to work hard on the one hand—and on the other, that of not being able to render a good account of our stewardship in the other and better world, if we oppress and tyrannize over them." [54] In view of all his connections, business and personal, with the Fontaines, there is every reason to believe that Henry was impregnated with such sentiments. One of the numerous Acts to revive the duties on imported slaves was favorably reported by the Propositions and Grievances Committee in 1769 and passed by the Burgesses. But such Acts could not effectively prohibit the trade, especially in view of the opposing lobby in London evidenced by petitions of the Bristol and Liverpool merchants.[55] On April 1, 1772, the Burgesses went so far as to send a direct petition to the throne, but Henry could hardly have expected it to be received favorably by George III.

At the Public Record Office at London may still be seen the original petition which has survived the vicissitudes of the passing years. In the unctuous phraseology which the petitioners were now beginning to employ almost tongue in cheek, the House begged leave "with all Humility" to approach the "Royal Presence" and referred to the many instances of His Majesty's "benevolent Intentions and most

[297]

gracious Disposition to promote the Prosperity and Happiness" of his subjects in the colonies. Getting down to earth, they implored the assistance of George III "in averting a Calamity of a most alarming Nature. The Importation of Slaves into the Colonies from the Coast of Africa hath long been considered as a Trade of great Inhumanity, and, under its present Encouragement, we have too much reason to fear will endanger the very Existence of your Majesty's American Dominions."

Then, with a sly humor, the Burgesses stated that they were sensible that some of the King's subjects in Great Britain "may reap Emoluments from this Sort of Traffick," but, they continued, when they considered that the slave trade greatly retarded the settlement of the colonies with more useful inhabitants and might in time have the most destructive influence, they presumed to hope that the interest of a few would be disregarded when compared with the security and happiness of such numbers of His Majesty's dutiful and loyal subjects. The King was urged to remove all restraints on the governors of Virginia which prevented their assent to laws that might have so "pernicious a Commerce." [56]

To this moving petition the British government did not give the dignity of a direct reply. However, in a letter to Governor Dunmore of July 1, 1772, the Earl of Hillsborough, the Colonial Secretary, recalled that a similar petition two years before to the Board of Trade had been rejected, and accurately prophesied that the same thing would happen again.[57]

It was during this period when the agitation against the slave trade was at its height in the colony that a Virginia Quaker leader, Robert Pleasants, sent Henry a copy of a book by a pioneer Abolitionist, Anthony Benezet. A French-born Quaker, Benezet had published and widely circulated a series of vigorous and disturbing pamphlets against the slave trade. The tracts were all the more effective because their benevolent author had not written in a vindictive tone. It was apparently a collection of these pamphlets which Robert Pleasants gave Henry, and evoked a noteworthy reply.[58]

Pleasants, a middle-aged planter on the James River, was a mem-

[298]

ber of a family known for their philanthropy. One of his Quaker ancestors had been among the first Virginians to be persecuted for their religious convictions. Although a large slaveholder, Pleasants had educated his Negroes, then freed them at a cost of some three thousand pounds.[59] As a Quaker, he especially admired Henry's rôle as a popular leader, and he felt at liberty to send Henry a copy of the Benezet book.

Henry's reply was candid and self-searching; courageous, also, for he did not label as confidential sentiments which might have caused his political ruin:

Hanover, Jan.ʸ 18.th 1773

DEAR SIR

I take this opp? to acknowledge the receipt of A Benezets Book against the Slave Trade. I thank you for it. It is not a little surprising that Christianity, whose chief excellence consists in softning the human heart, in cherishing & improving its finer Feelings, should encourage a Practice so totally repugnant to the first Impression of right & wrong. What adds to the wonder is that this Abominable Practice has been introduced in yᵉ. most enlightened Ages, Times that seem to have pretentions to boast of high Improvements in the Arts, Sciences, & refined Morality, h[ave] brought into general use, & guarded by many Laws, a Species of Violence & Tyranny, which our more rude & barbarous, but more honest Ancestors detested. Is it not amazing, that at a time, when yᵉ Rights of Humanity are defined & understood with precision, in a Country above all others fond of Liberty, that in such an Age, & such a Country we find Men, professing a Religion yᵉ most humane, mild, meek, gentle & generous; adopting a Principle as repugnant to humanity as it is inconsistant with the Bible and destructive to Liberty.

Every thinking honest Man rejects it in Speculation, how few in Practice from conscienscious Motives? The World in general has denied yᵉ People a share of its honours, but the Wise will ascribe to yᵉ a just Tribute of virtuous Praise, for yᵉ Practice of a train of Virtues among which yʳ disagreement to Slavery will be principally ranked.—I cannot but wish well to a people whose System imitates yᵉ Example of him whose Life was perfect.—And believe m[e], I shall honour the Quakers for their

[299]

noble Effort to abolish Slavery. It is equally calculated to promote moral & political Good.

Would any one believe that I am Master of Slaves of my own purchase! I am drawn along by y.ᵉ general inconvenience of living without them, I will not, I cannot justify it. However culpable my Conduct, I will so far pay my devoir to Virtue, as to own the excellence & rectitude of her Precepts, & to lament my want of conforming to them.—

I believe a time will come when an opp.ᵗ will be offered to abolish this lamentable Evil.—Every thing we can do is to improve it, if it happens in our day, if not, let us transmit to our descendants together with our Slaves, a pity for their unhappy Lot, & an abhorrence for Slavery. If we cannot reduce this wished for Reformation to practice, let us treat the unhappy victims with lenity, it is y.ᵉ furthest advance we can make toward Justice [We owe to the] purity of our Religion to shew that it is at variance with that Law which warrants Slavery.—

Here is an instance that silent Meetings (y.ᵉ scoff of rever.ᵈ Doct.ʳˢ) have done y.ᵗ w.ᶜʰ learned & elaborate Preaching could not effect, so much preferable are the genuine dictates of Conscience & a steady attention to its feelings above y.ᵉ teachings of those Men who pretend to have found a better Guide. I exhort you to persevere in so worthy a resolution, Some of your People disagree, or at least are lukewarm in the abolition of Slavery. Many treat y.ᵉ Resolution of your Meeting with redicule, & among those who throw Contempt on it, are Clergymen, whose surest Guard against both Redicule & Contempt is a certain Act of Assembly.—

I know not where to stop, I could say many things on this Subject; a serious review of which gives a gloomy perspective to future times. Excuse this Scrawl, and believe me with esteem,

Y.ʳ hbl Serv.ᵗ

PATRICK HENRY jun.ʳ

The Quaker Abolitionists were mild but persistent. On February 22, 1774, a year after Henry acknowledged receipt of Anthony Benezet's book, Pleasants wrote his Quaker correspondent that he had had very little opportunity for some months of being in Henry's company. But he expected to call on Henry at Scotchtown the next week when attending a Quaker meeting near by, and to "present

Henry with Benezet's last two collections" (of anti-slavery writings).

"[I] have much reason to believe both that as well as the other Books sent him will be very kindly accepted," Pleasants added.[60]

Three years later, in 1777, Pleasants would write Henry, then wartime Governor of Virginia, urging gradual emancipation of the slaves. The new Virginia Declaration of Rights, Pleasants believed to be "indeed noble, and I can but wish and hope, thy great abilities and interest may be exerted towards a full and clear explanation and confirmation thereof." [61]

Within a few weeks after writing Pleasants, Patrick was called to the deathbed of his father. In the large Henry family, life at times seemed to be a chronicle of births, marriages, and deaths. Early in February, 1769, the Scotch Parson Douglas of Goochland County had preached the funeral sermon from II Chronicles, 34:3 for two of Colonel Henry's daughters.[62] Unidentified among Patrick's bevy of sisters, they were probably young unmarried girls. The next year John Henry had announced his plan to leave the colony, apparently on a business trip in connection with his map of Virginia. He hoped to go abroad, but a few months later he was pressed as of old by financial difficulties. Still somewhat sanguine, however, he quoted some gentlemen, well acquainted in England, as believing many thousands of his map might be sold in Great Britain and France. Colonel Henry was then ailing as well as impoverished and his son's account book for the next year shows Patrick again serving as security for his father. He died about February 1, 1773, as is indicated by a bill to Patrick and William Henry, his executors, for fifteen yards of black bombazine, three pairs of black buckles, a pair of bone buckles, black cloth, etc.[63]

Sadly Patrick and his brother had prepared their father for his last earthly rites. He was a cultured and honorable, though somewhat visionary, gentleman, and several months before his death was diverting himself by reading Tyro's Latin Dictionary.[64] For his son Patrick, he set a standard of sound education and cultural appreciation on which the younger man was still building. In other respects, too,

Colonel Henry had striven to elevate his son, and it was good that he could live to see Patrick become one of the leading men of the colony. Upon him Colonel Henry had depended for much of his support during his latter years, and they had maintained an affectionate relationship. Colonel Meredith later described Patrick as the most dutiful of sons.[65]

On the slavery issue Henry, Lee, Jefferson, and their Quaker friends were as yet voices crying in the wilderness. But liberalism did accord with the spirit of the age, and there was a growing restiveness under British rule. Lord Dunmore, with his usual stubbornness or obtuseness, continued to make few efforts to placate the people. There was always a group of Court followers, however, that liked his imitation of royalty, and the people of Williamsburg, according to the glowing account in the *Virginia Gazette,* greeted with "inexpressible pleasure and satisfaction" the arrival in early 1774 of the Right Honorable the Countess of Dunmore, her son Lord Fincastle, and her other children. There was an illumination in honor of the new arrivals and the burgesses, called soon after, were glad of the excuse to give another ball.[66]

The convening of the Burgesses that May was, we may be sure, reluctantly requested by the Governor. With his usual talent for bungling, Dunmore had tried to settle a boundary dispute between Virginia and Pennsylvania, and merely aggravated the difficulties. He sent a military force to the disputed area which succeeded in killing several friendly Indians and helped to provoke further intrastate quarrels and an Indian war. The beleaguered Governor convened the Assembly on May 5, 1774. Thus he played into the hands of Henry and other burgesses seeking action on certain new phases of the mounting Anglo-American quarrel. The Assembly rejected the harassed Dunmore's appeal to raise troops to meet the Pennsylvanians and to punish the Indians now attacking the outlying settlers. But the House did busy itself with some ordinary business which it wished to transact before grappling with graver issues that, as in the past, would probably lead to its dissolution by the Governor.

These issues were immediately connected with the ill-advised effort of the British government to aid the powerful East India Company, and with the resultant Boston Tea Party. The ministry of Lord North, started in 1770 as a "forlorn hope," had become firmly entrenched. George III now largely directed its policy and, by a none too subtle use of patronage and corruption, was able to maintain docile majorities in Parliament. When Parliament repealed the Townshend duties with the exception of that on tea, Henry could only speculate on the results of its retention. But by 1773 the powerful East India Company was in financial straits. They had 17,000,000 pounds of tea stored in Great Britain on which they would have to pay a duty before selling it there. The ministry, therefore, permitted the removal of the English duty and shipment of the tea to America where it could be sold at a price that would underbid competing merchants. Obviously, the government, while helping the East India Company, was tempting the colonies to acknowledge the principle of parliamentary taxation. But the Americans would not rise to the bait: in several cities the cargoes of tea were not allowed to land and in Boston the tea chests were dumped into the harbor by citizens dressed as Mohawk Indians. Instead of attempting to punish only the persons involved, Parliament passed in the spring of 1774 the famous "Intolerable Acts." These Acts closed the port of Boston until the colony paid compensation for the destroyed tea, virtually abrogated the Massachusetts charter with its hard-won rights of self-government, and otherwise put the colony in a strait jacket. The North ministry, ignorant or heedless as usual, thinking that it was suppressing sedition in a colony, found that it was fanning rebellion in America.

News of the closing of the port of Boston and the anticipated destruction of its trade reached Williamsburg before May 19, 1774.[67] Henry joined in the outburst of indignation at the grim news. The liberal caucus was determined to take notice of the British action before the Port Bill took effect on June 1. "The lead in the House, on these subjects, was no longer left to the old members," Jefferson wrote. Henry, Richard Henry Lee, Francis Lightfoot Lee, Jefferson, and three or four other members agreed that they must take a bold

[303]

stand in line with Massachusetts. They decided to consult on proper measures in the council room of the Capitol, where they would have the benefit of the library. They were convinced of the need to arouse the people from "the lethargy into which they had fallen, as to passing events," and believed that the appointment of a day of general fasting and praying would be most likely to provoke popular interest. There had been no occasion of such solemnity since the distressing days of the war of 1755, Jefferson explained, and a new generation had since grown up. "With the help therefore of Rushworth, whom we rummaged over for the revolutionary precedents & forms of the Puritans of that day, preserved by him," Jefferson continued, "we cooked up a resolution, somewhat modernizing their phrazes, for appointing the 1st day of June, on which the Port bill was to commence, for a day of fasting, humiliation and prayer, to implore heaven to avert from us the evils of civil war, to inspire us with firmness in support of our rights, and to turn the hearts of the King & Parliament to moderation and justice." [68]

In order to give greater emphasis to their proposition, they prevailed on the grave and religious Treasurer Nicholas to move the resolution. This he did on May 24, 1774, and it was passed without opposition. It set aside June first for the day of fasting and prayer to avert the threatened destruction of American civil rights and the evils of civil war and to unite the people with one heart and mind in opposition "by all just and proper means" to every injury to these rights. They prayed that the King and Parliament would be inspired from above "with Wisdom, Moderation, and Justice, to remove from the loyal People of America all cause of danger, from a continued pursuit of Measures pregnant with their ruin." [69]

George Mason of Westmoreland County, future author of the Virginia Bill of Rights, shared Henry's interest in western land speculation. In late May, 1774, he came to Williamsburg in connection with his charter rights to some land and while there spent a memorable evening with Henry. The meeting helped to cement a political alliance that, with few interruptions, would remain unbroken until Mason's death.[70]

Mason, like his friend George Washington, lived on an estate overlooking the Potomac River. So many of the prominent Virginia families then owned great plantations spreading along the Tidewater rivers that it is startling to find in contemporary records the high proportion of small landholders owning few or no slaves. That the great families did keep a large measure of control through the pre-Revolutionary and Revolutionary periods was due to such obvious factors as their entrenched position, their ability and courage. But no one should overlook the infusion of liberalism which made them leaders in making needed changes in the body politic. These landed grandees, grown into lords within their own sphere, were quick to resent any abridgment of their rights by distant English officials. When chafing at British political and economic bonds, these Virginia Revolutionary leaders were largely moved by selfish considerations, but there was also genuine altruism, and this was symbolized by George Mason, the hazel-eyed, dark-complexioned planter, now arrived at a dignified middle age, whose path crossed Henry's at Williamsburg.[71]

Mason had served in the Burgesses, but for some years his influence had been chiefly that of the widely read, philosophical plantation master who entertained freely and left his imprint on his numerous guests—his neighbor, George Washington, and other well-placed Virginians. That March, 1773, Mason's beloved first wife had died, the patrician Ann Eilbeck with the delicate features and pink and white complexion, who gazes at us from an old canvas. Apparently shocked out of his retirement, Mason resumed his active political position in 1775, fulfilling the destiny of a gentleman who, as Jefferson noted, was "of the first order of wisdom among those who acted on the theater of the Revolution." [72] And, in the preceding May, 1774, he was in the capital during the immediate events leading to the dissolution of the Burgesses by Lord Dunmore. There he wrote on the twenty-sixth to a Westmoreland neighbor an illuminating analysis of Henry's rôle in the swiftly moving events.

[305]

Arriving in Williamsburg on Sunday, May 22, Mason had found everyone engrossed with the unhappy news of the Boston Port Bill. The dissolution of the Burgesses was generally expected, but he had reason to think that the House would first be able to transact the public business and not adjourn until late June.

"What ever resolves or measures are intended for the preservation of our rights and liberties," Mason informed his neighbor, "will be reserved for the conclusion of the session. Matters of that sort here are conducted and prepared with a great deal of privacy, and by very few members; of whom Patrick Henry is the principal."

That night Mason was requested to spend an evening with the small group of Whig leaders, and he had an opportunity to talk with Henry and to learn his sentiments. He also found opportunities to hear Henry speak in the House.

"He is by far the most powerful speaker I ever heard," Mason wrote. "Every word he says not only engages but commands the attention; and your passions are no longer your own when he addresses them. But his eloquence is the smallest part of his merit. He is in my opinion the first man upon this continent, as well in abilities as public virtues, and had he lived in Rome about the time of the first Punic War, when the Roman people had arrived at their meridian glory, and their virtue not tarnished, Mr. Henry's talents must have put him at the head of that glorious commonwealth." [73]

From this letter and the other evidence of Henry's mounting influence, it is clear that he was the leader in the advanced measures now proposed in Virginia.

The next day the members of the House met at the Raleigh Tavern, where they adopted a significant statement of principles. With the Anglo-American quarrel fast getting out of hand, neither side now stopped to weigh words. The British disregard of American constitutional rights by subjecting the people to taxation without representation was labeled by the unofficial assembly as a determined plan to reduce the colonials to "slavery." The Boston Port Bill was "a most dangerous attempt to destroy the constitutional liberty and rights of all North America." The shipment of tea to America was also severely criticized and their countrymen were urged not to purchase or use any kind of East Indian commodities except saltpeter and spices.

It was the next few sentences, however, that emphasized the note of unity which Henry and other members of the liberal caucus were stressing. The attack upon Massachusetts to compel submission to arbitrary taxes was branded as an attack upon all the colonies. It threatened ruin to the rights of them all, "unless the united wisdom of the whole be applied." The Virginia Committee of Correspondence was authorized to suggest to the committees in other colonies the appointment of delegates to a general congress. This congress was to meet annually at a convenient place and to deliberate on the general measures demanded by the united interest of the colonies.

It was also added, none too delicately, that a "tender regard" for British merchants and manufacturers prevented the Virginians from going further at that time. They earnestly hoped that the British would not persist in the unconstitutional principle of taxes in the colonies without colonial consent and thus compel the Americans to cut off all commercial intercourse with Great Britain.[74]

The Virginia call for the intercolonial congress was not the first at this period. Yet it was to her credit that the Burgesses in the extralegal sessions took the lead in calling an annual intercolonial congress looking to a permanent union. The assemblies of Rhode Island and Massachusetts in the middle of June followed the Virginia example, and from the Committees of Correspondence in several states the Old Dominion received letters of approval. The Philadelphia Committee, for example, wrote on June 13 that "all America look up to Virginia to take the Lead on the present Occasion"; the North Carolina Committee stated a week later that "we cannot enough applaud the generous Spirit exhibited by the Colony of Virginia upon this Emergency, and wish the Example may be as diffusive as it is truly laudable." [75]

Two days after the meeting in the Raleigh Tavern, letters to

Williamsburg conveyed the desire of the beleaguered Bostonians for immediate non-intercourse with Great Britain. The twenty-five burgesses remaining in town therefore called a convention of the people to meet in the capital on August 1.[76] And now events moved fast. Already on January 20 the *Virginia Gazette* had published "A Lady's Adieu to her TEA TABLE:

> Farewell the Tea Board, with its gaudy Equipage,
> Of Cups and Saucers, Cream Bucket, Sugar Tongs
> The pretty Tea Chest also, lately stor'd
> With Hysen, Congo, and best Double Fine
> Full Many a joyous Moment have I sat by ye,
> Hearing the Girl's Tattle, the Old Maids talk Scandal
> And the spruce Coxcomb laugh at—may be—nothing. . . .

No more would the lady "dish out the once-lov'd Liquor," now detestable because she had been taught and believed

> Its Use will fasten slavish Chains upon my Country.
> And LIBERTY's the Goddess I would choose
> To reign triumphant in AMERICA.[77]

Though not everyone joined in the chorus of patriotic paeans, on July 6 the Earl of Dartmouth wrote Governor Dunmore that he had hoped the other colonies would disregard the action taken at Boston but he now doubted it. He was afraid that the conduct of the Burgesses both before and after its dissolution would set an example to other colonies, "as it has already become in other instances." [78]

In Virginia the liberals were able to form virtually a united front. In view of the various Associations forming in the colony, the growing discontent even of those "well affected to government," and the increased danger from a savage enemy (the Indians), even conservative members of the Council cautiously advised the Governor on June 25 to issue writs for a new assembly.[79] The Westmoreland citizens sent grain to the distressed Bostonians,[80] and one correspondent even suggested in the *Virginia Gazette* that horse racing cease so that the money could be spent for relief of the Boston people.[81] For Virginians the ultimate sacrifice! There was a hardening of opinion both in America and in England.

"It was a year of fine harangues," Horace Walpole wrote in April, 1774. Walpole referred especially to the harangue by Alexander Wedderburn against Ben Franklin, actually a personal diatribe by the British Solicitor-General before a committee of the Privy Council; and to the speeches in the Commons by Edmund Burke on the tea duty and by Lord George Germain on the government of Massachusetts. Whatever hopes there may have been of conciliating the colonies were dispelled by the despotic measures now taken by the British government. On March 14 Lord North had introduced the bill for closing the harbor of Boston, and it was soon followed by another bill intended to destroy self-government in Massachusetts. Why should men of a mercantile cast collect together and debate on political matters when they ought to be minding their private business? asked a rising government leader, Lord George Germain. He followed with an oratorical outburst favoring further restriction on self-government in the Massachusetts colony which led Lord North to thank the speaker for a suggestion "worthy of his great mind." [82]

To the great majority of M.P.'s the members of the colonial assemblies were ignorant if not riotous rabble. In vain Edmund Burke argued that the Commons was engaged in the proscription of a province, that it would be expanded into the proscription of a nation.[83] Heedlessly, and with little thought of the extreme reaction that they might arouse in America, Parliament proceeded to pass a series of Draconian measures. Not only did they close the port of Boston and emasculate the Massachusetts charter but provisions were made for colonial officials charged with capital crimes to be tried in England, and for quartering British soldiers on the Massachusetts populace. Moreover, in a separate Act, well meaning but provocative, Parliament created the province of Quebec with a legislative council appointed by the Crown, and the Catholic Church established by law. The new province was to include not only French Canadian territory ceded in 1763

[309]

but the region between the Ohio River and the Great Lakes. Thus old religious prejudices were stirred up as well as the apprehensions of colonies with western land claims, of the frontiersmen, traders, and land speculators like Henry.

"The acts relative to Boston are exceedingly arbitrary and unjust but the toleration of the Catholic religion in Canada and the Extension of that Province is a full proof of . . . the disposition of our pious [King] and his Ministry," wrote an influential Virginia merchant, Thomas Adams, on August 20, 1774, to a London correspondent.[84]

Already the so-called Intolerable Acts had led to numerous meetings and resolutions of protest, including many in Virginia counties. Among them was a meeting of the Hanover freeholders at the courthouse on Wednesday, July 20. This gathering offered evidence, if any were needed, of how fortunate Henry was to have such liberal constituents; they stimulated Henry and he them. The freeholders thanked Henry and John Syme for their spirited conduct at the late session of the Burgesses and appointed them to represent Hanover at the August convention. The further resolutions are so eloquently worded that one regrets the necessity of deletions:

> We are free men; we have a right to be so, and to enjoy all the privileges and immunities of our fellow subject in England, and while we retain a just sense of that freedom, and those rights and privileges necessary for its safety and security, we shall never give up the right of taxation. Let it suffice to say, one for all, *we will never be taxed but by our own representatives;* this is the great badge of freedom, and British America hath been hitherto distinguished by it. . . . The sphere of life in which we move hath not afforded us lights sufficient to determine with certainty concerning those things from which the troubles at Boston originated. Whether the people there were warrented by justice when they destroyed the tea we know not; but this we know, that the parliament, by their proceedings, have made us and all North America parties in the present dispute, and deeply interested in the event of it; insomuch, that if our sister colony of Massachusetts Bay is enslaved we cannot long remain free. . . .
> Let it, therefore, be your great object to obtain a speedy re-

[310]

peal of those acts, and for this purpose we recommend the adoption of such measures as may produce the hearty union of all our countrymen and sister colonies. UNITED WE STAND, DIVIDED WE FALL. . . .

We judge it conducive to the interests of America, that a general congress of deputies from all the colonies be held, in order to form a plan for guarding the claims of the colonists, and their constitutional rights. . . . The arm of power, which is now stretched forth against us, is indeed formidable; but we do not despair. Our cause is good; and if it is served with constancy and fidelity, it cannot fail of success. We promise you our best support, and we will heartily join in such measures as a majority of our countrymen shall adopt for securing the public liberty. . . .[85]

The motto *"UNITED WE STAND, DIVIDED WE FALL,"* later to be so familiar to Americans, had been used in somewhat similar form by John Dickinson in 1768.[86] The resolutions also contain an indictment of the slave trade as "most dangerous to the virtue and welfare of this country" and urged that it be "totally discouraged." Altogether, the Hanover resolutions show the strong influence, direct or indirect, of Henry and of the forces affecting him.

The convention met at Williamsburg on August 1, 1774. Within a week this efficient body elected the seven Virginia representatives to the congress in Philadelphia and prepared for them a statement of instructions. "We never before had so full a meeting of delegates at any one time," George Washington wrote from Williamsburg on the fifth.[87] And never had the Virginia leaders, liberal and moderate, acted with greater unanimity. The rising young Jefferson, to be sure, had been taken ill with dysentery on the hot summer journey to the capital. But Jefferson dispatched to two friends at the convention copies of his noteworthy "A Summary View of the Rights of British America." One copy, sent to Henry, was not heard of further, and he may have carelessly lost it. Another, forwarded to Jefferson's cousin Peyton Randolph was laid on the table for perusal by the delegates. The paper shows the influence of the ideas of Richard Bland, as originated by Bland or as popularized by Henry. But, above all, the

"Summary View" is the work of a bold and liberal mind, with "a range of inquiry not then very frequent, and marching far beyond the politics of the day."

Jefferson argued that when colonial assemblies were forcibly dissolved the power reverted to the people who could use it "in any . . . way" they think proper. George III had "no right to land a single armed man" on American shores; those sent were liable to the colonial laws. Defiantly, after his full and learned statement of grievances and historical precedents, Jefferson added: "Let those flatter, who fear: it is not an American art. To give praise where it is not due might be well from the venal, but would ill beseem those who are asserting the rights of human nature." [88]

Although Jefferson's paper was widely read and influenced the future Revolutionary thought, it was considered too rash for adoption by the convention. The seven elected delegates, however, were representative of the best brains, experience, and character among the liberal and moderate factions: Speaker Peyton Randolph, Richard Henry Lee, George Washington, Patrick Henry, Richard Bland, Benjamin Harrison, and Edmund Pendleton. Randolph stood first with 104 votes, as shown in a surviving record of one poll of the delegates, and the others in the order listed. Henry, with 89 votes, stood fourth; Jefferson, with 51, was not chosen.[89] The conservatives and moderates still pulled their weight.

The convention next approved a set of instructions for their delegates to the Continental Congress which were probably as drastic as could be carried with a united front. There is every reason to believe that, if Henry did not write these instructions, he strongly influenced them. They called for a cessation on November 1 of British imports and of purchase of newly entered slaves. If American grievances were not adjusted before August 10, 1775, the export of Virginia tobacco and of all American products to Great Britain was to be halted. Much of the time of the convention must have been taken up with debate on how to enforce the trade embargo without critically injuring Virginia's economic life.

[312]

The session ended, Henry had three weeks in which to return to Hanover and set his affairs in order. Then he and Pendleton were to meet Washington at Mount Vernon for the long ride to Philadelphia.[90]

⟨≈⟩

Public Crisis and Private Sorrow

Every grievance of any one colony must be held and considered by the whole as a grievance to the whole.

—————JOSEPH HAWLEY of Massachusetts

Where liberty . . . is the prize, who would shun the warfare, who would stoop to waste a coward thought on life?

—————DR. JOSEPH WARREN of Massachusetts

IN THE diary of that taciturn and "elusive" gentleman,[1] George Washington, one finds these entries on important dates in the history of Patrick Henry and of the nation:

June 8, 1765 (the only entry in the diary for the week following Henry's Stamp Act speech): "Sowed Turnips for forward use."

August 7, 1765 (when the agitation against the Stamp Act was reaching a crescendo): "began to seperate the Male from Female hemp . . .—rather too late."

March 23, 1775 (the date of Henry's "Give me Liberty" speech at St. John's Church, Richmond, which Washington heard): "Dined at Mr. Patrick Coote's and lodged where I had done the Night before."

From Washington's diary, so singularly and almost comically lacking in details of his political career, we do learn that Patrick Henry, Edmund Pendleton, and George Mason arrived at Mount Vernon late in the evening of August 30, 1774. The three statesmen stayed overnight and engaged in conversation of a nature that we may safely conjecture. Henry knew what to expect from Pendleton, not a die-hard conservative, while from Mason and Washington he received warming encouragement. He and the scholarly squire of Gunston Hall were already forming a mutual admiration society, and Mason's liberalism was affecting the less erudite Washington. Of sound though somewhat slow judgment, Washington had decided that it was time for the colonies to make a stand, and the soldier who had remained steadfast in all the rout and horror of Braddock's defeat was not to be shaken from his position.

The next day the distinguished guests lingered for midday dinner.[2] Then Henry set out with Washington and Pendleton for the Continental Congress, reportedly after a parting admonition from Mrs. Washington, "I hope you will all stand firm. I know George will." [3]

The late southern summer was a dusty, sticky time for a long horseback ride. That afternoon the party crossed the Potomac River and reached Upper Marlboro in Prince Georges County, Maryland. During the next two days they dined at Annapolis, were ferried over the broad Chesapeake, and stopped at Newtown, now Chestertown, on the Eastern shore. To avoid the heat, the gentlemen did much of their riding before noon, and September 2 they made a bracing early morning trip of sixteen miles to Downe's Crossroads. They dined at the Buck Tavern and slept at New Castle, Delaware. That day they made some forty miles and by breakfast the next morning were at Christiana Ferry, now Wilmington, Delaware. From Wilmington they jogged to Chester for dinner.[4]

Now the Virginians were getting close to Philadelphia, and they were joined, according to a local diarist, by delegates from several other colonies. Some six miles out of the city they met with a reception which even outdid that accorded the Adamses and other Massachusetts representatives who had already ridden in from the northward. The Virginians, with other delegates from North Carolina, Maryland, and Delaware, were met by officers of all the Philadelphia military companies and other gentlemen on horseback to the number of five hundred. Two miles from the city, they were also greeted by the company of riflemen and infantry with a band of musicians and conducted proudly into Philadelphia.[5] The journey ending in such fanfare totaled about one hundred and fifty miles, made in a little over four days.

Comfortable Philadelphia, whose conservatism did not always extend to food and drink, was outdoing itself in entertaining many of the leading men in America. First, the Henry party was conducted to the New Tavern or City Tavern on the west side of Second Street above Walnut. It would not be the last time Henry was feted at this pretentious hostelry, described, when it had been completed the previous year, as the finest in America; there were several large clubrooms, two of which could be thrown together to make a dining room fifty feet long.[6] Well-fed and flattered, the Virginians were then escorted the short distance to the brick residence of young Dr. William Shippen. The Shippen mansion, the Shippen-Wistar House still lovingly preserved in Philadelphia, was by rights becoming a center for the Virginia delegation. When studying in London, Dr. Shippen had married Alice, sister of Richard Henry Lee, and the Shippens were related to the Willing family, a daughter of whom had married the ill-starred William Byrd III. Whether or not Dr. Shippen could extend his generous hospitality to Henry as well as Lee for the coming six-week session of the Congress we do not know. But Henry must have been entertained further at the mansion, certainly on the day after his arrival, since his companion, George Washington, speaks of staying for breakfast and dinner.[7]

With young Dr. Shippen, born in Henry's natal year, Patrick found congenial ties. Unlike many of the well-placed Philadelphians, Shippen was a strong Whig. Recently, he had written his wife's brother, William Lee, in England that "we have publish'd your paragraph on politicks as a stimulus to our delegates to be united & firm, which we generally seem determined on, as our only salvation." Later Henry would learn that Dr. Shippen had been made director-general of hospitals for the Continental armies. In Shippen, too, he found a fellow sufferer for a progressive cause: the Doctor, as a pioneer dissector of cadavers and the first American lecturer on anatomy, had with difficulty restrained the onslaught of an ignorant mob, which had got the wild idea that he was "snatching" bodies from graveyards in the city.[8]

As for introductions to other Philadelphians, Henry had hardly thought, when defending the usually obscure Virginia Quakers and sharing their aversion to slavery, that he would secure connections with Friends who were prominent and influential. Besides such introductions as came through Richard Henry Lee, who had arrived at Dr. Shippen's shortly before, the Virginia delegates had been given letters by Henry's Quaker supporter, Robert Pleasants, to influential Philadelphia Friends. Pleasants commended the Virginians to Israel Pemberton as men who had deserved well of their country, and referred to Bland, Henry, and Lee as "great speakers in our House of Assembly . . . and very able advocates for us at the time we made application for relief from militia fines." Another letter, to William Fisher, then Mayor of Philadelphia, was in similar vein, and in a third to Anthony Benezet, Pleasants particularly mentioned Patrick Henry "to whose character and Centiments thou art not altogether a stranger." Any marks of friendship showed to Henry and the other Virginia delegates ("which no doubt will be agreeable to every man in a strange country") would not be unworthily bestowed and might promote the good opinion they generally entertained of the Friends.

In the tall, blue-eyed Israel Pemberton, Henry established contact with a wealthy merchant actively interested in various humanitarian movements. But the strong-minded Pemberton, while he did not defend the actions of the British government after the Boston Port Bill, was determined to keep the Society of Friends clear of radical influences. The so-called "King of the Quakers," he wielded an influence which Henry would find detrimental to the Revolutionary cause. Anthony Benezet, however, must have proved little different from Henry's conception of the pious Philadelphia Quaker who wrote the anti-slavery pamphlets. Benezet, now about seventy years old, was not a self-righteous meddler but a thin little man whose face

[317]

bore "the imprint of a tranquil soul and a clear conscience." The introduction to him was but one of many broadening influences that Henry could take advantage of during the crowded weeks of the convention sessions.[9]

The Congress had been scheduled to open on Thursday, September 1, but there were not enough delegates present to meet until the following Monday. Four of the Virginia delegates, Peyton Randolph, Benjamin Harrison, Richard Henry Lee, and Richard Bland, had arrived on the afternoon of September 2, early enough for John Adams, an honest but sometimes caustic Massachusetts delegate, to gather some impressions for his diary. "The gentlemen from Virginia appear to be the most spirited and consistent of any." Harrison, Adams continued, would have come on foot rather than not at all; Bland would have come, upon this occasion, if it had been to Jericho. Richard Henry Lee was a masterly man, tall and spare; Bland, learned and bookish; and Randolph, large and "well looking." [10] To this Silas Deane, a Connecticut delegate, added that Randolph was open and affable and of majestic deportment, commanding "respect and esteem by his very aspect." [11] Already, Randolph had built up a prestige which would do much to explain his election as President of the Congress.

Deane further described Harrison as "an uncommonly large man . . . rather rough in his dress and speech." [12] Later, John Adams would find in Harrison some of the characteristics that led him to cross swords with Henry in Virginia, and Adams would depict the master of the extensive Berkeley plantation as "an indolent, luxurious, heavy gentleman, of no use in Congress or committee, but a great embarrassment to both." [13] A harsh judgment in view of some notable contributions that Harrison would make to the Revolutionary cause, but he would not see eye to eye with Henry and Adams.

Henry, Pendleton, and Washington arrived in Philadelphia too late for Adams to describe them in detail before he became absorbed with the daily meetings. But Caesar Rodney, a pale, reedlike, though spirited, Delaware delegate, noted that the seven Virginia representatives were present at the opening session "and more sensible fine fellows you'd never wish to see." The Bostonians had been condemned by many for their violence, but as compared "to those from Virginia, South Carolina and Rhode Island, they were moderate men." [14] Rodney did not perceive that the Bostonians, and notably the Adamses, were now playing a muted note.

After late arrivals had straggled in, there were fifty-six delegates present, representing all the colonies except distant Georgia. Henry probably had been introduced to a few of them when he rode to New York for the abortive congress of 1770; others he knew by reputation, and he could now measure them all by the yardstick of ability and firmness for colonial rights. Although Henry was a member of the House of Burgesses when it comprised a galaxy of lofty talents and ideals hardly ever surpassed in a provincial assembly, the convention was a still abler and more representative body. In education and experience, in numerical strength and representation of various political and economic viewpoints, it had never been equaled in America. Stephen Hopkins, a long-time popular leader in Rhode Island, had served in the old Albany congress of 1754. Nine delegates, including John Dickinson of Pennsylvania, Caesar Rodney of Delaware, and three South Carolinians, Thomas Lynch, Christopher Gadsden, and John Rutledge, had been members of the Stamp Act Congress. Two delegates, Washington and John Adams, would be the first two presidents of the United States, and one, Richard Henry Lee, would offer the resolution for American independence. Nor is this to minimize the good if not brilliant capacities, the integrity and experience of a number of representatives from various other colonies.

For Henry there was an added interest in that twenty-two of the delegates were attorneys. It was his first opportunity to meet many of his brother lawyers from other colonies. They brought skill in debating and writing legislative programs and, we trust, not too much of the "nibbling and quibbling" of which John Adams later complained. "There is no greater mortification than to sit with half a dozen wits, deliberating upon a petition, address, or memorial." [15]

On the whole, the delegates were moderately liberal in tone. Most of them would play noteworthy rôles on the Whig side in the critical struggles ahead. Only a few would carry caution to the point of weakness; one, Joseph Galloway of Pennsylvania, would become an outstanding Loyalist. Like Henry, Galloway had a zeal for western land development but his efforts to reconcile the interest of the colonies and the empire led him far from these colleagues to an ultimate burial, as an exile, in a distant Hertfordshire churchyard.[16]

Of the delegations from the various sections, those from New England and the South were the strongest advocates of dynamic action; those from the Middle colonies were inclined to what, in Henry's eyes, was conciliation or worse. Versatile and canny Ben Franklin, the best known American in Europe, was still a colonial agent in England. Sam Adams and his younger cousin, John, two of the ablest Whig leaders in the Northern delegation, usually preferred to stay in the background. The capable South Carolina and Virginia delegations had an exceptional opportunity to prove their mettle. Henry could again show that the man and the hour had met.

For the first time Henry met the Whig leaders of Massachusetts, which had stood in the forefront with Virginia during the mounting struggle for colonial rights. The two Adamses in particular he found congenial spirits. Sam Adams was not only a master at manipulating the local caucus and town meeting, he could also write political propaganda with a Jeremiah-like touch that may have reminded Henry of Samuel Davies. As yet it did not matter greatly that dour Sam was not a constructive statesman, that he was better at tearing down an old government than building a new one. Nowhere in America was there a more talented plotter and organizer of revolutions, nowhere a more passionate and unswerving adherent to a cause.

"I doubt whether there is a greater incendiary in the King's dominion," Governor Hutchinson of Massachusetts wrote early in 1771 of this latter day Puritan.[17] As a tireless agitator for the Revolutionary cause, Adams was superior to Henry, but he was less practical in business affairs, less capable of arousing men to emotional heights. Adams had long been of the opinion that the colonies must fight.

Now, in September, 1774, he was in Philadelphia wearing a new wig, new suit, new shoes, new silk hose, and even a purse with some fifteen or twenty johannes, all supplied by provident friends.[18] Suspected of being too radical and democratic, he stayed in the background, as did his cousin John Adams.

John, a stout, vigorous man of about middle height, was a lawyer of high character and capacity for large affairs. He was now a rising leader of the Whig party in America. After becoming a member of the Massachusetts delegation he had said, "We shall have to resist by force." [19] Playing his hand cleverly, he joined Sam Adams in looking for overt leaders of their program among the more conservative and respected Southern delegates. Henry did not entirely fit this Southern pattern, but Adams was attracted by his obvious abilities as a popular leader.

While voicing his advanced opinions, Henry could not forget that he was dependent on the caprices of the electorate. Virginia voters, like others, could move almost full circle from liberalism to ultra-conservatism. Although Henry had good reason to believe that the people at home wanted the Virginia delegates to take a firm stand for colonial rights, it was encouraging—and challenging—to see letters such as one from a Virginia officer, Adam Stephen. Writing shortly before the convention to Richard Henry Lee, Stephen urged the necessity for military preparation and added this fervent wish for the congress: "I expect to see the spirit of the Amphictyons shine as that illustrious council did in their purest times, before debauched with the Persian gold. The fate of America depends upon your meeting; and the eyes of the European world hang upon you, waiting the event." [20] Strengthened by such assurances and exhortations, so in keeping with his own actions and inclinations, Henry began work on a note of confidence that never forsook him during the seven-week session.

At the very first session, on September 5, the proceedings took a turn to his liking. Carpenters' Hall, meeting place of Philadelphia mechanics, was chosen as the assembly place instead of the State

House favored by some conservatives. Charles Thomson, the Philadelphia Sam Adams, was selected as Secretary of the Congress, although he had not been elected a member of the Pennsylvania delegation. "The Virginians and Carolinians Rutlidge [John Rutledge] excepted, seem much among the Bostonians, and have at their Instance adopted the two above Measures," noted Joseph Galloway, a Philadelphia conservative leader, to whom Thomson was anathema.[21]

When a meeting had been held in the city, not long ago, to consider action on the Boston Port Bill, Henry learned it was Thomson above all who had courageously overcome opposition in order to align Philadelphia in a limited support of the Boston radicals. As his violent speech was being drowned out by the cries of the conservatives, Thomson had conveniently fainted and been carried from the floor. It was strategy more to be expected of ladies. On the whole, the hard-pressed Philadelphia Whigs felt that they had made some progress with their plan of leading the local people "step by step till they had advanced too far to retreat." Now Thomson, their chieftain, had been called from a honeymoon with a second wife (a cousin of John Dickinson's, reputed to have brought her husband £5,000 sterling) to become amanuensis for the Congress.[22]

The hopes of the Galloway party were further dampened and those of the Whigs elevated by the choice of a chairman. Thomas Lynch, a South Carolinian of about sixty, rose from his seat. A planter of great wealth, with baronial holdings in land and slaves, he was nevertheless dressed in American-made clothes and was plain and sensible in his manner. "There is a gentleman present," Lynch stated, "who has presided with great dignity over a respectable society and to the great advantage of America." And he proposed that the Honorable Peyton Randolph, late Speaker of the Virginia House of Burgesses, be appointed chairman. He doubted not that the motion would be carried unanimously, and so it was.[23] The stout, distinguished-looking Randolph took his chair with the same easy assurance with which he had presided over the Burgesses. Two questions of procedure were then decided which set a standard for the future. It was agreed that the convention should be called the Congress and that Randolph should be addressed as the President.

The stage was now prepared for Henry's first speeches in the Congress. Leaving the Shippen house, he had met the other delegates at ten A.M. in the City Tavern, then walked with them the few blocks to Carpenters' Hall.[24] It was a Georgian brick building, in the form of a Greek cross, and, in addition to the friendly political atmosphere, Henry must have been impressed by the comfortable assembly room, the excellent library upstairs, and the long entry adjoining the meeting hall where delegates could stretch their legs.

Henry settled in his Windsor chair while the choice of the convention hall was made and Thomson elected.[25] Both selections had been privately arranged, Galloway sourly wrote, and for Henry they probably confirmed plans of which he had already been informed. Choice of Randolph was another encouraging move.

Meantime, Thomson, an Irish-born teacher, later a merchant, had been found by a doorkeeper of Congress as he alighted from his horse on Chestnut Street. Surprised, Thomson followed the messenger to Carpenters' Hall and took his place at the Secretary's desk. That clerical position he would hold for nearly fifteen years while the Continental Congress directed a revolution and started the American people on the venturesome path of a new government.[26] As he now began his minutes, the members of the assembly were faced with a problem which would again and again perplex American statesmen: should voting in the assembly be by colonies or by population and other resources? Confronted with such a difficult question, no one seemed willing to break the silence. At last a grave-looking member, dressed in a plain dark suit of minister's gray and with unpowdered wig, rose from his seat. Attention was fixed upon him; Thomson regretted that a country parson (or so he appeared) should so mistake his talents and audience. But as he spoke, he revealed such powers of eloquence and persuasion that the inquiry was murmured in the rectangular assembly room: "Who is it? Who is it?" From a few members who knew him came the reply: "It is Patrick Henry."

We are met here in a time and on an occasion of great difficulty

[323]

and distress, Henry declared. Our public circumstances are like those of a man in deep embarrassment and trouble, who calls his friends together to devise what is best to be done for his relief. One would propose one thing, and another a different one, while perhaps a third would think of something better suited to his unhappy circumstances. This he would embrace, and think no more of the rejected schemes with which he would have nothing to do.[27]

Henry's remarks, in this fragmentary version, were hardly momentous, but Thomson followed his suggestions when writing the minutes. He took down what Congress adopted and omitted the further proceedings. It was a practical decision, understandable at that time of quill pens and unsatisfactory shorthand, but as a result some important parts of the deliberations were not recorded.

Henry's remarks assumed further importance in a condensed abstract given by the diary of John Adams. Henry rose, so Adams noted, and said that it was the first general congress that had ever been held and that no former congress could be a precedent. They would have occasion for more general congresses, and a precedent ought to be established now. It would be a great injustice if a little colony should have the same weight in the councils of America as a great one. Therefore, Henry favored the appointment of a committee (to bring in a plan for equitable representation).[28]

The next day, Tuesday, September 6, Congress again met at ten A.M. and debate was continued on the crucial question of the voting rights of each colony. Henry now stood to deliver one of the most significant speeches during the convention.

"By the oppression of Parliament," he insisted, according to John Adams' version, "all government is dissolved. Fleets and armies and the present state of things show that government is dissolved. Where are your landmarks, your boundaries of Colonies? We are in a state of nature, sir. I do propose that a scale should be laid down; that part of North America which was once Massachusetts Bay, and that part which was once Virginia, ought to be considered as having a weight. Will not people complain? Ten thousand Virginians have not outweighed one thousand others.

"I will submit, however; I am determined to submit, if I am overruled.

"A worthy gentleman (ego) near me seems to admit the necessity of obtaining a more adequate representation.

"I hope future ages will quote our proceedings with applause. It is one of the great duties of the democratical part of the constitution to keep itself pure. It is known in my Province that some other Colonies are not so numerous or rich as they are. I am for giving all the satisfaction in my power.

"The distinctions between Virginians, Pennsylvanians, New Yorkers, and New Englanders, are no more. I am not a Virginian, but an American." [29]

In taking the broad viewpoint that he was an American, not a Virginian, Henry propounded a thought for which much of his life had been a preparation. The statement is not surprising to anyone who has noted the progressive ideas in his memorandum of (*circa*) 1766 or followed the subsequent widening of his experience. It has been argued that when stating that he was an American, he was actually developing a provincial argument in favor of special representation for Virginia. No doubt his remarks were influenced by practical politics, but it seems fair to give them a larger and more inspiring connotation. They did represent an advanced idea, so that in many respects he spoke for the future rather than for the present.

On the specific point of whether the vote should be by colonies or by population, the debate was now joined. Governor Ward of little Rhode Island pointed out that there were a great number of counties in Virginia very unequal in wealth and numbers, yet each having the right to send two representatives to the Burgesses.[30] Christopher Gadsden from another small state, South Carolina, could see no way of voting but by colonies.[31]

Two of the Virginia delegates, Lee and Bland, now showed that they were anxious for the convention not to split on lesser issues. Both of them pointed out that the convention lacked the proper information for determining the vote according to wealth and numbers.

"The question is, whether the rights and liberties of America shall be contended for, or given up to arbitrary power," Bland pointed out with his usual discrimination.[32]

"I agree that authentic accounts cannot be had, if by authority is meant attestations of officers of the Crown," Henry interpolated. "I go upon the supposition that government is at an end. All distinctions are thrown down. All America is thrown into one mass. We must aim at the minutiae of rectitude." [33]

Henry's argument that government was at an end disturbed John Jay, an acute-minded New Yorker. A refined-looking, graceful young man of Huguenot descent, he was a representative of the conservative colonial merchants who feared independence might bring mob rule. Jay replied that the measure of arbitrary power was not full; it must run over, before they undertook to frame a new constitution. But he praised the virtuous spirit and abilities of Virginia and favored giving her full weight, an argument advanced no less strongly because of his residence in the large state of New York. It was determined to give each colony one vote, but with the understanding that the decision not be a precedent for the future.[34]

Nothing further is known of the wording of Henry's opening speeches in the Congress. But Silas Deane wrote lyrical praise of them in a letter to his wife and added illuminating comparisons with his Virginia colleagues. Bland and Washington were "tolerable" speakers in public. Washington talked very modestly in a cool but determined style. Pendleton, as we would expect, was "polite in address, and elegant if not eloquent in style and elocution." And Henry, Deane added, was "the compleatest speaker I have ever heard. If his future speeches are equal to the small samples he has hitherto given us, they will be worth preserving." In a letter, Deane said that he could give no idea of the music of Henry's voice or "the highwrought yet natural elegance of his style and manner."

In Virginia and to the southward Henry and Lee were "styled the *Demosthenes* and *Cicero* of America," Deane continued. "God grant they may not, like them, plead in vain for the Liberties of their Country." [35]

The opening sessions had so far been devoted chiefly to questions

[326]

of organization and procedure. That the impression made by Henry only augmented his previous reputation was shown by his committee appointments. A committee of eleven was chosen, on September 7, to deal with the various statutes affecting the colonial trade and manufactures. Henry was assigned to this committee along with Christopher Gadsden, the dedicated South Carolinian who favored taking up his firelock and marching on Boston, Silas Deane, and other delegates of sound though not brilliant ability.[36] A grand committee of twenty-four members, including the Adamses, Lee, Pendleton, and Galloway, was also appointed to prepare a report on the rights of the colonies, and soon became involved in complicated questions relating to the degree of application of the British constitution to America; charters, compacts, and natural rights.[37] On the seventeenth, Henry's Committee on Statutes made its report, and two days later he was added to the important Committee on Rights. Two more North Carolina delegates, William Hooper and William Hewes, had arrived, and they had been appointed to this committee; Henry from Virginia and representatives from Pennsylvania and Massachusetts were added as a concession to the three most populous states. Not until September 24 did this grand committee make its report, other delegates meantime chafing at the delay. Henry was appointed to the committee in time to get the repercussions at least of its meaningful controversies, for instance on whether natural rights should be included in the report; John Adams insisted on retention, Galloway and Deane of New York dissented.[38]

During the two weeks of intensive committee work, Congress held only a few general sessions. But there were some periods of high emotion, with enough activity otherwise to satisfy, if not exhaust, the most perfervid delegates. Before adjournment on September 6, an express arrived with a report of the British bombardment of Boston. "I cannot say that all faces gather paleness," Silas Deane wrote his wife, "but they all gather indignation, and every tongue pronounces revenge." Henry, like the other delegates, seemed to consider the bombardment of the Massachusetts port as if it were in his own colony. The Reverend Jacob Duché, chaplain of the Congress, read to the tense convention the apt lines from the Thirty-fifth Psalm, "Plead my cause, O Lord, with them that strive with me . . ." and followed with a ten-minute extemporaneous prayer so pertinent and so "sublime" that it was "worth riding one hundred miles to hear." Although the rumor of the bombardment proved unfounded, it was obvious that the delegates were not to be frightened from their duties by the threat of war.[39]

While Henry's committee duties were not yet as heavy as those of John Adams, he had reason enough to agree with Adams' entry in his diary on the fourteenth: "We go to congress at nine, and there we stay, most earnestly engaged in debates upon the most abstruse mysteries of state, until three in the afternoon; then we adjourn, and go to dine with some of the nobles of Pennsylvania at four o'clock, and feast upon ten thousand delicacies, and sit drinking Madeira, Claret, and Burgundy till six or seven, and then go home fatigued to death with business, company, and care. Yet I hold out surprisingly." [40]

On Thursday, September 22, a crucial day in their committee work, John Adams, Henry, and other Virginians dined with Chief Justice Chew of Pennsylvania—one of many Lucullan feasts in honor of the visiting delegates: "Turtle, and every other thing, flummery, jellies, sweetmeats of twenty sorts, trifles, whipped sillabubs, floating islands, fools, &c. and then a dessert of fruits, raisins, almonds, pears, peaches. Wines most excellent and admirable." Adams, who drank Madeira at a great rate, "found no inconvenience in it." [41] Henry was probably among the Virginia and New Jersey delegates who dined at old Dr. Shippen's on Monday, September 26. John Adams, who was present, was still working to line up delegates for the advanced Whig cause, and an impression of his delicate maneuvering is given in a letter which he wrote that day to William Tudor:

> We have had numberless prejudices to remove here. We have been obliged to act with great delicacy and caution . . . to keep ourselves out of sight, and to feel pulses and sound the depths; to insinuate our sentiments, designs, and desires, by means of

[328]

other persons; sometimes of one Province, and sometimes of another.

Adams like a good Puritan continued to stick to his cause, but with the endless entertainments piled on the heavy convention duties he was "wearied to death." The business of Congress was "tedious beyond expression," he wrote. Every delegate had to "show his oratory, his criticism, and his political abilities." Every question was discussed "with a moderation, an acuteness, a minuteness equal to that of Queen Elizabeth's privy council." Let a motion be made that two and two make five, and he supposed they would be "entertained with logic and rhetoric, law, history, politics, and mathematics." [42]

Actually, the impatient Adams was seeing the situation too close at hand. On September 20, Richard Henry Lee wrote his brother William in London that the proceedings of the Congress were "yet on honor to be kept secret, but we have great hopes that their vigor and unanimity will prove the ruin of our ministerial Enemies and the salvation of American Liberty. About a fortnight more will produce a publication of our plan. . . ." [43]

The optimism of Lee and doubtless Henry had been largely produced by the reading in Congress on September 17 of some revolutionary resolves from Suffolk County, Massachusetts, and their subsequent endorsement by the convention. Even John Adams had a fit of elation! [44] In the resolves from the Massachusetts county (which included beleaguered Boston) its delegates declared that "the power but not the justice . . . of Great Britain" which had of old driven their ancestors from British shores now pursued the children. The late Acts of Parliament with regard to Massachusetts were in violation of the laws of nature, the British constitution and the charter of the province, and its people were not obligated to obey them. Commercial non-intercourse with Great Britain was recommended until the rights of Massachusetts were fully restored. [45]

The Suffolk Resolves were shrewdly presented to the Congress in such a manner that to reject them would appear to be leaving the Bostonians to an abject fate. A motion was passed by the delegates

approving the conduct of their Massachusetts countrymen in opposition to "the wicked ministerial measures" and recommending per-
severance in the same "firm and temperate conduct" as expressed in
the Suffolk Resolves. Richard Henry Lee may have had a hand in
this motion, if so with Henry's strong approval, and its unanimous
passage gave notable encouragement to the advanced liberals in the
convention.[46] They were in a position to win a narrow victory when
the real crisis of the convention came on September 28, 1774.

On the twenty-eighth, Joseph Galloway proposed his famous Plan
of Union for the colonies. Offered by the influential Pennsylvania
delegate, it was in some respects similar to that presented at Albany
a generation before by another distinguished Pennsylvanian, Ben
Franklin. There was to be a colonial union with a president-general
appointed by the King; and a grand council elected by the assemblies of the various colonies and with intracontinental powers similar
to those of the British Parliament in England. But the assent of the
appointive President-General was necessary for all Acts of the Grand
Council, and it was to be "an inferior and distinct branch of the British legislature, united and incorporated with it" for the general regulations affecting the colonies. Such legislation might originate in
either the Council or Parliament, but the approval of both was man-
datory.[47]

This plan offered a plausible scheme for unity within the British
Empire. It was defended by Galloway with an ability and subtlety
that made a strong appeal to the more conservative delegates. At the
last, before outlining the details of his plan, Galloway pleaded with
the delegates in words that would be prophetic of his own vicissitudes:

> I therefore beseech you, by the respect you are bound to pay to
> the instructions of your constituents, by the regard you have for
> the honour and safety of your country, and as you wish to avoid
> a war with Great-Britain which must terminate, at all events in
> the ruin of America, not to rely on a denial of the authority of
> Parliament, a refusal to be represented, and on a non-importa-
> tion agreement; because whatever protestations, in that case,
> may be made to the contrary, it will prove to the world that we

intend to throw off our allegiance to the State, and to involve
the two countries in all the horrors of a civil war.[48]

The motion for Galloway's plan was seconded by James Duane of
New York, and was supported by John Jay and Edward Rutledge.[49]
If the plan had been proposed before the reception of the Suffolk
Resolves, it apparently would have passed. As it was, the plan is said
to have failed by one vote; only Henry is known to have opposed it
in the debate. John Adams' account of his speech, while sketchy and,
it appears, not literally accurate, gives some impression of Henry's
argument: "The original constitution of the colonies was founded on
the broadest and most generous base," Henry declared. "The regulation of our trade was compensation enough for all the protection
we ever experienced from her [England].

"We shall liberate our constituents from a corrupt House of Commons, but throw them into the arms of an American Legislature, that
may be bribed by that nation which avows, in the face of the world,
that bribery is a part of her system of government.

"Before we are obliged to pay taxes as they do, let us be as free
as they; let us have our trade with all the world.

"We are not to consent by the representatives of representatives.

"I am inclined to think the present measures lead to war." [50]

The advocates of the Galloway Plan succeeded nevertheless in getting a vote for future consideration of the proposal, but what Galloway regarded as "the violent party" won such power in the convention that the motion was not included in the *Journal*.[51] Samuel Adams
wielded much power in defeat of the plan, and he and Henry deserve a large share of credit for defeat of the measure which would
have left America a dependency of Great Britain.[52] From what Henry
stated after his return to Hanover [53] and from other evidence, it
seems clear that he believed the Intolerable Acts, with earlier offensive measures, proved that the British would not give home rule to
America. This could only be secured by independence, and the Americans possessed the necessary political capacity and material resources
to assure its success.

[331]

Congress also adopted a non-importation, non-exportation, and non-consumption agreement or Association against Great Britain, and the enforcement was left in the hands of local committees usually under the control of the radicals. It also passed a Declaration of Rights and Grievances addressed to the people of Great Britain, a memorial to the American colonies, and a petition to the King.[54] Henry was a member of the committee which drew up this petition; that it was not satisfactorily prepared and had to be rewritten, was for a long time supposed to have been Henry's fault. But this accusation is based on a letter written a half-century later by Thomas Jefferson and is not adequately sustained by the evidence.[55]

On October 11 John Adams spent the evening with Henry at his lodgings, consulting in regard to the petition to the King. Adams declared that Henry "has high notions, talks of exalted minds, etc. He has a horrid opinion of Galloway, Jay, and the Rutledges. Their system, he says, would ruin the cause of America. He is very impatient to see such fellows, and not be at liberty to describe them in their true colors." [56]

On the other hand, when Henry was later queried as to the abilities of the Philadelphia delegates, he said that [John?] Rutledge was the greatest orator. And Henry added that, while Colonel Washington had no pretensions to eloquence, he had more solid judgment and information.[57] Already ties of respect and of similar aspirations were being formed between Henry and Washington that would remain unbroken throughout their long political careers.

The Continental Congress had at the outset been only a convention of ambassadors of distinct communities, but in the words of John Dickinson the colonists had "now taken such grounds that Great Britain must relax, or inevitably involve herself in a civil war." [58] At Philadelphia the delegates had built a framework to which they could add as emergencies required. Before adjournment, they called another continental congress to meet the following May, 1775.

After the Continental Congress had completed its business, Henry and John Adams took a memorable leave of each other. Adams expressed his conviction that, however necessary the American resolves, declarations of rights, remonstrances, associations, and the like might be to cement the union of the colonies, they would be wastepaper in England. Henry replied that they might make some impression on the English people, but agreed that they would be totally lost upon the government. Adams had just received a short and hurried letter from Major Joseph Hawley of Northampton, Massachusetts, which contained "a few broken hints" as to the course he felt the colonies should follow. The paper, prepared before the middle of August, 1774, begins as follows:

> We must fight, if we can't otherwise rid ourselves of British taxation, all revenues, or the constitution or form of government enacted for us by the British parliament. It is evil against right, —utterly intolerable to every man who has any idea or feeling of right or liberty.

Hawley's paper also contains statements to the effect that America's salvation depended upon "an established, persevering union of the colonies" and that "every grievance of any one colony must be held and considered by the whole as a grievance to the whole. This will be a difficult matter but it must be done."

Henry listened with keen attention to the paper. As Adams read the words "We must fight," Henry raised his head and vehemently asserted "By G—d, I am of that man's mind." He took Hawley's letter in his hand and he read it with a solemn pronouncement that he agreed entirely with the writer.

Adams said that he felt Henry had uttered a sacred oath upon a very great occasion. Adams could have sworn the oath as religiously as Henry, and he considered it as by no means inconsistent with the statement in Wirt's book that Henry never took the sacred name in vain.

Adams declared that the other delegates from Virginia returned home in full confidence that all the American grievances would be redressed.[59]

"We shall infallibly carry all our points, you will be completely relieved; all the offensive acts will be repealed; the army and fleet will be recalled, and Britain will give up her foolish project," Richard Henry Lee said to Adams in parting.

"Only George Washington was in doubt," Adams declared. Although he never spoke in public, Washington joined privately with the delegates who advocated a non-exportation and non-importation agreement. Washington thought that with both plans the Americans would prevail; without either, the issue was doubtful.[60]

Thus Richard Henry Lee felt that the Americans would carry their points without war, Washington was in doubt, and Henry felt that it would be necessary to fight.

Further proof that Henry had now mentally prepared himself for a final break with England is found in an incident that occurred back in Virginia. Not long, it seems, after Henry returned to Hanover, he found himself one day at the home of Colonel John Overton. Nearly all Virginia landed gentlemen still seemed to become colonels, and we are informed that Colonel Samuel Overton and Colonel Morris were also present, as well as the untitled John Hawkins. It was natural for the conversation to turn to the political crisis.

"Do you suppose that Great Britain would drive her colonies to extremities? And if so, what would be the issue of the war?" Colonel Samuel Overton asked Henry.

Henry looked around to see who was present, then replied confidentially (in words which appear to be recalled with substantial accuracy): "She will drive us to extremities—no accommodation will take place—hostilities will soon commence—and a desperate and bloody touch it will be."

"But do you think, Mr. Henry, that an infant nation as we are, without discipline, or ammunition, ships of war or money to procure them—do you think it possible, thus circumstanced, to oppose successfully the fleets and armies of Great Britain?"

"I will be candid with you," Henry replied. "I doubt whether we shall be able, alone, to cope with so powerful a nation. But," he continued, rising from his chair with great animation, "where is France? Where is Spain? Where is Holland? The natural enemies of Great

Britain—where will they be all this while? Do you suppose they will stand by, idle and indifferent spectators to the contest?

"Will Louis XVI be asleep all this time?" Henry continued. "Believe me, no! When Louis XVI shall be satisfied by our serious opposition, and our Declaration of Independence, that all prospect of reconciliation is gone, then, and not till then, will he furnish us with arms, ammunition and clothing; and not with these only, but he will send his fleet and arms to fight our battles for us; he will form with us a treaty offensive and defensive, against our unnatural mother. Spain and Holland will join the confederation! Our independence will be established, and we shall take our stand among the nations of the earth!"

At the word independence, Colonel Overton recalled, the company appeared to be startled. Never before had they heard any such drastic proposal even suggested.[61]

Even the critical John Adams had written regretfully of his departure on October 28 from "the happy, the peaceful, the elegant, the hospitable, and polite city of Philadelphia." Henry must have left there in an even more grateful mood. But he had ample reason to hasten home: not merely because of the impending session of the General Assembly but because of other grave events of a private and public nature. Lord Dunmore had summoned the Assembly to meet on August 11, 1774, but prorogued it to November 3. Henry, hurrying home from Philadelphia, knew that when the Burgesses and the Governor dealt with current issues the sparks would fly. Characteristically, however, Lord Dunmore avoided further conflict—and assertion of popular rights—by postponing the session, first until November 7, then to November 10, and again until February 1, 1775. The November proroguings were too late to prevent many upcountry members from making the long trip to Williamsburg. It was not surprising in view of the trend of events that the Governor on January 19 postponed the February session until May, 1775.[62] But by then the aggravated issues were being settled on the battlefield rather than in legislative halls.

[335]

How correct was Henry's forecast of a coming war, events soon proved. Hostilities had already broken out on the frontier, a training school for the grim warfare beginning the next year. The details of the Indian war as they reached the Henry family are disclosed in letters written by his mother and his sister Mrs. Anne Christian.[63] From Scotchtown in October, 1774, Mrs. Henry, somewhat at loose ends since the death of her husband, had gone to Botetourt County to visit her daughter Anne. While she was there an Indian war broke out and the Christians, with many of their friends and relatives, were again exposed to the threat of a savage foe.

Since Pontiac's War of a decade before, there had been an uneasy peace with the northwestern Indians. But their smoldering animosity was fanned by the building of backwoodsmen's cabins in the Indian hunting grounds. War broke out in 1774 on the western Virginia frontier, and no help came from neighboring Pennsylvania, irritated by Lord Dunmore's handling of their boundary dispute. Dunmore, mindful also of his own land speculations in the area, moved vigorously against the Indians. He led personally one expedition which got unwisely shunted down the Ohio and missed the battle of Point Pleasant. One of his officers, doubtless disappointed not to be present for the fighting, was Captain Alexander McClanahan, brother-in-law of Henry's ill wife. Less than thirty years before, when Augusta Court had lately been opened at Staunton, Alexander's father, Robert McClanahan, had obtained a license to keep an ordinary, the log cabin hostelry just opposite the courthouse. The guests, many in hunting shirts, sat on wooden benches; the tables were split logs attached together; the beef, pork, venison, hominy, cabbage, and potatoes were served in pewter or wooden platters. No forks and knives were provided "but each gent whipped out his jack knife and helped himself as best he could, fingers being freely used." Charge for the meal was the equivalent of 12½ cents, fixed by the court; coffee was not available, but rum was $1.50 a gallon, whiskey a dollar, and consumed by most of the sturdy customers without foundering.[64]

The ordinary keeper of the 1740's, Robert McClanahan, had later become one of the prominent men of the Valley, high sheriff and commander of the militia. Upon the outbreak of the Indian war twenty-five of the drafted men in Augusta County refused to march, preferring "to run the hazzard of the fine." But Robert McClanahan's son, Alexander, commanded one of the two "noble Companies" from the countryside which ventured out cheerfully with Lord Dunmore toward the Shawnee towns, only to miss the bad fighting.[65]

The other expedition against the Indians, composed of Virginia frontiersmen in hunting shirts and moccasins, assembled near the present Lewisburg, West Virginia, under General Andrew Lewis. In this force William Christian and his brother-in-law, William Fleming, served as colonels, while in the ranks were many of Henry's supporters. The little army was undisciplined, but in marksmanship, in courage and physique, perhaps it was never surpassed in America. Resolutely the men marched to meet the Indians.

Back home, their families had to make out the best they could against the threat of torch and scalping knife. Mrs. John Henry came back with her daughter from the exposed Christian place to Hanover, stopping en route with Mrs. William Fleming in Botetourt. From Scotchtown, on October 15, 1774, Mrs. Henry wrote Mrs. Fleming thanking her for her hospitality and assuring her that the lowland people had their own troubles and fears in regard to Great Britain. "Perhaps our good God will bring us out of these many evils, which threaten us not only from the mountains but from the seas." The Hanover people had been very sickly, but Mrs. Henry hoped that the sickly season was over. Her dear Annie [Christian] had been ailing for two or three days with a fever. The dear children, however, were very well. Her son Patrick had left for Philadelphia nearly seven weeks before. "The affairs are kept with great secrecy, nobody being allowed to be present." To this, Anne Christian added in a letter of the same date to a sister-in-law that she had not heard from her, "nor from the Fronteer which makes me very uneasie I heard a flying report that there were 4 Families killd on new river but hope it false.

"My brother Pat is not returnd from Philadelphia yet his Wife is extremely ill," Anne continued.[66]

[337]

Patrick had signed Sarah's name to several deeds during the past two years,[67] and it is obvious that her condition was pitiful. There is a hint of how distressing her illness was to Patrick in a statement which he made a few years later to a friend: he had been obliged, he said, to give up everything that recalled her memory.[68]

While Henry had to face the realities of his personal tragedy, he was confronted with the gravest crisis of his political career. In addition to closing the port of Boston and virtually crushing self-government in Massachusetts, the British were taking further drastic steps to intimidate the Americans. As usual throughout history, extremes on the one hand bred extremes on the other. On November 16, the *Virginia Gazette* printed the resolve of the Continental Congress urging that committees be chosen "to observe the conduct of persons in regard to the Association." There was no record, at least in the Hanover area, of the tarring and feathering used in many colonies to terrify dissident citizens. But already, on October 13, two Virginians had deemed it wise to print in the *Gazette* public apologies for their statements reflecting upon the measures pursued by the colony and their delegates to the Continental Congress. Coming close home, on December 15 both Malcolm Hart and Paul Thilman of Hanover were quoted as being forced to confess and recant their Tory expressions. The local committee considered a charge against Paul Thilman, the Hanover jailer, for violating the Association, for contemptuous behavior to many respectable gentlemen who questioned him, and for other offenses. He was found guilty and, faced with an economic interdict or exile, he "heartily and sincerely" professed and declared that he was truly sorry for his conduct.[69]

While no blood had yet been shed, the issues between the British and the Americans were being sharply drawn. It would not be many months before Lord Dunmore would be proclaiming:

Virginia, to wit:
WHEREAS, I have been informed, from undoubted Authority, that a certain Patrick Henry, of the County of Hanover, and a Number of deluded Followers, have taken up Arms . . . and styling themselves an Independent Company, have marched out

[338]

of their County, encamped, and put themselves in a Posture of War, and have written and dispatched Letters to divers Parts of the Country, exciting the People to join in these outrageous and rebellious Practices, to the great terrour of all His Majesty's faithful Subjects, and in open Defiance of Law and Government; and have committed other Acts of Violence . . .[69]

And Dunmore would denounce Henry to the ministry as "a man of desperate circumstances, who had been very active in encouraging disobedience and exciting a spirit of revolt among the people for many years past." [70]

If the Americans won, Henry would be acclaimed as a founding father, one of the great men of history. If they failed, he would be a traitor, and probably hang on an English gibbet.

LIST OF PRINCIPAL SOURCES

In writing the Patrick Henry biography, I owe much to the knowledge obtained from graduate study under distinguished professors at the Universities of Virginia, Illinois, North Carolina, and Chicago, and from experience gained in teaching American history to a generation of college students. Even with this background, the research and writing for the first volume in America and Great Britain has required eight years. It will be impractical to give a complete Bibliography, covering all the extensive data studied, until the publication of the second volume. But I have appended below a list of the most useful sources, along with abbreviated titles used in the following Notes, where these titles are not clear from the context.

British Sources

These consist chiefly of parish, city, and national government records; contemporary newspapers, diaries, merchants' accounts, and ecclesiastical correspondence. The most valuable data was found in Aberdeen and near-by Foveran Parish; at Edinburgh, Glasgow, and Bristol; and at London, especially in the British Museum, the Public Record Office, and the archives of the British Ecclesiastical Commission. The libraries at Aberdeen, Glasgow, Bristol, and the British Museum generously provided many printed records and other books, newspapers, pamphlets, and pictures, difficult if not impossible to obtain elsewhere.

American Sources
Manuscripts

The most important sources for Patrick Henry material are the Virginia State Library, the Virginia Historical Society, and the Valentine Museum, all in Richmond; the Library of Congress, Washington; the New York Public Library; the University of Virginia; Duke University; the University of North Carolina; and various Virginia courthouses. Henry was not only an orator and statesman but a lawyer, landowner and speculator,

[341]

with something of the back countryman's wanderlust. Manuscripts relating to him were found in over thirty Virginia courthouses. Photostats of much of this material are in the Virginia State Library, but it was necessary to spend many months in examining papers, often unindexed, in courthouses mostly in Piedmont Virginia or near by, but extending as far as Abingdon in Washington County. The old suit papers preserved at the Federal Courthouse in Richmond, the Philadelphia libraries and archives, and the records compiled by Colonial Williamsburg were mines of information.

In addition, I circularized the principal archival centers in the United States and in cases where advisable, I personally explored them. I made an effort to examine contemporary manuscripts, even when they were not known to contain Henry information. Thus I could get a "feeling" for the times and uncover valuable data in unexpected sources. The information even extended to contemporary modes of speech. An early Louisa County clerk, for instance, euphoniously wrote "Pahtrick" on a legal record, in accord with the local pronunciation; and Patrick Henry spelled the name of a Hanover client "N. Barkley" (Berkeley).

Selected Sources

Abernethy, Thomas Perkins, *Western Lands and the American Revolution.*

Adams, Charles Francis, *The Works of John Adams.* (Adams, *Works.*)

Anderson, William, *The Scottish Nation.*

Ballagh, James Curtis, *The Letters of Richard Henry Lee.*

Becker, Carl, *The Eve of the Revolution.*

Boyd, Julian, editor, *The Papers of Thomas Jefferson.* (Boyd, *Jefferson Papers.*)

Brant, Irving, *James Madison.*

Bridenbaugh, Carl, *Seat of Empire, The Political Rôle of Eighteenth Century Williamsburg.*

Brydon, G. M., *Virginia's Mother Church.*

Burnaby, A., *Travels through North America.* (*Burnaby's Travels.*)

Burnett, E. C., *Letters of Members of the Continental Congress.* (Burnett, *Letters.*)

Byrd, William, *A Journey to the Land of Eden and Other Papers.*

Campbell, Charles, *History of the Colony and Ancient Dominion of Virginia.*

Chamberlayne, Churchill Gibson, *Vestry Book of St. Paul's Parish, Hanover County, Virginia 1706-1786.*

Chitwood, Oliver P., *A History of Colonial America.*

Clement, Maude Carter, *The History of Pittsylvania County Virginia.*

Dabney, John Blair, Ms. Pamphlet copy of extracts from the manuscript, edited by Charles W. Dabney. Virginia State Library.

Dictionary of American Biography. (DAB.)

Dictionary of National Biography. (DNB.)

Executive Journals of the Council of Colonial Virginia. (Council Journal.)

Fitzpatrick, John C., editor, *The Diaries of George Washington. (Washington Diaries.)*

Foote, Rev. William Henry, *Sketches of Virginia, Historical and Biographical.*

Ford, P. L., editor, *The Writings of Thomas Jefferson.* (Ford, *Jefferson's Writings.*)

Ford, W. C., editor, *Journals of the Continental Congress. (Journal.)*

Freeman, Douglas Southall, *George Washington.*

Frothingham, Richard, *The Rise of the Republic of the United States.*

Gewehr, Wesley Marsh, *The Great Awakening in Virginia.*

Gipson, L. H., *The British Empire Before the American Revolution.*

Gipson, L. H., *The Coming of the Revolution, 1763-1775,* in Henry Steele Commager and Richard B. Morris, editors, *The New American Nation Series.* Contains an excellent bibliography.

Glazebrook, Eugenia, *Virginia Migrations, Hanover County.* Glazebrook, *Hanover.*

Gwathmey, John H., *Twelve Virginia Counties.*

Harris, Malcolm H., *A History of Louisa County Virginia.* (Harris, *Louisa.*)

Hening, William Waller, *The Statutes at Large; being a Collection of all the Laws of Virginia from the First Session of the Legislature, in the Year 1619. (Hening's Statutes.)*

Henry's Account Book. (Account Book.)

Henry, William Wirt, *Patrick Henry, Life, Correspondence and Speeches.* (Henry, *Henry.*)

Hill, Helen, *George Mason.*

Hunter, Mrs. W. W., *The Four John Symes of Virginia,* Ms.

Journal of House of Burgesses. (JHB.)

Kimball, Marie, *Thomas Jefferson.*

Lecky, W. E. H., *A History of England in the Eighteenth Century.*

Malone, Dumas, *Jefferson the Virginian.*

Mays, David John, *Edmund Pendleton.*

Meade, Bishop William, *Old Churches, Ministers and Families of Virginia*. (Meade, *Old Churches*.)

Morgan, Edmund, *The Stamp Act Crisis*.

Morgan, George, *The True Patrick Henry*. (Morgan, *Henry*.)

Perry, W. S., editor, *Historical Collections of the American Colonial Church*. (Perry, *Historical Collections*.)

Preston Manuscript. Unpublished biography of Elizabeth Henry by her descendant, Miss Nelly Preston. (Preston Ms.)

Swem, Earl Gregg, *Virginia Historical Index*.

Sydnor, Charles S., *Gentleman Freeholders Political Practices in Washington's Virginia*.

Tyler, Moses Coit, *Patrick Henry*.

Virginia Gazette, (Va. Gazette.)

Virginia Gazette Index.

Virginia Land Office Records. (L.O. Records.)

Virginia Magazine of History and Biography. (Va. Mag.)

William and Mary Quarterly. (Wm. and Mary.)

Wirt, William, *The Life of Patrick Henry*. (Wirt, *Henry*.)

NOTES

Chapter 1

THE EARLIER SCOTTISH INFLUENCES

1. Quoted in Norman Macpherson, *The Chapel, Crown, and other Ancient Buildings of King's College,* pp. 3-5. The author also refers to the college kirk and steeple, both of "hewin stone curiouslie wrought," and to the college bells with their "musicall harmonie." *Ibid.*

2. From a story handed down in the immediate neighborhood which at least has the flavor of the occasion. The story was repeated to the writer on June 15, 1951, by Miss Mary Haw, who lives near Hanover Courthouse. She had been given the story by Lancy Jones from Hilly Farm of which The Glebe, the Rev. Patrick Henry's place, was a part.

3. For sources of the data given on the Parson's Cause in this chapter see chap. VIII.

4. Maury's letter dated Dec. 12, 1763, is in James Maury-Camm Letterbook, Alderman Library, University of Virginia. Photostatic copy through courtesy of William H. Gaines, Jr., and Graduate History Club, University of Virginia. The general tenor of Henry's speech is given in Commissary William Robinson's letter to the Bishop of London, Aug. 12, 1765. W. S. Perry, *Historical Collections of the American Colonial Church* hereafter cited as *Historical Collections,* I, 514. A few changes for convenience in reading have been made in capitalization, punctuation, etc., and the words have been put in direct discourse.

5. Henry, *Henry,* I, 41. Letter of Frank Ruffin to Paul Carrington Cameron, Hillsboro, N.C., June 1, 1870, in 18 *William and Mary Quarterly* (hereafter cited as *Wm. and Mary*), Series 1, pp. 270-274. Frank Ruffin knew several of Henry's descendants in the Roane family, including his grandson, William H. Roane; also John Roane, Jr., who died in King William County, Va., in 1838, aged 72. Ruffin stated that the only sentence he ever heard from Patrick Henry's speech in the Parson's Cause was: "Such is the avarice, such the insatiate thirst for gold of these ecclesi-

astical harpies that they would snatch the last hoe cake from the widow and the orphan."

6. For sources of the data on Col. Henry in this paragraph see esp. pp. 14-16 and accompanying notes. His Latin dictionary, later owned by his son Patrick, is in the Virginia State Library.

7. See pp. 121-123.

8. Personal visit to Aberdeen in summer of 1948.

9. From original in Library of Congress. That Margaret had not kept in close touch with Patrick, however, is indicated by the fact that the letter is addressed to him in Scotchtown, Hanover County, where he had not lived for some fourteen years.

The Mrs. Meredith to whom Margaret Donald referred was Patrick's sister, Jane, who married Samuel Meredith; Betsy Henry was Patrick's sister Elizabeth.

10. For this data on David Henry and his relationship to Patrick, see 62 *The Gentleman's Magazine*, part I, 578-579, and part II, 697-698; also William Anderson, *The Scottish Nation*, II, 463-464. The reference to several of David Henry's relatives who came to America doubtless helps to explain his connection with various Henry families now in the United States.

11. William Wirt Henry Papers, Va. Historical Society, Richmond, Va.

12. See pp. 9-10. There are no records of Alexander Henry and Jean Robertson having any adult male children except John, Patrick's father, and the Rev. Patrick. The obituary notices of David Henry (see Note 10) show that he was born at Foveran on Dec. 26, 1710. Fragmentary records still surviving state that on Dec. 27, 1709, Alexander Henry "in Foveran" had a son baptized David. All the evidence seems to indicate that this was David, the printer, and there was a mistake in the obituary as to the birth year. Parochial Registers, County of Aberdeen, Foveran, New Register House, Edinburgh.

13. Proof that John Henry held a bursary or scholarship at King's College is found in its alumni records. See p. 15.

14. William Robbie, *Aberdeen, Its Traditions and History*, pp. 258-259. The data on the Hendrys who received parish relief is from the Kirk Session Reports, Foveran Church, Newburgh, Scotland.

15. Kirk Session Reports, Foveran Church.

16. Dr. Douglas Simpson, Librarian, University of Aberdeen, a scholarly writer on the local history. To Dr. Simpson I am indebted for much valuable assistance, both when I was in Aberdeenshire and after my return to the United States.

17. Margaret Hendry was assessed £1, one of the largest amounts on

the list and identical with that for Helen Udny. Most of the parishioners were assessed a few shillings or less. Moreover, on Apr. 3, 1687, a John Hendry was assessed six shillings, which was over a fourth the allotment for the entire congregation. Kirk Session Reports, Foveran Church.

18. Although many of the parishioners were Episcopalians, they were under the legal discipline of the state church, the Presbyterian Kirk.

19. The Robertson name is frequently found in the Aberdeenshire records.

20. "Foveran" is apparently derived from the Gaelic "fueran," a spring. J. A. Henderson, *Aberdeenshire Epitaphs*, pp. 309-310.

21. An early Scandinavian poet, Einar Skulason, describes a raid on Apardion (Aberdeen) in 1153:

> "I heard the overthrow of people;
> The Clash of broken arms was heard
> The King destroyed the peace
> Of the dwellers in Apardion."
> —*Scottish Notes and Queries*, March, 1894

22. Data from Alexander Murray and Ian Duiguid, Newburgh, Scotland.

23. The Scottish Jacobites termed him James VIII. He was the son of James II of England and VII of Scotland, last of the Stuart Kings.

24. Data from Dr. Douglas Simpson, Aberdeen.

25. I happened to be in Aberdeen in 1948 during one of the services commemorating the ordination of Bishop Seabury.

26. Some thirty years later, in 1755, the population was estimated at 15,730. W. E. H. Lecky, *A History of England in the Eighteenth Century*, II, 273.

27. *Aberdeen Journal Notes and Queries*, V, 232.

28. William Watt, *A History of Aberdeen and Banff*, p. 310.

29. For this data on John Henry's preparation for and admission to King's College, I am indebted to Dr. Douglas Simpson. See also p. 15.

30. This description is taken from a picture of King's College about 1670, in the College Library.

31. See Walter Scott, *Legend of Montrose*.

32. Thomas Carlyle, *Frederick the Great (1900)*, VII, 215. Keith was the Earl whose family was seated in Aberdeenshire. The oatmeal tradition is not to be accepted literally. Peter Ledingham, sacristan at King's College, stated that "in the old days the boys had to provide a bag of oatmeal and a bag of potatoes which were cooked in the Buttery and were about all they had to live on. Every month they would go home to replenish their supplies." Interview on June 25, 1948.

33. In his will now at the Valentine Museum, Richmond, Va., he signed himself Patrick Henry, M.A. See also Records of the Marischal College and University, II, 294-295. I am indebted to R. G. Cant, Deputy Keeper of the Muniments, University of St. Andrews, Scotland, for seeking possible records of the Rev. Patrick Henry in the printed records of several British universities.

34. Alumni records of King's and Marischal colleges. For John Henry's college record see especially Peter John Anderson, ed., *Alumni in Arts of the University and King's College of Aberdeen, 1596-1860*, pp. 58-59.

35. The original papal bull of 1494 directed that the projected university be conducted like those at Paris and Bologna ("sicut in Parisieni et Boloniensi"). *Aberdeen University Students' Handbook for 1947-1948*, pp. 56-58. See also Lecky, *op. cit.*, II, 272-274.

36. Robert S. Rait, *History of the Universities of Aberdeen*, p. 187; Andrew Lang, *A History of Scotland*, pp. 409-410.

37. During the eighteenth century Henrys and the variants, Hendrys or Hendries, abounded in Aberdeenshire, both the town and countryside. The Gordon surname in that region was borne by noblemen of the "wild" strain from which Lord Byron was descended and by humble dependents. There were gradations, though of less degree, among the Henrys, or Hendrys and Hendries. Even in Foveran Parish where lived some of Patrick's kin, there is a tradition of two different Henry families, perhaps of markedly different social background. Data from Alexander Murray, Newburgh, Scotland, June, 1948.

One family, now removed to Aberdeen and beyond, lived in a stone cottage at Foveran (surviving in recent years) and trace back to a blacksmith and a shoemaker. They may not have been of the same family as David Henry. At any rate, their descendants were fired with zeal for education and advancement. One became a minister and teacher in New Zealand; another, George Henry, a missionary to Africa. His aged nephew, William Fraser of Aberdeen, showed a picture of George standing by Livingstone's tomb in central Africa. His uncle, he said, "wanted to better himself and see the wu-r-rld," so went to Africa. Another of this present-day family, then 82 years old, said that there were three Henry lads at the college in her grandmother's time. She could remember the books piled up in her house—they were "a very booky family." Interviews of William Fraser, 87 Osborne Place, and Mrs. Annie Watson (née Forbes) of 27 Hammersfield Avenue, Aberdeen, in June, 1948. Mrs. Watson, then 82 years old, stated that she is the niece of James Henry, the minister who went to New Zealand.

[348]

38. Data from King's College records, kindly supplied by Dr. Douglas Simpson. Article on James Blair, *Dictionary of American Biography* (hereafter cited as *DAB*). 9 *Wm. and Mary* (Ser. 2), p. 301.

39. Article on Patrick Ferguson in *Dictionary of National Biography* (hereafter cited as *DNB*). Lyman Draper, *King's Mountain and Its Heroes*, pp. 73, 287. Personal visit to Kings Mountain battlefield, June, 1956.

40. Governor William Gooch's sister landed at Hampton in Jan., 1729/30, and Governor Dinwiddie at York in 1751. Governor William Gooch to his brother Thomas, Jan. 7, 1729/30, *Va. Gazette* (Hunter ed.), Nov. 22, 1751. This and other travel data was generously provided by Colonial Williamsburg, Inc.

41. *Henry v. Kimbrow-Caveat*. Entered Feb. 9, 1727. Colonial Papers, Va. State Library. *Executive Journal of the Council of Colonial Virginia* (hereafter cited as *Council Journal*), IV, 178-179, June 13, 1728.

42. On Mar. 27, 1735 (8 George II), John Henry bought from Nicholas Meriwether 110 acres of wild land on Roundabout Creek in upper Hanover County (now Louisa) for two shillings. Hanover County Records, Va. State Library.

43. Brant, *Madison*, I, 60; and Mays, *Pendleton*, I, 139-141. For extracts from Robertson's account book while running the school see 33 *Va. Mag.*, pp. 194-195. See also John H. Gwathmey, *Twelve Virginia Counties*, p. 126.

44. Albert J. Beveridge, *The Life of John Marshall*, I, 16-19. Marshall also studied briefly under a young Scottish minister, James Thompson, and at the school in Westmoreland County of the Rev. Archibald Campbell, "a sound classical scholar equipped with all the learning which the Scottish universities could give." *Ibid.* pp. 53, 57.

45. King's College records, courtesy of Dr. Douglas Simpson. William Smith in *DAB*.

46. This letter was formerly in the records of the Bishop of London at Fulham Palace but is now in the archives of the British Ecclesiastical Commission, London. It states in part: "My Lord, I take this opportunity of the bearer . . . to beg leave to signify to your Lordship that I am under the greatest obligations to love & honour you, not only as my most Reverend and worthy Diosesan, but more particularly for the large share of your favour & indulgence I was honour^d with both before and after my admission into the number of your Clergy which I was still more sensible of upon my arrival here when I found your letters concerning me both to the Governour & Commissary there too exceeding kind." The Rev. Patrick went on to say that "The Character" which his "Lordship was

pleased to give" him had been "very much" to his "advantage . . . in the discharge of my office. . . ." Allowance must be made for the exaggerated style of the period and the difficulty in securing worthy ministers for the colonies. Nevertheless, it does appear that the Bishop of London found the Rev. Patrick worthy of special recommendation.

Chapter 2

THE ENGLISH AND HANOVER PROGENITORS

1. William Byrd, *A Journey to the Land of Eden* (1928 ed.), pp. 363-364. Byrd refers to John Syme as "of the family of the Saracens." In the 18th century Saracen was sometimes used to mean an ignorant and tasteless person, a barbarian, Goth, Vandal. *The Oxford English Dictionary*, IX, 106.

2. For data on John Syme's career in Virginia and his widow, Sarah's, remarriage, see *Council Journal*, IV, esp. pp. 39, 83, 288, 339; I *Tyler's Quarterly*, No. 2, pp. 121-122; 13 and 14 Virginia Land Office Records (hereafter cited as L.O. Records); *Journal of House of Burgesses* (hereafter cited as *JHB*), *1712-1726* and *1727-1740*. The marriage was sometime between Byrd's visit in Oct., 1732, and Nov. 1, 1734. *Council Journal*, IV, 339.

There is a record of a John Syme, probably the Virginia emigrant, in the alumni records of Aberdeen University. See also Kirk Session Reports, Foveran Parish, for 1698. The fact that John Henry joined Syme at Studley after coming to America may indicate that Syme was from Aberdeenshire.

3. *Burnaby's Travels* (reprint of 3rd ed.), pp. 57-58.

4. For this data on Mrs. Henry see p. 337; Henry, *Henry*, I, 6; Charles Campbell, *History of the Colony and Ancient Dominion of Virginia*, p. 520. Campbell, whose book was published in 1860, was a great-nephew of Philip Aylett who married Patrick Henry's daughter Elizabeth. From information in Campbell's book and his papers in the William and Mary Library, it is evident that he got much information on Henry from family sources. A copy of Henry's mother's will is filed at Amherst Courthouse, Virginia.

5. R. T. Barton, ed., *Virginia Colonial Decisions*, II, p. B214.

6. In addition to his landed holdings as cited, Syme had inherited considerable property from his first wife. Although Sarah and John Henry lost part of this estate in subsequent litigation, she retained an interest in

it at least, it appears, until John Syme, Jr., assumed active control. Barton, *op. cit.*, pp. B213-B223; and pp. 46-47.

7. 15 L.O. Records, p. 151.

8. *Council Journal*, IV, 353.

9. Henry, *Henry*, I, 1. Also personal research in England during 1948, including trips to the West Country and to Yorkshire and to various English archives. My conclusion that the Winstons were very probably from the West Country is confirmed by still later research by thorough English genealogists. Mrs. C. S. Pillsbury of Minneapolis, a descendant of the Hanover Winstons, has generously permitted me to examine the results of this study which she promoted.

10. N. C. P. Tyack, *The Trade Relations of Bristol with Virginia during the Seventeenth Century*. M.A. thesis, Bristol University, pp. 36-41. See also Abbot Emerson Smith, *Colonists in Bondage, White Servitude and Convict Labor in America, 1607-1776;* 35 *Va.* Mag. pp. 299-300. Data secured from city archives, Bristol, England during the summer of 1948.

11. See Note 10.

12. See L.O. Records, Richmond for the latter part of the seventeenth century. In addition to the longer studies listed in Note 10, see O. P. Chitwood, *A History of Colonial America* (1948 ed.), pp. 412-417.

13. Personal visit to Bristol in summer of 1948.

14. Reminiscences of Henry collected by Nathaniel Pope. Library of Congress. Morgan, *Henry,* pp. 30-31.

15. *Va. Gazette,* Purdie and Dixon, publishers (hereafter cited as P&D), Jan. 13, 1774.

16. In the Bristol and L.O. Records, Richmond.

17. Chitwood, *op. cit.* p. 416.

18. Shipping records in contemporary issues of *Va. Gazette;* Tyack, *op. cit.* See Note 10.

19. Another of Sir Henry's descendants was Lady Arabella Churchill, mistress of James II and mother of the Duke of Berwick, the Spanish general.

20. A. L. Rowse, *The Early Churchills,* pp. 7-8.

21. In Henry St. George, *Visitation of London,* II, 358, Dr. Thomas Winston is listed as a grandson of Richard Winston "gent." of Painswick, and there is a sketch of the Winston coat of arms, certified by Sir William Segar, "Knight Garter Principall King of Arms." See also the sketch of Thomas Winston in *DNB*, LXII, 212. A little earlier, in 1573 or as the Latin record gives it "anno Elizabethae 15," we find a Thomas Winston marrying in Standish where Sir Henry Winston's family was seated. See

W. P. W. Phillimore, ed., *Gloucestershire Parish Records*, VI and XVI, for references to Thomas and numerous other Winstons and Winstones (the name is spelled interchangeably).

22. Near the church are some old houses, many shops and large business establishments. Several of the adjacent city squares were in 1943 either razed or reduced to hollow shells after the German bombing.

23. York County Deeds, Orders, Wills, IV, 97. August 24, 1666.

24. In 1666 a William Winston, evidently the emigrant, signed his name as a witness to a will. *Ibid.*, p. 165.

25. The tract, with some adjoining land purchased by Winston from David Crafford, totaled 266 acres. 7 L.O. Records, p. 594.

26. 8 L.O. Records, pp. 129-130.

27. The reference to William Winston's land on Totopotomoy Creek is in 8 L.O. Records, p. 314. See also 9 L.O. Records, pp. 59, 60, 231, 232, and 562.

28. 9 L.O. Records, pp. 376-377.

29. *Ibid;* C. G. Chamberlayne, *Vestry Book of St. Paul's Parish*, pp. 22-66, *passim;* 31 *Va. Mag.*, p. 229; and Clayton Torrence, *Winstons of Virginia*, pp. 18-22. There is some question whether or not Isaac Winston was the son of Anthony Winston who died in 1725. Torrence *(ibid.)* believed that Isaac was probably the son. Certainly Isaac was the descendant of William Winston, the Virginia progenitor. See also George Wythe Munford, *The Two Parsons*, pp. 65-68. Processioners were reputable citizens appointed every four years to walk over land boundaries.

30. Anthony Winston, son of William, died on Dec. 14, 1725. C. G. Chamberlayne, *St. Peter's Parish*, p. 448. See also references in Note 29.

31. Munford, *op. cit.*, pp. 65-68.

32. *Ibid.*

33. Data on distinguished Winstons and Dabneys in recent generations is found in the *DAB* and *Who's Who in America*. See also William A. Dabney, *The Dabneys of Virginia;* John B. Dabney, *Sketches and Reminiscences of the Dabney and Morris Families* (pamphlet—photostatic copy, Va. State Library); L.O. Records; and *Council Journal*.

34. The name Cornelius, frequently found among the early Dabneys, suggests a Flemish connection. Numerous Flemish emigrants came to eastern England in the late Middle Ages and perhaps one married a Dabney in that region. The name was not confined to that area, however, for I found several Dabneys listed in the 17th century records of St. James Church, Bristol.

35. Charles W. Dabney, ed., *The John Blair Dabney Manuscript, 1795-1868*, pp. 9-10. Pamphlet copy in the Va. State Library. For a full

discussion of the family origins which explodes the theory that they were descended from the Huguenot d'Aubignés, see Charles W. Dabney, "Origin of the Dabney Family of Virginia," 45 *Va. Mag.*, pp. 121, *passim*. The fond claim that the first Dabney came to Virginia after the revocation in 1685 of the Edict of Nantes giving religious tolerance to the Huguenots unfortunately runs counter to the fact that he was in Virginia a generation before.

36. "Strange News from Virginia . . . A True Account of the Life and Death of Nathaniel Bacon, Esq." Handwritten copy in Library of Congress.

37. 23 *Va. Mag.*, p. 402.

38. For a vivid account of Bacon's Rebellion, see T. J. Wertenbaker, *Torchbearer of the Revolution.* For a brief summary of the causes, see Chitwood, *op. cit.*, and W. F. Craven, *The Southern Colonies in the Seventeenth Century.*

39. Wertenbaker, *op. cit.*, p. 62.

40. "A True Narrative of The . . . Late Rebellion in Virginia by His Majestyes Commissioners" in 4 *Va. Mag.* (Oct., 1896), p. 153.

41. Wertenbaker, *op. cit.*, pp. 94, 157, 197 and 199; T. J. Wertenbaker, *Virginia Under the Stuarts*, pp. 193, *passim*.

42. The excerpt from Bacon's Manifesto, with a comparison of Bacon and Berkeley, is taken from Armistead C. Gordon, *Men and Events*, pp. 47-49. The personal description of Bacon is in "A True Narrative," *op. cit.*, p. 122.

43. *Va. Gazette* (P&D), Feb. 23, 1769, p. 1. For a description of Bacon's death see "A True Narrative," *op. cit.*, p. 153, and Wertenbaker, *Torchbearer*, p. 178.

44. 5 L.O. Records, p. 406.

45. See references to the Virginia colonial Dabneys in Note 33 and Harris, *Louisa*, pp. 305-307, *passim*.

46. John Syme obtained the chief portion of his father's estate which the elder Syme had either made or acquired through his first marriage to Mildred Meriwether. *Hening's Statutes* VIII, 54-57; Mrs. W. W. Hunter, *The Four John Symes* (Ms.). Mrs. Hunter, of R.F.D. 2, Fresno, Ohio, is a descendant of John Syme and her Ms. is based on original sources.

47. For a brief account of early Albemarle land patents see Rev. Edgar Woods, *Albemarle County in Virginia*, pp. 4-5.

48. Dumas Malone, *Jefferson, the Virginian*, pp. 17-18; Marie Kimball, *Jefferson: The Road to Glory*, I, 18, *passim*.

49. This land was in three grants. One was to John Henry and John Moor for 2,000 acres on the branches of Mechamp Creek, Camp Creek, and Bunches Creek in what was then part of Hanover and is now Albemarle. Another grant, for 6,000 acres, was to Henry and William Robertson in Hanover beyond "the West Mountains joining 400 acres already surveyed" for Robertson and "joining some Surveys of the said Henry." There is no proof that Henry fulfilled his claims to all this land, but later in 1735 he definitely acquired 1,250 acres on Buck Mountain Creek or near by.

There is a claim, never definitely substantiated, that John Henry built the Michie Tavern which has been removed in late years from a beautiful spot near Earleysville in Albemarle County to the hillside below Monticello. The tavern was built on John Henry's original Buck Mountain Creek tract, but there is no definite proof that the building was erected by him, or that his son Patrick ever had a home there as asserted. *Council Journal*, IV, 353, and 16 L.O. Records, p. 5. Data from Mrs. Charles J. Milton, Michie Tavern, and from Miss Mary Rawlings, the Charlottesville historian. Professor E. J. Oglesby of Charlottesville generously took Miss Rawlings and me on August 14, 1955, to the former site of the Michie Tavern between Earleysville and Free Union, and data was given me there by John A. Via, present owner of the site. See also Louisa County Deed Book A, pp. 223-225; *Va. Gazette*, Feb. 10, 1737 (advertisement by John Thomson mentioning John Henry's Buck Mountain Creek lands). The reference to John Henry's overseer in Albemarle is in Patrick Henry's Account Book, entry for John Henry in 1762.

50. The Goochland grant was in co-ownership with Isaac Winston and William Robertson. *Council Journal*, IV, 364. See also *ibid.*, p. 380, and 17 L.O. Records, pp. 213-214. By this time it was customary to grant land in return for small payments instead of the fifty acres for each settler imported. The grants were controlled by the Council in their own interests, and an applicant might be refused if its aristocratic members did not consider him of sufficient standing. For information on the Virginia land grants during the colonial period, I am indebted to Dr. Manning C. Voorhis of Randolph-Macon Woman's College. He made an exhaustive study of the subject for his Ph.D. dissertation at the University of Virginia.

51. Henry, *Henry*, II, 634.

52. *Ibid.*, I, 7.

Chapter 3

EARLY PLANTATION LIFE

1. *Maryland Historical Magazine*, VII, 4-5.

2. Maude H. Woodfin, *Another Secret Diary of William Byrd*, p. 147. This is an approximate description. A lock of Henry's hair, in the possession of a descendant, Mrs. Sam Creath, Paces, Va., is of a reddish-sandy color.

3. The foundations were uncovered in 1936, the bicentennial of Henry's birth. The insurance policy for 1796, probably indicating few substantial changes since Patrick's birth, shows a two-story brick house, 30 by 40 feet, a great outside nursery, an outside kitchen, a store, dairy, and so on. Data on the Studley estate was given me in June, 1947, by Mrs. Melvin Hall, a co-owner; by her brother-in-law, H. A. Hall, then 76 years old, who was reared in the neighborhood; by William R. Shelton of Rural Plains; and by the late Dr. I. K. Redd of Hanover who was born at Studley. See also microfilm of Mutual Assurance Society policy for Peter Lyons, Va. State Library. There is a personal description of the place (*circa* 1850) by Charles Campbell in the Campbell Papers, Box 4, Wm. and Mary Library.

4. *Hening's Statutes*, VIII, 56, Oct., 1764.

5. W. S. Perry, *Historical Collections*, I, 279-280. The New Kent minister was replying to a questionnaire sent in 1724 by the Bishop of London.

6. *Va. Gazette* (No. 480), Oct. 10, 1745.

7. *Va. Gazette*, Nov. 2, 1739. Advertisement by John Shelton.

8. *Va. Gazette* (P&D), Mar. 31, 1768.

9. Henry Adams, *John Randolph*, p. 4.

10. *Va. Gazette*, Oct. 7, 1737; also Dec. 9, 1737, after the celebration. It was in many respects typical of a number of neighborhood festivities which young Patrick must have attended during the following years.

11. For a list of Virginia colonial governors or their equivalent see Matthew Page Andrews, *Virginia, the Old Dominion*, pp. 593-594.

12. Henry was made an acting justice on April 27, 1737 (*Council Journal*, IV, 391) and received a new commission in 1741 (*ibid.*, V, 56, 126). He was appointed sheriff in 1744 (*ibid.*, p. 150). He was again commissioned as a member of the county court in 1752 (*ibid.*, p. 391) and was presiding justice in 1763 when his son appeared in the Parson's Cause. See p. 125, *et seq*.

13. Chamberlayne, *St. Paul's Parish*, p. 148. In that following Oc-

tober, Henry was "Sworn a Vestry-man for this parish, took the Oaths directed by Law, and signed the Test." *Ibid.*, pp. 151-152.

14. He is listed as Major Henry on June 1, 1737 *et seq.* Chamberlayne, *St. Paul's Parish*, pp. 151-152. The first reference to him here as Colonel is on Oct. 18, 1747 (*ibid.*, p. 197), and he is so described in numerous records thereafter including a letter from Governor Botetourt to the Earl of Hillsborough, Oct. 22, 1769. Colonial Office Papers, Public Record Office, London.

15. For these records of Isaac Winston, see *Council Journal*, IV, 95, 179, 364; V, 289; and 14 L.O. Records, pp. 471-472. Numerous other details of Isaac's life may be found in the records cited, in Henrico Courthouse, in the *Va. Gazette*, etc.

16. See pp. 103-104.

17. *Council Journal*, V, 388-391.

18. *JHB, 1752-1758,* pp. 29, 61, 62.

19. *Council Journal*, V, 391-392. On Apr. 30, 1752.

20. Cases listed here are drawn from Goochland Order Book, VII, 638-640; and Goochland Loose Papers, Va. State Library. Although the surviving Hanover Records are deficient in such material, similar examples may be found in Louisa and adjoining courthouses. There is illuminating information on the county justices in Charles S. Sydnor, *Gentlemen Freeholders, Political Practices in Washington's Virginia.* Dr. Sydnor's untimely death was a real loss to American scholarship.

21. Data in 1947 from the late Dr. I. K. Redd of Ellerson, Hanover County.

22. Hanovertown was created a town in 1761. *JHB, 1761-1765,* p. 165. See also Lucile Wheeler, "Hanovertown" (with illustrations) in *Richmond Times Dispatch,* June 29, 1947. There is much information on early Hanover history in the special edition of the *Herald Progress,* published at Ashland, Va., in Aug., 1938. See also *Hening's Statutes,* VII, 601; and *Va. Gazette,* Sept. 14, 1739.

23. A photostat of this plat was supplied me through the courtesy of H. McGowan King, Hanover County.

24. Interview of Haddon Alexander, Old Church, Va., on Aug. 12, 1947; advertisements relating to John Syme in *Va. Gazette,* Nov. 2, 1769; Mar. 8, 1770; and Feb. 4, 1773.

25. Journal of Baron Von Closen, aide to General Rochambeau in 10 *Wm. and Mary* (Ser. 3), pp. 215-216.

26. *The Present State of Virginia—1726.* Public Record Office, London. Sainsbury Transcripts, Library of Congress. With minor exceptions, all white men and Negroes over 16 years old were tithable or chargeable

for paying any public, county, and parish charges. *Hening's Statutes*, III, 258-259 and IV, 133.

27. In Va. State Library.

28. There is interesting data on the large Hanover landholders of the colonial period in Gwathmey, *op. cit.*, pp. 93-94, and, of course, the land grants at the State Capitol are a mine of information.

29. Hanover Records, 1733-1735, Va. State Library.

30. *Ibid.*

31. There is a comprehensive Henry genealogy to the time of its publication in Henry, *Henry*, II, Appendix I. W. W. Henry, however, does not include a complete record of the children, who died early, of John and Patrick. *The Douglas Register, 1750-1797*, contains a record of burial on Feb. 3, 1769 by the Rev. William Douglas of two daughters of John Henry. Possibly one of these is Sarah, listed by W. W. Henry as marrying Thomas Thomas of Bristol, England, for Sarah's date of death is unknown. John's other nine children, cited by W. W. Henry, are known to have died after the two mentioned by Mr. Douglas. Thus John appears to have had at least eleven children. In Morgan, *Henry*, opposite p. 406, there is a photograph of a page in the Henry family Bible, showing that Patrick had a daughter Jane Robertson, who is not listed by W. W. Henry. She died on Jan. 19, 1798, when only four days old. Including this infant child, Patrick Henry had seventeen children, six by his first wife and eleven by his second.

32. Meredith Memo. Quoted in Morgan, *Henry*, p. 431. Actually John Henry had at least nine daughters. See Note 31.

33. Copy of letter of Commissary William Dawson to Anglican ministers in Virginia. In Papers of Bishop of London.

34. *Va. Gazette*, Mar. 27, 1745.

35. News of the Jacobite defeat at Culloden is in the *Va. Gazette*, July 31, 1745. The celebration at Newcastle is described in a letter of Aug. 28, 1746. X *Tyler's Quarterly*, p. 117.

36. Wirt, *Henry*, p. 14, quoting letter in 1805 from Nathaniel Pope.

37. *Va. Gazette*, Dec. 9, 1737.

38. Alexander Gammie, *The Churches of Aberdeen*, p. 307.

39. Mrs. W. W. Hunter (see chap. II, Note 46), wrote me on April 12, 1954, that he was born in 1729. Mrs. Hunter generously supplied a chronological outline of events in the Syme family, 1715-1836, based on contemporary records. See also *Winston & Ux* v. *Henry* in Barton, *Colonial Decisions*, p. B213.

40. A generation later it would take General Rochambeau's party over half a day to ride from Newcastle to a plantation some 10 miles from Mount

Brilliant. They had to travel through "a forest of full grown trees" in which they could barely cut their way. For miles they saw few or no inhabitants—only some confusing crossroads, a lime kiln, and a "pitiful little Negro cabin." 10 *Wm. and Mary* (Ser. 3), pp. 215-216.

41. Louisa County Deed Book, 1742-1754, Part I, 223-225; *ibid.*, Part II, 288-289; Goochland County Deed Book, V, 185-187.

42. 28 L.O. Records, pp. 701-702.

43. In Nov. 18, 1748, he was listed as a vestryman of St. Paul's, but he is not included for a meeting on Nov. 20, 1749. Two years later another vestryman was elected "in the room" of Col. Henry "who hath left this parish." Chamberlayne, *St. Paul's Parish*, pp. 202, 205, 207, 329.

44. Mount Brilliant, in the southeastern section of Hanover County, is about a mile from the ruined Auburn Mills on the South Anna River and only a few miles from the Goochland and Henrico county lines. The data on the former Mount Brilliant estate was largely obtained by interviews in 1947 with Jerry Rada and Anton Vitex, owners of portions of the Henry estate. Rada, then 56 years old, had lived in the neighborhood nearly fifty years. He said that in 1944 or 1945 he was cultivating deeper than usual with the new tractor and found the house site. There were over a hundred old bricks on the spot and several pieces of pottery and china in the environs. The house site had been pointed out to him by Ely Harris, the previous owner of the place, who had died in 1913 when about 70 years old; also by a number of other old people including Eddie Snead who died about 1937 when some 91 years old.

Rada spoke of finding some perfect arrowheads, an Indian bead, and a tomahawk in the vicinity.

H. McGowan King, Hanover County, described a visit about 1932 to Mount Brilliant. An old man, at least 70, he thought, named Talley, pointed out the site of the Henry house. It was a depression on the crest of a hill not far from the South Anna River which corresponded with the site pointed out by Rada and Vitex. At or near this spot King found some old English coins and an instrument which he and a number of other persons thought was a surveying instrument. Personal interview, Aug. 31, 1947.

The aged Ely Harris told Rada that the original house was English style, a story and a half with dormer windows. After Rada's present residence was built about 150 years ago, the old Mount Brilliant house was torn down and some of the timbers used to make a barn. They were large mortised and hand-hewn timbers with wooden pins in them instead of nails and were all or nearly all oak, as he recalls. The barn in which they were used has been torn down but he showed me a piece of the hewn framing.

I found several pieces of china and a few pieces of brick several hundred feet from the house site. Perhaps they were at or near the site of an outdoor kitchen. About a quarter mile toward the river Rada stated that there is another house site, perhaps of slave quarters.

45. For data on John Syme, Jr.'s residence in upper Hanover County see Mrs. W. W. Hunter, *The Four John Symes.*

Chapter 4

ARTISTIC ROMANCING OR THE MORE PROSAIC FACTS?

1. Mason L. Weems, *Life of George Washington,* pp. 15-16. Article on Weems in *DAB.*

2. John P. Kennedy, *Memoirs of William Wirt,* pp. 76-77.

3. Van Wyck Brooks, *The World of Washington Irving,* pp. 282-284.

4. These reminiscences are chiefly in the Wirt Papers at the Library of Congress. Some helpful data on Henry is contained in a letter, written by Nathaniel Pope to Wirt Sept. 26, 1805. This letter is now at the Va. Historical Society. See also the W. W. Henry Papers, Va. Historical Society.

5. The language of John Roane, Jr., "was like Patrick Henry's whose reputation Mr. Wirt has injured by trying to brighten it." Frank Ruffin to Paul Cameron, June 1, 1870. 18 *Wm. and Mary* (Ser. 1), pp. 270-274. See p. 6 for Ruffin's contacts with Henry's Roane descendants.

Meredith's statement is printed in Morgan, *Henry,* pp. 431-434. Meredith was about four years older than Henry and lived within four miles of him until Henry left Hanover. *Ibid.,* p. 432.

6. Wirt, *Henry,* 18. But there is more testimony of a different sort by Judge Roane. He wrote that Henry's dress was in accordance with "the customs of the times in which he lived." "I can myself remember," Roane continued, "when there was only one four-wheeled carriage, and two pair of boots (called shoe boots) in the wealthy and fashionable County of Essex. I myself delighted to go barefooted and in trousers until I went to College; and I have heard my father say, that his father, when possessed of perhaps 100 Negroes, and when he was a Col. of militia and Justice of the quorum, would in his shirt and trousers (in summer) visit two or three of his plantations and return home to breakfast." Morgan, *Henry,* p. 439. Perhaps Wirt gave undue attention to Nathaniel Pope's description of

Henry when serving at his father-in-law's tavern or those of him when he first served in the Burgesses and lived in Louisa. See pp. 90-91, 226.

7. "From all quarters the testimony appears to be to this effect—that he was an indolent, dreamy, frolicsome creature, with a mortal enmity to books, supplemented by a passionate regard for fishing-rods and shot-guns, disorderly in dress, slouching, vagrant, unambitious; a roamer in woods, a loiterer on riverbanks; having more tastes and aspirations in common with trappers and frontiersmen than with the toilers of civilized life; giving no hint nor token, by word or act, of the possession of any intellectual gift that could raise him above mediocrity, or even lift him up to it." M. C. Tyler, *Patrick Henry*, pp. 4-5.

The Encyclopedias *Americana* and *Britannica* and, to a less extent, Philip A. Bruce, *The Virginia Plutarch*, are among numerous other publications which have been influenced by the inaccurate accounts of Henry's early years. "He was a frolicsome and vagrant youth . . ." *Americana* (1945 ed.), XIV, 107. "A mediocre student in the country school and under his father's tutorship." *Britannica* (1947 ed.), XI, 446. "He is commonly thought to have been something of a saunterer in his youth, with a decided aversion to study; and yet he is known to have relished the Latin classics and had even mastered some Greek." Bruce, *op. cit.*, I, 174.

8. Wirt, *Henry*, p. 18.

9. *Ibid.*, pp. 18-19.

10. Weems, *op. cit.*, pp. 23-24.

11. Wirt, *Henry*, p. 19.

12. Meredith Memo in Morgan, *Henry*, p. 431.

13. *Ibid.*, p. 431.

14. William R. Shelton of Rural Plains told me that within his lifetime one could walk out on the plantation before breakfast and kill all the partridges he could carry. He and H. A. Hall both gave me a vivid impression of the abundant game in the lower country within their memory. And, as for the Mount Brilliant neighborhood, Jerry Rada told me that when he was a boy there was still a plentiful supply of deer weighing about 125 pounds, wild turkey, partridges, squirrels, and rabbits. For a description of the abundant game in Virginia during 1759-1760 see *Burnaby's Travels*, pp. 42-43.

15. *Southern Literary Messenger*, XIII, 527-528.

16. Roane Memo in Morgan, *Henry*, p. 438.

17. Henry's playmates were Charles Dabney and his brother. In his Ms. Charles Dabney tells this incident, describing the spot on the South Anna. Morgan, *Henry*, p. 30.

18. Nathaniel Pope, quoted in *ibid.*, pp. 30-31.

19. Personal interview on July 15, 1954, of James W. Christopher, Route 2, Beaverdam, Va. He said that the canoe was found some forty years earlier. A similar canoe, uncovered in late years, is on display at the Valentine Museum.

20. James W. Christopher found this inscription carved near the front door of the mill: "M. Crew 1750." He stated that there is evidence the timber antedates that time. Christopher, who operated the mill about 1913, believes that a dam was there when Henry was a boy. Personal interview of Christopher and visit to the mill, July 15, 1945.

21. Morgan, *Henry*, p. 31.

22. Charles Campbell, *History of Virginia*, pp. 521-522. See also Wirt, *Henry*, p. 17. Wirt adds without stating his authority that Patrick's "love of solitude, in his youth, was often observed. Even when hunting with a party . . . his choice was to take his stand alone, where he might wait for the passing game, and indulge himself, meanwhile, in the luxury of thinking. Not that he was averse to society; on the contrary, he had, at times, a very high zest for it." *Ibid.*

23. Campbell, *op. cit.*, p. 522. For examples of the influence of Wirt's exaggerated stories about Henry's love of hunting and fishing cf. p. 70.

24. Meredith Memo in Morgan, *Henry*, p. 431.

25. "I am informed that P. Henry was a tolerable performer upon the violin. Capt. Dabney says he performed very well upon an Instrument called a Lute and the Rocky Mills Family [the Symes] all say that he played well upon the Harpsichord and Piano." Nathaniel Pope to William Wirt, Sept. 12, 1805, in Library of Congress. "I have no doubt, from report, but Mr. H. had been a good performer, but I never heard him play on a violin, or any other instrument, or even sing or hum a tune. His daughters played on musical instruments, but these seemed not much to engage his attention." Roane Memo in *ibid.*, p. 438.

26. *Ibid.*, p. 438.

27. *Ibid.*

28. *Ibid.*, p. 448.

29. *Ibid.*, p. 341.

30. Burton Hendrick, *The Lees of Virginia*, pp. 85-86.

31. Morgan, *Henry*, p. 434.

32. Samuel Davies, the noted Presbyterian minister of Hanover, said that John Henry was better acquainted with Horace than the Bible. 33 *Va. Mag.*, pp. 44-45.

33. Printed in the *Evangelical and Literary Magazine*, III, 173, which states that the letter was found in an old copy of Giatices' *Annotations on the New Testament.*

[361]

34. Indicating that he must have had some reading knowledge of Greek and Latin as well as devotion to classical literature were the following titles: Watson's *Horace, Juvenal* and *Juvenalis, Decalo dis Mortis, Homeri Ilias*, Ovid's *Metamorphoses, Selecta Colequorum* and *Roman Antiquities*. There was also a "parcel" of Latin and Greek books valued at £1.16, and these volumes dealing with Greece or Greek literature: Milner's *Greek Grammar, Antiquity of Greece*, Barkley's *Greek Rudem'ts*, and Hardy, *N. Test. Grecum*. Morgan, *Henry*, pp. 464-468. The Henry inventories are still preserved at Charlotte Courthouse, Va.

35. See Note 34.

36. Wirt, *Henry*, p. 16.

37. Fontaine Ms., Cornell University.

38. Henry, *Henry*, I, 10. The book with the French inscription is in the Va. State Library.

39. "He [Henry] was delighted with the 'Life and Opinions of Tristram Shandy,' which I have known him to read several hours together, lying with his back upon a bed. He had a most retentive memory, making whatever he read his own. I never heard him quote verbatim any passages from history or poetry, but he would give you the fact or sentiment in his own expressive language. He had a most extraordinary talent for collecting the sentiments of his company upon any subject, without discovering his own, and he would effect this by interrogations which to the company often appeared to be irrelevant to the subject." Henry, *Henry*, I, 9-10,

Chapter 5

Orator and Statesman: The Seeds Being Sown

1. Samuel E. Morison and Henry S. Commager, *The Growth of the American Republic* (3rd ed.), I, 128.

2. Henry Aylett Sampson, *Sonnets and Other Poems*, p. 122.

3. Henry, *Henry*, I, 265.

4. *Ibid.*, pp. 280-281.

5. Fontaine Ms., Cornell University.

6. Chamberlayne, *St. Paul's Parish*, p. 147. Parson Henry had left St. George's Parish on Apr. 28, 1734. *Minute Book of St. George's Parish* at University of Va. Library.

7. Chamberlayne, *St. Paul's Parish*, pp. 187, 194, 195.

8. Copy in Library of Congress.

9. A pamphlet copy of a portion of this sermon is at the Va. Historical quoting Nathaniel Pope.

Society. In a footnote it is stated that Mr. Henry lived about a mile from the dead parishioner and was often with him during his sickness.

10. The Rev. Mr. Henry was listed as also buying a bottle of snuff. Photostat of Merchants' Ledger, Hanover County, 1750-1751, at Va. State Library. In the *Journal* of A. Gordon, Mr. Henry is charged for two gross of corks. See A. Gordon, *Journal for Ledger A, 1750:1751* is at the University of N.C. Library.

11. Mr. Henry adds that if we thus employ ourselves worthily "we may depend on it, that when posting Time hath summ'd up our years, we shall *finish our course* with a good deal of *joy*, in looking back on that part of our life which we have spent well: and our pleasure will be inexpressible in looking up to JESUS, who will then be ready to receive our departing spirits to dwell with himself, till a joyful resurrection shall fix both soul and body in . . ." The Rev. Patrick Henry's sermon. See above Note 9.

12. Munford, *The Two Parsons*, pp. 66-67.

13. Wirt, *Henry*, p. 15. He quotes information given him by Nathaniel Pope, a companion of Patrick's "childhood and youth." Preface, pp. 3-5. The anecdote is also repeated by the careful W. W. Henry in his *Henry*, I, 6-7.

14. *Ibid.*, II, 502. Alexander was president of Hampden-Sydney College, and later a professor at the College of New Jersey Theological Seminary. For a biographical sketch see Alexander Weddell, *Va. Historical Portraiture*, pp. 365-366.

15. Data from a descendant of Elizabeth Henry, Miss Nelly Preston, Seven Mile Ford, Va. Miss Preston has written a biographical account of Elizabeth Henry (hereafter cited as Preston Ms.). See also Morgan, *Henry*, p. ix, and Thomas L. Preston, *A Sketch of Mrs. Elizabeth Russell* (pamphlet).

16. For examples of oratorical talent passed down to Henry's Aylett descendants see 18 *Wm. and Mary* (Ser. 1), pp. 270-274, and J. B. Jones, *A Rebel War Clerk's Diary*, I, 20. The oratorical gift inherited through Elizabeth Henry by the Prestons is referred to in Morgan, *Henry*, pp. 236-237.

17. The Rev. William Henry Foote, *Sketches of Virginia, Historical and Biographical* (hereafter cited as Foote, *Sketches of Virginia*), Ser. I, pp. 121-123, 161.

18. Henry, *Henry*, I, 12; Harris, *Louisa*, pp. 178-179, 182; Chamberlayne, *St. Paul's Parish*, pp. 354-355, 391-392, 428; Capt. Samuel Morris in Henry, Account Book, 1762-1770; Foote, *op. cit.*, pp. 161-168.

19. Henry, *Henry*, I, 11, 12; Foote, *loc. cit.*

20. See references in Note 19, and Harris, *Louisa*, pp. 178-179.

21. 1 *Wm. and Mary* (Ser. 2), pp. 266-277.

22. M. W. Hazeltine, ed., *Orations from Homer to William McKinley*, V, pp. 1975-1987.

23. Several of Whitefield's sermons were printed in pamphlet form by John Parks of Williamsburg, grandfather of Henry's wife, Sarah Shelton.

24. George Whitefield in *DAB* and *DNB;* The Rev. John Tillie, *Memoirs of Reverend George Whitefield.*

25. Meredith Memo in Morgan, *Henry*, p. 432.

26. 1 *Wm. and Mary* (Ser. 2), pp. 272-273; Foote, *op. cit.*, p. 160.

27. 1 *Wm. and Mary* (Ser. 2), p. 273.

28. Meredith Memo in Morgan, *Henry*, p. 432; Henry, *Henry*, I, 15-16; Harris, *Louisa*, pp. 180-181; Campbell, *Virginia*, p. 522.

29. Henry, *Henry*, I, 15; Foote, *op. cit.*, p. 172.

30. There is a picture of Davies in the frontispiece of Foote, *op. cit.*, Ser. 2. See also Henry, *Henry*, I, 15.

31. *Ibid.*

32. For the data on Davies in the preceding paragraphs see *ibid.*, pp. 12-16; Minutes of the Hanover Presbytery, 1755-1769, pp. 18-19 (photostat at Va. State Library); Samuel Davies in *DAB;* Perry, *Historical Collections*, I, 395-396. Davies' sermons used here are in *Sermons on Important Subjects by the late Reverend Samuel Davies* (1828), I, 161, *passim.*

33. *Ibid.*, p. 65.

34. Henry, *Henry*, I, 281.

35. Davies' *Sermons, op. cit.*

Chapter 6

DIFFICULT YEARS

1. Douglas S. Freeman, *George Washington: A Biography*, I, 260.

2. Meredith Memo in Morgan, *Henry*, p. 432.

3. Charles M. Andrews, *Materials in Public Records Office of Great Britain*, II, 323. In addition, I have examined numerous accounts for Virginia stores of the period preserved in the local court records, the state, and college archives. They all indicate that the stores offered a variety of goods, usually even more than the general store of later times.

4. A. Gordon, *Journal.* "The Rev'd Part'k Henry" purchased 1 gross corks, "2 pr. callimanco shoes," snuff, a saddle, etc.

5. Meredith Memo in Morgan, *Henry*, p. 432; Wirt, *Henry*, p. 23.

6. Data secured in the summer of 1947 from Haddon Alexander and Julian Meade Ruffin, both of Old Church, Va. See Note 7.

7. Information in 1947 from Haddon Alexander who lived at Clifton near Old Church on property which he said John Syme once owned. Alexander stated that Henry lived at the original Clifton house (destroyed in 1878) when a storekeeper.

8. Wirt, *Henry*, pp. 20-21.

9. Lyman Chalkley, *Chronicles of the Scotch-Irish Settlement in Virginia, extracted from the original court records of Augusta County*, I, 337.

10. Wirt, *Henry*, p. 21.

11. "That he employed part of his leisure in storing his mind with information from books, cannot be doubted. Behind the counter he could con the news furnished by the *Virginia Gazette*, and he probably dipped sometimes into the *Gentleman's Magazine*." Campbell, *Virginia*, p. 523.

12. "Whenever a company of his customers met in the store, (which frequently happened on the last day of the week) and were themselves sufficiently gay and animated to talk and act as nature prompted, without concealment, without reserve, he would take no part in their discussions, but listen with a silence as deep and attentive as if under the influence of some potent charm. If, on the contrary, they were dull and silent, he would, without betraying his drift, task himself to set them in motion, and excite them to remark, collision and exclamation." Wirt, *Henry*, pp. 21-22.

13. *Ibid.*, p. 22.

14. Colonel Meredith wrote that William and Patrick "did not continue business longer than one year, when it was found necessary to abandon it, as they had injured themselves by granting too extensive credit." Morgan, *Henry*, p. 432. See also Wirt, *Henry*, p. 23, and Campbell, *op. cit.*, p. 522.

15. Morgan, *Henry*, p. 38.

16. Henry's store Account Book is at the Valentine Museum.

17. Meredith Memo in Morgan, *Henry*, p. 432.

18. *Ibid.;* Henry, *Henry*, I, 16.

19. Tyler, *Henry*, p. 6.

20. Preston Ms.

21. Wirt, *Henry*, p. 24.

22. Henry, *Henry*, I, 16.

23. Data from William R. Shelton, Rural Plains. The Sheltons have owned some old books in late years, including a few possibly obtained through John Parks. The available family, state and parish records all indicate that the Hanover Sheltons had considerable more cultural and propertied interests than sometimes intimated. One of them, John Shelton,

was reader of St. Paul's Parish, New Kent County, as early as 1705. Chamberlyne, *St. Paul's Parish*, p. 7. Data from William R. Shelton and Misses Berta and Mary Shelton of the family which still owns historic Rural Plains.

24. Data from William R. Shelton.

25. William R. Shelton was able to give the traditional description of Sarah as a pretty girl. Mr. Shelton and John Fontaine, a descendant of Sarah, were able to give descriptions of numerous Shelton kinfolk living within a few generations after her. The appearance of these men and women indicated a prevailing family type as described.

26. This tradition was repeated to me by the late Dr. I. K. Redd of Hanover County.

27. An Anglican prayer book, once owned by the Rev. Patrick Henry, is in the Valentine Museum. Perhaps it was used by Parson Henry when marrying young Patrick and Sarah. See also *Hening's Statutes, 1748-1755,* pp. 81-84.

28. Data from William R. Shelton.

29. Perry, *Historical Collections,* I, 414-419.

30. See Note. 27.

31. Entry for John Shelton in Henry's legal Account Book; Henry, *Henry,* I, 16-17.

32. For a good account of soil exhaustion in Virginia during the period see Avery Craven, *Soil Exhaustion as a Factor in the Agricultural History of Virginia and Maryland.* University of Illinois Studies.

33. Edmund Winston Memo in Library of Congress.

34. Data from the late Dr. I. K. Redd, Hanover, and family tradition all seems to indicate that Martha was born in 1755. See also Henry, *Henry,* II, 634; and p. 277.

35. John E. Bakeless, *Daniel Boone,* p. 30.

36. One of the oldest in the county, the building still boasts heart pine framing and hand-hewn timbers. There are two old mantels and some wooden pins, used instead of nails; also, on the outside, some hand-wrought nails. An old elm in the front yard was probably standing when the Henry children were toddling thereabouts.

37. Only one dormer is left, but William R. Shelton says there were three in front and back. The single chimney, between the east and middle rooms, is of special interest. A full six feet in width and breadth, it contains fireplaces on each side. Here Sarah must have cooked and, with Patrick and the children, hovered for warmth and companionship. On the walls were doubtless hung Patrick's gun, tools, and household articles,

[366]

much as in a frontiersman's cabin. Personal visit to Pine Slash, Dec. 8, 1948, with William R. Shelton.

38. Data from William R. Shelton.

39. Henry, *Henry*, I, 17.

40. Eugenia Glazebrook, *Virginia Migrations, Hanover County*, II, 47-48 (hereafter cited as Glazebrook, *Hanover*). The Syme correspondence listed is from pre-Revolutionary suit papers, Federal Courthouse, Richmond, Va.

41. Copy of Sparks Transcripts at Va. State Library. On Oct. 10 the *Va. Gazette* reported that 150 Indians had appeared in the neighborhood of Fort Cumberland and killed or captured upwards of twenty families.

42. *JHB, 1752-1758*, pp. xxii, 293.

43. Kimball, *Jefferson*, I, 35-36.

44. Glazebrook, *op. cit.*, II, 44; copy in U.S. Circuit Court, District of Virginia, judgment against John Syme in *Warre, Ex. v. Syme*.

45. In the list of goods some items seem reasonable enough when ordered by a large planter now raising a family: 300 yds. cotton, "5 m 20d nails," 5 Doz best Broad Hoes, "2 small coarce saddles," and so on for a total of several dozen articles bought in quantity. We can sympathize with Syme also in his order for "2 Casks Beer" and "20 yds. Diaper ¾ wide." But even though he was a leading gentleman of Hanover, married to a Meriwether and narrowly defeated for the Burgesses, should he not have cut his suit closer to the cloth? Did he need to order, for instance, "1 Silver soup spoon, 1 Dozn. Silver Table spoons, 1 Silver Punch Ladle & Strainer" and "13 yds Green Cloath" livery for his servants with "11 yds. Green Plush, 40 yds. Green Plains, 1 Dozn. Pair Green Stockings"? Glazebrook, *op. cit.*, II, 45.

46. *Ibid.*, pp. 46-47.

47. W. A. Crozier, *Virginia Colonial Militia*, quoting *Md. Gazette*, June 17, 1756.

48. *JHB, 1761-1765*, p. 221.

49. *Ibid.*, pp. 330, 339.

50. In addition to Patrick and his wife, there appear to have been at least two children by 1759. Henry, *Henry*, II, 636; Wirt, *Henry*, p. 26.

51. There is excellent data on the Virginia economic difficulties at this time in David J. Mays, *Edmund Pendleton*, I, 142-155. The contemporary British newspapers and the *Va. Gazette* contain various references to the French privateers and other wartime deterrents to the Virginia trade. In the Bishop of London's Papers, there is a revealing fragment of a letter from the Rev. Thomas Dawson in Virginia to the Bishop. Dated 1757, the letter noted that "as our ships frequently miscarry in these

troublesome times" Dawson was sending another copy by a man-of-war. See also 8 *Wm. and Mary* (Ser. 1), pp. 88-90.

52. Mays, *op. cit.*, I, 143; Chitwood, *Colonial America*, p. 621; *Hening's Statutes, 1756-1763*, pp. 240-241, Sept. 1758.

53. The well-authenticated Hanover tradition is that the store was situated at the crossroads about a mile south of Hanover Courthouse, where the courthouse road joined the former Fredericksburg-Williamsburg highway. This old road on which many colonial worthies journeyed back and forth to the capital may still be traced alongside the Pamunkey in lower Hanover. The purported site of Patrick's store, just off the present U.S. 2 Highway, has been pointed out even in recent years by local inhabitants. Data in 1945 from Miss Sallie Woolfolk who had it from the late Miss Molly Haw; also from Judge Leon Bazile, and from H. McGowan King, Hanover, who was given it by the late George P. Haw. The Haw family were identified for generations with the area near Hanover Courthouse.

54. Wirt, *Henry*, pp. 30-31.

55. Henry Account Book at Valentine Museum.

56. Other charges made against Henry during the year were such as would be expected of a family living with difficulty on a very modest scale: 2 pair worsted and one of yarn hose, a comb, a felt hat which Patrick or one of his boys probably wore in all weather long after it lost any pretense of style, a "cheese," buttons, shalloon, and "part of a hat ⅓" which Sarah probably finished sewing. There is also an entry in October indicating that he had exchanged some of his "A.F. Carge" [doubtless tobacco] for bed cords.

57. Account Book. See also Chamberlayne, *St. Paul's Parish*, pp. 326-327 *et seq.*

58. *Ibid.*

59. Henry, *Henry*, I, 17.

60. *Ibid;* Wirt, *Henry*, p. 31.

61. *Ibid.*, p. 26.

62. From memo in letter by Jefferson to Wirt, April 12, 1812. Photostat at University of Va. Library.

63. Jefferson to Wirt, Aug. 5, 1815. Photostat at University of Va. Library.

64. G. T. Curtis, *Life of Daniel Webster*, I, 584.

65. Pope to Wirt. Va. Historical Society.

66. Account Book.

Chapter 7

ADMISSION TO THE BAR

1. Jefferson did not come to William and Mary until Mar. 25, 1760. Kimball, *Jefferson*, I, 44. See also Wirt, *Henry*, p. 30. On April 15 Henry was admitted to the Goochland bar, quite likely after admission to that of his native Hanover. Record from Goochland Order Book reprinted in IX *Tyler's Quarterly*, p. 97.

2. For a daily record of the weather during this period see *Burnaby's Travels*, pp. 218-219.

3. Malone, *Jefferson*, I, 48.

4. For a good description of the Capitol see Fred Shelley, ed., "The Journal of Ebenezer Hazard in Virginia, 1777," in *Va. Mag.* (Oct., 1954).

5. *JHB, 1758-1761*, p. 168; *Burnaby's Travels*, p. 33.

6. *Hening's Statutes*, I, 302, Act VII, Session of Nov., 1645. There is a good discussion of the legislation relating to Virginia colonial lawyers in Robert M. Hughes, "The Historical Evolution of the Board of Law Examiners and Its Influence on Legal Education" in *American Bar Proceedings*, 1914.

7. Charles R. Warren, *A History of the American Bar*, p. 4.

8. *Hening's Statutes*, Act VI, Session of Dec., 1656.

9. Hughes, "The Board of Law Examiners," *op. cit.*

10. *Ibid.*

11. There is comparative data on the legal career of Henry and two other noteworthy lawyers of the period in Clement Eaton, "A Mirror of the Southern Colonial Lawyer: The Fee Books of Patrick Henry, Thomas Jefferson, and Waightstill Avery," 8 *Wm. and Mary* (Ser. 3), pp. 520-534.

12. Edmund Winston Memo in Library of Congress.

13. George Dabney Memo, Library of Congress. Dabney also noted that Henry borrowed "some Law Books" from Judge Edmund Pendleton to use in preparing for the bar. On the other hand, Henry's son-in-law, Judge Spencer Roane, wrote that he did not believe Henry read law under Pendleton or was under any obligation to him. Roane did not know Henry at that early period, as did the trustworthy Dabney, but the latter was possibly mistaken. Judge Roane served with Pendleton on the Virginia Court of Appeals. Roane Memo in Morgan, *Henry*, pp. 439-440.

14. *Ibid.*, p. 433.

15. Edmund Winston Memo in Library of Congress.

16. Wirt, *Henry*, p. 30.

17. Wirt quoted Nathaniel Pope as saying the time was nine months and Judge Tyler that it was only one month, adding "This [latter] I had from his [Henry's] own lips. In this time, he read Coke upon Littleton, and the Virginia laws." *Ibid.*, p. 28.

18. Henry, *Henry*, I, 20, citing *Southern Literary Messenger*, XIX, 317. Letter of June 2, 1793.

19. Henry, *Henry*, I, 22 citing "Memorandum for Mr. Wirt" in *Historical Magazine*, Aug., 1867. On the other hand, the aged Jefferson said in 1824: "There were four examiners, Wythe, Pendleton, Peyton Randolph and John Randolph. Wythe and Pendleton at once rejected his application; the two Randolphs were, by his importunity, prevailed upon to sign the license; and having obtained their signature, he again applied to Pendleton, and after much entreaty and many promises of future study, succeeded also in obtaining his. He then turned out for a practicing Lawyer." Henry, *Henry*, I, 22-23.

20. Goochland Order Book, April 15, 1760.

21. George Dabney Memo.

22. Wirt, *Henry*, pp. 29-30. Wirt's account was given him by Judge John Tyler who had it directly from Henry. Allowing for any minor lapses in memory or for dramatization by Wirt, it is still the most valuable account of Henry's experience with the examiners.

23. Tyler, *Henry*, pp. 23-24; Wirt, *Henry*, pp. 28-30. An edition of the Virginia Laws had been printed by William Parks, Sarah's grandfather, and in that day when books were few and highly valued may well have been owned by the Sheltons and perused by Henry. Among numerous other books either printed by Parks or at least sold at his bookstore was George Webb, *Office and Authority of a Justice of Peace*. This volume Patrick may have found at his father's home, if not at the Sheltons', since the latter appear to have inherited Parks' books. Data from William R. Shelton, Rural Plains.

24. After being relegated to an outhouse, many of the Goochland court records were providentially removed to the Va. State Library. There this writer found them before they could be indexed or cleaned, and their very disarray was indicative of the conditions under which Patrick began his practice. Particles of mica shining in them recalled the day when Henry and his legal brethren would sand their papers instead of blotting them. Some other debris was doubtless trimmings from quill pens which generations of county clerks had to sharpen at intervals, elm leaves from the courthouse green, and the traces of courthouse mice.

25. Data from Miss Margaret Kean Miller, clerk, Goochland County. See also Richard Cunningham Wight, *The Story of Goochland*.

26. Goochland Order Book VII, p. 497. Jan. 21, 1755.

27. The Order Books at Goochland Courthouse for 1730-1760 prove that a number of the early Huguenot families in that area were still living there. At a court held on Nov. 18, 1747, Paul Michaux, ferryman (on the James River) was paid 1,040 lbs. of tobacco. Goochland Order Book VI, p. 399.

Two descendants of Valentine Wood and his wife, Lucy Henry, have generously supplied a present-day picture of Woodville and helpful family data. These descendants are Miss Marion D. Wood, Decatur, Ill., and Miss Emily Dunn, Virginia Beach, Va.

28. In *Harding* v. *Prewitt,* Henry set forth in his declaration that his client, Harding, agreed with Prewitt to satisfy him for his trouble provided he would take into his care sundry stores belonging to Harding and sell them for the best price he could get on the plaintiff's account. The defendant thereupon sold and disposed of "Sundry negroes" for a considerable sum of money which ought to have been applied to the benefit of the plaintiff. "Yet the said Deft." Henry averred, "contriving & fraudulently intending to Defraud the Said Pltf. in this Behalf hath not paid the said money arising by such Sale to the said pltf. but the same to his own private use doth unjustly keep and Detain whereby the Said pltf. hath suffer'd imprisonment and undergone grevious hardships to his Damage two hundred pounds & thereon he brings suit. Henry Pr. Pltf."

29. In Goochland Papers.

30. *Ibid.*

31. *Ibid.*

32. *Robinson* v. *Winston. Ibid.*

33. *Dabney* v. *Norvell. Ibid.*

34. At Valentine Museum, Richmond.

35. Henry, *Henry*, I, 25.

36. 11 *Wm. and Mary* (Ser. 1), p. 98.

37. Account Book, 1760-1762, pp. 1, 2.

38. For the suits listed in this paragraph, see Account Book, entries for 1760. William Coles lived at Rock Castle on the North Anna River. Data from Judge Leon Bazile, Hanover.

39. Account Book, 1760-1762, p. 17.

40. Copy of will furnished by John Fontaine, descendant of the Winston Family; Torrence, *Winston of Virginia*, pp. 22-24.

41. Wirt, *Henry*, p. 31. There are no available records to indicate that

Henry did not remain at the tavern until his removal to Louisa County in 1765.

42. Arthur Lee to Richard Henry Lee, Dec. 29, 1760. University of Va. Library.

43. C. F. Adams, ed., *Works of John Adams* (hereafter cited as Adams, *Works*), II, 117-118.

44. A. L. Cross, *A Shorter History of Great Britain*, p. 507.

45. James Buchanan, of Shockoe on the James where the city of Richmond was spreading, gave Henry several such cases, one for Donald and Company of Glasgow, and paid him the £2.8.9 charged. Gideon Marr of frontier Albemarle gave him eight suits, at 15 shillings each, which probably required much riding and other tedious work in the rough mountain country where his friend, Tom Jefferson, would soon start practice. Henry also handled eleven minor cases for James George of Goochland with aggregate fees of £9.11.8, of which only 15s. had been paid by the end of the year. His largest client in 1761, however, was Alexander Baine of Henrico, charged £16.19.0½. This account covers 26 items, on which no payment was made until the next year; Baine was doubtless waiting for Henry's collections. Besides what appear to have been debt actions, the account contained charges for drawing conveyances for land, Negroes, and a spring in Goochland and for appearing in a suit in Albemarle. Account Book, 1761.

46. *Ibid.*

47. *Ibid.*, 1762. Dolly Madison in *DAB*.

48. Goochland Papers.

49. *Va. Gazette*, Dec. 4, 1766.

50. *John Henry* v. *John Horn*, suit entered on Feb. 24, 1763. Goochland County Papers. Meredith Memo in Morgan, *Henry*, pp. 433-444. There are numerous records of William Henry at Fluvanna Courthouse.

51. Account Book, 1763.

52. *Ibid.*

53. *Ibid.*

54. *Ibid.*

55. *Ibid.*

56. L. H. Gipson, *The British Empire Before the American Revolution*, II, 133-134. This and other related volumes of Gipson's full and definitive work are indispensable for a thorough study of the period. There is excellent material on Robert Carter in Louis Morton, *Robert Carter of Nomini Hall*. The portrait probably by Reynolds is in the frontispiece, with descriptive details on p. 34.

57. Glazebrook, *Hanover*, II, 50-51, 133-134.

58. A copy of this list of sterling judgments is in the Va. State Library.

59. William Wirt Henry wrote that there were 92 pages in the fee book through 1763, but by the time he made his tabulations 16 had been cut out and carried off by relic hunters or "otherwise lost." He, therefore, estimated for the missing pages the average number of cases in each of the others. Henry, *Henry*, I, 24-25.

60. The tabulation which I have made includes estimates for missing pages of the account books similar to those made by W. W. Henry.

61. Jefferson to Wirt, Apr. 12, 1812. Ford, *Jefferson*, IX, 343.

62. Account Book, 1761.

Chapter 8

THE PARSON'S CAUSE

1. Some of the brick headers still retain their original glazing.

2. Perry, *Historical Collections*, I, 334-335.

3. Jarratt's *Autobiography*, with an Introduction and Notes by Douglass Adair, is in 9 *Wm. and Mary* (Ser. 3), pp. 346-393. See also Jarratt in *DAB* and Rt. Rev. William Meade, *Old Churches, Ministers and Families of Virginia*, I, 470.

4. Blair to the Bishop of London, Mar. 11, 1736. British Ecclesiastical Commission, London.

5. Harris, *Louisa*, p. 164.

6. *Council Journal*, V, 100-101.

7. Margaret N. Armstrong, *Trelawney, A Man's Life*, p. 3.

8. *Council Journal*, V, 86.

9. William Dawson, who had served as a professor at William and Mary since the 1720's and as Blair's assistant, was chosen Commissary (and president at the college) on Blair's death in 1743. Lyon G. Tyler, ed., *Encyclopedia of Virginia Biography*, I, 156.

10. Rev. Patrick Henry to Bishop of London, Sept. 4, 1735. British Ecclesiastical Commission, London. See also Perry, *op. cit.*, I, 357-359, 365, *passim*; and correspondence of Blair and Dawson, Bishop of London's Papers.

11. Dinwiddie to the Bishop of London, Sept. 12, 1757. Perry, *op. cit.*, I, 454-458. Dawson to the Bishop of London, July 9, 1757. *Ibid.*, pp. 451-454.

12. Camm to the Bishop of London, June 4, 1752. *Ibid.*, pp. 386-388. Kay to the Bishop of London, June 14, 1752. *Ibid.*, pp. 389-393. XIII *Tyler's Quarterly*, pp. 246-247.

13. *Hening's Statutes,* 1748-1755, pp. 568-569. The tobacco law of 1748 had been approved by the King. For a good discussion, see C. R. Lingley, *The Transition in Virginia From Colony to Commonwealth,* pp. 21-34.

14. The clergy petitioned Governor Dinwiddie to veto the measure. He thereupon told several of them that the law was "contrary to common Justice and his Instructions." But Dinwiddie, absorbed with arming the colony for the French war following Braddock's defeat, felt that he must pass the bill "for Fear of having the People upon his Back." Glenn Curtis Smith, *The Parson's Cause,* p. 9. (Pamphlet in Va. State Library with valuable treatment of the Parson's Cause.)

15. The Clergy of Virginia to the Bishop of London, Feb. 25, 1756. Perry, *op. cit.,* I, 440-446.

16. *JHB, 1758-1761,* pp. 16-18, 34-35.

17. *Hening's Statutes,* VII, 240-241; John Camm in *DAB; 19 Wm. and Mary* (Ser. 1), p. 29.

18. *JHB, 1752-1758,* pp. 143-144; see also pp. 136, 141.

19. W. C. Ford, ed., *A Fragment on the Pistole Fee, claimed by the Governor of Virginia, 1753* by Richard Bland. From a letter by Bland to an unknown addressee. (Pamphlet in Va. State Library.) Recalling the days of John Hampden and the Great Rebellion against Charles I, Bland wrote, "Ship-money was not opposed because of the demand but because of the illegality of it." See also the sketch of Richard Bland in the *DAB* by Dr. E. G. Swem, an authority on Virginia history.

20. Copy of Bland's letter in Va. State Library.

21. Comparing Bland's writing with the *Farmer's Letters* by John Dickinson of Pennsylvania, Jefferson added, "Still there was more sound matter in his pamphlet than the celebrated 'Letters' which were truly but an ignis fatuus, leading us from true principles." A. A. Lipscomb, ed., *Writings of Jefferson,* XIV, 338. Jefferson to Wirt, Aug. 5, 1815.

22. Lyon G. Tyler in 19 *Wm. and Mary* (Ser. 1), pp. 16-17.

23. Perry, *op. cit.,* I, 464.

24. Commissary Robinson to the Bishop of London, Aug. 17, 1764. *Ibid.,* pp. 489-501.

25. In the hope of cutting off Mr. White from further legal recourse, it was even entered on the court record that he had been paid in tobacco, not money—"a known falsehood both contrary to what appeared in Court and to the mind of the Jury." *Ibid.,* p. 497.

26. The extracts from the Maury Bible records are in 10 *Wm. and Mary* (Ser. 1), pp. 122-123. See also 1 *Wm. and Mary* (Ser. 2), p. 279; and Ann Maury, translator and compiler, *Memoirs of a Huguenot Family.*

27. Malone, *Jefferson*, I, 40-43; Henry, *Henry*, I, 28-35; photostat of *vestry book, Fredericksville Parish*, Louisa County, Va. State Library.

28. Harris, *Louisa*, pp. 112, 113, 179, 410.

29. The Henry fee book contains no record of payments by Johnson after 1763 until Sept. 12, 1768 when Henry made this entry: "To cash for my dues" £5. Account Book, 1762-1770, p. 29.

30. James Maury-Camm Letterbook, University of Va. Library. Letter of Dec. 12, 1763.

31. *Ibid.*

32. Henry, *Henry*, I, 37; copy of John Blair Dabney Ms., Va. State Library; J. B. Dabney, *Sketches and Reminiscences;* George Dabney Memo in Library of Congress.

33. Chamberlayne, *St. Paul's Parish*, pp. 449-453, 464-465, 468 *et seq.* A John Wingfield is listed among the "Desenters from the Church of England and others" in Albemarle, Amherst, and Buckingham counties who sent a petition to the Virginia Assembly on Nov. 9, 1776. The original petition is in the Va. State Library. Harris, *Louisa*, p. 171, and genealogical data supplied by Guy L. Wingfield and Miss Adrienne Wingfield, Lynchburg, Va., descendants of the early Albemarle County Wingfields.

34. Harris, *Louisa*, p. 429, *passim;* data from Judge Leon Bazile of Hanover, an authority on the county history. A John Thornton was clerk of New Kent County in 1729. Chamberlayne, *St. Paul's Parish*, p. 635.

35. *Ibid.*, pp. 426, 434, 442, 443, 478.

36. The remaining jurors are listed in Henry, *Henry*, I, 37, along with the names of the known Dissenters among them. These Dissenters were George Dabney, Samuel Morris, and Roger Shackleford. For further data on the jurors as listed by W. W. Henry see esp. Chamberlayne, *St. Paul's Parish*, Maury's letter to Camm, *op. cit.*, and Henry's Account Book. Swem's *Index* continues to be an invaluable guide to information on these and other families treated in the Virginia historical magazines.

37. Henry, *Henry*, I, 37; Wirt, *Henry*, p. 36.

38. It is most probable that several of the burgesses from Hanover or near by were present. See also Harris, *Louisa*, p. 42.

39. Wirt, *Henry*, p. 36. The conversation has been put in direct discourse. See also Henry, *Henry*, I, 36-37.

40. Nathaniel Pope in his letter to Wirt *(op. cit.)*, says Colonel William Winston told him that the Rev. Mr. Henry took his seat on the bench in the courtroom. But W. W. Henry quotes the commonly accepted version by Colonel Meredith. Pope also makes the statement which seems improbable on the face of it that Patrick Henry was employed on the day of trial and he refers to Parson Maury as "Mr. Maury."

41. The statement that Patrick had never before spoken in public is obviously wrong in view of the numerous court hearings in his earlier cases. Also we may well doubt that he was so overawed by the Rev. Mr. Henry. Nevertheless, his uncle had been outstanding in opposition to the Two Penny Act and Patrick, when he could differentiate causes and individuals, was considerate of the feelings of his opponents.

42. Lyons is sometimes listed as an alumnus of Trinity College, Dublin, but in answer to my query their register could find no record of his attendance. Further data on Lyons may be found in VIII *Tyler's Quarterly*, pp. 184-185; Weddell, *Va. Portraiture*, pp. 302-323; and Morgan, *Henry*, pp. 303-304.

43. Henry, *Henry*, I, 37-38; Wirt, *Henry*, p. 37.

44. *Ibid.*, pp. 37-38.

45. *Ibid.*

46. *Ibid.*, pp. 38-39.

47. *Ibid.*, pp. 40-41.

48. *Ibid.*, pp. 41-42.

49. "You'll observe," Maury wrote at this point, "I do not pretend to remember Henry's words, but take this to have been the Sum & Substance of this part of his laboured Oration." Maury to Camm, *op. cit.* (See Note 30 above.) Maury's quotations from Henry have been put in direct discourse.

The substance of Henry's speech with other details is further confirmed by Edmund Winston in his memo.

50. Maury to Camm, *ibid.*

51. See pp. 5-6.

52. Henry, *Henry*, I, 43.

53. Wirt, *Henry*, p. 40.

54. The form of address was customary for the Bishop of London but Carter doubtless used it with an ironic relish. G. C. Smith, *Parson's Cause*, pp. 28-29.

55. *Ibid.*

56. Jefferson to Wirt, Aug. 5, 1815. Lipscomb, *op. cit.*, XIV, 336.

57. For a bibliography of the writings of Bland, Camm, and Landon Carter during this period see the Index to the *Va. Gazette*; Clinton Rossiter, *Seedtime of the Republic*, esp. p. 258; and *JHB, 1761-1765*, p. xlviii.

58. 19 *Wm. and Mary* (Ser. 1), p. 24.

59. Maury also wrote Camm, "You see, then, it is so clear a point in this person's opinion that the ready road to popularity here is to trample under foot the interests of religion, the rights of the Church, and the pre-

rogative of the crowd." Maury to Camm, *op. cit.*; Henry, *Henry*, I, 43-44.

60. *Ibid.*, pp. 44-45.

61. *Ibid.*

62. *Ibid.*, pp. 45-46. Joseph Henry Smith, *Appeals to the Privy Council from the American Plantations*, esp. pp. 623-627.

63. *JHB, 1758-1761*, p. xviii.

64. Wirt to Jefferson, Feb. 27, 1814. IX *Tyler's Quarterly*, p. 88. Henry, *Henry*, I, 43.

65. Thomas Trevillian, George Dabney, and Benjamin Anderson, three of the jurors in the Parson's Cause, were listed as members of the Hanover Committee of Safety on Nov. 8, 1775. Samuel Meredith, another member of the committee, had given information in the case. 5 *Wm. and Mary* (Ser. 1), pp. 94-106.

Chapter 9

A BACKWOODS LEADER

1. Harris, *Louisa*, p. 143.

2. For a significant discussion, see Frederick J. Turner, *The Frontier in American History*, esp. chaps. 1 and 3; also T. P. Abernethy, *The Three Virginia Frontiers*, and Wertenbaker, *The Old South, The Founding of American Civilization*, esp. chap. IV.

3. *Hening's Statutes*, VII, section 4, pp. 517-518, Nov., 1762. The mention of Henry as a possible candidate for the Burgesses from Hanover is in *JHB, 1761-1765*, p. 271.

4. Rupert Hughes, *Washington*, I, 367-368.

5. *Hening's Statutes*, VII, section 19, p. 526, Nov., 1762.

6. *JHB, 1761-1765*, pp. 269-273; also see pp. 202, 205, 230.

7. *Ibid.*, p. 269.

8. List of Judgments for Sterling Money, obtained in the General Court of Virginia by Persons residing in Great Britain. Va. State Library.

9. *JHB, 1761-1765*, p. 272.

10. Wirt, *Henry*, pp. 51-52, quoting Judge John Tyler. It seems incredible that Edmund Pendleton, who lived in adjoining Caroline County, knew nothing of Henry. Some other committee members must have heard of his argument against the parsons.

11. 15 *Va. Magazine*, p. 356.

12. Wirt, *Henry*, p. 52. Wirt also quotes Judge Edmund Winston as giving this version of the incident:

"Some time after, a member of the house, speaking to me of this occurrence, said, he had, for a day or two, observed an ill-dressed young man
sauntering in the lobby; that he seemed to be a stranger to every body,
and he had not the curiosity to inquire his name; but that, attending when
the case of the contested election came on, he was surprised to find this
same person counsel for one of the parties; and still more so, when he
delivered an argument superior to anything he had ever heard." *Ibid.,*
citing Winston Memo.

13. *JHB, 1761-1765,* p. 272.

14. Letter from Theodorick Bland, Sr., to unnamed addressee, June
27, 1765, in Archibald Campbell, ed., *Bland Papers,* p. 27.

15. Account Book, 1762-1770, p. 96.

16. Lecky, *England in the Eighteenth Century* (1906 ed.), IV,
73-74.

17. The members of Parliament were not required, as was usual practice in the House of Burgesses, to live in the district from which they were
elected. No systematic attempt had been made in recent generations to
apportion representation according to changes in wealth and population.
While thriving cities such as Liverpool and Manchester had no representation at all, decayed boroughs with little or no population continued to
send up their members to Westminster.

Of some 558 members of the House of Commons at the outbreak of
the American Revolution, over half were nominated by a few hundred
peers and influential commoners. The Duke of Norfolk was represented by
eleven members, Lord Lonsdale by nine, and the Duke of Rutland and
Lord Carrington by six each. G. E. Howard, *Preliminaries of the American Revolution,* pp. 35-36.

18. K. Y. Feiling, *History of England,* p. 701. See also L. B. Namier,
England in the Age of the American Revolution, passim.

19. Howard, *op. cit.,* pp. 106, 107; Chitwood, *Colonial America,* pp.
511-512.

20. There is excellent data on this colonial smuggling in L. H. Gipson, *The Coming of the Revolution, 1763-1775.* For a brief discussion
see Morison and Commager, *Growth of the American Republic,* chap.
VI, esp. p. 132.

21. Adams, *Works,* X, 314-320, 323-338, and esp. 348, 351.

22. Chitwood, *op. cit.,* pp. 624-627.

23. Carl Becker, *The Eve of the Revolution,* p. 15. Chitwood, *op. cit.,*
p. 624. There is a more favorable view in Gipson, Coming of the Revolution, pp. 56-57.

24. Morison and Commager, *op. cit.,* I, 128-130.

25. *Ibid.*, p. 144.

26. These aggressive elements included, as we shall detail, numerous relatives, clients, and other associates of Henry.

27. J. S. Bassett, *Short History of the United States*, p. 163.

28. Howard, *op. cit.*, pp. 113-114.

29. *JHB, 1761-1765*, pp. 256-257. Bland's name was added on Nov. 20, 1764. *Ibid.*, p. 264. The remaining members were Benjamin Harrison and Archibald Cary. *Ibid.*, p. 257.

30. Edmund Lee, *Lee of Virginia*, p. 175. Edmund Lee credits his ancestor with bringing the question before the House and with being selected to draw up the memorials to the King and the House of Commons. Richard Henry Lee is listed second in the committee, or next after the Attorney-General, which probably indicates that he proposed its appointment. *Journal*, p. 257. Charles Campbell in his *History of Virginia*, p. 657, says that Wythe prepared the remonstrance to the Commons "in conformity with his radical principles" but that "it was greatly modified by the Assembly."

31. See pp. 150-152.

32. *JHB, 1761-1765*, p. lviii.

33. The *Journal* (*ibid.*, p. 294) speaks of amendments by the House to the memorials to the Lords and Commons. The "ready compliance" to the royal requisitions was at the price of some concessions by the royal governors. They were careful not to offend the Burgesses as, for instance, by opposing the Two Penny Acts. See also Percy Scott Flippen, *The Royal Government in Virginia 1624-1775*, pp. 132-135.

34. The memorial to the House of Lords was written along similar lines. *JHB, 1761-1765*, pp. lv-lvi.

35. *Ibid.*, pp. lvi-lvii.

36. His speech praising the Americans as "sons of liberty" had "stirred the dull House for perhaps three minutes." Becker, *op. cit.*, p. 47. The vote in favor of the ministry was 205 to 49.

37. Becker, *Ibid.* This volume and Lecky, *op. cit.*, vol. IV, contain good accounts of the Stamp Act question with opposing arguments.

38. Few in either England or America actually wanted colonial representatives seated at Westminster.

39. Lecky, *op. cit.*, p. 76.

40. *Ibid.*

41. *Ibid.*, p. 79.

42. Howard, *op. cit.*, p. 136, quoting Cobbett-Hansard, *Parliamentary History*, XVI, 40.

43. The text of the Stamp Act is in the *Va. Gazette* and *JHB, 1761-*

1765, lix-lxiv. The chief English arguments favoring the stamp tax are given in Gipson, *Coming of the Revolution*, esp. pp. 76-77.

44. Howard, *op. cit.*, p. 137.

45. Carl Van Doren, *Benjamin Franklin*, quoting A. H. Smith, ed., *The Writings of Benjamin Franklin*, IV, 390.

46. Howard, *op. cit.*, p. 138.

47. *Ibid.*, pp. 140-141.

48. *JHB, 1761-1765*, p. 315.

49. See James Matthews, "Mulattoe," in Account Book, 1762-1770, p. 53; also p. 55; and entries for John Gilbert, Louisa carpenter, Account Book, 1762-1770.

50. Johnson's strong remarks were made according to the evidence of several witnesses at his house on the evening of Louisa court day in Nov., 1759. The proceedings of the House to which he referred were in the preceding September. Capitalization of the statements quoted has been changed to modern form. *JHB, 1758-1761*, pp. 88-90, 114.

51. *Ibid.*, p. 114.

52. "Notwithstanding the opposition of the people to the stamp act, yet the placemen, the large landed proprietors who were the professed adherents of government, still held the control of this legislature. Disgusted by the delays and sophistries of this class during the preceding session, one of the Johnsons, two brothers that represented Louisa County, declared his intention to bring into the house Patrick Henry, who was equally distinguished by his eloquence and by an opposition to the claims of parliament, verging on sedition. Johnson accordingly, by accepting the office of coroner, vacated his seat in favor of Henry." Campbell, *Virginia*, pp. 538-539. Campbell, whose history was published in 1860, had exceptionally good sources of information from Henry family and elsewhere, as noted.

53. In his letter to William Wirt from Hanover Courthouse, Sept. 26, 1805, Nathaniel Pope wrote that the previous day he had sought information on Henry from Colonel William O. Winston of Hanover. Winston "was intimate with Mr. Henry," Pope said, "from his childhood untill he removed to Prince Edward" (in 1777) and "was nearly related to him." "Col. Winston also says that Patrick Henry was a resident of Hanover at the time he was first elected for Louisa where he had a Freehold at a place called the Round-about . . . & that [torn] and forty other Freeholders residents of Hanover who had Freeholds in Louisa went up to vote for him." Pope to Wirt, Va. Historical Society.

Henry's name was brought forward by William Venable, a prominent citizen of Louisa. Patrick was elected to the Burgesses although not a resident of Louisa. Henry, *Henry* I, 70. A bond executed in Aug. 1765, describes Henry as a resident of Hanover County. *Ibid.*

Chapter 10

THE STAMP ACT SPEECH

1. *JHB, 1761-1765,* pp. 351-353; 356-360.
2. Curtis P. Nettels, *The Roots of American Civilization,* p. 460.
3. On May 20, 1765, the *Journal* states that "a Member returned on a new writ, having taken the Oaths appointed to be taken by Act of Parliament, instead of the Oaths of Allegiance and Supremacy, and taken and subscribed the Oath of Abjuration, and also subscribed the Test was admitted to his Place in the House."
4. The *JHB* states that one new member was admitted on Saturday, May 18, and another on Monday, May 20. After the notice of admission of the second member on May 20, it adds that Mr. Ward was added to the Committee of Claims and Mr. Henry to the Committee on Courts of Justice. If the two new committee members are listed in order of their admission to the House, as seems natural, then Henry became a member of the Burgesses on May 20. *JHB, 1761-1765,* pp. 343-345.
5. Carl Bridenbaugh, *Seat of Empire,* p. 38.
6. *Ibid.*
7. *JHB, 1761-1765,* pp. 313-314.
8. It was significant to note the number of seats held by a relatively few families, with their relatives and adherents in the Tidewater or elsewhere. Robert Bolling was a burgess from Dinwiddie and Robert Bolling, Jr., from Buckingham, near where the James finally burst out of its mountain confines; Mann Page was from "The College" and John Page from baronial Rosewell across the blue York in Gloucester; Lewis Burwell from Carter's Grove in James City and Burwell Bassett from the hospitable New Kent neighborhood below Studley where George Washington had lately acquired his bride; Richard Bland, Sr., and Richard Bland, Jr., from Prince George, with its growing river mart of Petersburg. There were also two Carters from the Northern Neck; two Paynes, Henry's associates in Goochland; two Riddicks from Nansemond on the eastern Carolina border; two Cabells from the upper James (though listed *in absentia*); and a bevy of Lees, chiefly from Northern Virginia. For convenient data on individuals and families listed in this Note see Meade, *Old Churches* and the appropriate references in E. G. Swem, *Virginia Historical Index.*

9. *Ibid.* Among the leading members were Richard Bland, chairman of the important Committee of Privileges and Elections, and Peyton Randolph, head of the large and influential Committee of Propositions and Grievances and second ranking member of the Election Committee. Other members with influential committee assignments included Edmund Pendleton and Landon Carter.

10. *JHB, 1761-1765*, pp. 230-231.

11. *Ibid.*, p. 231. Data on Wythe generously supplied by Oscar L. Shewmake, Richmond, Va.

12. "Journal of a French Traveller in the Colonies, 1765," in *Amer. Hist. Review*, vol. 26 (1920-1921), pp. 740-741.

13. *Ibid.*, pp. 742-743.

14. *Ibid.*

15. *Ibid.*, pp. 741-742. Of William Byrd III and his gambling associates the traveler also wrote, "This gentleman from a man of the greatest property of any in America has reduced himself to that Degree by gameing, that few or nobody will credit him for ever so small a sum of money. he was obliged to sell 400 fine Negroes a few days before my arrival. there were many sets made at me to get me in for the box but I had the good look [luck] to Keep Clear of it, but Could not avoid playing some rubbers at whist."

16. *JHB, 1761-1765*, pp. 345-354.

17. Ford, *Jefferson's Writings*, IX, 339, 465-466; *JHB, 1761-1765*, pp. 350-351.

18. *JHB, 1761-1765*, pp. 350-351, 356.

19. There is a copy of Robinson's portrait in Weddell, *Va. Portraiture*, p. 169. See also "The Robinson Family of Middlesex" in 17 *Va. Mag.*, pp. 318-319.

20. *JHB, 1758-1761*, pp. 66-67.

21. Opinion of Judge Leon Bazille, the Hanover County historian, with which this writer concurs.

22. *JHB, 1761-1765*, pp. 354-355, 357.

23. *Ibid.*, pp. 355-356.

24. "When the Assembly met, they seemed quite at a loss how to act in the matter, postponed taking it into consideration till they had dispatched the necessary business." Extract from *South Carolina Gazette*, July 15, 1765, at Colonial Williamsburg, Inc. For a reference to the forces favoring inaction, see Henry, *Henry*, I, 78-79.

25. The petitions have a suppliant tone even after allowing for the obsequious forms then commonly used in such documents.

26. "At the close of the sessions, when there was but a thin house,

many members being absent preparing to return home, Mr. Henry brought in a number of resolves." William Gordon, *The History of the Rise, Progress, and Establishment of the Independence of the United States of America*, I, 117.

27. *South Carolina Gazette*, July 15, 1765.

28. Henry, *Henry*, I, 78.

29. Letter of William Robinson to the Bishop of London, Aug. 17, 1764, in Perry, *Historical Collections*, I, 497.

30. Henry, *Henry*, I, 78.

31. This document, with Henry's endorsement, is now preserved at the Girard Trust Company, Philadelphia. See also photograph of the resolutions in frontispiece of the *JHB, 1761-1765;* also of Henry's endorsement in Morgan, *Henry*, p. 100.

32. On November 15 John Syme had written to his British agents concerning certain Virginia shippers that "Their Minds are as Unsettled as the Markets on our River, for the tobacco . . . forgetting you have advanced Money for them, they only think of the present time." The shippers cited were all associates of Henry: "Mr. Dandridge," Anthony Winston, and L. Pope. "Times are very hard," Syme added. Horse breeding, by which he supplemented his income, was in a poor way, for horses now fell "every Day in their value." Glazebrook, *Hanover*, II, 55-56.

33. *Ibid.*, p. 56.

34. Avery Craven and Walter Johnson, *The United States, Experiment in Democracy*, p. 88.

35. When Henkels of Philadelphia auctioned some of Henry's effects, then belonging to his great-granddaughter, Mrs. M. B. Harrison, they included Coke's Second Part of the *Institutions of the Laws of England*, folio, London, 1642. This was advertised, doubtless on the basis of family information, as the identical book on the flyleaf of which Henry drew up his Stamp Act Resolutions. *Boston Transcript*, Dec. 21, 1910.

36. The similarities in Henry's speech and the Memorials of the 1764 Assembly are noted in Irving Brant, *James Madison*, I, 420-421. He makes comparisons substantially as follows:

Memorials of Burgesses, Dec., 1764: "knows what Taxes such People can bear, or the easiest mode of raising them."

Henry's Stamp Act resolutions: "know what taxes the People are able to bear, and the easiest Mode of raising them."

Burgesses' memorials: "they cannot now be deprived of a right they have so long enjoyed, and which they have never forfeited."

Henry's resolutions: "The same hath never been forfeited or in any way given up."

Burgesses' memorials: "The representatives themselves must be affected by every tax imposed by the people."
Henry's resolutions: "Persons chosen by themselves to represent them, who . . . are equally affected by such Taxes themselves."

Burgesses' memorials: "our ancestors brought with them every Right and Privilege."
Henry's resolutions: "the first Adventurers and Settlers of this his Majesties' Colony . . . brought with them and transmitted to their Posterity . . . all the priviledges." (*JHB, 1761-5,* photograph of Henry's resolutions in frontispiece; also pp. 302-303 and *liv.*

I have used the copy of the resolutions left in the Henry papers rather than the copy in the *Journal* which has slight variations chiefly in spelling and capitalization. Henry stated on the back of his copy that he wrote the resolutions "alone, unadvised, and unassisted," and Brant, *op. cit.,* p. 186, criticizes him for concealing his paraphrasing. But Henry's reliance on the earlier document must have been obvious to informed persons of the time. Perhaps he felt no need to mention this. It may perhaps be inferred that he meant only to imply that he had no assistance in the actual writing of his resolutions.

After making his criticism of the purported paraphrasing, Brant adds, "He (Henry) took the words of his conservative predecessors, uttered when it was safe to utter them, and demanded that they repeat them when it was no longer safe to do so—that is, after the bill had become a law. They refused, and he defeated them." *Ibid.,* p. 186.

That Henry possibly felt his reliance on the Burgesses' memorials was too obvious to require mention is further indicated by the comment of William Wirt, *Henry,* pp. 53-54. He explains the circumstances of the passage, then adds, "It is evident that, while they affirm, in clear and strong terms, the constitutional exemption of the colony from taxation by the British parliament, they breathe nevertheless, a tone so suppliant, and exhibit such a picture of anticipated suffering . . . as to indicate that no opposition beyond remonstrance was, at this time, meditated." Wirt then notes that "the reader will remark that the first four resolutions, as left by Mr. Henry, do little more than reaffirm the principles advanced in" the memorials of 1764; that is, they deny the right assumed by the British parliament, and assert the exclusive right of the colony to tax itself. There is an important difference, however, between these state papers and the resolutions, in the point of time and the circumstances under which they were brought forward, for the address and other state papers were prepared before the stamp act had passed; they do nothing more, therefore, than call in question, by a course of respectful and submissive reasoning, the propriety of exercising the right, before it had been exercised; and they are, moreover, addressed to the legislature of Great Britain, by the way of prevention, and in a strain of decent remonstrance and argument. But at the time when Mr. Henry offered his resolutions, the stamp act had passed; and the resolutions were intended for the people of the colonies. It will also be observed, that the fifth resolution, as given by Mr. Henry, contains the bold assertion, that every attempt to vest the power of taxation over the colonies in any person or persons whatsoever, other than the general assembly, had a manifest tendency to destroy British, as well as American freedom; which was asserting, in effect, that the act which had passed was an encroachment on the rights and liberties of the people, and amounted to a direct charge of tyranny and despotism against the British king, lords, and commons." *Ibid.*, pp. 165-166.

In one of the 1764 memorials, there is also a statement which bears some resemblance to Henry's strong assertion in his fifth resolution. The memorial declares that "British Patriots will never consent to the Exercise of anticonstitutional Power, which even in the remote Corner may be dangerous in its Example to the interior Parts of the British Empire, and will certainly be detrimental to its Commerce." *JHB, 1761-1765,* p. 304. This phrasing, with that which preceded it in the memorials, is not nearly so vigorous, either in the actual words or implication as in Henry's fifth resolution: "Therefore that the General Assembly of this colony have the *only and sole* exclusive right and Power to lay Taxes and Impositions upon the Inhabitants of this Colony and that every attempt to vest such Power in any Person or Persons whatsoever other than the General Assembly aforesaid has a manifest Tendency to destroy British as well as American Freedom."

It should also be repeated that Henry's resolutions were proposed after the passage of the Stamp Act and by many of his opponents were considered inflammatory or even treasonable.

37. Wirt, *Henry*, p. 65, quoting Judge Winston "on the authority of Henry himself."

38. "Mr. Johnston always claimed the credit of being the first man who discovered the great but hidden powers of that unrivalled orator. He had great difficulty in persuading Mr. Henry that he was the only man who was fitted to make such a speech. . . ." Meade, *Old Churches*, II, 240.

39. This may help to explain Edmund Randolph's assertion that Flem-

ing wrote Henry's resolutions. Randolph, "History of Virginia" (Ms.). See Notes 40 and 41. The Ms. history is reprinted in 10 *Va. Mag.*

40. W. W. Henry, who later had the Patrick Henry copy of the resolutions in his possession, does not say that they were in his grandfather's handwriting. But he does specifically state that the endorsement on the back is Henry's. Henry, *Henry*, I, 81. The handwriting of the Stamp Act resolutions bears a strong resemblance to that in John Fleming's ledger now preserved at the Va. Historical Society.

41. Considering what we know otherwise of Fleming's and Johnston's ability and their rôles in the proceedings, it would appear that they were most responsible for the additional resolutions. But Munford, although then less known, had literary ability, as evidenced later by his popular play, *The Candidates*.

42. *JHB, 1761-1765*, pp. 356-358; Carrington Memo in Library of Congress.

43. H. B. Grigsby, *Virginia Convention of 1776*, quoted in Weddell, *op. cit.*, pp. 225-228 (with accompanying picture of Randolph).

44. Copied from photostat of Henry's copy in frontispiece of *JHB, 1761-1765*. In the few instances where these resolutions were defaced or illegible, I used the copy in Henry, *Henry*, I, 80-81. He had access to the original copy left by his grandfather, Patrick Henry.

45. Tyler, *Henry*, p. 61-63.

46. This is Tyler's theory. *Ibid.*, p. 67.

47. Fauquier to the Board of Trade, June 5, 1765, in *JHB, 1761-1765*, pp. lxvii-lxviii.

48. Morgan, *Henry*, p. 100.

49. Jefferson also incorrectly included Pendleton in the list of Henry's opponents during the debate. William Wirt let the mistake slip into his account despite the fact that Wirt had received from James Madison Pendleton's letter stating that he was absent. But Wirt persisted in accepting the recollections of Jefferson and made no reference to Pendleton's own statement that he had left the House when "the business of the session was supposed to be over—except for the concluding ceremonies and many Members retired." Mays, *Pendleton*, I, 161-163.

It was just as well that Henry did not have to face the cool, resourceful arguments of the masterful Pendleton, "the ablest man in debate" that Jefferson had ever met. Never vanquished, if he lost the main fight Pendleton returned "to make it a drawn one, by dexterous manoeuvres, skirmishes in detail, and the recovery of small advantages." Ford, *Jefferson* (1904), I, 59. Pendleton, a conservative though not reactionary leader, would have certainly opposed Henry if he had been present during the debate.

50. They did not disagree with Henry's party "as to the grievance complained of," but wanted to await an answer to their previous petition. This reply "possibly might rend[er] the proposed proceedings unnecessary." Carrington Memo.

51. *JHB, 1761-1765,* p. lxv. Especially since the vote was so close, more recognition should be given George Johnston and the other burgesses who supported Henry so staunchly at this critical juncture. Johnston, a resident of the new town of Alexandria, had a well-provided farm near by on the Potomac River, not far above Mount Vernon. He was one of the leading attorneys of his section and, besides numerous lawbooks, his large library was well stocked with volumes of Pope, Addison, and other classical authors. He had been a burgess from Fairfax County since 1758 and was a weighty speaker and debater. To Johnston, experienced, cultivated, liberal-minded, Henry might logically turn for help, even as he could to John Fleming of Cumberland. For Fleming lived at Maiden's Adventure, across the river from Goochland, and practiced with Henry at many a county court. Fleming was himself a lawyer with a large clientele and a burgess from 1755 until his death in 1767. Upon Fleming, patriotic and strong-minded, Henry could also rely for advice and support. Noblesse oblige! Although the careers of both Johnston and Fleming would be cut short in a few years, three of their sons, fine young officers, would be sacrificed in the coming Revolution.

Without straining the point of heredity it may likewise be noted that Henry, Fleming, and Johnston were all of Scottish descent. And, perhaps more significant, they were all from the newer counties, as distinguished from the conservative Tidewater. 10 *Va. Mag.,* pp. 11-12, 389-394.

52. Fauquier to the Board of Trade, *JHB, 1761-1765,* lxvii-lxviii.

53. Carrington Memo; Henry, *Henry,* I, 86-87; Beveridge, *Marshall,* I, 62-65.

54. Carrington Memo; Henry, *Henry,* I, 86-87.

55. Carrington Memo.

56. P. L. Ford, ed., *Autobiography of Thomas Jefferson,* p. 8. The editor adds useful notes.

57. Jefferson, to Wirt, Aug. 14, 1814. Ford, *Jefferson's Writings,* IX, 468.

58. Fauquier to the Board of Trade, *op. cit.,* Note 52. Edmund Pendleton wrote that a letter was received near the end of the session from Montague, agent of the Burgesses in Great Britain, transmitting them a copy of the Stamp Act. Mays, *Pendleton,* I, 161.

59. Fauquier to the Board of Trade, *op. cit.*, Note. 52.

60. Henry Cabot Lodge, *Daniel Webster*, p. 200.

61. "Journal of a French Traveller," in *op. cit.*, vol. 26, pp. 726-747; vol. 27, pp. 70-89.

62. This account was reprinted in *The General Advertizer* for the *New York Thursday's Gazette*, Oct. 31, 1765. See *Amer. Hist. Review*, vol. 26, p. 727.

63. Perry, *op. cit.*, I, 514-515.

64. W. Gordon, *op. cit.*, p. 118.

65. Edmund Randolph, in his Ms. history (see 10 *Va. Mag.*, pp. 9-13), although not quoting Henry as apologizing to the treason accusation, says that Henry replied: "And George the Third may he never have either." Randolph had good sources of information, but he did not hear Henry's speech.

66. John Daly Burk, *History of Virginia*, III, 305-310.

67. *JHB, 1761-1765*, p. lxviii; *Bristol Journal*, Aug. 10, 1765; *Glasgow Journal*, Oct. 31, 1765.

68. *Bristol Journal*, Aug. 10, 1765.

69. Wirt, *Henry*, pp. 72-73.

70. 15 *Va. Mag.*, p. 356.

71. Carrington Memo. The last surviving person known to have heard Henry's speech was William Taylor, long-time clerk and respected citizen of Lunenburg County, Virginia. When he died in 1820 a Richmond newspaper could find nothing better to say of him than that he had voted for Henry's Stamp Act resolutions. Data from the late Mrs. Annie Taylor Burwell of Warrenton, N.C., a descendant of William Taylor. *Richmond Enquirer*, Sept. 22, 1820. Landon Bell, *The Old Free State*, II, 363-364.

72. Hugh Blair Grigsby as cited in Morgan, *Henry*, p. 99.

73. Henry, *Henry*, I, 109-110, quoting letter of Judge John Tyler to Wirt.

74. Adams, *Works*, I, 66.

Chapter 11

THE ROAD TO REVOLUTION

1. James Truslow Adams, *Revolutionary New England*, p. 320.

2. This quotation is from the *Va. Gazette* (P&D), Mar. 31, 1768. A number of Dickinson's *Farmer's Letters* were reprinted in the *Gazette* during Jan.-Mar., 1768. For the Dickinson letter reprinted in the *Va. Gazette* on Mar. 31, 1768, see P. L. Ford, ed., *The Writings of John*

Dickinson, I, 400. For earlier expression by Dickinson of somewhat similar ideas, see *ibid.*, p. 262 in *Address to The Committee of Correspondence in Barbados* (1766), and *ibid.*, p. 202 in *Address On The Stamp Act* (Nov., 1765).

3. See pp. 176-177.

4. *Bristol Journal*, Aug. 10, 1765. *London Gazetteer*, Aug. 13, 1765. Extract of a letter from Virginia, June 14. Abstract in New York Public Library.

5. Letter from New York dated July 11 in *Md. Gazette*, July 25, 1765. Also *Boston Gazette*, July 22.

6. Fauquier to Conway, Nov. 3, 1765, Public Record Office, London. Jefferson describes his breakfasts with Wythe and Small in his *Autobiography*.

7. Letter from Virginia, June 14, 1765 in *London Gazetteer*, Aug. 13.

8. Henry to George Thomas, Feb. 18, 1764. In New York Public Library. This is Henry's earliest letter on non-political matters which is known to be extant.

9. Account Book 1762-1770, pp. 26, 59, 61, 65, 67, 150.

10. Comparing the resolutions left by Henry and the finally amended ones printed in the *JHB* with those sent northward, it is found that the latter more closely resemble Henry's. Obviously, the resolutions dispatched northward were made from an earlier copy than that finally amended. The copy sent to the North, however, omitted the third resolution in Henry's copy and several words and includes other minor differences. This appears to have been the result of hasty copying. See *Massachusetts Gazette*, July 4, 1765.

11. The resolutions published in Glasgow are the same as those disseminated in the North. The third resolution is omitted as in the Northern versions, and there are only minor differences otherwise, as in capitalization, which would be expected from separate printers. Altogether, there is strong evidence that the Northern version was perhaps sent out to be published for propaganda purposes without the statement that the last two violent resolutions were not passed by the Assembly. When Joseph Royle, the conservative editor of the *Va. Gazette* "complained that the other papers were stuffed with false news about Virginia, the radicals replied that 'If Mr. Royle had been pleased to publish those Resolves, the Authenticity of his Intelligence,' would have been indisputed, and he would not have had any Reason of complaint on the Score." Edmund Morgan, *The Stamp Act Crisis*, p. 98, quoting *Md. Gazette*, Oct. 3, 1765. Morgan's book should be studied for other illuminating material.

12. Gordon, *History of the U.S.*, pp. 117-121. The statement that

the resolves were enclosed in the letter does not conform with Gordon's account of the resolves being brought from New York by the "Irish Gentleman." Possibly the *Newport Mercury* was disguising its source of information.

13. For details on the Massachusetts background see E. Morgan, *op. cit.*, pp. 99-105, *passim*.

14. Richard Frothingham, *The Rise of the Republic*, p. 181.

15. C. G. Carter, ed., *The Correspondence of General Thomas Gage with the Secretaries of State, 1763-1775*, p. 67.

16. For example, in 1764 the Massachusetts House had sent a circular letter to the other colonies urging united action through their agents in England against the Sugar Act and the proposed Stamp Act. E. Morgan, *op. cit.*, p. 102.

17. The congress was to meet on Oct. 10, only three weeks before Nov. 1 when the law would become effective.

18. See letter of Governor Bernard of Massachusetts to the Lords of Trade, quoted in W. Gordon, *op. cit.*, pp. 117-121; also E. Morgan, *op. cit.*, p. 104.

19. The New Jersey legislature was about to adjourn and was moved more by uncertainty than ill-will. George Bancroft, *History of the United States*, III, 120; Howard, *Preliminaries of the Revolution*, pp. 146-147.

20. *Ibid.*, p. 146.

21. Bancroft, *loc. cit.*

22. Shakespeare, 2 *Henry IV*, Act I, Scene 1.

23. Howard, *op. cit.*, p. 147; Frothingham, *op. cit.*, p. 182; D. D. Wallace, *History of South Carolina*, II, esp. pp. 66-67.

24. E. Morgan, *op. cit.*, p. 27.

25. *Ibid.*, pp. 27-28; Howard, *op. cit.*, pp. 109-110. For interesting details on the Rhode Island slave dealers' use of rum in the African trade see U. B. Phillips, *American Negro Slavery*, p. 28, *passim*.

26. In Nov., 1764, Stephen Hopkins, the popularly elected Governor of Rhode Island, had published a forceful pamphlet against the proposed Stamp Act. Issued by authority of the Rhode Island Assembly, this pamphlet had been widely reprinted in the colonies. Howard, *op. cit.*, pp. 133-134.

27. E. Morgan, *op. cit.*, p. 98.

28. A New York correspondent in *Boston Post Boy*, Aug. 2, 1765. The effect on the press was dwelt on as early as Apr. 11 in a letter written from New York and published in the *Bristol Journal* for June 8. The writer noted that the Stamp Act resolves which they had just received, "must make the ears of every American (who conceived himself to be a

free man according to the British constitution) to tingle, and fill him with astonishment." Then he continued with regard to the tax on printed matter:

"The articles that more particularly effect the press, and will probably greatly lessen the business of it, are the following viz. On every news-paper or pamphlet of half a sheet or under, one half-penny sterling: on every ditto above half a sheet and not exceeding a sheet, one penny sterling: on every pamphlet and paper more than one sheet and not exceeding six sheets in octavo, or a lesser page, or twelve sheets in quarto, or twenty in folio, a duty of two shillings sterling for every sheet in one copy: on every advertisement in any news-paper, or other paper, or pamphlet, two shillings: on every almanack or calendar, for any one year or less, printed on one side of one sheet, two-pence sterling: on every almanac for one year four pence sterling: on every ditto for several years, each four pence sterling, &c . . ."

29. These organizations were Sons of Liberty and their associates. During his speech in Parliament opposing the Stamp Act, Isaac Barré had referred to the American opponents of the tax as "sons of liberty."

30. J. T. A. Adams, *op. cit.*, p. 231, quoting Gov. Bernard's correspondence and Ingersoll Papers.

31. *Ibid.*

32. Frothingham, *op. cit.*, p. 183.

33. Howard, *op. cit.*, p. 147; E. Morgan, *op. cit.*, p. 98.

34. For these resolutions see *Pennsylvania Gazette*, Sept. 26; *Boston Gazette*, Oct. 21; *Mass. Gazette*, Oct. 31; and Howard, *op. cit.*, p. 148. The influence of Henry's resolutions is obvious from the wording.

35. For a reference to the "great commotions" in the colonies and the causes thereof see *Glasgow Journal*, Oct. 31, 1765, letter from a Philadelphia gentleman to a friend in Bristol.

36. J. T. A. Adams, *op. cit.*, p. 335.

37. *Ibid.*

38. The boycott was especially strong in commercial towns where merchants signed agreements not to import British goods. New York City was a leader in this movement, followed by Philadelphia and Boston. Many artisans and farmers also pledged themselves to encourage the production and use of American products. Nettels, *Roots of American Civilization*, p. 631.

39. The editor added a disclaimer that if there was any error in them "the Fault lies not here." *Md. Gazette*, July 4, 1766.

40. The present Boswell's Tavern, Virginia.

41. See the "French" traveler's account, June 6, 1765, in *Amer. Hist. Review,* and Account Book, 1762-1770, p. 144.

42. *Ibid.*

43. Extract from a letter from Virginia to England, Jan. 6, 1765. Quoted in *Mass. Gazette,* July 25, 1765.

44. Account Book, 1762-1770.

45. *Ibid.*

46. *Ibid.*

47. *Syme* v. *Pearson* and various debt suits against Henry's Winston relatives. Goochland Loose Papers, Va. State Library; *JHB, 1761-1765,* p. 255, Oct. 15, 1764.

48. Henry, the first son of Valentine Wood and Lucy Wood, had been christened on March 22 with a number of Henrys probably in attendance. *Douglas Register,* p. 323.

49. Goochland Papers, Va. State Library.

50. Henry, *Henry,* I,

51. Harris, *Louisa,* pp. 51-68.

52. In his unpublished letter to the *Va. Gazette* the writer had spoken of its efforts in the Aug. 30 issue to deceive their Northern brethren into believing that the people of the colony were not "so well disposed to assert their just and constitutional Rights, as it has been truly represented they are." Then he had continued in this strong vein: "It is expected that you will retract, the injurious Censure that Paragraph of your Paper was meant to convey, by publishing this in your next Gazette; which is the best Atonement you can make for so unjust and dishonourable an Imputation. And this you may regard, as proceeding from no false telligencer; but, from a Person better acquainted with the Actions and Intentions of the People of Virginia, than a resident Printer in Williamsburg, can be or than the servile Dictator, of the above mentioned Paragraph, seems to be." The author of the letter asked the *Md. Gazette* to publish it since it had not yet appeared in the *Va. Gazette* and, some time having elapsed they could not now be reasonably expected to do so. The writer signed himself "A Virginian" but he cannot be definitely identified.

53. Bernard's address was delivered on Sept. 25 to the Massachusetts Assembly.

54. Fauquier to Lords of Trade, Nov. 3, 1765, Public Record Office, London; also copy in *JHB, 1761-1765,* pp. lxviii-lxix. *Va. Gazette* (P&D), Oct. 25, 1765.

55. For accounts of the congress in its New York setting see Frothingham, *op. cit.,* pp. 184-190 and E. Morgan, *op. cit.,* pp. 103-113.

56. In the first resolution passed by the congress it acknowledged "all

due subordination" to Parliament. The Virginia, North Carolina, and Georgia governors prevented their assemblies from meeting to elect delegates. New Hampshire declined to attend but formally approved the proceedings of the congress.

57. Howard, *op. cit.*, p. 155.

58. *Va. Gazette Day Book*, Apr. 16, May 16, and Oct. 16, 1764. University of Va. Library.

59. Clinton Rossiter, "Richard Bland: The Whig in America" in *Wm. and Mary* (Jan. 1953), pp. 37-38. Rossiter has (*ibid.*, pp. 33-79) a detailed, fully documented treatment of Bland's writings. See also Rossiter, *Seedtime of the Republic*.

60. Reprint in 1922, edited by E. G. Swem.

61. *Ibid.*

62. "Indeed, in 1765 some of the 'best people' in America might have been found either in the mob or encouraging it to rise up against British 'tyranny.'" John C. Miller, *Origins of the American Revolution*, p. 131. Laurens, a great merchant, was opposed to the Stamp Act but also to the "burglary and robbery" of the opposing rioters. Wallace, *op. cit.*, II, 67.

63. *Va. Gazette* (P&D), July 25 and Oct. 3, 1766.

64. The original Westmoreland Association is in the Va. Historical Society archives.

65. There is a good account of the Ritchie episode in Freeman, *Washington*, III, 153-156. See also *Va. Gazette (Rind)*, May 16 and 30, 1766. If Ritchie did not retract, the committee from the Sons of Liberty had resolved to strip him naked to the waist, tie him to the tail of a cart, and draw him to the pillory where he would be left an hour. He was informed that this or further measures would be taken against him if necessary.

66. Henry, *Henry*, I, 96-97; T. J. Wertenbaker, *Norfolk, Historic Southern Port*, pp. 52-53; *Va. Gazette*, Apr. 4, 1766.

67. Miller, *op. cit.*, pp. 142-143.

68. *Boston Gazette*, Dec. 2, quoting New York dispatch of Nov. 25.

69. The petitions, or references thereto, of numerous English merchants and artisans are in G. S. Callender, *Selections from the Economic History of the United States, 1765-1860*, pp. 145-148 and F. J. Hinkhouse, *The Preliminaries of the American Revolution as Seen in the English Press, 1763-1775*, esp. chap. II and p. 62. See also Dora M. Clark, *British Opinion and the American Revolution*.

70. Howard, *op. cit.*, p. 163.

71. *Ibid.*

72. Feiling, *England*, pp. 704-705. There is a good account of the fight for repeal in Miller, *op. cit.*, chap. 7.

73. *Ibid.*, p. 156.

74. *Va. Gazette* on Apr. 18, 1766, carried an Annapolis dispatch of Apr. 10 announcing the passage of the repeal bill by the House of Commons.

75. On April 11.

Chapter 12

A Maturing Statesman

1. Letter of Mar. 27, 1768, from Lee to a correspondent identified only as "A gentleman, of influence in England." James C. Ballagh, *Letters of Richard Henry Lee*, p. 26.

2. *JHB, 1766-1769*, p. 12.

3. William Byrd, *A Journey to the Land of Eden*, pp. 318-319.

4. 9 *Wm. and Mary* (Ser. 3), p. 361.

5. The account of Chiswell's funeral is taken from the John Blair Dabney Ms. Routlidge was killed at Mosby's Tavern in Cumberland County. Williamsburg dispatch of July 18, 1766, in *Glasgow Journal*, Nov. 13, 1766. Mosby's Tavern was at the old Cumberland Courthouse on Deep Creek. Notes by John Randolph in an interleaved almanac now at Va. Historical Society. The notes were made from colonial Virginia newspapers. Dabney states that Chiswell seized a sword and ran Routlidge through the body. On the other hand, it was claimed by several witnesses that during the altercation he ran against Chiswell's extended sword. *Va. Gazette* (P&D) Sept. 12, 1766. See also *Gazette*, July 4 and Aug. 1, 1766; Daniel Call, *Cases in the Court of Appeal*, IV, p. xvii; and Kimball, *Jefferson*, I, 133. A recent account of the affray, with evidence that makes Routlidge seem somewhat less culpable than formerly believed, is in Herbert Bradshaw, *History of Prince Edward County*, pp. 100-102. This full and readable study contains much material on a county with which Henry was identified.

6. *JHB, 1766-1769*, pp. 5-11.

7. *Va. Gazette* (P&D) Oct. 24, 1766.

8. *JHB, 1761-1765*, pp. 3-4.

9. *JHB, 1766-1769*, p. 3. For Richard Anderson, see Harris, *Louisa*, pp. 18, 21, *passim;* and Account Book, 1762-1770.

10. The question was aired in the *Gazette* (Aug. 1 and Sept. 5, 1766) by Nicholas and by other letter writers signing themselves "Philautos," "An Honest Buckskin," and "A Freeholder." The latter wrote

alarmingly of a balance due from the Treasurer in Nov., 1753, of £8,319.13.11 with no specie on hand, of creditors being paid in paper money or not at all, and of the "suspicions" among people for many years that much of Robinson's influence was obtained by "indirect methods." See also T. P. Abernethy, *Western Lands and the American Revolution*, pp. 151-154.

11. Campbell, *Virginia*, p. 545.

12. Fauquier to Lords of Trade. Colonial Office Papers, Public Record Office, London.

13. *Va. Gazette* (P&D), Oct. 30, 1766.

14. Fauquier to Lords of Trade.

15. *JHB, 1766-1769*, p. 11. At the time this appeared a victory for the conservatives, but Randolph, as we shall note, developed into a moderate leader of the Revolutionary party. Moreover, a bill proposed at the 1766 session and finally passed in 1769 provided a salary for the Speaker. While giving a certain dignity to the office, this law also made him far more amenable to the House and aided the liberty party. *Ibid.*, pp. 60, 298.

16. Campbell, *op. cit.*, p. 545.

17. George Dabney Ms. Wirt Papers, Library of Congress.

18. *JHB, 1766-1769*, p. 24. The motion also provided that "the Speaker shall not be concerned as an officer of the Treasury in any Manner whatsoever." Nov. 12, 1766. See also George Dabney Ms.

19. Ballagh, *op. cit.*, p. 56.

20. *Ibid.*, pp. 18-22.

21. *JHB, 1766-1769*, pp. xii-xiii, quoting R. H. Lee, *Memoir of Richard Henry Lee.*

22. Among the eleven members of the committee were also Francis Lightfoot Lee, John Fleming, and Paul Carrington, with George Wythe and Richard Bland from the moderate opposition. To this committee, appointed on the second day of the session, Edward Moseley and Edmund Pendleton were added on November 18. *JHB, 1766-1769*, pp. 14, 30.

23. *Ibid.*, p. 65.

24. *Ibid.*, pp. 66-67. There were 13,700 acres in King and Queen, Spotsylvania, and Caroline; 4,250 in Hanover, 1,200 in King William, and so on.

25. Mays, *Pendleton*, I, 181. He made a long and thorough study of the Robinson papers in the U.S. District Court at Richmond and elsewhere to which all students of the period are indebted.

26. *Ibid.*, 183-184.

27. The great majority of the debts were concentrated in a few Tide-

water counties, especially Robinson's own King and Queen and adjoining King William.

"As to the influence of Robinson on members of the General Assembly because of his loans to them, I can be no more definite. I don't see how a man heavily indebted to Robinson could fail to be influenced thereby. On the other hand, most of the people to whom Robinson loaned money were good friends of his, and I am sure he would have made the loans even though he knew at the time it would not affect their votes. Truth is, Mr. Robinson was exceedingly generous, and I doubt if he turned anybody down. This business of political favors is a rather intangible thing, and I doubt if we shall ever be able to put our fingers on specific cases where loans actually influenced votes. We have two troubles, of course; one, that so many records have been destroyed, and two, that people who deal in political influence as it affects themselves, talk about it in a back room and rarely make memos." Letter from David Mays, Richmond, Nov. 9, 1953.

28. Meredith owed £30.15 and Dr. Hinde 22,062 pounds of tobacco. Hinde was the Henry family physician in the early 1770's and probably earlier. Henry's client and future father-in-law, Col. West Dandridge, is listed as owing £27.5 for most of which he denied liability. Richard Henry Lee owed only £12. For these and other details see Pendleton's list of the Robinson debtors in 1766 and those still remaining in 1792 in Mays, *op. cit*, I, 358-375.

29. *Ibid.*, p. 185.

30. *JHB, 1766-1769*, pp. 66-67.

31. *Ibid.*, p. 67.

32. Henry was the lowest ranking among the eighteen members of this committee. He also ranked thirteenth among the forty-five members of the Committee of Propositions and Grievances. *Ibid.*, pp. 14, 15.

Two cases well illustrate the routine work to which he devoted much of his time in committee. In a petition on Nov. 11 from "sundry" inhabitants of Fauquier County, complaint was made that the grist mills, hedges, and stops on certain streams prevented the fish from coming up them, and the matter was referred to the Committee on Propositions and Grievances. The Elections Committee had to deal with the failure of the sheriff of distant Hampshire and Frederick counties to order an election for the Burgesses. Colonel Thomas Preston had promised "to contrive" the writs in due time to the sheriff but his "traveling Chair" broke down in Hanover. *Ibid.*, pp. 18-23.

33. A letter to the Burgesses with a copy of the proceedings of the Stamp Act Congress was ordered to be laid on the table where it could be perused by the members. *Ibid.*, p. 13.

34. *Ibid.*, p. 13.

35. A portion of Halifax County, however, was now made into a new county named Pittsylvania in honor of William Pitt, and a parish in the county was named for Lord Camden, another staunch opponent of the Stamp Act. *Ibid.*, pp. 9, 75 and M. C. Clements, *History of Pittsylvania County, Virginia*, pp. 93-94.

36. See p. 202.

37. Morgan, *Henry*, p. 434, Meredith Memo. Col. Henry's teaching assistant was one Walker, a Scotsman. *Ibid.* Fithian notes in his Journal for Dec. 13, 1773, that it had been "the custom heretofore [of the Virginians] to have all their Tutors, and Schoolmasters from Scotland, tho' they begin to be willing to employ their own countrymen."

38. In the memorial, probably prepared with Patrick's help, John Henry set forth the advantages of his maps for travel and navigation. He said that they would contribute greatly to the honor of the Virginia colony as well as to the interest of Great Britain by the more speedy settlement of her recent acquisitions upon the American continent.

39. See pp. 283-284.

40. *JHB, 1766-1769*, p. 60.

41. Helen Hill, *George Mason*, esp. pp. 17, 31-32.

42. *JHB, 1766-1769*, p. 72.

43. Louisa Order Book, May 12, 1766. In Meade, *Old Churches*, II, 41-42, are copies, taken from a Fredericksville parish vestry book, of tests required of the Louisa vestrymen.

44. "If anyone doubts the truths asserted here," Henry said, "I beseech him to reflect wherefore is it, that a country, I say the happyest for situation on the continent, blest with a soil producing not only the necessarys but the luxurys of life; full of rivers, havens and inlets, that invite the visits of commerce for the products of industry; and bordered with extended plains, that instead of lonely scattered huts, might be covered with magnificent citys; wherefore is it that a country producing the choicest grain, stock, wool, fish, hemp, flax, metals of the North, together with the corn, pulp, rice, wine, fruits and most of those delicacys found in southern climes, should want the common conveniencys, the necessarys of life. I will not enumerate the good things our country may produce. Let me ask what it will not produce? The truth is anything but inhabitants sensible of its value." Henry, *Henry*, I, 114.

45. *Ibid.*

46. *Ibid.*, pp. 115-116.

47. Allowance should be made for the fact that Jefferson made the

statement that Henry could not write in 1824, only two years before the former's death.

48. Hanover was represented by John Syme and Samuel Meredith; Halifax by Walter Coles. *JHB, 1766-1769*, pp. 79-80. The *JHB* lists 47 of the 116 members as absent. Both burgesses were absent from 15 counties, mostly in the westerly regions difficult of access to Williamsburg in March.

49. *Ibid.*, pp. 97, 120-121.

50. *Ibid.*, p. 108.

51. *Ibid.*, pp. 119-120.

52. *Ibid.*, p. 123.

53. *Ibid.*, pp. 115-116. "The business of Paper Money becomes every day more and more Serious." Letter of Richard Corbin to Robert Cary Aug. 22, 1762. Copy in Corbin Letter Book, Va. Historical Society. Corbin states that the merchants here have drawn up a memorial to the Lords of Trade and elaborates on the difficulties of the creditor class through use of paper money. For an opinion on the currency question to which Henry would probably have agreed, see E. James Ferguson, "Currency Finance: An Interpretation of Colonial Monetary Practices," in 10 *Wm. and Mary* (Ser. 3), esp. pp. 160, 162, 166, 174-179. He questions the old view of the "sound" money advocates and holds that the colonies benefited from a controlled use of paper money.

54. Receipt signed by George Thomas, July 20, 1771. Valentine Museum.

55. Fauquier to Shelburne, Nov. 7, 1767. Public Record Office, London.

Chapter 13

FRONTIER LANDS AND CONNECTIONS

1. The original indenture, dated Oct. 21, 1765, is at Louisa Courthouse. Patrick paid John Henry £100 current money for the plantation on both sides of Roundabout Creek.

2. The entries for John Gilbert, Louisa carpenter, show no payments after Dec. 1, 1765. Account Book, 1762-1770, p. 137.

3. "Genealogy Roane Family." Contributed by W. W. Henry. In 5 *Va. Mag.*, pp. 89-90.

4. The data on the Johnson homes and family is based on personal visits to the Louisa area described and, in particular, on very generous assistance by Mrs. Josephine Neal, Louisa. She is a descendant of Sheriff Thomas Johnson and lives on the site of Roundabout Castle, about two miles by air line from Roundabout, the Henry place. She was born at

Roundabout Castle, which was burned in 1913, and also recalls the other Johnson place, previously Meriwether's, before the house was destroyed.

5. The Roundabout house had a large front room from which a stairway led to a half-story upstairs. The shingle roof sloped down in the back, and in the rear of the front room was another large room, one story in height. To the left of the front room as one entered the front door was a lean-to or passageway connecting with a third large room. There was a fireplace to the right in the front room and another to the right in the back room; also a chimney at the end of the house to the left. The present stable at Roundabout was partly made from old hand-hewn beams of the original house. A mantel and other objects from Roundabout may still be found in the county, and this writer has a large handmade brick, picked up at the foundation. Personal visits to the Roundabout site. Data from Mrs. Josephine Neal who recalls the original house destroyed about 1920. Photographs of original house kindly supplied by John G. May, Jr., Richmond. Description by Captain W. T. Meade, Louisa, in Morgan, *Henry*, pp. 113-114. Accounts of John Gilbert, carpenter, and John Anderson, mason, in Account Book, 1762-1770, p. 137. Henry, *Henry*, I, 123. There were probably one or more outbuildings which could be used for guests. Capt. Meade, *op. cit.*

6. Much useful data on early Louisa County history may be found in Harris, *Louisa*. Many colonial records have been preserved at Louisa Courthouse. I am indebted to W. B. Gilmer, Louisa, for helpful information on the county history based on official records and early county newspapers. The Mutual Assurance Society, Richmond, has records (see microfilm at Va. State Library) of some colonial homes in Louisa County.

7. Harris, *Louisa*, p. 135.

8. *Ibid*, pp. 179-184, 410. Herbert C. Bradshaw, "Princeton University's Place in the History of Virginia" in *Richmond Times-Dispatch* Mar. 2, 1947. Records of Hanover Presbytery, Va. State Library. Personal visit to Providence Church. Data on the Todd relationships of Mrs. Mary Todd Lincoln is given in Albert J. Beveridge, *Abraham Lincoln*, I, 307-309.

9. Patrick's young cousin Isaac Coles, who boarded with him in 1767, was charged for an elk skin, and credit was given two of Henry's debtors in Louisa about this time for dressing deerskins and for two quarters of venison. Account Book, 1762-1770, pp. 150, 151, 188.

10. Reminiscences of Capt. William Perkins in Morgan, *Henry*, pp. 113-114.

11. Wirt, *Henry*, pp. 48-49, quoting an anonymous correspondent, perhaps Jefferson.

12. *Ibid.*, pp. 49-50.

13. This was late in 1768, when Henry is believed to have already returned to Hanover, but the only farm he is known to have owned in this area was at Roundabout. For his barter transactions in that year, see account with George Donald, Richmond, in Account Book, 1762-1770.

14. Bridenbaugh, *Seat of Empire*, p. 1.

15. *Ibid.*

16. Proclamation by Fauquier. Copy in Colonial Office Papers. Public Record Office, London.

17. *JHB, 1766-1769*, pp. 37, 69-70.

18. C. W. Alvord, *The Mississippi Valley in British Politics*, II, 110-111; 5 *Va. Mag.*, pp. 175-180, 241-244.

19. The Va. Council granted on July 12, 1749 the petition of William Winston, Jr., Isaac Winston, Jr., Peter Fontaine, Jr., Edmund Winston, and Samuel Redd to take up and survey 50,000 acres between the Ohio and Mississippi rivers. *Council Journal, V, 297.*

20. For this data on John Syme, I am greatly indebted to his descendant, Mrs. W. W. Hunter, *The Four John Symes* (Ms.)

21. List of Judgments for Sterling Money. Va. State Library.

22. For the information on Henry's Holston land interests see Account Book, 1762-1770, p. 28, and Chalkley, *Chronicles of the Scotch-Irish in Virginia*, III, 462, 478.

23. Account Book, 1762-1770, p. 28. In his lengthy notation herein on the John Shelton account Henry stated: "The land was long since lost for non payment of quit rents and except one tract of it had not been seen since it was surveyed (viz. about 20 years). I made a journey thither in company with Wm. Henry, Wm. Christian, etc. etc., to search for it but could find one tract only."

24. *Ibid.*

25. Lewis Preston Summers, *History of Southwest Virginia, 1746-1786*, pp. 796-807 and esp. p. 807, quoting "Journal of Doctor Thomas Walker—1749-1750."

26. Summers, *op. cit.*, p. 797.

27. The scalp is displayed in the old City Hall near Independence Hall.

28. R. L. Kincaid, *The Wilderness Road*, pp. 56-57.

29. Preston Ms. Data from Miss Nelly Preston.

30. Freeman, *Washington*, II, 191-207.

31. See Note 29. Abernethy, *Western Lands*, pp. 4, 5, 7, *passim.*

32. Preston Ms.

33. *JHB, 1766-1769*, pp. xxvi-xxviii. This contains a detailed account of the negotiations of the Virginia commissioners, Dr. Walker and Andrew Lewis, in connection with the Treaty of Hard Labour.

34. Account Book, 1762-1770. Henry added that "After many contests and much altercation with the Indians, our own people, government here, and administration at home, an extension of territory was purchased from the Indians, and the lands above were taken into this Colony, except part of one tract which the line split." See also Henry, *Henry*, I, 121.

For details of further negotiations regarding Henry's claim see *JHB*, *1770-1772*, pp. viii-xxvi. There is an explanatory map in the frontispiece.

35. Henry to Fleming, June 10, 1767. Copy in W. W. Henry Papers, Va. Historical Society. In a postscript Henry added, "I have mention'd your going out to sundry other gentlemen & everybody is fond of it."

36. Data from the late Mrs. William R. Shelton, Hanover County, a descendant of the Shelton-Alexander McClanahan marriage. See also Frederick Johnston, *Old Virginia Clerks*, pp. 51-53.

37. For this data on Israel and William Christian, see contemporary vols. of the *JHB*, esp. 1761-65; William Heth Whitsitt, *The Life and Times of Judge Caleb Wallace*, pp. 59-60; *Pa. Gazette*, Oct. 19, 1763; Israel Christian in Henry's Account Book, 1762-1770; Joseph A. Waddell, *Annals of Augusta*; and Chalkley, *op. cit.*

38. Henry, *Henry*, I, 122.

39. List of Judgments for Sterling Money. Va. State Library.

40. Preston Ms.; data from Miss Nelly Preston; 7 *Va. Mag.*, p. 253; Chalkley, *op. cit.*, I, 130, 133; Henry, *Henry*, II, 640.

41. Henry, *Henry*, II, 641. Otis Bowyer to W. W. Henry, Feb. 26, 1896, in W. W. Henry Papers, Va. Historical Society; Chalkley, *op. cit.*, pp. 90, 310, *passim*. Luke Bowyer is listed as a witness to the deed of Oct. 21, 1765, at Louisa Courthouse by which John Henry sold some Roundabout property to Patrick. Bowyer was not admitted to practice in Augusta until Aug. 18, 1768, (Chalkley, *op. cit.*, p. 310) and very probably studied law under Patrick prior to that time.

42. William Fleming in *DAB*; data from Miss Nelly Preston; Fleming Papers, Washington and Lee University.

43. This letter, dated Hanover, Mar. 22, 1773, was apparently written to William Fleming. Fleming Papers, Washington and Lee University. Deed of land in 1773 of Wm. Christian to Patrick Henry. Botetourt County Deed Book, I, 471.

44. I. B. Cohen, *An Economic and Social Survey of Botetourt County*, esp. pp. 9-18; Waddell, *op. cit.*, pp. 36-235.

45. Abernethy, *Western Lands*, p. 61, 80, *passim*; William Fleming in *DAB*.

46. There is no record, however, of the bill's becoming a law. *JHB*, *1766-1769*, p. 122.

47. There was a specific reference to Orders of Council for which the terms had not been fulfilled. The resolutions also requested the Governor to discourage all future monopolies of land within the colony. *JHB, 1766-1769*, pp. 318-319.

48. "Your Memorialists further beg Leave to represent to your Lordship, that Lands which have been granted by Patents regularly obtained, according to the known and fixed Rules of this Government, if the said Line were to take Place, would be entirely dismembered from this Colony, allotted to the Indians, and entirely left to the Proprietors, who were authorized by Law, and encouraged by the Royal Instruction of his late Majesty to his Governor to explore and settle this new Country at the Risque of their Lives, and at a great Expense." In *Colonial Papers, 1741-1775*, Va. State Library. See also *JHB, 1766-1769*, pp. 335-336.

49. See p. 229.

50. In Wirt Papers, Library of Congress.

51. *Ibid.*

52. See p. 228.

53. Jefferson's mother was Jane Randolph, daughter of Isham Randolph of Goochland. The marriage bonds of Jane and Peter Jefferson, dated Oct. 3, 1739, now framed and hung on the wall at Goochland Courthouse, state that they were sealed and delivered in the presence of "H. Wood." Henry Wood was the father of Valentine Wood, clerk of Goochland Court, who married Patrick's sister Lucy.

54. *Colonial Papers, 1741-1775*, Va. State Library.

55. Three years later Samuel Meredith and William Christian, along with their patriotic but spendthrift commander, William Byrd III, and James Walker, petitioned the Council for land to which they were entitled for service in the French war.

56. Archibald Henderson, *The Conquest of the Old Southwest*, pp. 210-211; Alvord, *op. cit.*, II, pp. 202-203.

57. *Ibid.*, pp. 193-194; Abernethy, *Western Lands*, pp. 113-115.

58. See Note 57.

Chapter 14

A Man of Varied Interests

1. Lecky was referring to the time from Oct., 1766, when Charles Townshend seized active control of the ministry. Lecky, *England in the Eighteenth Century*, III, 379.

2. Henry Aylett Sampson, *Sonnets and Other Poems*, p. 122.

3. The *Va. Gazette* (P&D), May 9, 1766, contains a London letter

with a long account of Pitt's speech favoring repeal of the Stamp Act. There is also this statement on Pitt's oratorical style: "As he always begins very low and everybody was in agitation on his first rising, I could not hear his introduction until he said . . ."

4. "As an orator, Henry had much in common with Chatham, whose voice was melodious and whose gesture and delivery were superb. Arthur S. McDowall says: 'The most remarkable characteristic of his speaking was its union of dramatic power with a striking moral ascendancy; and this was the salient characteristic of his life as well as oratory.' Grattan said: 'He lighted upon his subject and reached the point by the flashings of his mind, which were felt but could not be followed.' In this he was Henry over again." Morgan, *Henry*, p. 131.

5. "We are here under great anxiety concerning the fate of the Stamp Act, which has been under the consideration of the House for this month and upwards; and indeed a close application there has been concerning it, and many warm debates it has occassioned. Mr. Pitt acquited himself gloriously in the affair, and has been a great friend to the Americans; he stood forth nobly, arguing for a total repeal of the Stamp Act, and an extension of trade to North America. Those who had the happiness to hear him speak thought there could not a man exist who displayed so much patriotism as he did." *Va. Gazette* (P&D), April 11, 1766. Extract of a letter from Bristol, February 14, 1766.

6. *Va. Gazette* (P&D), May 9, 1766.

7. *Ibid.*

8. Pitt also weakened his influence when he accepted the title of the Earl of Chatham and entered the House of Lords.

9. Morison and Commager, *Growth of the American Republic*, I, 155.

10. The House brushed aside Burke's warning that the ministry would find out their mistake. "You will never see a shilling from America." Cavendish, *Reports*, I, 39.

11. Howard, *Preliminaries of the Revolution*, pp. 184-185.

12. *Ibid.*, pp. 185-186. Ford, *Writings of John Dickinson*, I, 324-325, 355-357, *et seq.*

13. The quotation is by John Marshall in *McCulloch* v. *Maryland*.

14. *Va. Gazette Day Book*, University of Va. Library.

15. *Ibid.*

16. James E. Pate, "Richard Bland's Inquiry into the Rights of the British Colonies" in 2 *Wm. and Mary* (Ser. 2), p. 27. For a fuller treatment see E. G. Swem, ed., *Bland's Inquiry*.

17. "The more I have thought and read on the subject," Franklin wrote, "the more I find myself confirmed in the opinion that no middle

ground can well be maintained; I mean not clearly with intelligible arguments. Something might be made of either of the extremes: that Parliament has a power to make all laws for us, or that it has a power to make no laws for us; and I think the arguments for the latter more numerous and weighty than those for the former." Carl Van Doren, *Benjamin Franklin*, p. 378, quoting *Writings*, V, 113-115.

18. Moncure Conway to W. W. Henry, Sept. 18, 1894, in Va. Historical Society. Conway quotes the Ms. diary of Rachel Wilson shown him by John Bright's daughter.

19. *JHB, 1766-1769*, p. 104.

20. See pp. 216-220.

21. *Ibid.*

22. *John Blair Dabney Ms.*

23. Harris, *Louisa*, pp. 214-216. For references to Henry's Quaker clients, see Account Book, 1763-1770, pp. 4, 29.

24. Robert Taylor Semple, *The Baptists in Virginia* (revised ed.), pp. 41-44. James B. Taylor, *Virginia Baptist Ministers*, I, 48-54, 78, 106, 126, *passim*. The work of Samuel Harris, early Baptist evangelist born at Hanover in 1724 is noted in Clement, *History of Pittsylvania County*, pp. 126, *et seq.* For the Louisa Baptists see Harris, *Louisa*.

25. Semple, *op. cit.*, esp. p. 44. Two Baptist evangelists of this period, not of obscure families, were John Waller of Spotsylvania County and William Marshall, an uncle of the Chief Justice. Taylor, *op. cit.*, I, 78, 105.

26. Quoted in Mays, *Pendleton*, I, 262-265. It has good data on the Baptist movement in counties near Hanover. See also Wesley Marsh Gewehr, *The Great Awakening in Va.*

27. "They were democratic in politics, as well as religion, and whole hearted in their sympathy with the colonial cause as against England." H. J. Eckenrode, *Separation of Church and State in Virginia*, p. 38. In chap. V Eckenrode has an excellent summary of the pre-Revolutionary Baptist movement.

28. The accounts by the early Baptist historians in Virginia, such as Semple, are naturally colored by the sufferings of their co-religionists. These accounts should be checked in Gewehr, *The Great Awakening* and contemporary records. Many devout Anglicans believed with good reason that the Baptists were trying not merely to secure religious liberty but to cripple the Anglican Church in the colony. See G. M. Brydon, *Virginia's Mother Church*, esp. II, chap. VIII.

29. The Rev. John Corbley. Taylor, *op. cit.*, I, 26. See also Note 30.

30. Mays, *Pendleton*, I, 263.

31. Semple, *op. cit.*, p. 41.

32. Henry, *Henry*, I, 118-119.

33. Taylor, *op. cit.*, I, 51, states that Weatherford was arrested in Chesterfield by Colonel Cary and thrown into prison. There is a monument at Chesterfield Courthouse, commemorating the Baptist ministers imprisoned there.

34. Roane Memo in Morgan, *Henry*, p. 440.

35. Mays, *op. cit.*, I, 262-264.

36. Thomas Elliott Campbell, *Colonial Caroline*. This volume, while lacking certain specific documentation, is obviously the result of wide study of Caroline history. It should be balanced against the picture of Edmund Pendleton and his associates given in Mays' *Pendleton*.

37. Spotsylvania Order Book.

38. Henry, *Henry*, I, 119.

39. W. L. Hopkins, *Hopkins of Virginia*, pp. 39-40.

40. Semple, *op. cit.*, p. 80. Brydon, *op. cit.*, shows that the Virginia Anglican Church took no part as an organization in the persecution of the Baptists. He also shows that they participated in only a few instances in the arrests and physical violence.

41. Campbell, *Caroline*, p. 226.

42. *JHB, 1766-1769*, pp. 205, 252.

43. *Ibid.*, *1770-1772*, pp. 20, 157, 160, 161.

44. *Ibid.*, p. 245.

45. Gewehr, *op. cit.*, p. 126. In his thorough, well-documented volume, Gewehr has an excellent treatment of the Baptist movement in this period. See esp. chap. V, with sketch map (opposite p. 106) of the religious revival areas.

46. *Ibid.*, p. 128.

47. *JHB, 1770-1772*, p. 188.

48. *Ibid.*, p. 194. For an evidence of Nicholas' friendship with Henry, see p. 259.

49. *JHB, 1773-1776*, pp. 92-102. Eckenrode, *op. cit.*, pp. 39, *et seq.*

50. Henry, *Henry*, I, 123. The approximate date is indicated by entries in his Account Book about this time.

51. John Sanderson, *Biography of the Signers of the Declaration of Independence*, vol. 16, in New York Public Library.

52. The June and December sessions were for criminal cases involving persons other than slaves. For an excellent discussion of the General Court by a scholarly practicing lawyer, see Mays, *op. cit.*, I, chap. 13. Also see *Hening's Statutes*, vols. 5 and 6.

53. *Hening's Statutes*, VI, 143.

54. See Account Books, 1762-1770 and 1770-1774.

55. Clement, *op. cit.*, pp. 98-99.

56. See R. D. Meade's review of Mays' *Pendleton* in *Journal of Southern History*, vol. 19, pp. 74-75.

57. *Va. Gazette* (P&D), Sept. 24, Oct. 1, 8, and 16, 1767.

58. Mays, *op. cit.*, I, 230, quoting Michie's Preface to *Call's* [Va.] *Reports* (1900).

59. Henry, *Henry*, I, 123.

60. Morgan, *Henry*, p. 440.

61. Henry, *Henry*, I, 124.

62. Wirt, *Henry*, pp. 81-82.

63. Henry, *Henry*, I, 125-127, quoting letter from Tucker to William Wirt in 1805.

64. *Ibid.*, 126-127.

65. Account Book, 1770-1774, section 2, p. 12.

66. *Ibid.*, pp. 35, 34, 31, 4, 22.

67. *Ibid.*, pp. 14, 24, 16, 23, 12, 3.

68. *Ibid.* The records on Henry's sale of the gelding are on p. 3; the suit against Andrew Lewis on p. 23.

69. *Ibid.*, p. 13.

70. *Ibid.*, p. 22.

71. *Ibid.*, p. 11.

72. *Va. Gazette* (P&D), Jan. 5, 1773.

73. Malone, *Jefferson*, I, 121-124. "The Honble Wm Byrd retains me generally," Jefferson wrote. *Ibid.*, p. 122.

74. The figures are tabulations of individual entries in the Account Books.

75. Account Book, 1770-1774.

76. Letter of June 14, 1771. Duplicate in Colonial Office Papers. Public Record Office, London.

77. *Va. Gazette* (P&D), Sept. 29, 1768.

78. *Ibid.*, Jan. 3, 1771.

79. They made an exception, however, in cases where they served gratis. *Va. Gazette* (P&D), May 20, 1773.

80. *Ibid.*

81. Mays, *op. cit.*, I, 248.

82. Goochland Loose Papers, Va. State Library; Account Book, 1770-1774, p. 10.

83. Wirt, *Henry*, pp. 80-81.

Chapter 15

MOUNTING POLITICAL AND PERSONAL PROBLEMS

1. *Va. Gazette*, (P&D), Mar. 3, 1768. Fauquier's will, expressing opposition to slavery and accenting the scientific interests that had won him a membership in the Royal Society, proved further his influence for a broad and liberal culture. A copy is on file in Yorktown, Va. See R. D. Meade, "Governor Fauquier, Friend of Jefferson," in *Richmond Times-Dispatch Magazine*, July 17, 1935.

2. *JHB, 1766-1769*, p. 140.

3. See Account Book, 1762-1770; Henry, *Henry*, I, 21, 146, and above pp. 229-232.

4. Howard, *Preliminaries of the Revolution*, pp. 175-176.

5. These counties were Chesterfield, Henrico, Dinwiddie, and Amelia. *JHB, 1766-1769*, p. 145. Bland was a representative of Prince George County, adjoining Dinwiddie.

6. Prince William County, near Lee's own Westmoreland, was represented in the Burgesses by Henry Lee and Foushee Tebbs. *Ibid.*, pp. 136, 148.

7. *Ibid.*, pp. 165-171. Apr. 14, 1768.

8. In the memorial to the Commons there is a protest against imposition by them of "an internal tax of any kind," a plain intimation that even the Townshend duties were labeled internal taxes. *Ibid.*, p. 170.

9. "The Notion of a virtual Representation hath been so often and fully refuted, that it surely is unnecessary to multiply Works on that Head: if the Property, the Liberties, the Lives of Millions of his Majesty's most dutiful Subjects are merely ideal, how deplorable must be their condition." *Ibid.*, p. 170.

10. Morison and Commager, *Growth of the American Republic*, I, 151-162, has a good discussion of the constitutional issue.

11. H. J. Eckenrode, *The Revolution in Virginia*, p. 28. Eckenrode states that Richard Bland wrote the complaint. Probably he did compose most if not all of it, but there is no positive proof.

12. The *Liberty* had entered the harbor with six pipes of "good saleable Madeira" for the coffeehouse trade and more of the "very best" or "best" for Hancock and the Treasurer of the Province. Becker, *Eve of the Revolution*, p. 124. Peter Cunningham, ed., *Letters of Horace Walpole*, V, 115, 116, 120, 121 (on Botetourt's gambling).

13. *Ibid.*, 120-121. The gossipy Walpole had good information on opinion in English governing circles.

[407]

14. Miller, *Origins of the Revolution*, p. 316.

15. "I congratulate you and my country on the appointment of Lord Botetourt to the Government of Virginia. . . . He is a very amiable character, remarkable for his very great Attention to business, as he was said never to have been absent from the House of Commons during the twenty years he was a member of it . . . and he had been as remarkable since he came into the House of Peers, for his close attendance there. He was never married, has been ever commended for his hospitality and affability. . . ." Letter from Colonel George Mercer to James Mercer, Aug. 15, 1768. Copy at Colonial Williamsburg, Inc., of original in Public Record Office, London.

"Lord Botetourt is arrived amongst us with the greatest advantages imaginable. . . . He hath been received & welcomed in a manner which gives him great pleasure." William Nelson, York, to John Norton, London, Nov. 14, 1768, in Frances Mason, ed., *John Norton and Sons, Merchants of London and Virginia*, pp. 75-77.

16. "My political creed was published to the world in the different applications to Government from our former Assembly, and I am so little inclined to depart from one jot or tittle of it, that I would avow it with my last breath." Nicholas to Arthur Lee, May 31, 1769. *Southern Literary Messenger*, vol. 27 (Sept. 1858), p. 184.

17. "Our long expected Governor at length arrived, his lordship's good sense, affability, and politeness give general pleasure, but how far his political opinions may agree with those of Virginia remains yet to be known." R. H. Lee to John Dickinson, Nov. 26, 1768. Ballagh, *Lee*, pp. 30, 31.

18. *JHB, 1766-1769*, p. 185.

Nathaniel Macon, long-time congressman for whom the two Randolph-Macon colleges were partly named, was a member of a branch of this family which had settled in Warren County, N.C. See William E. Dodd, *Nathaniel Macon*.

19. George Dabney Ms.

20. Henry, *Henry*, I, 134.

21. The pageant, supposed to dazzle, seemed rather to offend. Campbell, *Virginia*, p. 556. See also Weddell, *Va. Portraiture*, pp. 192-195 (with copy of Botetourt portrait).

22. Campbell, *Virginia*, p. 556.

23. Kimball, *Jefferson*, I, 187. W. W. Henry properly notes that the advanced party was strengthened by the addition of Jefferson. Henry, *Henry*, I, 136.

24. When the Massachusetts Assembly met at Boston in June, 1768,

the members found British ships in the harbor and a British regiment quartered in the city.

25. Lee, *Memoirs of R. H. Lee*, I, 69.

26. "Say the time-serving Men as the Assembly have denied, and the King has asserted those rights, the matter ought to lie without their taking the least notice of it, Lee wrote Dickinson, Nov. 26, 1768. This was on the supposition, Lee added, that the principle admitted would never again be carried into execution." Ballagh, *Lee*, pp. 30-31.

27. Lee to Dickinson, Nov. 26, 1768. *Ibid.*, pp. 30-31.

28. Ford, *Jefferson's Writings*, X, 327-328, quoting Jefferson's conversation in 1824 with Daniel Webster.

29. *Ibid.*, IX, 340-341.

30. *JHB, 1766-1769*, pp. 214-215. May 16, 1769.

31. This seems true even though the Burgesses had outlined the material to be included in the address.

32. The address does not appear to be in Henry's style.

33. *JHB, 1766-1769*, p. 218.

34. Hill, *Mason*, pp. 99-101.

35. The conservative leader, Edmund Pendleton, had left for home several days before and had thus been absent also at the adoption of the resolutions and address to the King. If he had been present during these stirring days, he might have slightly modified the proceedings. It should be emphasized, however, that he was not a stiff reactionary, a blind opponent of change. See Mays, *Pendleton*.

The *JHB* prints the Signers of the Address in two parallel lists, with speaker Randolph at the top of the left list and Henry of that opposite. In the *Va. Gazette* (P&D) for May 18, however, Henry's name is printed eleventh, after several members who were more conservative and less conspicuous. Perhaps there was an effort to play down the role of the liberal leaders and to emphasize the unanimity of the proceedings.

36. *JHB, 1766-1769*, pp. xl-xliii.

37. "The Farmer" of course referred to John Dickinson and his *Letters of a Pennsylvania Farmer*, and "The Monitor" to the letters, so signed, by Arthur Lee. His letters, in defense of the Whig cause, were voluminously reprinted in the *Va. Gazette*.

38. In an age of excessive drinking even pious New Englanders were not exempt. On June 5 the Massachusetts House of Representatives had celebrated the King's birthday by a great drinking party, attended by a number of the Council and the clergy. There were twenty-two toasts embracing every subject from the Royal Family, Chatham, Burke, Paoli and his brave Corsicans to "The Farmer of Pennsylvania." *Essex* (Mass.)

Gazette, Aug. 8, 1769. Kimball, "Some Genial and Drinking Customs" in 2 *Wm. and Mary* (Ser. 3), p. 353; Helen Bullock, *The Williamsburg Art of Cookery*, esp. pp. 213-216.

39. Ballagh, *op. cit.*, p. 37.

40. Roane Memo in Morgan, *Henry*, p. 442. Roane was born in 1762. The burgesses may have been unable to regulate tobacco chewing in the gallery, but when they met again in November they did pass a rule regulating its use on the floor. Under the rules as drawn up by Henry's Committee of Privileges and Elections, Edmund Pendleton, chairman, reporting, it was provided that no member should chew tobacco in the House while the Speaker was in the chair or during a Committee of the Whole House. Other rules, long commended by precedent and example, required members to keep strictly to the point in debate, to avoid all indecent and disrespectful language, and to speak no more than twice in the same debate without permission. *JHB, 1766-1769*, pp. 323-324.

41. *Ibid.*, pp. 228-230. Edmund Pendleton was made chairman of the Committee on Privileges and Elections and was the third ranking member of the Committee of Propositions and Grievances and the new Committee on Religion. Treasurer Nicholas was chairman of the latter committee and among the highest ranking members of the two others. Richard Henry Lee and Archibald Cary were two more ranking members of the three committees. *Ibid.* Membership in the committees was usually continued as long as the burgesses served in the House and those who held important assignments were strongly entrenched in their power. For a significant discussion see Sydnor, *Gentlemen Freeholders*.

42. *Va. Gazette*, July 27, 1769.

43. Martha Jacquelin, York [Yorktown] to John Norton, London, Aug. 14, 1769. Mason, *op. cit.*, pp. 101-103.

44. Bill to Henry from Sampson and George Matthews. Va. Historical Society. Account Book, 1762-1770, pp. 113, 167.

45. The ball was given at the Capitol and the guests "chiefly dressed in Virginia cloth, made a genteel appearance." *Va. Gazette*, Dec. 14, 1769.

46. Letter of May 26, 1769. Quoted in *Essex* (Mass.) *Gazette*, June 27, 1769.

47. *Ibid.*, Aug. 8, 1769, quoting Boston dispatch of June 13. The North Carolina resolves, based on those of Virginia, are in *ibid.*, Jan. 22, 1770.

48. On Nov. 13, 1769. Quoted in Frothingham, *Rise of the Republic*, p. 238.

49. "I believe to fear that the Spirit of Association in America will

grow cool in some of the Colonies: especially at N. York; where the Dutch Blood, thirsting for present Gain, seems still to flow in their Veins, & hath raised much Noise to the Northward about it, But I blush on reading what you say abt the Virginians: that their Invoices rather encrese than diminish. I wish such People were of any other Country than of mine." William Nelson to John Norton, London, July 19, 1770. Mason, *op. cit.*, pp. 137-138.

50. George Otto Trevelyan, *The American Revolution*, I, 199.

51. Wilkes' letter from King's Bench Prison thanking the Middlesex voters for re-electing him is on the first page of the *Va. Gazette* (P&D), May 18, 1769. On page 2 are the Virginia resolves of May 16 and an account of the dissolution of the Burgesses and the formation of the Association.

52. Hill, *op. cit.*, pp. 273-274. Mason was writing on Dec. 6, 1770, to thank an English relative who had sent him a copy of Junius' letters. There were several editions published about this time among which Henry's was probably numbered.

53. *The Letters of Junius* (Boston, 1827), pp. 32-34.

54. *Va. Gazette* (Rind), Jan. 18, 1770, pp. 1-2. The letter in the *Gazette* is from the *London Public Ledger*, Oct. 19, 1769. It is signed by "Senius" apparently another pen name of Junius. The lines beginning "what can enoble" are slightly changed from a quotation in Pope's *Essay on Man*, epistle IV, lines 215-216.

55. *Va. Gazette* (Rind), Mar. 8, 1770.

56. *Ibid.*, Nov. 8, 1770.

57. Henry's accounts show that in May, 1769, he charged Nicholas for nine days' attendance as a burgess £4.10 and eight days traveling £4, and in November for forty days' attendance £20 and eight days' traveling £4. Account Book, 1762-1770, p. 163.

58. The bill from the two Matthews, *ibid.* (1768-1769), with references to the purchase of a gallon of timothy seed and bag (⅜) and the flaxseed (⅙ per half-bushel with bag) show that Henry was continuing active farm operations, apparently with an overseer. Earlier, in 1764, he had listed accounts with William Crane "formerly my Overseer in 1763" and with James Matthews who finished Crane's time. Account Book, 1762-1770, p. 80.

59. Bill of John Buchanan, Merchant, against Henry, Oct. 16, 1770, in Library of Congress.

60. Bill of Sampson and George Matthews against Henry, Dec. 16, 1769, at Va. Historical Society.

61. John, born in 1750, was the son of Col. Peter Fontaine of Han-

over. Peter had married Elizabeth, daughter of Patrick's uncle William Winston and his wife, Sarah Dabney. Mary Selden Kennedy, *The Seldens of Virginia and Allied Families*, I, 668-669. Data from John Fontaine, then of Wilson, N.C., a descendant of the Henrys and Fontaines. Sarah Dabney Winston was not only Patrick Henry's aunt by marriage but his cousin through his grandmother Dabney.

62. See above, p. 600; and Account Book, 1762-1770, p. 41.

63. The will of the Rev. Peter Fontaine and other valuable data on Fontaines is in Maury, *Memoirs of a Huguenot Family*, esp. pp. 151, 338-340, 351-355, 363. William Wallace Scott, *History of Orange County, Virginia*, pp. 104-113, contains the journal of John Fontaine on the expedition to the Shenandoah. See also Kennedy, *The Seldens of Virginia*, esp. pp. 667-670; Peyton Neale Clark, *Old King William Families;* 22 *Va. Mag.*, p. 195; Dabney, *The Dabneys of Virginia*, pp. 55-56; Byrd, *A Journey to the Land of Eden* and *Another Secret Diary* (Woodfin, ed.). The comments of Col. Peter Fontaine on tobacco and slavery are in Maury, *op. cit.*, pp. 363-365. For will of Isaac Winston, see pp. 103-104.

64. When Sarah Henry died in 1775, Martha was married but still under twenty-one years of age. Since Patrick had bought Scotchtown in 1771 and home weddings were customary on such remote plantations, with large mansions, it is likely that Martha was married there. Henry, *Henry*, I, 149, 318.

65. Sometime before his death in 1766, John Chiswell sold Scotchtown to John Robinson. Robinson's executors sold the estate in sections, and the house tract was presumably sold to John Payne who conveyed it to Patrick Henry in 1771. Many of the earliest Hanover records were destroyed, but John Payne is known to have owned Scotchtown about this time and the owners at all other periods are listed in the records. Henry, *Henry*, I, 149, 618; Allen C. Clark, *Life and Letters of Dolly Madison*, pp. 9-10; Weddell, *Virginia Historical Portraiture*, p. 323; *Va. Gazette* (P&D), Dec. 21, 1769, Jan. 11 and July 19, 1770.

I am grateful to Judge Leon Bazile, Hanover County, for a documented memo on the owners of Scotchtown, with other very helpful data. See also Account Book, 1770-1774, p. 7, for an entry regarding Scotchtown by Henry in 1771.

66. See below p. 294 and references in Note 65. Fork Church, so called for its proximity to the fork or confluence of the North and South Anna rivers, is 2.5 miles from Scotchtown on a county road.

Although in a lonely situation by any standard, the Scotchtown estate was formerly located on an old road to Charlottesville. "Ten or fifteen miles west or northwest of the Court House and east of the South Anna on the road leading from Richmond to Charlottesville, we may find a place though nothing more than an old farm, yet styled Scotchtown." "A Western Pioneer" in *Richmond Whig*, Sept. 23, 1843. See Mays, *Pendleton*, I, 384.

67. Preston Ms. Henry, *Henry*, I, 149.

68. *Ibid.*

69. *Council Journal*, IV, 83, 128.

70. Byrd, *A Journey to the Land of Eden*, pp. 327-328.

71. Personal visits to Scotchtown. Advertisement of a sale of Scotchtown by administrators of John Robinson. *Va. Gazette* (P&D), July 19, 1770; and Edith Sale, *Interior of Virginia Houses of Colonial Times*, pp. 485-493.

72. *Memoirs and Letters of Dolly Madison* (1886), ed. by her great-niece [Lucia B. Cutts], pp. 4-5. Miss Sally Campbell spoke to me of the marble mantelpiece at Scotchtown which was destroyed, of the white paling fence which was pulled down, and the large oak trees cut down, both by Capt. Edmund Taylor, one of the later owners. There was also boxwood in front of the house, a brick smokehouse and outside kitchen, a tanyard, and an old mill on New Found River.

73. Data in the Aylett family Bible shows that Elizabeth Henry Aylett died Sept. 24, 1842, aged 73 years, 5 months, 1 day (and was, therefore, born on Apr. 23, 1769). The Bible is in the possession of her descendant, John Fontaine. Edward Henry, the last child of Sarah and Patrick, was known to have been born within a few years after Elizabeth. Since Sarah's ill-health was a cause for the purchase of Scotchtown in 1771 and became increasingly worse, it seems safe to place the birth of her last child about 1771. Henry, *Henry*, I, 149, and II, 635-636. Preston Ms. In a letter of Sept. 13 [1771?] to her daughter Mrs. Anne Christian, Mrs. John Henry spoke of having already told her that Patrick had bought Scotchtown. She said also that "Littel Edward is a fine child. I nursed him while they were gone." W. W. Henry Papers, Va. Historical Society.

74. Preston Ms. Data from Miss Nelly Preston, and from Miss Mary Rawlings, Charlottesville. Miss Rawlings' great-grandfather, Maj. James Watson of Green Spring, Louisa County, married Sarah Shelton Henry's cousin, Elizabeth Shelton. The facts on Elizabeth's opinion of Henry were related to Miss Rawlings by Thomas Watson of Green Spring, who was born about 1800. The quotation on how long the cradle was rocking in Henry's household is from Miss Rawlings, expressing Elizabeth Shelton's viewpoint.

75. Meredith Memo in Morgan, *Henry*, p. 432.

76. Fleming Papers, Washington and Lee University.

77. Interview of Miss Sally Campbell. She was born at Glen Cairn in 1855, and her grandmother from whom she had the data on Mrs. Henry was Mrs. Harriett Brown (née Sheppard), born Aug. 3, 1799. Miss Campbell pronounced Patrick "Pähtrick."

The neighborhood story of Mrs. Henry's insanity is repeated by several reliable witnesses. Mrs. Fenton Noland (née Lucy Landon Cooke) of Airwell, Hanover County, said that she had heard Mrs. Henry was crazy and confined in the basement at Scotchtown with a Negro nurse. Mrs. Noland, then 85 years old, was descended from prominent families long identified with upper Hanover County. Personal interview, June 16, 1951.

Rosewell Page, Jr., of near-by Oakland in upper Hanover, referred to the county legend that Mrs. Henry was crazy and kept in the basement at Scotchtown by a Negro woman. Personal interview, June 16, 1951. Miss Bertie Shelton of the Rural Plains family told me in 1956 that she knew the story of Mrs. Henry's insanity was repeated in the upper part of the county. Sam Schroetter, Jr., of Charlottesville told me the same year that he had heard the story from someone living near Scotchtown.

A brief history of Scotchtown, written in recent years when the property was owned by Miss Lavinia Sheppard Taylor, is at the Va. Historical Society. This account contains a number of obvious inaccuracies, but it does refer to the tradition that an early owner kept his wife confined in the dungeon under the large hallway.

Chapter 16

WOULD COLONIALISM SUFFICE?

1. For this statistical data see reprint of John Henry's map in Abernethy, *Western Lands*, opposite p. 2.

2. *Va. Gazette* (P&D), Dec. 21 and 28, 1769.

3. *Murdochs, Donald, & Co.* v. *Edmund Winston*. Papers in Box 12. U.S. District Court, Richmond.

4. Botetourt was asked to inform the House if the government was committed to confirm any Orders of Council for granting lands between the Alleghenies and a line from the western boundary of North Carolina and the junction of the Ohio River with the Mississippi. This was in the area where Henry had acquired the tract from John Shelton. Fearing that he might be dispossessed, Henry heartily concurred in the request that Botetourt "be pleased in future to discourage all Monopolies of Lands within the Colony." *JHB, 1766-1769*, pp. 318, 319.

5. *Ibid.*, pp. 318, 319, Dec. 5 and 13, 1769.

[414]

6. For the legislative Acts providing for these internal improvements see *ibid.*, *1770-1772*, pp. 315-316.

7. *Ibid.*

8. *Ibid.*, pp. vii-viii.

9. *Ibid.*, pp. 35, 137. So far as known, it was Henry's first trip outside of Virginia. Possibly he crossed into what was then North Carolina territory when locating his Holston lands.

10. *New York Journal*, July 12, 1770.

11. This was the conventional route used a few years before by George Washington (Freeman, *Washington*, I, 157-168) and the British traveler, Burnaby. See Note 12.

12. *Burnaby's Travels*, pp. 80-82.

13. Henry, *Henry*, I, 114.

14. It was "beautifully laid out into fields of clover, grain, and flax." *Burnaby's Travels*, p. 88.

15. Ten years before, in 1760, Burnaby had described Philadelphia as having 3,000 houses and 18,000 or 20,000 inhabitants. He added that the streets were crowded with people and the river with vessels. *Burnaby's Travels*, pp. 89, 91.

16. Sketches of Lamb and McDougall in *DAB*; T. J. Wertenbaker, *Father Knickerbocker Rebels*, pp. 23-24.

17. *Ibid.*, p. 14.

18. *Ibid.*

19. Nelson to Hillsborough. Colonial Office Papers. Public Record Office, London. A correspondent, writing to the *Va. Gazette* on June 14, 1770, reported that in a late tour of several neighboring provinces he had found the "sensible" people greatly displeased with the Virginians for not adhering more strictly to the Association.

20. *Va. Gazette* (P&D), July 19, 1770.

21. Col. Severn Ayres' service in the Burgesses with Henry is noted in *JHB*, *1766-1769* and *1770-1772*. See also Adams, *Works*, II, 249-250.

22. Spotsylvania Order Book, 1768-1774, entry for Nov. 15, 1770; Mays, *Pendleton*, I, 262-267.

23. Account Book, 1770-1773.

24. There is a good biographical sketch of Dunmore in R. A. Brock, *Virginia and Virginians*, vol. I. See also Flippen, *The Royal Government in Virginia*, and Lyon Gardiner Tyler, *Williamsburg*, p. 55.

25. Rutherford Goodwin, *Williamsburg in Virginia*, p. 87.

26. *Ibid.*, p. 88.

27. Henry, *Henry*, I, 163-164.

28. *Ibid.*, pp. 164-165.

[415]

29. There is a good summary of the Gaspee affair in H. J. Carmen and H. C. Syreit, *A History of the American People*, I, 138-139.

30. Jefferson states that there may have been one or two members present whose names he could not recall. Ford, *Jefferson's Writings*, I, 7-8.

31. Ford, *Jefferson's Writings*, I, 8. Henry, *Henry*, I, 161-162.

32. Carr's grandmother was Mary Dabney. For further data on him see Harris, *Louisa*, pp. 296-297, *passim;* and Malone, *Jefferson*, I, 170-171, *passim*.

33. Henry, *Henry*, I, 164.

34. Henry is listed first in a committee including James Hatt of Norfolk, Treasure Nicholas, and Richard Bland. *JHB, 1773-1776*, pp. 12-14.

35. *Ibid.*, p. 22.

36. *Ibid.*, pp. 20-22, 33, 36, 39, 43, *passim;* and Henry, *Henry*, I, 157-159, 165.

37. *Va. Gazette* (P&D), Apr. 22, 1773.

38. Lee, *Memoirs of R. H. Lee*, pp. 17-19.

39. Campbell, *Virginia*, pp. 494-495; Maury, *Memoirs*, 351-352; 364-365; *Memoirs and Letters of Dolly Madison*, p. 8.

40. *King* v. *Taffy*. Goochland Papers. Va. State Library; *JHB, 1766-1769*, pp. 259, 268-269; *New York Journal*, Feb. 22, 1770.

41. *Va. Gazette* (P&D), Sept. 21, 1769.

42. Goochland Order Book, June 25, 1733.

43. Louisa County Deed Book D, May 18, 1767; Account Book, 1762-1770.

44. Jerdone Memo. Book, 1766-1767. Va. State Library.

45. *JHB, 1766-1769*, pp. 83, 92, 95.

46. *Ibid.*, pp. 89, 107.

47. Francis Coleman Rosenberger, *Virginia Reader*, p. 311.

48. J. C. Ballagh, *A History of Slavery in Virginia*, pp. 10, 12, 24. See also John Henry's estimate of the slaves in 1770, above p. 283.

49. Chitwood, *Colonial America*, p. 419, quoting H. U. Faulkner, *American Economic History*, p. 75 note.

50. *Calendar of Records*. The Society of Merchant Venturers, Bristol. Vol. 11 (1701-1800), p. 41.

51. Archives of The Society of Merchant Venturers, Bristol. African Trade, Box V.

52. Maury, *op. cit.*, pp. 351-352.

53. Frederic [sic.] Bancroft, *Slave-Trading in the Old South*, p. 5.

54. Maury, *op. cit.*, pp. 364-365. Letter of June 7, 1754.

55. Several of these petitions are preserved in the Public Record Office, London.

56. *JHB, 1770-1772,* pp. 283-284. The original petition, signed by Speaker Peyton Randolph, is in Colonial Office Papers, Public Record Office, London.

57. Hillsborough to Dunmore. Colonial Office Papers. Public Record Office, London.

58. 1 *Wm. and Mary* (Ser. 2), 1921, pp. 107-109, *passim.* There is a copy of Henry's letter at the Library Company of Philadelphia. See also Henry, *Henry,* I, 151-153.

59. *Ibid.,* pp. 168-169.

60. *Ibid.,* pp. 108-109.

61. Copy of letter in W. W. Henry Papers. Va. Historical Society.

62. *Douglas Register,* pp. 334-338.

63. *Va. Gazette* (P&D), Dec. 13, 1770. Bill of Henderson, McCaul and Co. to William and Patrick Henry, executers of the deceased Col. John Henry. Va. Historical Society.

64. This dictionary which later belonged to Patrick Henry is in the Va. State Library.

65. Henry, *Henry,* I, 156; Meredith Memo in Morgan, *Henry,* p. 432.

66. John Esten Cooke, *Virginia,* pp. 417-418.

67. *Va. Gazette,* (P&D), May 19, 1774.

68. Ford, *Jefferson's Writings,* I, 9-10. See also Bernard Mayo, *Jefferson Himself,* pp. 49-50. This is a useful summary of Jefferson's many-sided career in his own words.

69. *JHB, 1773-1776,* pp. xv, 124.

70. Kate Rowland, *George Mason,* I, 169-170.

71. *Ibid.,* p. 57.

72. *Ibid.;* Hill, *Mason,* p. 152; Ford, *Jefferson's Writings,* I, 57.

73. Rowland, *op. cit.,* I, 168-169.

74. *JHB, 1773-1776,* pp. xiii-xiv.

75. *Ibid.,* pp. 151-154.

76. *Ibid.,* pp. 149-150.

77. *Va. Gazette* (P&D), Jan. 20, 1774.

78. Dartmouth to Dunmore, July 6, 1774. Colonial Office Papers. Public Record Office, London.

79. The Council of Virginia to Dunmore. Colonial Office Papers. Public Record Office, London.

80. *Va. Gazette* (Rind), July 21, 1774.

81. *Ibid.*

82. Trevelyan, *American Revolution*, I, 166-167.

83. *Ibid.*, p. 167.

84. Massie Papers. Va. Historical Society.

85. *Va. Gazette* (Rind), July 28, 1774.

86. In his *An Address Read At A Meeting Of Merchants To Consider Non-Importation* (Apr. 25, 1768), Dickinson concluded as follows: "Let us never forget that our Strength depends on our Union and our Liberty on our Strength. 'United we conquer divided we die.' " See Ford, *Writings of John Dickinson*, I, 417.

87. *Va. Gazette* (P&D), Aug. 4, 1774, gives names of the commissioners and states that £1,000 was raised by subscription to defray their expenses at the congress. Washington to Thomas Johnson of Maryland. Freeman, *Washington*, III, 367.

88. See Julian Boyd, *Jefferson Papers*, I, 121-137 and Appendix I for the text of *A Summary View* with some useful notes; see also comments in Malone, *Jefferson*, I, 180-190.

89. Freeman, *op. cit.*, III, illustration and note, following p. 373.

90. See below p. 315.

Chapter 17

PUBLIC CRISIS AND PRIVATE SORROW

1. W. E. Woodward, *George Washington, The Image and the Man*, p. 80.

2. For these entries from Washington's diary see John C. Fitzpatrick, ed., *The Diaries of George Washington*, I, 212, 213, and II, 189.

3. *Ibid.*, II, 162; Freeman, *Washington*, III, 370-372; Mays, *Pendleton*, I, 276-278; Henry, *Henry*, I, 213.

4. There is a log of the journey to Philadelphia in *Washington Diaries*, II, 162. See also Mays, *op. cit.*, I, 280-283. "On Thursday the 1st of this month, after a very warm, disagreeable ride, I arrived in Town together with some of the Virginia gentn." E. C. Burnett, *Letters of Members of the Continental Congress* (hereafter cited as Burnett, *Letters*), I, 27, quoting Caesar Rodney of Delaware.

5. This account by the local diarist, Christopher Marshall, is in *Pa. Magazine of History*, vol. 56, p. 124.

6. *Ibid.*, I am indebted to David A. Kimball of the historical division, National Park Service, Independence Hall, for a copy of a contemporary print of the City Tavern. Mr. Dennis Kurjack, Mr. William C. Everhart and Mr. Kimball of this office were all generous in supplying valuable

data from the contemporary records and other sources. See also J. Thomas Scharf and Thompson Westcott, *History of Philadelphia, 1609-1884*, I, 291-292; and H. D. Eberlein and C. Van D. Hubbard, *Portrait of a Colonial City, Philadelphia, 1670-1838*, esp. pp. 301-307 (with accompanying photograph of Shippen-Wistar house).

"The streets of this town are vastly more regular and elegant than those in Boston, and the houses are more grand, as well as neat. They are almost all painted, brick buildings and all." Adams, *Works*, II, 347. Aug. 20, 1774.

7. Dr. William Shippen in *DAB; Washington Diaries*, II, 162; also see pp. 162-168. Esther Armes, ed. and compiler, *Nancy Shippen, Her Journal Book*, pp. 15, 16, 24, 36, 54-59.

8. *Ibid.*, pp. 302-303. Eberlein and Hubbard, *op. cit.*, pp. 302-303.

9. The letters from Robert Pleasants to Benezet, Fisher, and Pemberton (addressed to "Dear Uncle") are in 1 *Wm. and Mary* (Ser. 2), pp. 107-108, 176. There is a description of Anthony Benezet when he called in 1781 on the French generals at Philadelphia in 10 *Wm. and Mary* (Ser. 3), p. 208. See also Theodore Thayer, *Israel Pemberton, King of the Quakers*, esp. pp. 3, 5, 195, *et seq.*

10. Adams, *Works*, II, 362. Notes for Friday and Saturday, Sept. 2 and 3, 1774.

11. Burnett, *Letters*, I, 28.

12. *Ibid.*, p. 28.

13. Adams, *Works*, III, 31.

14. *Ibid.*, II, 364 (description of Rodney); Burnett, *Letters*, I, 28.

15. A list of delegates to the Stamp Act Congress is in Frothingham, *Rise of the Republic*, p. 185. See also Adams, *Works*, II, 357 and 401; and *Journal of the Continental Congress* (hereafter cited as *Journal*), esp. pp. 13-14.

16. Joseph Galloway in *DAB*.

17. Frothingham, *op. cit.*, pp. 167-168; Samuel Adams in *DAB;* John C. Miller, *Sam Adams*, pp. 238-240, 315, *passim*.

18. *Ibid.*; Adams, *Works*, esp. vol. II, 163-164. Trevelyan, *American Revolution*, I, 91-92.

19. Frothingham, *op. cit.*, p. 359; John Adams in *DAB;* Adams, *Works*, esp. vol. II, containing his diary, 1755-1776; Gilbert Chinard, *John Adams*, pp. 70-78, *passim*.

20. Frothingham, *op. cit.*, p. 359.

21. Burnett, *Letters*, I, 9.

22. Miller, *Origins of the American Revolution*, pp. 364-366; Adams, *Works*, II, 358-359; Charles Thomson in *DAB*.

23. *Journal*, p. 14; Thomas Lynch in *DAB*; Adams, *Works*, II, 323. Lynch's reference to Randolph, as quoted by Adams, has been put in direct discourse.

24. *Ibid.*, p. 365.

25. There is an excellent history of Carpenters' Hall in Charles E. Peterson, "Notes on Carpenters' Hall," 1953. This brochure, fully documented and illustrated, by Mr. Peterson, then resident architect of the Independence National Historical Park Project, was reprinted in the *Transactions of the American Philosophical Society*, vol. 43, part 1. See also Scharf and Westcott, *History of Philadelphia*, I, 291-292.

26. Burnett, *Letters*, I, 10. *Journal*, I, 14. Charles Thomson in *DAB*.

27. Burnett, *Letters*, I, 10.

28. *Ibid.*; Adams, *Works*, II, 365.

29. *Ibid.*, pp. 366-367.

30. *Ibid.*, p. 367.

31. *Ibid.*

32. *Ibid.*

33. *Ibid.*, pp. 367-368.

34. *Journal*, I, 25; John Jay in *DAB*; Adams, *Works*, II, 368.

35. Burnett, *Letters*, I, 28-29.

36. *Journal*, I, 29. William Hooper of North Carolina was added on Sept. 14, giving a member from each state represented. *Ibid.*, p. 31.

37. Twenty-two members were appointed on Sept. 7 to the Committee on Rights. Two more members, from North Carolina, were added on Sept. 14, bringing the total membership to twenty-four. *Journal*, pp. 27, 28, 31.

38. *Ibid.*, pp. 28, 31, 41, 42; Burnett, *The Continental Congress*, p. 52.

39. Burnett, *Letters*, I, 18; Adams, *Works*, II, 368-369.

40. For other entertainments which Henry must have attended, see *Pa. Gazette*, Sept. 21, 1774, banquet at City Tavern, given by the gentlemen of Philadelphia; Adams, *Works*, II, 400, *passim*; Burnett, *Letters*, p. 24.

41. Benjamin Chew in *DAB*. See also Adams, *Works*, II, 380.

42. *Ibid.*, IX, 347; Burnett, *Letters*, pp. 66-67.

43. R. H. Lee to Wm. Lee, Sept. 20, 1774. In New York Public Library.

44. *Journal*, I, 31-37. Adams, *Works*, II, 381.

45. *Journal*, I, 31-37.

46. *Journal*, I, 39-40.

47. Galloway's motion and plan with his introductory speech is in *Journal*, I, 43-51. See also Adams, *Works*, II, 387-389 and Julian P.

Boyd, *Anglo-American Union Joseph Galloway's Plans to Preserve the British Empire, 1774-1778*, esp. pp. 28-39 and 112-114.

48. *Journal*, I, 47.

49. Adams, *Works*, II, 389-390.

50. *Ibid.*, 390.

51. Burnett, *Continental Congress*, 49-50 and *Letters*, I, 54-56; Henry, *Henry*, I, 234; Adams, *Works*, II, 377, 387-389.

52. Henry, *Henry*, I, 234-235; Adams, *Works*, II, 390.

53. See pp. 334-335.

54. The text of these agreements is in *Journal*, I, 63-121. There is also a letter to the inhabitants of the province of Quebec. For the text of the memorial to the people of Great Britain, see *Va. Gazette* (P&D), Nov. 3, 1774. The same text is likewise printed in the *Norwich* (England) *Mercury*, Jan. 7, 1775.

55. Moses Coit Tyler, Ithaca, N.Y., to W. W. Henry, Nov. 16, 1887, in W. W. Henry Papers, Va. Historical Society. John Adams to John Jay, Jan. 9, 1818. Adams, *Works*, X, 272-274. John Jay in *DAB*. Jefferson to Wirt in Burnett, *Letters*, I, 79; and John Dickinson in *DAB*.

56. Adams, *Works*, II, 396. Adams added: "Henry said he had no public education; at fifteen he read Vergil and Livy, and has not looked into a Latin book since. His father left him at that age, and he has been struggling through life ever since." *Ibid*.

57. Henry, *Henry*, I, 247, quoting Ms. letter of Nathaniel Pope to William Wirt. Capt. George Dabney had queried Henry, and gave his reply to Pope.

58. John Dickinson to Arthur Lee, Oct. 27, 1774 in Burnett, *Letters*, I, 83.

On Sept. 26, 1774, Joseph Reed, later a member of Congress from Philadelphia, wrote a Mr. De Berdt: "We are indeed on the melancholy verge of civil war. United as one man, and breathing a spirit of the most animating kind, the Colonies are resolved to risk the consequences of opposition to the late edicts of Parliament. All ranks of people, from the highest to the lowest, speak the same language, and I believe will act the same part. I know of no power in this country that can protect an opposer of the public voice and conduct. A spirit and resolution is manifested which would not have disgraced the Romans in their best days. I hope they will mingle with them prudence and temperance so as to avoid extremities as long as possible. No man dares open his mouth against non-importation. Now the Congress have recommended it, it will not stop here;—non-exportation to England, Ireland, and the West Indies, and, if necessary, non-consumption of English fabrics, will be the bloodless and defensive war of the Colonies so long as hostilities are forborne by administration; but when they commence, (if unhappily they should,) terrible consequences are to be apprehended. God only knows what will be the event of all these things. If Parliament will repeal the tea duty, and put Boston in its former station, all will be well, and the tea will be paid for. Nothing else will save this country and Britain too. My head and heart are both full." W. B. Reed, *Life of Jos. Reed.*

59. Kennedy, *Memoirs of the Life of William Wirt,* II, 47-48. In Burnett, *Letters,* I, lxiv, it is stated that the Virginia delegates planned to leave Philadelphia on Sunday, Oct. 23. Richard Henry Lee signed his name and Henry's on Oct. 26 to the petition to the King; Washington his name and that of three other Virginia delegates.

60. *Ibid.*

61. Wirt, *Henry,* pp. 95-96.

62. For a record of these proroguings see *JHB, 1773-1776,* pp. 165-172.

63. Henry, *Henry,* I, 249; Fleming Papers, Washington and Lee University.

64. The data on Robert McClanahan's ordinary is from an account by Joseph H. Waddell in 7 *Va. Mag.,* p. 112.

65. The account of the Augusta County contingent in Dunmore's War, including Alexander McClanahan's company, is in a letter of the Rev. John Brown to Col. William Preston, Smithfield, Aug. 22, 1774. Thwaites and Kellog, *Documentary History of Dunmore's War,* pp. 159-161.

66. Letter of Mrs. Anne Christian to Mrs. Anne Fleming, Oct. 15, 1774. Fleming Papers, Washington and Lee University.

67. The following deeds for Patrick and Sarah Henry are signed only by Patrick: Patrick and Sarah Henry to John Perkins, Aug. 15, 1770, Louisa County Deed Book J, pp. 541-542; Patrick and Sarah Henry to Lewis Walden, July 1, 1773, Louisa County Deed Book D½, pp. 519-520; Patrick and Sarah Henry to Humphrey Parish, July 19, 1773, Louisa County Deed Book D½, pp. 594-595.

In Deed Book E, Aug. 22, 1774, pp. 38-39, is a deed of Patrick and Sarah to Nathaniel Thacker in which Sarah's signature appears to have been made by Patrick.

68. *Va. Gazette* (P&D), Dec. 15, 1774.

69. Dunmore's proclamation is in the *Va. Gazette* (Dixon and Hunter), May 13, 1775.

70. The original letter from Dunmore is in the Public Record Office, London.

INDEX

[423]

INDEX

[424]

INDEX

INDEX

INDEX